CW00665725

NO ONE LEFT
TO LIE TO

ALSO BY CHRISTOPHER HITCHENS

BOOKS

Hostage to History: Cyprus from the Ottomans to Kissinger
Blood, Class and Empire: The Enduring Anglo-American Relationship
Imperial Spoils: The Curious Case of the Elgin Marbles
Why Orwell Matters
No One Left to Lie To: The Triangulations of William Jefferson Clinton
Letters to a Young Contrarian
The Trial of Henry Kissinger
Thomas Jefferson: Author of America
Thomas Paine's "Rights of Man": A Biography
god Is Not Great: How Religion Poisons Everything
The Portable Atheist
Hitch-22: A Memoir
Arguably: Essays
Mortality

PAMPHLETS

Karl Marx and the Paris Commune
The Monarchy: A Critique of Britain's Favorite Fetish
The Missionary Position: Mother Teresa in Theory and Practice
A Long Short War: The Postponed Liberation of Iraq

ESSAYS

Prepared for the Worst: Essays and Minority Reports
For the Sake of Argument
Unacknowledged Legislation: Writers in the Public Sphere
Love, Poverty and War: Journeys and Essays

COLLABORATIONS

James Callaghan: The Road to Number Ten (with Peter Kellner)
Blaming the Victims (edited with Edward Said)
When the Borders Bleed: The Struggle of the Kurds (photographs by Ed Kash)
International Territory: The United Nations (photographs by Adam Bartos)
Vanity Fair's Hollywood (with Graydon Carter and David Friend)

NO ONE LEFT TO LIE TO

THE TRIANGULATIONS OF WILLIAM JEFFERSON CLINTON

Foreword by Douglas Brinkley

Christopher Hitchens

Atlantic Books
London

First published in 1999 by Verso, an imprint of New Left Books.

Published in hardback and e-book in Great Britain in 2012 by Atlantic Books, an imprint of Atlantic Books Ltd.

10 9 8 7 6 5 4 3 2 1

A CIP catalogue record for this book is available from the British Library.

E-book ISBN: 978-0-85789-843-2
Hardback ISBN: 978-0-85789-841-8

Printed in Great Britain by the MPG Books Group

Atlantic Books
An imprint of Atlantic Books Ltd
Ormond House
26–27 Boswell Street
London
WC1N 3JZ

www.atlantic-books.co.uk

For Laura Antonia and Sophia Mando,
my daughters

Contents

Foreword

Let's be clear right off the bat: Christopher Hitchens was duty-bound to slay Washington, D.C., scoundrels. Somewhere around the time that the Warren Commission said there was no conspiracy to kill Kennedy and the Johnson administration insisted there was light at the end of the Vietnam tunnel, Hitchens made a pact with himself to be a principled avatar of subjective journalism. If a major politician dared to insult the intelligentsia's sense of enlightened reason, he or she would have to contend with the crocodile-snapping wrath of Hitchens. So when five-term Arkansas governor Bill Clinton became U.S. president in 1993, full of "I didn't inhale" denials, he was destined to encounter the bite. What Clinton couldn't have expected was that Hitchens—in this clever and devastating polemic—would gnaw off a big chunk of his ass for the ages. For unlike most Clinton-era diatribes that reeked of partisan sniping of-the-moment, Hitchens managed to write a classic takedown of our forty-second president— on par with Norman Mailer's *The Presidential Papers* (pathetic LBJ) and Hunter S. Thompson's *Fear and Loathing: On the Campaign Trail '72* (poor Nixon)— with the prose durability of history. Or, more simply put, its bottle vintage holds up well.

What *No One Left to Lie To* shares with the Mailer and Thompson titles is a wicked sense of humor, razorblade indictments, idiopathic anger, high élan, and a wheelbarrow full of indisputable facts. Hitchens proves to be a dangerous foe to Clinton precisely because he avoids the protest *modus operandi* of the antiwar 1960s. Instead of being unwashed and plastered in DayGlo, he embodies the refined English gentleman, swirling a scotch-and-Perrier ("the perfect delivery system") in a leather armchair, utilizing the polished grammar of an Oxford don in dissent, passing judgment from history's throne. In these chapters, the hubristic Hitchens dismantles the Clinton propaganda machine of the 1990s, like a veteran safecracker going click-back click-click-back click until he gets the goods. Detractors of Hitchens over the years have misguidedly tattooed him with the anarchistic "bomb-thrower" label. It's overwrought. While it's true that Hitchens unleashes his disdain for Clinton right out of the gate here, deriding him on Page One as a bird-dogging "crooked president," the beauty of this deft polemic is that our avenging hero proceeds to prove the relative merits of this harsh prosecution.

Hemingway famously wrote that real writers have a built-in bullshit detector—no one has ever accused Hitchens of not reading faces. What goaded him the most was that Clinton, the so-called New Democrat, with the help of his Machiavellian-Svengali consultant Dick Morris, decided the way to hold political power was by making promises to the Left while delivering to the Right. This rotten strategy was called Triangulation. All Clinton gave a damn about, Hitchens maintains, was holding on to power. As a man of the Left, an English-American columnist and critic for *The Nation* and *Vanity Fair*, Hitchens *wanted* to be sympathetic to Clinton. His well-honed sense of ethics, however, made that impossible. He refused to be a Beltway liberal muted by the "moral and political blackmail" of Bill and Hillary Clinton's "eight years of reptilian rule."

I distinctly remember defending Clinton to Hitchens one evening at a Ruth's Chris Steak House dinner around the time of the 9/11 attacks. Having reviewed Martin Walker's *The President We Deserve* for *The Washington Post*, I argued that Clinton would receive kudos from history for his fiscal responsibility, defense of the middle class, and an approach to world peace that favored trade over the use of military force. I even suggested that Vice President Al Gore made a terrible error during his 2000 presidential campaign by not using Clinton more. I mistakenly speculated that the Clinton Library would someday become a major tourist attraction in the South, like Graceland. "Douglas," he said softly, "*nobody* wants to see the NAFTA pen under glass. The winning artifact is Monica Lewinsky's blue dress. And you'll never see it exhibited in Little Rock."

To Hitchens, there were no sacred cows in Clintonland. With tomahawk flying, he scalps Clinton for the welfare bill ("more hasty, callous, short-term, and ill-considered than anything the Republicans could have hoped to carry on their own"), the escalated war on drugs, the willy-nilly bombing of a suspected Osama bin Laden chemical plant in Sudan on the day of the president's testimony in his perjury trial, and the bombing of Saddam Hussein's Iraq on the eve of the House of Representatives' vote on his impeachment. The low-road that Clinton operated on, Hitchens argues, set new non-standards, even in the snake-oil world of American politics. With utter contempt, Hitchens recalls how during the heat of the 1992 New Hampshire primary (where Clinton was tanking in the polls because of the Gennifer Flowers flap), the president-to-be rushed back to Arkansas to order the execution of the mentally disabled Rickey Ray Rector. "This moment deserves to be remembered," Hitchens writes, "because it introduces a Clintonian mannerism of *faux* 'concern' that has since become tediously familiar," and "because it marks the first of many times that Clinton would deliberately opt for death as a means of distraction from sex."

No One Left to Lie To was scandalous when first published in 1999. The Democratic Party, still trying to sweep Lewinsky under the carpet, didn't take kindly to a TV gadabout metaphorically waving the semen-flecked Blue Dress around as a grim reminder that the Arkansas hustler was still renting out the Lincoln Bedroom to the highest bidder. Hitchens took to the airwaves, claiming that Clinton wasn't just a serial liar; he actually "reacted with extreme indignation when confronted with the disclosure of the fact." To be around Clinton, he told viewers, was to subject oneself to the devil of corrosive expediency. It's not so much that Clinton surrounded himself with sycophantic yes men—all narcissistic presidents do that. It's that Clinton insisted, no matter the proposition, that his associates and supporters—indeed, all liberals—march in lockstep with his diabolic ways. To do otherwise was a sign of rank disloyalty to the House of Clinton. It was Nixon redux.

History must be careful not to credit Hitchens with this book's arch title. As the story goes, Hitchens was in a Miami airport on December 10, 1998, when he saw David Schippers, chief investigative counsel for the House Judiciary Committee, on television. The old-style Chicago law-and-order pol was on a roll. "The president, then, has lied under oath in a civil deposition, lied under oath in a criminal grand jury," Schippers said. "He lied to the people, he lied to the Cabinet, he lied to his top aides, and now he's lied under oath to the Congress of the United States. *There's no one left to lie to.*"

Bingo. Hitchens thought Schippers was spot-on. The more he reflected, the angrier he got. The writing process for *No One Left to Lie To* took only days; he banged it out in a fury. Using his disgust at Clinton's shameless gall as fuel, he defended the twenty-two-year-old intern Monica Lewinsky, who had over forty romantic encounters in the Oval Office with the president, from bogus charges that she was a slutty stalker. That Clinton had determined to demolish her on the electric chair of public opinion infuriated Hitchens. So he acted. He came to the rescue of a damsel in distress, protecting the modern-day Hester Prynne. It was Clinton, he said, the philanderer-in-chief, who deserved persecution for lying under oath.

There was something a bit New Age Chivalrous about it all. In 2002, Lewinsky wrote Hitchens, on pink stationery, mailed to him c/o *The Nation*, a note of gratitude for writing *No One Left to Lie To* and defending her as a talking head in the HBO film *Monica in Black and White*. "I'm not sure you've seen the HBO documentary I participated in," Lewinsky wrote Hitchens. "I wanted to thank you for being the only journalist to stand up against the Clinton spin machine (mainly Blumenthal) and reveal the genesis of the stalker story on television. Though I'm not sure people were ready to change their minds in '99, I hope they heard you in the documentary. Your credibility superseded his denials."

Clinton is for Hitchens emblematic of an official Washington overrun with lobbyists, Tammany-bribers, and bagmen of a thousand stripes. But Hitchens doesn't merely knock Clinton down like most polemicists. Instead, he drives over him with an 18-wheel Peterbilt, shifts gears to reverse, and then flattens the reputation of the Arkansas "boy wonder" again and again. Anyone who gets misty-eyed when Fleetwood Mac's "Don't Stop," the Clinton theme song, comes on the radio shouldn't read this exposé.

Hitchens tries a criminal case against Clinton (a.k.a. "Slick Willie") with gusto. No stone is left unturned. He catalogues all of Bubba's lies. He shames so-called FOBs ("friends of Bill") such as Terry McAuliffe and Sidney Blumenthal for embracing the two-faced and conniving Clinton under the assumption that an alternative president would be far worse. Was America really worse for wear because Nixon was forced to resign in 1974 and Gerald Ford became president? Would Vice President Al Gore really have been that bad for America compared with the craven

Clinton? The heart of this long-form pamphlet is about adults turning a blind eye to abuse of power for convenience's sake. What concerned Hitchens more than Clinton the man is the way once-decent public servants abandoned Golden Rule morality to be near the White House center of power. Hitchens rebukes the faux separation, promulgated by Clinton's apologists during the impeachment proceedings of 1998, of the Arkansan's private and public behavior. "Clinton's private vileness," he writes, "meshed exactly with his brutal and opportunistic public style."

Anyone who defends Clinton's bad behavior gets the stern Sherman-esque backhand. It's liberating to think that the powerful will be held accountable by those few true-blooded journalists like Hitchens who have guts; he was willing to burn a Rolodex-worth of sources to deliver the conviction. What Hitchens, in the end, loathes most are fellow reporters who cover up lies with balderdash. Who is holding the fourth estate's patsies' feet to the fire? In our Red-Blue political divide, American journalists often seem to pick sides. Just turn on Fox News and MSNBC any night of the week to get the score. Hitchens is reminding the press that for democracy to flourish, even in a diluted form, its members must be islands unto themselves. There is no more telling line in *No One Left to Lie To* than Hitchens saying: "The pact which a journalist makes is, finally, with the public. I did not move to Washington in order to keep quiet."

A cheer not free of lampoon hit Hitchens after the publication of *No One Left to Lie To*. While Clintonistas denounced him as a drunken gadfly willing to sell his soul for book sales, the one-time darling of *The Nation* was now also embraced by the neoconservative *The Weekly Standard*. Trying to pigeonhole him into a single school of thought was an exercise in futility. "My own opinion is enough for me, and I claim the right to have it defended against any consensus, any majority, any where, any place, any time," Hitchens noted in *Vanity Fair*. "And anyone who disagrees with this can pick a number, get in line, and kiss my ass."

Having absorbed a bus-load of Democratic Party grief for bashing Clinton's power-at-any-cost character, Hitchens felt vindicated when, on January 26, 2008, the former president made a racially divisive comment in the run-up to the South Carolina presidential primary. Out of the blue, Clinton reminded America that "Jesse Jackson won South Carolina twice, in '84 and '88"—grossly mischaracterizing Barack Obama's predicted victory over his wife, Hillary Clinton, as a *negro* thing. So much for a post-racial America: Clinton had marginalized Obama as the black candidate. The incident, Hitchens believed, was part-and-parcel to Clinton's longtime "southern strategy" that entailed publicly empathizing with African-Americans while nevertheless playing golf at a whites-only country club. In chapter two ("Chameleon in Black and White") Hitchens documents the heinous ways Clinton employed racially divisive stunts to get white redneck support in the 1992 run for the nomination. Examples are legion. Clinton had the temerity to invite himself to Jesse Jackson's Rainbow Coalition Conference just to deliberately insult Sister Souljah for writing vile rap lyrics: a ploy to attract the Bubba vote who worried the Arkansas governor might be a McGovernite. Clinton even told a Native American poet that he was one-quarter Cherokee just to garner Indian support. "The claim," Hitchens writes, "never advanced before, would have made him the first Native American president.... His opportunist defenders, having helped him with a reversible chameleon-like change in the color of his skin, still found themselves stuck with the content of his character."

Most of the tin-roof Clinton cheerleaders of the 1990s and beyond will be essentially forgotten in history. How many among us, even a presidential historian like myself, can name a Chester Arthur donor or a Millard Fillmore cabinet official? But everyone knows the wit and wisdom of Dorothy Parker and Ambrose Bierce and H.L. Mencken. Like these esteemed literary predecessors, Hitchens will be anthologized and read for years to come. Three versions of Clinton's impeachment drama (maybe more to come) will remain essential: Clinton's own *My Life*, Kenneth Starr's *Official Report of the Independent Counsel's Investigation of the President*, and Hitchens's *No One Left to Lie To*. Hopefully Hitchens's book will continue to be read in journalism and history classes, not for its nitty-gritty anti-Clinton invective and switchblade putdowns, but to remind politicians that there are still reporters out there who will expose your most sordid shenanigans with a shit-rain of honest ridicule. Hitchens salutes a few of them—Jamin Raskin, Marc Cooper, and Graydon Carter among them—in these pages.

Clinton was impeached by the House but acquitted by the Senate. Although he was barred from practicing law, prison time isn't in his biography. But he paid a peculiar price for his Lewinsky-era corruption: Hitchens's eternal scorn, which, since his death from esophageal cancer in 2011, is resounding louder than ever with a thunderously appreciative reading public. In the post–Cold War era, Hitchens was the polemicist who mattered most. He understood better than anyone that today's news is tomorrow's history. "He used to say to me at certain moments," his wife, Carol Blue, recalled, "whether it be in the back of a pickup truck driving into Romania from Hungary on Boxing Day 1989, or driving through the Krajina in Bosnia in 1992, or in February 1999 during the close of the Clinton impeachment hearings: 'It's history, Blue.'"

Douglas Brinkley
February 2012

Acknowledgments

Thanks are due to all those on the Left who saw the menace of Clinton, and who resisted the moral and political blackmail which silenced and shamed the liberal herd. In particular, I should like to thank Perry Anderson, Marc Cooper, Patrick Caddell, Doug Ireland, Bruce Shapiro, Barbara Ehrenreich, Gwendolyn Mink, Sam Husseini (for his especial help on the health-care racket), Robin Blackburn, Roger Morris, Joseph Heller, and Jamin Raskin. Many honorable conservative friends also deserve my thanks, for repudiating Clintonism even when it served their immediate and (I would say) exorbitant political needs. They might prefer not to be thanked by name.

The experience of beginning such an essay in a state of relative composure, and then finishing it amid the collapsing scenery of a show-trial and an unfolding scandal of multinational proportions— only hinted at here—was a vertiginous one. I could not have attempted it or undergone it without

Acknowledgments

Carol Blue, whose instinct for justice and whose contempt for falsity has been my loving insurance for a decade.

Christopher Hitchens
Washington, D.C., March 1999

Preface

This little book has no "hidden agenda." It is offered in the most cheerful and open polemical spirit, as an attack on a crooked president and a corrupt and reactionary administration. Necessarily, it also engages with the stratagems that have been employed to shield that president and that administration. And it maintains, even insists, that the two most salient elements of Clintonism—the personal crookery on the one hand, and the cowardice and conservatism on the other—are indissolubly related. I have found it frankly astonishing and sometimes alarming, not just since January of 1998 but since January of 1992, to encounter the dust storm of bogus arguments that face anyone prepared to make such a simple case. A brief explanation—by no means to be mistaken for an apologia—may be helpful.

Some years ago, I was approached, as were my editors at *Vanity Fair*, by a woman claiming to be the mother of a child by Clinton. (I decline to use the word "illegitimate" as a description of a baby, and may as well say at once that this is not my only difference with the supposedly moral majority, or indeed with any other congregation or—the *mot juste*—"flock.") The woman seemed superficially convincing; the attached photographs had an almost offputting resemblance to the putative father; the child was— if only by the rightly discredited test of *Plessy v. Ferguson*—black. The mother had, at the time of his conception, been reduced to selling her body for money. We had a little editorial conference about it. Did Hitchens want to go to Australia, where the woman then was? Well, Hitchens had always wanted to go to Australia. But here are the reasons why I turned down such a tempting increment on my frequent-flyer mileage program.

First of all—and even assuming the truth of the story—the little boy had been conceived when Mr. Clinton was the governor of Arkansas. At that time, the bold governor had not begun his highly popular campaign against defenseless indigent mothers. Nor had he emerged as the upright scourge of the "dead-beat dad" or absent father. The woman—perhaps because she had African genes and worked as a prostitute—had not been rewarded with a state job, even of the lowly kind bestowed on Gennifer Flowers. There seemed, in other words, to be no political irony or contradiction of the sort that sometimes licenses a righteous press in the exposure of iniquity. There was, further, the question of Mrs. and Miss

Clinton. If Hillary Clinton, hardened as she doubt-less was (I would now say, as she undoubtedly *is*), was going to find that she had a sudden step-daughter, that might perhaps be one thing. But Chelsea Clinton was then aged about twelve. An unexpected black half-brother (quite close to her own age) might have been just the right surprise for her. On the other hand, it might not. I didn't feel it was my job to decide this. My friends Graydon Carter and Elise O'Shaughnessy, I'm pleased to say, were in com-plete agreement. A great story in one way: but also a story we would always have regretted breaking. Even when I *did* go to Australia for the magazine, some-time later, I took care to leave the woman's accusing dossier behind.

Like a number of other people in Washington, I had heard a third-hand version of her tale during the elec-tion of 1992. In the briefly famous documentary *The War Room*, which hymns the spinning skills of thugs like James Carville, George Stephanopoulos can be seen "live" on the telephone, deftly fending off a nut-case Ross Perot supporter who has called in about the "bastard." The caller may not have said "black bas-tard," but one didn't have to be unduly tender-minded to notice that Clinton—however much he had tried to charm and woo them—still had enemies on the Right. Some of these enemies had allowed themselves to become infected, or were infected already, with the filthy taint of racism. That seemed an additional reason for maintaining a certain...reserve. I wasn't to know that, by the middle of 1998, Clinton's hacks would be using the bigotry of some of his critics, in the same way that Johnnie Cochran had employed the sick racist cop Mark Fuhrman, to change the subject and to "whiten" the sepulcher.

Just as the Republican case against the president seemed to be lapsing into incoherence, in the first days of 1999, Matt Drudge uncorked the black baby again. Indeed, he curtain-raised this nonexclusive at the annual gathering of the cultural and political Right, held in San Diego as a rival attraction to the pulverizing tedium and self-regard of the Clintonian "Renaissance Weekend" at Hilton Head. Once put to the most perfunctory forensic test, the whole story collapsed within the space of twenty-four hours. Mr. Clinton's DNA—famously found dabbled on the costly Gap garment of a credulous intern—was sufficiently knowable from the indices of the Starr Report for a preliminary finding to be possible. There was nothing like a "match" between the two genetic attributes. Once again, and for reasons of professional rather than political feeling, I felt glad that Graydon Carter and I had put privacy (and scruples that arose partly from the fatherhood of our own daughters) ahead of sensation all those years ago.

Still, I couldn't help but notice that White House spokesmen, when bluntly asked about the Drudge story by reporters, reacted as if it *could* be true. There was nothing about their Leader, they seemed to convey by the etiolated remains of their body language, that might not one day need a "privacy" defense, however hastily or wildly concocted. It turned out, however, that Mr. Drudge had done them another unintended favor. Nothing is more helpful, to a person with a record of economizing with the truth, than a false and malicious and disprovable allegation. And Drudge—whose want of discrimination in this respect is almost a trademark—openly says that he'll print anything and let the customers decide what's actually kosher. This form of pretended "consumer sovereignty" is fraudulent in the same way that its analogues are. (It means, for one thing, that you have no right to claim that you were correct, or truthful, or brave. All you did was pass it on, like a leaker or some other kind of conduit. The death of any intelligent or principled journalism is foreshadowed by such promiscuity.) In the old days, true enough, the Washington press corps was a megaphone for "official sources." Now, it's a megaphone for official sources *and* traders from the toilet.

Just such a symbiosis—comparable to his affectless equidistance between Left and Right, Republican and Democrat, white-collar crime and blue-collar crime, true and false, sacred and profane, bought and paid for, public and private, *quid* and *quo*—happened to serve Mr. Clinton well on the day in January 1998 that his presidency went into eclipse, or seemed about to do so. He made the most ample possible use of the natural reticence and decency that is felt by people who open a bedroom or bathroom door without knocking. (And this, even though he was the occupant of said bathroom and bedroom.) He also made a masterly use of the apparent contrast between the trivial and the serious. But on this occasion, and having watched it for some years, I felt confident that I could see through his shell game. On the first day, and in the presence of witnesses, I said: "This time he's going to be impeached." And, in support of my own much underrated and even mocked prescience, I will quote what the *Los Angeles Times* was kind enough to print under my name on January 28, 1998:

> Montesquieu remarked that if a great city or a great state should fall as the result of an apparent "accident," then there would be a general reason why it required only an accident to make it fall. This may appear to be a tautology, but it actually holds up very well as a means of analyzing what we lazily refer to as a "sex scandal."
>
> If a rust-free zipper were enough on its own to cripple a politician, then quite clearly Bill Clinton

would be remembered, if at all, as a mediocre Governor of the great state of Arkansas. It is therefore silly to describe the present unseemly furor as a prurient outburst over one man's apparently self-destructive sexual compulsions.

Until recently, this same man was fairly successfully fighting a delaying action against two long-standing complaints. The first was that he had imported unsavory Arkansas business practices to Washington, along with some of the unsavory practitioners like the disgraced Webster Hubbell. The second was that he viewed stray women employees as spoils along the trail.

Think of these two strands as wires, neither of them especially "live." (Everybody knew something about both, and few people believed that there was no substance to either story, but a fairly general benefit of the doubt was still being awarded.) Now the two wires have touched, and crossed, and crackled. Vernon Jordan's fellow board-members at Revlon gave a suspiciously large "consultancy" contract to Hubbell at just the moment when his usefulness as anybody's attorney had come to an end. (He was, after all, not just quitting the Department of Justice but going straight to jail.) And now this same well of Revlon is revisited by the busy Mr. Jordan when it comes time to furnish Monica Lewinsky with a soft landing. So, does this represent a Clinton machine *modus operandi* when it comes to potentially embarrassing witnesses? Kenneth Starr would be failing in his mandate as Independent Counsel if he did not put the question, and press hard for an answer. Even more to the point, so would we. This was all waiting to happen....

Or consider Dick Morris, Clinton's other best friend. The tarts from the "escort service" we could have—with a slight shudder—overlooked. But Morris's carryings-on in the Jefferson Hotel were an allegory of the way business was being conducted at the Democratic National Committee and even in the franchising of the Lincoln Bedroom. His exorbitant political bills necessitated the debauching, not just of himself, but of a whole presidential election. So that dirty little story served to illuminate the dirty big story. As does this one....

Had Clinton begun by saying: "Yes, I did love Gennifer, but that's my business," many of us would have rejoiced and defended him. Instead, he disowned and insulted her and said he'd been innocent of that adultery, and treated the voters as if they were saps. Having apparently put Ms. Lewinsky into the quick-fix world of Jordan and Morris, he is in no position to claim that it's a private emotional matter, and has no right to confuse his business with that of the country's. Which is why he has a scandal on "his" hands, and is also why we need feel no pang when he falsely claims that the press and public are wasting his valuable time, when the truth is exactly the other way about.

I sat back after writing that, and sat back rather pleased with myself after reading it in print, and thought that some people would take my point even if they didn't agree with it, and then went through a year in which, not once but several times every day, I was informed that Clinton had lied only to protect his wife and daughter (and, OK, himself) from shame! In the course of that same year, his wife and daughter were exposed by Clinton to repeated shame and humiliation. Dick Morris emerged as the only person to whom Clinton told the truth. Vernon Jordan emerged as the crucial witness in a matter of obstruction of justice. "Notice how they always trash the accusers," said Erik Tarloff to me one day. Erik has contributed to speeches for Clinton and Gore and is married to Laura D'Andrea Tyson, former chair of Clinton's Council of Economic Advisers. "They destroy their reputations. If Monica hadn't had that blue dress, they were getting ready to portray her as a fantasist and an erotomaniac. Imagine what we'd all be thinking of her now." Nor was this an exaggeration. In parallel with its Robert Rubin/Alan Greenspan presentation of bankerly orthodoxy and unshakable respectability, the Clinton administration always had its banana republic side. For all the talk about historic presidential "philandering," it is hard to recall any other White House which has had to maintain a quasi-governmental or para-state division devoted exclusively to the bullying and defamation of women. Like my old friend, there were many who "didn't like to think about it." Even Clinton's best friend, the notably unfastidious Dick Morris, once told CNBC:

> Under Betsey Wright's supervision in the 1992 Clinton campaign, there was an entire operation funded with over $100,000 of campaign money, which included federal matching funds, to hire private detectives to go into the personal lives of women who were alleged to have had sex with Bill Clinton. To develop compromising material—black-mailing information, basically—to coerce them into signing affidavits saying they did not have sex with Bill Clinton.

"Having sex" was the most fragrant and presentable way of describing the experience of certain women, like the Arkansas nursing-home supervisor Juanita Broaddrick, who was raped by Clinton while he was state attorney general in 1978. [See Chapter Six.] Even as the 1999 impeachment trial was in progress, NBC was withholding a long interview with this extremely credible and principled lady, whose affidavit sat in the "evidence room" at the House of Representatives. No Democrat ever went to look at the evidence, and this was not because of its presumed untruth. (By then, the use of the mantra "consensual sex" had become part of consensual, or consensus, politics.) And women who told the truth were accused, at best, of trying to lure a sitting president into a "perjury trap." As if it were necessary to trick Clinton into telling a lie....

Of course, in a time of "sexual McCarthyism" there's probably some advantage in being prudent. Take this little item, which appeared deadpan on page A10 of the *Washington Post* on January 30, 1999. It concerned the testimony of an "investigator" who had been hired to keep an eye on Ms. Kathleen Willey. Ms. Willey, some may recall, had been an admirer of President Clinton, had been the wife of a Democratic fund-raiser, had been a volunteer worker at the White House, had suddenly become a widow, had gone in distress to the Oval Office for comfort and for a discussion about the possibility of a paying job, and had been rewarded with a crushing embrace, some clichéd words of bar-room courtship, and the guiding by the presidential mitt of her own hand onto his distended penis. (That is, if you believe her story. It could all have been channeled into her mind by the Christian Coalition or the Aryan Nations, who then manipulated this staunch Democratic liberal into confessing her embarrassment on *60 Minutes*.) Whatever the truth of her story—and smoking guns should perhaps not be mentioned right away— she found her life altered once she had gone public. Her car tires ruined...her cat gone missing...some unexpected attention from a major Clinton fundraising crony named Nathan Landow...nothing you could quite put a name to. As the *Washington Post* unsensationally put it:

> Jarrett Stern, a private investigator, told ABC News in an interview broadcast last night that he was hired for an unspecified project by Landow, a wealthy Maryland developer who has raised hundreds of thousands of dollars for Clinton-Gore campaigns. Stern's lawyer, Edouard Bouquet of Bethesda, told the network his client felt uneasy about what he was asked to do and called Willey, using an alias, to warn her someone was out to do her harm...
>
> Stern declined to detail what he had been asked to do in connection with Willey, but he told ABC that he "wholeheartedly" believes that Willey was approached with a menacing message by a stranger jogging near her Richmond home two days before her [Paula] Jones case testimony. Willey has said the man inquired about her children by name, about her

missing cat and about whether she'd gotten the tires on her car repaired after they were mysteriously vandalized by someone who drove masses of nails into all four of them. "Don't you get the message?" she has said the man asked.

I. F. Stone once observed that the *Washington Post* was a great newspaper, because you never knew on what page you would find the Page One story. This tale made page ten on the Saturday before the United States Senate called its first witness. Let us imagine and even believe that Ms. Willey and M. Bouquet and Mr. Stern all conspired to tell a lie. You will still have to notice that it is they—lacking state power, or police power, or public-opinion power if it comes to that—who are the "sexual McCarthyites." They are McCarthyites by virtue of having made an allegation. The potential culprits—Mr. Landow or the most powerful man in the world, for whom he raised untold money—are the hapless victims. The charge of McCarthyism aimed at Ms. Willey and her unexpected corroborators could easily have been avoided. They could, after all, have kept quiet. And I almost wish that they had, because then I would not have been told by Gloria Steinem and Betty Friedan and many others that it was Clinton who dared not move outside or even inside his secure executive mansion, for fear of the female stalkers and lynchers

and inquisitors who dogged his every step. And out-
lets like *The Nation* would not have dishonored the
memory of McCarthy's victims—many of them men
and women of principle who were persecuted for
their principles and not for their deeds—by comparing their experience to the contemptible evasions of
a cheap crook. Mr. Nate Landow also tried to follow
the "McCarthyite" script as much as it lay within his
power. Confronted with questions about his lean-
ing on an inconvenient and vulnerable witness, he
eagerly sought the protection of the Fifth Amendment against self-incrimination. This and other legal
stratagems were not strange to him. Note what Dick
Morris said earlier: that when Clinton is in trouble he
resorts to the world of soft money for allies. (It is this
fact alone that destroys his claim to "privacy," and
ties together his public affluence and private squalor.)
Nathan Landow is the personification of that shady
and manipulative world. He paid a small fortune to
have Kathleen Willey flown by private jet from Rich-
mond to his mansion on Maryland's Eastern Shore,
where he "pressed her" about her deposition in the
Paula Jones case. His fund-raising organization,
IMPAC, was and remains a core group in the "money
primary" to which Democratic aspirants must submit. (He himself probably prefers Gore to Clinton.)
In 1996, he provided a microcosm of the soft-money
world in action.

The Cheyenne-Arapaho peoples of Oklahoma have been attempting for years to regain land that was illegally seized from them by the federal government in 1869. Democratic Party fund-raisers persuaded the tribes that an ideal means of gaining attention would be to donate $107,000 to the Clinton-Gore campaign. This contribution secured them a small place at a large lunch with other Clinton donors, but no action. According to the *Washington Post*, a Democratic political operative named Michael Copperthite then petitioned Landow to take up their cause. Landow first required them to register with the consulting firm of Peter Knight, who is Al Gore's chief moneyman and promoter, for a $100,000 retainer and a fee of $10,000 per month. Then he demanded that the Cheyenne-Arapaho sign a development deal with him, handing over 10 percent of all income produced on the recovered land, including the revenues from oil and gas. When news of this nasty deal—which was rejected by the tribes—became public, the Democratic National Committee was forced to return the money and the Senate Committee on Governmental Affairs issued a report describing the "fleecing" of the Indians by "a series of Democratic operators, who attempted to pick their pockets for legal fees, land development and additional contributions."

These are the sort of "Democratic operators" to

whom Clinton turns when he needs someone to take care of business. And, of course, Mr. Landow's daughter works at the White House, causing nobody to ask how she got her job. In Clinton's Washington there is always affirmative action for such people.

In the same week as the Landow-Willey revelations, the Court of Appeals decisively reinstated Judge Kenneth Starr's case against Webster Hubbell, his wife, and their two "advisers" for tax evasion. It might be said—probably was said—that when it comes to lying about taxes, "everybody does it." However, Mr. Hubbell's seeming motive in concealing a large tranche of income was not the wish to enjoy its fruits while free of tax. It was—how can one phrase this without sounding like the frightful Inspector Javert?—because he would have had difficulty explaining how he came by the money in the first place. The money, to which I had tried to call attention in my *Los Angeles Times* article a year previously, had been given him by Revlon and other normally tightfisted corporations not unconnected to the soft-money universe inhabited by Clinton. In their reinstatement of the suit, the majority on the Court of Appeals used the dread phrase "hush money" in a rather suggestive, albeit *prima facie*, manner. Many past presidents have appointed sordid underlings at the Department of Justice. One thinks of Bobby Kennedy; one thinks of Edwin

Meese. This time, however, almost nobody came forward to say that "they all do it." Perhaps this alibi had become subject, after a grueling workout, to a law that nobody can break with impunity: the law of diminishing returns. There was no sex involved, so Judge Starr was spared the routine yells about his pornographic and prurient obsessions. I continued to chant the slogan I had minted a year previously: "It's not the lipstick traces, stupid. It's the Revlon Connection."

Something like this may have occurred to Senator Russell Feingold of Wisconsin when, only two days later on January 28, he cast the only Democratic vote against dismissing the charges, and also the only Democratic vote in favor of calling witnesses to the Senate. One says "Democratic" vote, though in point of fact Senator Feingold is the only member of the Senate who is entitled to call himself an independent. In the elections of November 1998, he submitted himself for reelection having announced that he would accept no "soft money" donations. This brave decision, which almost cost him his seat, rallied many Wisconsin voters who had been raised in the grand tradition of LaFollette's mid-western populism—a populism of trustbusting rather than crowd-pleasing. His later Senate vote on impeachment, which represented the misgivings of at least five other senators who were more prudent as well as more susceptible to party discipline, forever negates the unending Clintonoid propaganda about a vast right-wing conspiracy, and also shames all those who were browbeaten into complicity: turned to stone by the waving of Medusa's Heads like Lott and Gingrich, and too slow to realize that such Gorgons were in fact Clinton's once-and-future allies, not his nemesis.

I began this prologue by disclaiming any "hidden agenda." But I think I might as well proclaim the open one. For more than a year, I watched people develop and circulate the most vulgar imaginable conspiracy theories, most of them directed at the work of an Independent Counsel, and all of them part-generated with public funds by a White House that shamelessly and simultaneously whined about its need to resume public business. I heard and saw the most damaging and defamatory muck being readied for the heads and shoulders of women who told, or who might consider telling, the plain truth. I observed, in some quite tasteful Washington surroundings, the incubation of sheer paranoia and rumor-mongering; most especially the ludicrous claim that Mr. Clinton's departure would lead—had no one read the Constitution?—to the accession of Bob Barr or Pat Robertson to the White House. (I also saw, rather satisfyingly, the same Mr. Robertson, and later all the fund-raisers of the Republican Party assembled in conclave in Palm Beach, Florida, as they beseeched the congressional party to leave Mr. Clinton alone, and in general to get with the program.) Not even this consolation, however, could make up for the pro-Clinton and anti-impeachment rally that took place in Washington on December 17, 1998. On that day, as nameless Iraqis died to make a Clinton holiday, and as the most pathetic lies were emitted from the White House, Jesse Jackson and other members of the stage-army of liberalism were gathered on the Capitol steps to wave banners and shout slogans in defense of Clinton's integrity and–yes–privacy. "A Camera in Every Bedroom," said one witless placard, perhaps confusing the off-the-record surveillance conducted by the White House with the on-the-record legal investigation to which Clinton had promised his "full cooperation." As the news of the bombing arrived, and sank in, the poor fools had an impromptu discussion about whether to proceed with their pointless rally, or to adjourn it. They went ahead. It is the argument of all these ensuing pages that the public and private faces of Clintonism are the same, as was proved on that awful day and on many others. It is the hope of these pages, also, that some of the honor of the Left can be rescued from the moral and intellectual shambles of the past seven years, in which the locusts have dined so long and so well.

Among the many occasions on which he telegraphed his personal and political character to the wider world, Clinton's speech at the funeral of Richard Nixon in April 1994 was salient. Speaking as he did after a fatuous harangue from Billy Graham, a piece of self-promoting sanctimony from Henry Kissinger, and a lachrymose performance from Robert Dole, Clinton seemed determined nonetheless to match their standard. There was fatuity in plenty: "Nixon would not allow America to quit the world." There was mawkishness and falsity to spare: "From these humble roots grew the force of a driving dream." There was one useful if alarming revelation: "Even in the final weeks of his life, he gave me his wise counsel, especially in regard to Russia." (One likes to picture Clinton getting pro-Yeltsin phone calls from the old maestro who always guessed the Russians wrong, and who also initiated the ongoing romance between Chinese Stalinism and United States multinational corporations. Perhaps that's what the calls were really about.) However, toward the close of this boilerplated and pharisaic homily, Clinton gave one hostage to fortune, which I scribbled down at the time:

Today is a day for his family, his friends, and his nation to remember President Nixon's life in totality. To them let me say: May the day of judging

President Nixon on anything less than his entire life and career come to a close.

How devoutly I wished that this prayer might be answered: the foul-mouthed anti-Semitism in the Oval Office along with the murder of Allende; the hush money and the Mafia conversations along with the aerial destruction of Indochina; the utter sexlessness along with the incurably dirty mind; the sense of incredulity and self-pity that rose to a shriek when even the least of his offenses was unearthed. I wrote down Clinton's sanctimonious words because I was sure that I would need them one day.

They were careless people, Tom and Daisy—they smashed up things and creatures and then retreated back into their money or their vast carelessness, or whatever it was that kept them together, and let other people clean up the mess they had made...
—F. Scott Fitzgerald, *The Great Gatsby*

ONE

Triangulation

To have the pleasure and the praise of electioneering ingenuity, and also to get paid for it, without too much anxiety whether the ingenuity will achieve its ultimate end, perhaps gives to some select persons a sort of satisfaction in their superiority to their more agitated fellow-men that is worthy to be classed with those generous enjoyments—of having the truth chiefly to yourself, and of seeing others in danger of drowning while you are high and dry.
—George Eliot, *Felix Holt, the Radical*

It is told of Huey Long that, contemplating a run for high office, he summoned the big wads and donors of his great state and enlightened them thus: "Those of you who come in with me now will receive a big piece of the pie. Those of you who delay, and commit yourselves later, will receive a smaller piece of pie. Those of you who don't come in at all will receive—Good Government!" A touch earthy and plebeian for modern tastes, perhaps, but there is no doubt that the Kingfish had a primal understanding of the essence of American politics. This essence, when distilled, consists of the manipulation of populism by elitism. That elite is most successful which can claim the heartiest allegiance of the fickle crowd; can present itself as most "in touch" with popular concerns; can anticipate the tides and pulses of opinion; can, in short, be the least apparently "elitist." It's no great distance from Huey Long's robust cry of "Every man a king!" to the insipid "inclusiveness" of "Putting People First," but the smarter elite managers have learned in the interlude that solid, measurable pledges have to be distinguished by a "reserve" tag that earmarks them for the bankrollers and backers. They have also learned that it can be imprudent to promise the voters too much.

Unless, that is, the voters should decide that they don't deserve or expect anything. On December 10, 1998, the majority counsel of the House Judiciary Committee, David Schippers, delivered one of the most remarkable speeches ever heard in the precincts. A leathery Chicago law 'n' order Democrat, Mr. Schippers represented the old-style, big-city, blue-collar sensibility which, in the age of Democrats Lite, it had been a priority for Mr. Clinton and his Sunbelt Dixiecrats to discard. The spirit of an earlier time, of a time before "smoking materials" had been banned from the White House, rasped from his delivery. After pedantically walking his hearers through a traditional prosecutor's review of an incorrigible perp (his address could be used in any civics class in the nation, if there were still such things as civics classes), Mr. Schippers paused and said:

> The President, then, has lied under oath in a civil deposition, lied under oath in a criminal grand jury. He lied to the people, he lied to his Cabinet, he lied to his top aides, and now he's lied under oath to the Congress of the United States. *There's no one left to lie to.*

Poor sap, I thought, as I watched this (alone in an unfazed crowd) on a screen at Miami airport. On what wheezing mule did *he* ride into town? So sincere and so annihilating, and so free from distressing sexual graphics, was his forensic presentation that, when it was over, Congressman John Conyers of the Democratic caucus silkily begged leave of the chair to compliment Mr. Schippers for his efforts. And that was that. Mr. Conyers went back to saying, as he'd said from the first, that the only person entitled to be affronted by the lie was—Mrs. Clinton. Eight days later, the Democratic leadership was telling the whole House that impeachment should not be discussed while the president and commander in chief was engaged in the weighty task of bombing Iraq.

Reluctant though many people still are to accept this conclusion, the two excuses offered by the Democrats are in fact one and the same. Excuse number one, endlessly repeated by liberals throughout 1998, holds that the matter is so private that it can only be arbitrated by the president's chief political ally and closest confidante (who can also avail herself, in case of need, of a presidential pardon). Excuse number two, taken up by the Democratic leadership and the White House as the missiles were striking Baghdad—as they had earlier struck Sudan and Afghanistan—was that the matter was so public as to impose a patriotic duty on every citizen to close ranks and keep silent. (Congressman Patrick Kennedy of Rhode Island, nephew of JFK and RFK and son of "Teddy," no doubt had Judith Exner, Sam Giancana, the Bay of Pigs, and Chappaquiddick in mind when he said that any insinuation of a connection between bombing and impeachment "bordered on treason.")

The task of reviewing the Clinton regime, then, involves the retracing of a frontier between "private" and "public," over a period when "privatization" was the most public slogan of the administration, at home and abroad. It also involves the humbler and more journalistic task of tracing and nailing a series of public lies about secret—not private—matters. Just as the necessary qualification for a good liar is a good memory, so the essential equipment of a would-be lie detector is a good timeline, and a decent archive.

Mr. Schippers was mistaken when he said that there was "no one left to lie to." He was wrong, not in the naive way that we teach children to distinguish truth from falsehood (and what a year it was for "what shall we tell the children?"). In that original, literal sense, he would have been wrong in leaving out Mr. Clinton's family, all of Mr. Clinton's foreign political visitors, and all viewers on the planet within reach of CNN. No, he was in error in that he failed to account for those who *wanted* to be lied to, and those who wished at all costs to believe. He also failed to account for Dick Morris—the sole human being to whom the mendacious president at once confided the truth. (Before, that is, he embarked on a seven-month exploitation of state power and high office to conceal such a "personal" question from others.)

The choice of Mr. Morris as confidant was suggestive, even significant. A cousin of Jules Feiffer and the late Roy Cohn (the Cohn genes were obviously dominant), Mr. Morris served for a long spell as Bill Clinton's pimp. He and Mr. Clinton shared some pretty foul evenings together, bloating and sating themselves at public expense while consigning the poor and defenseless to yet more misery. The kinds of grossness and greed in which they indulged are perfectly cognate with one another—selfish and fleshy and hypocritical and exploitative. "The Monster," Morris called Clinton when in private congress with his whore. "The creep," she called Morris when she could get away and have a decent bath. "The Big Creep" became Monica Lewinsky's post-pet telephone name for the Chief Executive. "The lesser evil" is the title that exalted liberalism has invented to describe this beautiful relationship and all that has flowed from it.

Mr. Morris's most valued gift to the president was his invention—perhaps I should say "coinage"—of the lucrative business known as "triangulation." And this same business has put a new spin on an old ball. The traditional handling of the relation between populism and elitism involves achieving a point of balance between those who support you, and those whom you support. Its classic pitfalls are the accusations that fall between flip and flop, or zig and zag. Its classic advantage is the straight plea for the benefit of the "lesser evil" calculus, which in most modern elections means a straight and preconditioned choice between one and another, or A and B, or Tweedledum and Tweedledee. The most apparently sophisticated and wised-up person, who is well accustomed to saying that "there's nothing to choose between them," can also be heard, under pressure, denouncing abstainers and waverers for doing the work of the extreme Right. In contrast, a potential Perot voter could be identified, in 1992, by his or her tendency to believe simultaneously that (a.) the two main parties were too much alike, resembling two cozily fused buttocks of the same giant *derrière*, and (b.) that the two matching hemispheres spent too much time in fratricidal strife. (Mr. Perot went his supporters one better, by demanding that the United States be run like a corporation—which it already is.) But thus is the corporatist attitude to politics inculcated, and thus failed a movement for a "Third Party" which, in its turn, had failed to recognize that there were not yet two. The same ethos can be imbibed from any edition of the *New York Times*, which invariably uses "partisan" as a pejorative and "bipartisan" as a compliment—and this, by the way, in its "objective" and "detached" news columns—but would indignantly repudiate the corollary: namely, that it views favorably the idea of a one-party system.

Let me give respective examples of the practice and theory of triangulation. The practice was captured vividly in a 1999 essay by Robert Reich, Clinton's first-term secretary of labor and one of the small core of liberal policy makers to have been a "Friend of Bill," or FOB, since the halcyon Rhodes Scholarship days of 1969. Mr. Reich here reminisces on the Cabinet discussions he attended in 1996, when the Clinton administration decided to remove many millions of mothers and children from the welfare rolls:

> When, during his 1992 presidential campaign, Bill Clinton vowed to "end welfare as we know it" by moving people "from welfare to work," he presumably did not have in mind the legislation that he signed into law in August 1996. The original idea had been to smooth the passage from welfare to work with guaranteed health care, child care, job training and a job paying enough to live on. The 1996 legislation contained none of these supports— no health care or child care for people coming off welfare, no job training, no assurance of a job paying a living wage, nor, for that matter, of a job at any wage. In effect, what was dubbed welfare "reform" merely ended the promise of help to the indigent and their children which Franklin D. Roosevelt had initiated more than sixty years before.

That is indeed how many of us remember the betrayal of the poor that year. Now here's Reich again, detailing the triangulation aspect of the decision:

In short, being "tough" on welfare was more important than being correct about welfare. The pledge
Clinton had made in 1992, to "end welfare as we
know it," and "move people from welfare to work,"
had fudged the issue. Was this toughness or compassion? It depended on how the words were interpreted.
Once elected, Clinton had two years in office with a
Congress controlled by Democrats, but, revealingly,
did not, during those years, forward to Congress a
bill to move people from welfare to work with all the
necessary supports, because he feared he could not
justify a reform that would, in fact, cost more than
the welfare system it was intended to replace.

So, as Mr. Reich goes on to relate in excruciating
detail, Mr. Clinton—who was at that stage twenty
points ahead in the opinion polls—signed legislation that was more hasty, callous, short-term, and
ill-considered than anything the Republicans could
have hoped to carry on their own. He thus made
sure that he had robbed them of an electoral issue,
and gained new access to the very donors who customarily sent money to the other party. (Mr. Reich
has good reason to remember this episode with pain.
His own wife said to him, when he got home after the
vote: "You know, your President is a real asshole.")
Yet, perhaps because of old loyalties and his Harvard
training in circumlocution, he lacks the brisk ability

to synthesize that is possessed by his spouse and also by the conservative theorist David Frum. Writing in Rupert Murdoch's *Weekly Standard* of February 1999, Mr. Frum saw through Clintonism and its triangulations with an almost world-weary ease:

> Since 1994, Clinton has offered the Democratic party a devilish bargain: Accept and defend policies you hate (welfare reform, the Defense of Marriage Act), condone and excuse crimes (perjury, campaign finance abuses) and I'll deliver you the executive branch of government...Again since 1994, Clinton has survived and even thrived by deftly balancing between right and left. He has assuaged the Left by continually proposing bold new programs—the expansion of Medicare to 55 year-olds, a national day-care program, the reversal of welfare reform, the hooking up to the Internet of every classroom, and now the socialization of the means of production via Social Security. And he has placated the Right by dropping every one of these programs as soon as he proposed it. Clinton makes speeches, Rubin and Greenspan make policy; the Left gets words, the Right gets deeds; and everybody is content.

I wouldn't describe myself as "content" with the above, or with those so easily satisfied and so credulous that they hailed the welfare bill as a "tough decision" one year, and then gave standing ovations to a cornucopia of vote-purchasing proposals in the "Lewinsky" budget that confirmed Frum's analysis so neatly a week after it was written. He is right, also, to remind people of the Defense of Marriage Act, a straight piece of gaybaiting demagogy and opportunism which Clinton rushed to sign, afterward purchasing seventy separate "spots" on Christian radio stations in order to brag about the fact. Nobody on the Left has noticed, with Frum's clarity, that it is the Left which swallows the soft promises of Clinton and the Right that demands, and gets, hard guarantees.

Clinton is the first modern politician to have assimilated the whole theory and practice of "triangulation," to have internalized it, and to have deployed it against both his own party and the Republicans, as well as against the democratic process itself. As the political waters dried out and sank around him, the president was able to maintain an edifice of personal power, and to appeal to the credibility of the office as a means of maintaining his own. It is no cause for astonishment that in this "project" he retained the warm support of Arthur Schlesinger, author of *The Imperial Presidency*. However, it might alarm the liberal Left to discover that the most acute depiction of presidential imperialism was penned by another clever young neoconservative during the 1996 election. Neatly pointing out that Clinton had been liberated by the eclipse of his congressional party in 1994 to raise his own funds and select his own "private" reelection program, Daniel Casse wrote in the July 1996 *Commentary*:

> Today, far from trying to rebuild the party, Clinton is trying to decouple the presidential engine from the Congressional train. *He has learned how the Republicans can be, at once, a steady source of new ideas and a perfect foil.* Having seen where majorities took his party over the past two decades, and what little benefit they brought him in his first months in office, he may even be quietly hoping that the Democrats remain a Congressional minority, and hence that much less likely to interfere with his second term.

Not since Walter Karp analyzed the antagonism between the Carter-era "Congressional Democrats" and "White House Democrats" had anyone so deftly touched on the open secret of party politics. At the close of the 1970s, Tip O'Neill's Hill managers had coldly decided they would rather deal with Reagan than Carter. Their Republican counterparts in the mid-1990s made clear their preference for Clinton

over Dole, if not quite over Bush. A flattering profile of Gore, written by the author of *Primary Colors*
in the *New Yorker* of October 26, 1998, stated without equivocation that he and Clinton, sure of their
commanding lead in the 1996 presidential race, had
consciously decided *not* to spend any of their surplus
money or time in campaigning for congressional
Democrats. This was partly because Mr. Gore did
not want to see Mr. Gephardt become Speaker, and
thus perhaps spoil his own chances in 2000. But the
decision also revealed the privatization of politics, as
did the annexation of the fund-raising function by a
president who kept his essential alliance with Dick
Morris (a conservative Republican and former adviser
to Jesse Helms) a secret even from his own staff.

Of course, for unanticipated reasons also having to
do with presidential privacy, by the summer of 1998
Mr. Clinton found that he suddenly *did* need partisan support on the Hill. So Casse was, if anything,
too subtle. (For Washington reasons that might one
day be worth analyzing more minutely, both he and
David Frum form part of a conservative subculture
that originates in Canada.) He was certainly too flattering to those who had not required anything so
subtle in the way of their own seduction. Even as
the three-dimensional evidence of "triangulation"
was all about them, many of the "core" Democratic
constituencies would still settle for the traditional

two-dimensional "lesser evil" cajolery: a quick flute of warm and flat champagne before the trousers were torn open ("Liar, liar—pants on fire") and the anxious, turgid member taken out and waved. Two vignettes introduce this "New Covenant":

On February 19, 1996—President's Day—Miss Monica Lewinsky was paying one of her off-the-record visits to the Oval Office. She testified ruefully that no romance, however perfunctory, occurred on this occasion. The president was compelled to take a long telephone call from a sugar grower in Florida named, she thought, "something like Fanuli." In the flat, decidedly nonerotic tones of the Kenneth Starr referral to Congress:

> Ms. Lewinsky's account is corroborated...Concerning Ms. Lewinsky's recollection of a call from a sugar grower named "Fanuli," the President talked with Alfonso Fanjul of Palm Beach, Florida, from 12.42 to 1.04 pm. Mr. Fanjul had telephoned a few minutes earlier, at 12.24 pm. The Fanjuls are prominent sugar growers in Florida.

Indeed, "the Fanjuls are prominent sugar growers in Florida." Heirs of a leading Batista-supporting dynasty in their native Cuba, they are the most prominent sugar growers in the United States. They also possess the distinction of having dumped the greatest quantity of phosphorus waste into the Everglades, and of having paid the heaviest fines for maltreating black stoop laborers from the Dominican Republic ($375,000) and for making illegal campaign contributions ($439,000). As friends of "affirmative action" for minorities, Alfonso and Jose Fanjul have benefitted from "minority set-aside" contracts for the Miami airport, and receive an annual taxpayer subvention of $65 million in sugar "price supports," which currently run at $1.4 billion yearly for the entire U.S. sugar industry. The brothers have different political sympathies. In 1992, Alfonso was Florida's financial co-chairman for the Clinton presidential campaign. Having been a vice-chairman for Bush/Quayle in 1988, in 1996 Jose was national vice-chairman of the Dole for President Finance Committee.

Alfonso Fanjul called Bill Clinton in the Oval Office, on President's Day (birthday of Washington and Lincoln), and got half an hour of ear time, even as the President's on-staff comfort-woman *du jour* was kept waiting.

Rightly is the Starr referral termed "pornographic," for its exposure of such private intimacies to public view. Even more lasciviously, Starr went on to detail the lipstick traces of the Revlon corporation in finding a well-cushioned post for a minx who was (in the only "exculpatory" statement that Clinton's hacks could seize upon) quoted as saying that "No one ever told me to lie; no one ever promised me a job." How correct the liberals are in adjudging these privy topics to be prurient and obscene. And how apt it is, in such a crisis, that a Puritan instinct for decent reticence should come to Clinton's aid.

My second anecdote concerns a moment in the White House, which was innocently related to me by George Stephanopoulos. It took place shortly after the State of the Union speech in 1996 when the president, having already apologized to the "business community" for burdening it with too much penal taxation, had gone further and declared that "the era of big government is over." There was every reason, in the White House at that stage, to adopt such a "triangulation" position and thereby deprive the Republicans of an old electoral mantra. But Stephanopoulos, prompted by electoral considerations as much as by any nostalgia for the despised New Deal, proposed a rider to the statement. Ought we not to add, he ventured, that we do not propose a policy of "Every Man For Himself"? To this, Ann Lewis, Clinton's director of communications, at once riposted scornfully that she could not approve any presidential utterance that used "man" to mean mankind. Ms. Lewis, the sister of Congressman Barney Frank and a loudly self-proclaimed feminist in her own right, was later to swallow, or better say retract, many of her own brave words about how "sex is sex," small print or no small print, and to come out forthrightly for the libidinous autonomy (and of course, "privacy") of the Big Banana. And thus we have the introduction of another theme that is critical to our story. *At all times, Clinton's retreat from egalitarian or even from "progressive" positions has been hedged by a bodyguard of political correctness.*

In his awful $2.5 million Random House turkey, artlessly entitled *Behind the Oval Office*, Dick Morris complains all the way to the till. "Triangulation," he writes, "is much misunderstood. It is not merely splitting the difference between left and right." This accurate objection—we are talking about a three-card monte and not an even split—must be read in the context of its preceding sentence: "Polls are not the instrument of the mob; they offer the prospect of leadership wedded to a finely-calibrated measurement of opinion."

By no means—let us agree once more with Mr. Morris—are polls the instrument of the mob. The mob would not know how to poll itself, nor could it afford the enormous outlay that modern polling requires. (Have you ever seen a poll asking whether or not the Federal Reserve is too secretive? Who would pay to ask such a question? Who would know how to answer it?) Instead, the polling business gives the patricians an idea of what the mob is thinking, and of how that thinking might be changed or, shall we say, "shaped." It is the essential weapon in the mastery of populism by the elite. It also allows for "fine calibration," and for capsules of "message" to be prescribed for variant constituencies.

In the 1992 election, Mr. Clinton raised discrete fortunes from a gorgeous mosaic of diversity and correctness. From David Mixner and the gays he wrung immense sums on the promise of lifting the ban on homosexual service in "the military"—a promise he betrayed with his repellent "don't ask, don't tell" policy. From a variety of feminist circles he took even larger totals for what was dubbed "The Year of the Woman," while he and his wife applauded Anita Hill for her bravery in "speaking out" about funny business behind the file cabinets. Some Jews—the more conservative and religious ones, to be precise—were massaged by Clinton's attack on George Bush's policy of withholding loan guarantees from the ultra-chauvinist Yitzhak Shamir. For the first time since Kennedy's day, Cuban-American extremists were brought into the Democratic tent by another attack on Bush from the right—this time a promise to extend the embargo on Cuba to third countries. Each of these initiatives yielded showers of fruit from the money tree. At the same time, Clinton also came to office seeming to promise universal health care, a post–Cold War sensitivity to human rights, a decent outrage about the Bush/Baker/Eagleburger cynicism in Bosnia, China, and Haiti, and on top of all that, "a government that looked more like America." Within weeks of the "People's Inaugural" in January 1993, Interior Secretary Bruce Babbitt arranged a deal on the Everglades with the Fanjul family, leaving Al Gore's famous "environmentalist" fans seething and impotent at the first of many, many disappointments.

TWO

Chameleon in Black and White

In his hot youth in the 1960s, Bill Clinton had been, on his own account, a strong supporter of the civil rights movement. Recalling those brave days during the April 1997 anniversary celebrations of Jackie Robinson's victory over Jim Crow in baseball, he told an invited audience:

> When I was a young person, both I and my family thought that the segregation which dominated our part of the country was wrong...So he was like— he was fabulous evidence for people in the South, when we were all arguing over the integration of the schools, the integration of all public facilities, basically the integration of our national life. Whenever some bigot would say something, you could always cite Jackie Robinson...You know, if you were arguing the integration side of the argument, you could always play the Jackie Robinson card and watch

the big husky redneck shut up [here the transcript shows a chuckle] because there was nothing they could say.

Actually, there would have been something the big husky redneck could have said. "Huh?" would have about covered it. Or perhaps, "Run along, kid." Jackie Robinson—a lifelong Republican—broke the color line in baseball in 1947, when Clinton was one. He retired from the game in 1956, when Clinton was nine. The Supreme Court had decided in favor of school integration two years before that. Perhaps the seven-year-old boy wonder did confront the hefty and the white-sheeted with his piping treble, but not even the fond memoirs of his doting mama record the fact.

As against that, at the close of Mr. Clinton's tenure as governor, Arkansas was the only state in the union that did not have a civil rights statute. It seems safe to say this did not trouble his conscience too heavily. Let us consult the most sympathetic biography of Clinton ever published, *The President We Deserve*, by the excellent British correspondent Martin Walker of *The Guardian*. (His book was simultaneously published in London, under the even happier title *The President They Deserve*.) Described as "truly sensational" by Sidney Blumenthal in the *New Yorker* (and thus by a reviewer who, we may be sure, intended no invasion of privacy), Walker's account of Clinton's rise covers his electoral defeat in Arkansas in 1980. Clinton had begun his two years at the State House by inviting the venomous old segregationist Orval Faubus, the former governor of Arkansas, to a place of honor at the inaugural ceremony (a step that might have caused Jackie Robinson to raise an eyebrow), but not even this was enough to protect him against vulgar, local accusations of "nigger-loving." The crunch moment came in the dying days of the Carter administration, when Cuban "Mariel boatlift" refugees were stuffed into an emergency holding pen at Fort Chaffee, and later protested against their confinement. As Walker phrases it: "The ominous black-and-white shots of dark-skinned Cuban rioters against white-faced police and Arkansans had carried a powerful subliminal message." The boyish governor knew what to do at once. (His conversion to friendship with Cuban refugees did not come until he met the Fanjul brothers.) He vowed to prevent any more Cubans from landing on Arkansas soil, and declared loudly that he would defy the federal government "even if they bring the whole United States Army down here." This echo of the rebel yell was correctly described by Paul Greenberg, columnist for the *Arkansas Democrat-Gazette*, as "a credible imitation of Orval E. Faubus." Walker tactfully omits that revealing moment, but goes on to describe, with insights from the Clinton inner circle, the conclusion that Bill and Hillary drew from the ensuing reverse at the polls: "The lessons were plain: Never be outnegatived again."

Perhaps, like the earlier TV impressions he cites, this dictum only occurs to Mr. Walker in the "subliminal" sense. But its provenance is well established. George Wallace, defeated by a less polished racist in an electoral tussle in long-ago Alabama, swore in public "never to be out-niggered again." This slogan was well known, and well understood, in all the former states of the Old Confederacy. And after 1980, Clinton clearly began to evolve a "Southern strategy" of his own.

In the 1992 run for the Democratic nomination, that strategy became plain for anyone willing to see it. Clinton took care to have himself photographed at an all-white golf club, and also standing at a prison farm photo-op, wearing his shades in the sunshine while a crowd of uniformed black convicts broke rocks in the sun. Taxed with long-time membership in the "exclusive" golf club—"inclusiveness" being only a buzz-word away—Clinton calmly replied that the club's "staff and facilities" were integrated, a "legally accurate" means of stating the obvious fact that at least the hired help was colored. He invited himself to Jesse Jackson's Rainbow Coalition conference, and there went out of his way (having alerted reporters in the meantime) to pick a fight with the inflammatory rap lyrics of Sister Souljah. Ambushed in this style, the Reverend Jackson exasperatedly—and rather presciently—described the hungry young candidate as "just an appetite." Clinton fashioned an electoral mantra out of the promise to "end welfare as we know it," making the morals of the underclass into the salient issue and none-too-subtly leaving the hue of that class to the imagination. Most memorably—I say this in spite of the fact that so many people have succeeded in forgetting it—he quit the thick of the New Hampshire primary, in January 1992, in order to fly back to Arkansas and give personal supervision to the execution of Rickey Ray Rector.

Rector was a black lumpen failure, convicted of a double murder, who had shot himself in the head on arrest and achieved the same result as a frontal lobotomy would have done. He understood his charge and trial and sentence not at all. Nursed back to life and condemned to death, he had spent a decade on Death Row in Cummins prison. His execution number came up in a week when Clinton, according to one report of the poll numbers, had lost twelve points as a result of the Gennifer Flowers disclosures. These two "numbers" were accordingly made to intersect. In 1988, Clinton had backed the ludicrous presidential campaign of Michael Dukakis, a personal coward and political dolt who had lost an easy argument about capital punishment in a public debate with George Bush, and who had also suffered from a sleazy "subliminal" campaign about a dusky parole-breaking rapist named Willie Horton. Official Democratic folklore (which also carefully forgot that Horton had first been used by Senator Al Gore as a weapon against Dukakis in the primaries) coagulated around the view that no candidate should ever be out-Hortoned again. The mass media ministered to this "perception." In the week of the Flowers revelations, *Time* magazine helpfully inquired: "Suppose Clinton does sew up the nomination by mid-March and the Republicans discover a Willie Horton in his background?" The quasi-sentient Rickey Ray Rector was to provide the perfect rebuttal to such annoying speculations about the governor's credibility.

A few columnists—the late Murray Kempton, Jimmy Breslin, and your humble servant among them—commented with disgust on this human sacrifice, but the press pack preferred to use Clinton's successful lying about Gennifer Flowers as the test of his fitness for high office. It was not until more than a year later that the whole story of Rector's last days was recounted by Marshall Frady in a long essay in the *New Yorker*. Served his traditional last meal, Rector had left the pecan pie on the side of the tray, as he incoherently explained to his queasy guards, "for later." Strapped to a gurney, he had tried to help his executioners find a viable vein (his blood vessels were impaired by an antipsychotic drug) before they inflicted a "cut-down" and slashed the crook of his arm with a scalpel to insert a catheter. It seems he thought they were physicians trying to help him. For many poor Americans of all colors, jail is the only place where doctors, lawyers, teachers, and chaplains are, however grudgingly, made available to them. An hour was spent on the cut-down process, before the death-giving chemicals could kick in. Warden Willis Sargent, a tough former Army non-com, was assailed by misgivings as the deadline approached. "Rickey's a harmless guy," he said. "This is not something I want to do." The police department witness, Lieutenant Rodney Pearson (Rector had shot a cop) found himself having second thoughts as he watched an obviously gravely retarded and uncomprehending prisoner being subjected to the "strap-down." The chaplain, Dennis Pigman, resigned from the prison system shortly afterward, saying: "I hate murder. I hate murderers. But to execute children? What was done to Rickey Ray Rector was in itself, absolutely, a crime. A horrible crime. We're not supposed to *execute children.*"

Well, that of course depends on the needs of the hour, and the requirements of a "New Democrat." Most nauseating, in Mr. Frady's account, was the lip-biting conduct of Governor Clinton himself. At all

times, he pretended—to Rector's lawyer Jeff Rosen-
zweig and to others who managed to reach him in
the closing moments—that this was a very painful
moment for him *personally*. But that same affectation exposed itself when he received a telephone
call from his friend Carolyn Staley, director of the
Governor's Commission on Adult Literacy. Hearing
on the radio that Rector's execution was stalled by
the snag of finding a usable vein, she telephoned her
friend Bill and he called her back and—well, I'll let
Mr. Frady tell it:

> She told him, "I just wanted to let you know that
> I'm praying for you about the execution tonight,"
> and he replied in a groan, "It's just awful. Just ter-
> rible, terrible." As she recalls it now, "I heard in his
> voice a self—a depth of anguish—I'd never, never
> heard in him before." She then told him, "You
> know, he's not even dead yet." "*What?*" she remem-
> bers him exclaiming. "*What?*" From his startlement,
> it was obvious to her that the conference in which
> he had been absorbed had not exactly been a "blow
> by blow" account of Rector's fate … Staley then told
> him, "Bill, I'm so sorry. We've had two executions
> this week, haven't *we*." She meant the Flowers allega-
> tions. "He just groaned," she remembers, and they
> moved on to discussing that topic. Ultimately, she
> says, the conversation wound up "much more about

the Gennifer Flowers matter" than about what was happening to Rector at that moment down at Cummins.

Easy to believe. One is compelled to acknowledge the versatility, and the quick-change between ostentatious pain-feeling and everyday political instinct. It was during those same closing moments that Clinton and his spouse decided on their celebrated *60 Minutes* strategy, and left Little Rock refreshed for a round of campaign and fund-raising appearances where the "character question" would be conveniently limited to a choice between a dizzy blonde and a "strong woman." This moment deserves to be remembered for a number of reasons: first because it introduces a Clintonian mannerism of *faux* "concern" that has since become tediously familiar, second because it illuminates his later attitude toward matters racial, and matters penal, and third because it marks the first of many times that Clinton would deliberately opt for death as a means of distraction from sex.

I followed Clinton from New Hampshire to Arkansas to California to New York that season, noticing with subdued admiration the ways in which his fans and staffers would recommend him in private. "He's already won the two invisible primaries," one was often told by the wised-up, "the money primary and the polling primary." This was true enough; the "donor community" had adopted him early, and the pundits likewise conferred the charismatic title of "front-runner" before a single New Hampshire ballot had been cast. Clinton actually lost that primary, which pundits and other political chin-pullers had hitherto described as a *sine qua non*, but it was then decided, in the circles that "counted," that this didn't count this time. Most amazing though, was the frequently heard observation that Clinton, as a Southerner, "understood black people." This extraordinary piece of condescension was convertible currency, as it turned out, because of the jolt delivered to consensus by the disorders in Los Angeles. Nervous voters everywhere found Bush's response to be insufficiently fuzzy. Clinton, it was widely assumed, would be more "caring" and "healing." The impression—again "subliminal"—helped him considerably. But an impression it was. Clinton gave the City of the Angels a wide berth, and limited his comments to some platitudes, taken from the playbook of neoconservatism, about the "culture of poverty" in South Central.

That very idiom—naturally concerned yet nonetheless strict—was to become the substratum of his now-celebrated "comfort level" with black Americans while in office. Obviously on good personal terms with Vernon Jordan and Ron Brown and Mike Espy (one of them a conduit to Pamela Harriman's opulent PAC, one of them the genius fund-extorter of the Democratic National Committee, and one of them a long-time friend of Tyson Foods), Clinton also rocked to Aretha Franklin on the Mall during his inauguration and invited Maya Angelou to deliver a piece of doggerel poetry at the ceremony itself. Well versed in the cant of Southern Baptist rhetorical uplift, the new president was capable of working the crowd at black church services, just as, infinitely protean in devotional matters, he never looked out of place standing next to Billy Graham or Mother Teresa. However, there were four occasions when push, to employ an old political cliche, came to shove.

The first of these moments took place when Clinton proposed Dr. Lani Guinier to head the Civil Rights Division of the Justice Department. Dr. Guinier was and is a legal scholar of some distinction. She and her husband had invited the Clintons to their wedding, and had helped introduce them to polite society on Martha's Vineyard. She had helped calm Jesse Jackson and other black leaders after Clinton had staged the Sister Souljah headline grabber. ("You got your story," Jackson had crisply told George Stephanopoulos and Paul Begala as he left the platform on that occasion.) However, in essays for the *Yale Law Review* and other journals, Dr. Guinier had made the unpardonable mistake of thinking aloud about proportional representation in Dixie. After being fed a misleading attack circulated by Abigail Thernstrom, a neoconservative opponent of affirmative action, the Republican Right pounced, and arraigned her as a "Quota Queen" opposed to majority—or at any rate majoritarian—rule. This was a slander. Dr. Guinier had expressed her opposition to quotas on principle, and had actually written on the need for electoral "weighting" arrangements to protect the *white* minority in South Africa. She was also in the process of making an excellent impression on the Republican senators who had originally believed the first-draft briefing papers circulated by extremists about her. None of this prevented Clinton's peremptory withdrawal, in June 1993, of her nomination:

> At the time of the nomination, I had not read her writings. I wish I had. The problem is that this battle will be waged based on her academic writings. And I cannot fight a battle that I know is divisive, that is an uphill battle, that is distracting to the country, if I do not believe in the ground of the battle. That is the only problem.

These were early days, and the delight of parsing a Clinton paragraph had not yet attained to the joy it has since become. Still, it is striking to note that Clinton did not "believe in the ground of the battle."

The ground of the battle, according to him, was "her academic writings." And these awkward texts he had, on his own admission, "not read." There was, in the tenses, a very slight suggestion that he might have read them *since* the nomination, in which case he could have discerned for himself, as a Yale Law graduate and a member of the bar, that what was being said about his friend was literally and figuratively untrue. But even that suggestion was overshadowed by a declared refusal to involve himself with anything that was "divisive," or that might involve "an uphill battle," or that could "distract the country." And this reluctance in turn would seem to exclude any very staunch commitment to racial equality, let alone to facing down "big husky rednecks" in the Deep South, as six-or-was-it-nine-year-old Bill had once known how to do.

The grace note was left to Mrs. Clinton, who happened to pass by Dr. Guinier in a corridor just as the news of the administration's retreat was sinking in. Waving to her old friend without breaking stride, the First Lady managed to blurt the words "Hey kiddo!" adding ten paces later that she was "half an hour late for a luncheon" before pushing on and leaving her to reflect. A final insult was also delivered, and recorded in Dr. Guinier's extremely literate and persuasive memoir, *Lift Every Voice:*

We had tried to get Vernon Jordan to come. Vernon had told me he could be helpful with Senator Alan Simpson. During a relaxed, one-on-one meeting in his law office, Vernon had offered to meet or call Simpson on my behalf should that become necessary. When Vernon was subsequently asked to follow up with Simpson, he reportedly said, "I don't do that kind of thing."

Oh but he does, he does... When the rich and spoiled daughters of donors and fund-raisers are given affirmative-action jobs at the White House, Mr. Jordan can't do enough of that kind of thing.

White House aversion to the "divisive" may have been genuine in its own terms, because the important civil rights post at Justice went unfilled for more than twelve months (nothing divisive about that, one is compelled to notice) before going to Deval Patrick. Mr. Patrick, who might without unfairness be described as one of the less prominent members of the administration, found himself short of "access" and "input" and other crucial resources. In January 1995, he decided not to accompany Mr. Clinton to Dr. King's birthplace in Atlanta for the annual birthday commemoration. He had discovered that the president's speech would not allude to civil rights, but would take the form of a stern lecture on good behavior to young black men. Mr. Patrick had failed to divine Mr. Clinton's original and essential "message," dating back to his days at the Democratic Leadership Council: It is time for some people in society to set a good example of moral continence, industry, and thrift. Since this admonition is not going to be delivered to the Fanjuls, or to Roger Tamraz, or to the Hollywood "benefit nights," it may as well be orated, with suitable notice for the networks, to a captive audience of another sort. (In *The Importance of Being Earnest*, Algernon languidly observes that if the lower orders will not set an example, it is difficult to see the point of them.)

Clinton's next test of loyalty to black friends and colleagues involved his surgeon-general, Dr. Joycelyn Elders. Never popular with the phalanx that concentrated around the "Contract With America," this lady was to make two mistakes. Charged with responsibility for matters of public health, she asked whether it might be wise to lift the prohibition, not of soft narcotics, but on any debate about decriminalizing them. The striking thing about Mr. Clinton's rapid response was not his stony opposition to decriminalization but his vehement opposition to the merest mention of the topic. It was the debate, not the proposal, that he forbade. In effect, he told

34

his surgeon-general to shut up. That was, had she but known how to recognize it, her "first strike." Nor was she allowed three. At another public forum, where the subject was sexual well-being among American teenagers, Dr. Elders proposed an open discussion of masturbation, as well as of the existing choice between latex sheaths and abstinence. The presidential firing that followed was swift and peremptory. It was as if the good doctor had publicly defiled the temple of her own body. One feels almost laughably heavy-footed in pointing out that Mrs. Clinton's prim little book, *It Takes a Village*, proposes sexual abstinence for the young, and that the president was earnestly seconding this very proposal while using an impressionable intern as the physical rather than moral equivalent of a blow-up doll.

The third instance—one exempts altogether the "National Initiative" of conversation about race and racism, which withered on the vine and lost the president's attention altogether—concerns Peter and Marian Wright Edelman. With a near peerless record in the civil rights movement (it was Marian Wright Edelman who first introduced Hillary Clinton to Vernon Jordan), this couple had worked unstintingly for Democratic liberalism and in the conviction that children should not suffer for the blunders or crimes or sheer failures of their parents.

By 1996, with welfarism and welfare mothers the main, if not sole, political culprits in a social land-scape rife with every other kind of depredation, this simple concept seemed as sinister as Sweden—almost as sinister as socialism itself. Going further than any Republican president had ever dared venture, and prompted every day by Dick Morris, who consid-ered this boldness to be the essence of triangulation, Clinton proposed that a sixty-year federal commit-ment to children in poverty be scrapped, and the whole problem be referred to the budget-conscious fifty states. A provision in the bill mandated that if a woman would not or could not give the name of her child's father, or objected to this invasion of her privacy, she could be stricken from the welfare rolls.

Shortly after the November elections, I was given an eyewitness account of the White House conclave at which the Clintonoid inner circle made its decision to sign the welfare bill. Not all the positions taken at this "defining" meeting were predictable: the stern-est and longest holdout against the act was mounted by Treasury Secretary Robert Rubin, though I sup-pose he did have reasons of New York exceptionalism for taking this stand. Another detail that my infor-mant let fall is worth "sharing." There was, he said, one argument that carried no weight in the room. This was the view, put forward by Mr. Morris, that failure to sign the bill would result in a Republican victory in November. "Dick won," he said, "but not because he persuaded anyone of that."

On September 11, Peter Edelman, after long service at the Department of Health and Human Services, had tendered his resignation. This gave him the distinction, along with two colleagues who resigned at the same time and for the same reasons, of being the only example of a departure on principle from either Clinton administration. Edelman resigned, not just because of the policy decision itself, but because of the extreme cynicism that lay behind it.

At about the same time, Dick Morris was caught by a tabloid newspaper in the Jefferson Hotel, wasting his substance (and perhaps other people's too) with harlots and high living. No relativist words about privacy or consenting adults were spoken on this occasion: it was an election season, after all, and the president dropped him from the team without compunction. But in compensation, he and his wife publicly lamented Mr. Morris's fate, and wished him back very soon (and got him back even sooner, though without advising anybody of the fact). I chanced to run into Peter Edelman at about the same time, and asked him out of curiosity: "Did you get any calls from Bill or Hillary asking you to stay, or saying they're sorry you went?" No, Mr. Edelman had not. Like Lani Guinier, who never heard from her old friends the Clintons again (apart from a machine-generated Christmas card), he had been triangulated out of political existence.

Mike Espy, another black Clinton appointment, was secretary for agriculture until he was accused of taking favors and gratuities from the agribusiness interests he was supposed to regulate and supervise. An application from the special prosecutor to investigate the whole pattern of political donations from Don Tyson and Tyson Foods was immediately rejected by Attorney General Janet Reno, a biddable mediocrity whose tenure at the Justice Department was itself something of a scandal. As a consequence, the evidence against Espy became rather a matter of nickels and dimes, and he was eventually acquitted. With the acquittal secure, Clinton found the courage to offer congratulations. But Mr. Espy was not as impressed as he might have been by this display of summer-soldier solidarity. He had, after all, been fired from the Cabinet as soon as the charges against him had been made. And Clinton had delegated the firing to his chief of staff Leon Panetta, afterward keeping his distance entirely. Mr. Espy could have consoled himself on one score, however. There could be no question of any discrimination in his case. His boss would always abandon a friend in trouble, regardless of race, color, or creed. Only men like Webster Hubbell received continued, solicitous attention, at least in the period elapsing between their indictments and the expiry of the statute of limitations.

During the 1990 midterm elections, the most blatantly racist electoral appeal was offered by Senator Jesse Helms of North Carolina. Nobody who was anywhere near a liberal mailing list between the years 1980 and 1996 could have avoided a solicitation from various Democrat-sponsored coalitions against "The New Right's Prince of Darkness." By hauling up buckets of sludge from the deepest wells of the racist and fundamentalist Old Confederacy, Helms had made himself the most visible and unapologetic target. But his last-ditch TV advertisement of 1994 became the standard by which the liberals measured cynicism. On screen, a pair of work-worn white hands were seen opening an envelope, and then sadly crumpling the enclosed missive. "You needed that job," said the sorrowful voice-over, "but it had to go to a minority." But I have found that most liberals are still shocked to hear that the author of the "white hands" TV incitement was—Dick Morris.

They have no right to be shocked. By late 1998, it was being openly said in Democratic and liberal quarters that the wronged President Clinton was being lynched, yes, just as Clarence Thomas had once been lynched, by a posse of big and husky rednecks. On the floor of the House, with the evident

approval of the Democratic leadership, Maxine
Waters said that the defense of this wronged man
was the moral equivalent of the fight against slavery
and segregation. During the Senate trial, the White
House fielded a young black woman attorney, Cheryl
Mills, to make essentially the same point. And when
the trial managers failed to call the president's secretary Betty Currie, the race card was played yet again.
Clinton's spinners successfully spread the word that
the senators feared to question a shy and dignified
black lady (whose life, incidentally, had been made
a hell of lawyer's bills by the actions of her boss) lest
she break down and cry. There was something brilliantly sordid about this last innuendo: nobody knew
better than the White House that a private deal had
been made between senators Lott and Daschle to
restrict the number of witnesses to three. And these
potentates had decided that Sidney Blumenthal was
a better test of Clinton's human shield than a fragile
secretary.

This sort of tactic works well enough for the daily
news cycle, and for the latest opinion poll. But it may
not be enough to satisfy the high-minded that they
are, as ever, on the right side. (Or, to put it another
way, that the side they are on is the right one.) The
niche market of the intellectuals—once described
by Harold Rosenberg as "the herd of independent
minds"—was to be served by its own designated

hero, the former playwright Arthur Miller. Writing in the *New York Times* on October 15, 1998, the author of *The Crucible* shared the following thoughts:

> Witch-hunts are always spooked by women's horrifying sexuality awakened by the superstud Devil. In Europe, where tens of thousands perished in the hunts, broadsides showed the Devil with two phalluses, one above the other. And of course mankind's original downfall came about when the Filthy One corrupted the mother of mankind. In Salem, witch-hunting ministers had the solemn duty to examine women's bodies for signs of the "Devil's Marks"—a suggestion of webbing, perhaps, between the toes, a mole behind an ear or between the legs, or a bite mark somewhere. I thought of this wonderfully holy exercise when Congress went pawing through Kenneth Starr's fiercely exact report on the President's intimate meetings with Monica Lewinsky. I guess nothing changes all that much.

Oh but surely, Mr. Miller, some things have changed? Just to take your observations in order, Miss Paula Jones—the witch or bitch in this case, depending on whether you take the verdict of James Carville or Edward Bennett—did not accuse the president of flaunting two phalluses. Indeed, she implied that it would have taken two of his phalluses to make one normal one, which could even be part of the reason why he paid her the sum of $840,000 to keep quiet. (This payment involved dipping into the "blind trust" maintained by his wife, and perhaps put aside for a rainy day after her success in the cattle-futures and other markets.) Stepping lightly over this point, Mr. Clinton has admitted to nothing at all *except* the defilement of his relations with his wife and the mother of his daughter, and has used the pain of them for Bible-bearing photo-ops on every Sunday morning since then. No woman's body was probed by the inquisitors of the Starr team, though there do seem to have been some very close examinations—and even a few bite marks, according to some—visited by the chief executive on certain females. Rather, the Starr team examined the body of the world's most powerful man, as a result of a legal process that had been initiated by one of the world's least powerful women and seconded on a 9–0 vote by the Supreme Court. You are right in describing the Starr findings as "fiercely exact," because not even the Alpha male defendant has challenged them. Yet Congress had no choice but to "paw through" said findings, which were lawfully commissioned by the Alpha male's usually complicit female attorney general. And the evidence there discovered—necessarily a bit grungy, as is common with investigations of sexual harassment, and with evasions of same—consisted not of "Devil's Marks" but of matching DNA.

The above does not prove that Clinton is The Evil One, but it does prove beyond a peradventure that Arthur Miller is The Stupid One. Would he let it go at that? He would not. Digging a deeper ditch for himself, and handing up the shovel, he continued:

> Then there is the color element. Mr. Clinton, according to Toni Morrison, the Nobel Prize-winning novelist, is our first black President, the first to come from the broken home, the alcoholic mother, the under-the-bridge shadows of our ranking systems.

Thus, we may have lost the mystical power to divine diabolism, but we can still divine blackness by the following symptoms: broken homes, alcoholic mothers, under-the-bridge habits, and (presumable from the rest of Arthur Miller's senescent musings) the tendency to sexual predation and to shameless perjury about same. I can remember a time when Ronald Reagan's genial caricature of the vodka-soaked welfare mother was considered "offensive" by all those with OK opinions, if only because half the white children in America had been brought up by caring nannies—sober and decent black ladies—who had to tend to their own children when they had finished with their day jobs. But in Reagan's day, the children of the most shiftless white or black mother were still guaranteed a federal minimum. And Reagan would never have dared to stage a *Primary Colors* photo-op execution—if only for fear of the fulminant liberal response that Clinton avoided. In the asinine remarks of Miller, the Left's hero of the 1950s, political correctness has achieved its own negation.

In July 1998, during the third and last televised forum of his national "dialogue" on race, Clinton was confronted by the Native American poet and novelist Sherman Alexie, who complained that many of his fellows were still living in the United States' version of the Third World. Responding, Clinton announced that his grandmother had been one-quarter Cherokee. This claim, never advanced before, would, if true, have made him the first Native American president. It didn't wash with Alexie, who later observed that people "are always talking about race in coded language. What they will do is come up to me and say they're Cherokee." Clinton did his best to be the first to laugh. Within weeks, Clinton's symbolic pandering brought him a balloon of black sympathy in the bell curves of the opinion polls. He had hired Jesse Jackson to replace Billy Graham as Minister of choice and to counsel his stricken daughter, and he had closed his "atonement" appeal for the

November 1998 elections at a fund-raiser in a black church in Baltimore, Maryland—an unconstitutional action for which he was later sued by Americans United for the Separation of Church and State. By these last-minute improvisations, he had, without calling any undue attention to the fact, become the first president to play the race card both ways—once traditionally and once, so to speak, in reverse. His opportunist defenders, having helped him with a reversible chameleonlike change in the color of his skin, still found themselves stuck with the content of his character.

THREE
The Policy Coup

History does not record the nature of the luncheon for which Hillary Clinton was so late that she could only spare a "Hey kiddo" for an endangered and isolated friend. But at that stage of 1993, she was, to outward appearances, all radiant energy and business in pursuit of health care for all. Many initiatives were put "on hold" because they were thought subordinate to this overarching objective. The late Les Aspin, Clinton's luckless and incompetent secretary of defense, once told me that he had planned to make a brief personal appearance in Sarajevo, in order to keep some small part of the empty campaign promise made by Clinton to the Bosnians, but had been ordered to stay at home lest attention be distracted from "Hillary's healthcare drive." To this day, many people believe that the insurance companies torpedoed a worthwhile if somewhat complex plan. In numerous self-pitying accounts, the First Lady and her underlings have spoken with feeling on the point. Perhaps you remember the highly successful "Harry and Louise" TV slots, where a painfully average couple pondered looming threats to their choice of family physician. As Mrs. Clinton put it in a fighting speech in the fall of 1993:

I know you've all seen the ads. You know, the kind of homey kitchen ads where you've got the couple sitting there talking about how the President's plan is going to take away choice and the President's plan is going to narrow options, and then that sort of heartfelt sigh by that woman at the end, "There must be a better way"—you know, you've seen that, right? What you *don't* get told in the ad is that it is paid for by insurance companies. It is time for you and for every American to stand up and say to the insurance industry: "Enough is enough, we want our healthcare system back!"

It is fortunate for the Clintons that this populist appeal was unsuccessful. Had the masses risen up against the insurance companies, they would have discovered that the four largest of them—Aetna, Prudential, Met Life, and Cigna—had helped finance and design the "managed-competition" scheme which the Clintons and their Jackson Hole Group had put forward in the first place. These corporations, and the Clintons, had also decided to exclude from consideration, right from the start, any "single-payer" or "Canadian-style" solution. A group of doctors at the Harvard Medical School, better known as Physicians for a National Health Program, devised a version of single-payer which combined comprehensive coverage, to include the 40 million uninsured Americans, with free choice in the selection of physicians. The Congressional Budget Office certified this plan as the most cost-effective on offer. Dr. David Himmelstein, one of the leaders of the group, met Mrs. Clinton in early 1993. It became clear, in the course of their conversation, that she wanted two things simultaneously: the insurance giants "on board," and the option of attacking said giants if things went wrong. Dr. Himmelstein laid out the advantages of his plan, and pointed out that some 70 percent of the public had shown support for such a scheme. "David," said the First Lady, before wearily dismissing him, "tell me something interesting."

The "triangulation" went like this. Harry and Louise sob-story ads were paid for by the Health Insurance Association of America (HIAA), a group made up of the smaller insurance providers. The major five insurance corporations spent even more money to support "managed competition" and to buy up HMOs as the likeliest investment for the future. The Clintons demagogically campaigned against the "insurance industry," while backing—and with the backing of—those large fish that were preparing to swallow the minnows. This strategy, invisible to the media (which in those days rather liked the image of Hillary versus the fat cats), was neatly summarized by Patrick Woodall of Ralph Nader's Public Citizen:

> The managed-competition-style plan the Clintons have chosen virtually guarantees that the five largest health-insurance companies—Aetna, Prudential, Met Life, Cigna, and The Travelers—will run the show in the health-care system.

And Robert Dreyfuss of Physicians for a National Health Program added:

> The Clintons are getting away with murder by portraying themselves as opponents of the insurance industry. It's only the small fry that oppose their plan. Under any managed-competition scheme, the small ones will be pushed out of the market very quickly.

As indeed it was to prove. Having come up with a plan that embodied the worst of bureaucracy and the worst of "free enterprise," and having seen it fail abjectly because of its abysmal and labyrinthine complexity, the Clintons dropped the subject of health care for good. The president threw away the pen that he told the Congress he would only use to sign a bill for universal and portable coverage, and instead proposed no bill or remedy at all. Thus was squandered a political consensus on health care which had taken a decade to build up, and which had been used by the Clintons as a short-term electoral vehicle against a foundering George Bush. Since they had been gambling, in effect, with other people's chips, the First Couple felt little pain.

The same could not be said for the general population, or for the medical profession, which was swiftly annexed by huge HMOs like Columbia Sunrise. Gag rules for doctors, the insistence on no-choice allocations of primary "caregivers," and actual bonuses paid to physicians and nurses and emergency rooms that denied care, or even restricted access to new treatments, soon followed. So did the exposure of extraordinary levels of corruption in the new health-care conglomerates. Until the impeachment crisis broke, no comment was made by the administration about any of these phenomena, which left most patients and most doctors measurably worse off than they had been in 1992.

By the fall of 1998, with his personal and legal problems mounting, the president could attract defenders of the caliber of Gore Vidal, who spoke darkly about a backdoor revenge mounted by the insurance oligarchy through the third-party agency of Kenneth Starr. Perhaps encouraged by this, Clinton belatedly came out for a Patients' Bill of Rights, proposed by many in Congress to protect Americans from the depredations of HMOs. This last triangulation—offering to help plug a wound that he had himself inflicted—was perhaps the most satisfying of all. In a strong field, it remains perhaps the most salient example of the Clintonian style of populism for the poor and reassurance for the rich or, if you prefer, big pieces of pie for the fat cats and "good government" for the rest.

Whether the "capital" is moral or political or just plain financial, the Clinton practice is to use other people's. Some good judges would cite campaign financing, even more than health care, as the classic demonstration of that principle in operation. Perhaps more than any one thing, the system of private political fund-raising licenses the plaintive yelp, routinely emitted by anyone indicted or accused, to the effect that "everybody does it." Even by this debased standard, however, the Clinton administration was to achieve prodigies of innovation and excess. It was also to show ingenuity in the confection of excuses and alibis. One of these excuses was "privacy." No sooner had the suggestion been made that the Clintons were auctioning off the Lincoln Bedroom than Neel Lattimore, then the First Lady's press secretary, replied with indignation: "This is their home, and they have guests visit them all the time. Mrs. Clinton and Chelsea have friends that spend the night, but these names are not available to the public." The vulgar "public," which actually owns the White House, has no right to peek inside. Second-order stonewall replies took the more traditional form of the "security" defense, the separation of powers defense, and the flat-out lie. The Center for Public Integrity in Washington, which first tried to ventilate the matter, was told by the social secretary's office that: "No one in the White House will release that kind of information about guests anyway. I think it's for security reasons." The president's associate counsel, Marvin Krislov, discovered that "The Office of the President is not an 'agency' for purposes of the Freedom of Information Act," a "finding" that was worth having for its own sake. And Amy Weiss Tobe, press secretary to the Democratic National Committee, said of the story: "This has become an urban myth, like the alligators in the sewers of New York. It is just not true."

There may be no carnivorous reptiles in the underground waterways of Manhattan, but it was eventually established that almost eighty major donors and fund-raisers had indeed been thrashing about in the Lincoln and the Queen's bedrooms at 1600 Pennsylvania Avenue. The invitations were sometimes

NO ONE LEFT TO LIE TO

offered as rewards, and sometimes as inducements. Steve Grossman, president of the Massachusetts Envelope Company and of the America-Israel Public Affairs Committee (AIPAC), contributed at least $400,000 to the Democratic Party and to Mr. Clinton's election campaigns between 1991 and 1996. Nor was an overnight stay at the White House— following a state dinner for the president of Brazil— his only reward. His wife, Barbara, was appointed by the president to the National Council of the Arts, and he himself became a "managing trustee" for the Democratic National Committee. Other beneficiaries-cum-benefactors included David Geffen and Steven Spielberg of DreamWorks ($389,000 and $236,500, respectively), the Waltons of Wal-Mart ($216,800), the Nortons of Norton Utilities ($350,750), and Larry and Shelia Lawrence of the Hotel del Coronado and associated real estate ($100,000, counting contributions from their companies and their company's employees). Despite the rumors about a liaison between the president and Mrs. Lawrence, the Clintons always insisted on high standards of propriety, stipulating for example that unmarried couples—even consenting ones— could not sleep together in Mr. Lincoln's chamber. Mr. Lawrence later achieved a brief celebrity by his triple crown of buying, lying, and dying: buying the ambassadorship to Switzerland, lying about his wartime service, and consequently being exhumed from Arlington Cemetery, where he had been mistakenly interred with full fund-raising honors.

The franchising of the Lincoln Bedroom gave way ultimately to the selling of the Oval Office itself. At forty-four separate "coffee" meetings between August 3, 1995 and August 23, 1996, President Clinton personally received the sweepings of the international black-bag community in his official quarters, and asked them for money. "Nice to see you again," he says to Roger Tamraz, pipeline artist and fugitive from justice, on one of the videos shot by the White House Communications Agency (WHCA). These videos became a source of controversy, for two reasons. During the Senate inquiry into the breach of campaign finance laws, in October 1997, the White House promised to turn over all materials relating to solicitation. The tapes, however, were not "discovered" by administration officials until the deadline was almost past. Then there was a further delay in handing them to the Justice Department. The legal deadline for Attorney General Reno to decide on whether or not to "expand" her inquiry was Friday, October 4. The tapes—the existence of which had been confirmed to Senate investigators the preceding Wednesday—were delivered to Justice on Saturday, October 5. No official explanation for this—at minimum—1,680-minute delay was ever offered by the White House.

The second reason for the brief notoriety of the tapes was the appearance on one of them of John Huang, a Chinese financier and fund-raiser with intimate connections in Beijing. He is shown shaking Clinton's hand on June 18, on the only tape which has no audio. Because the soundtrack was sadly missing, allegations from other witnesses that Mr. Huang opened the proceedings with a fund-raising appeal could not be confirmed. It is not legal to use the public-business spaces of the executive mansion—the Oval Office, the Roosevelt Room, and the Map Room—for the shaking down of the well-heeled, and most especially not for the shaking down of the well-heeled emissaries of foreign despotisms in China, Indonesia, and the Middle East. Donald L. Fowler, national co-chairman of the Democratic Party, shows a lively and acute awareness of this when, on a videotape from the Map Room on December 13, 1995, he is heard declining an offer of five checks from an unidentified guest as the President discusses golf. "As soon as this thing is over, I'll call you," says Fowler, while making a suggestive passing reference to the legal profession. "I'm sorry. I can't take this. I apologize to you, and we'll get it done." It got done, all right.

* * *

The pen of a Thomas Nast would be required to do justice to Lanny J. Davis, a "special counsel" to the White House. "Holding this type of event was legal and appropriate," he said on October 5, 1997. "There is no suggestion that there was any solicitation for money." On the same day he added: "These tapes are not inconsistent with what we have previously described to be the purpose of these coffees: to encourage people to support the President and his programs and that included financial support." So checks were written but only after the event and were thus, he maintained, "incidental." As for keeping those innocuous tapes from the later Senate inquiry: "That was inadvertent. We have always acted in good faith." Several senators mentioned the ominous words "obstruction of justice." (In late 1998, Mr. Davis's skills were required again to stave off impeachment, and he returned from private practice to the White House team. Shall I ever forget appearing with him on TV on the day of the impeachment vote, and hearing him say that there was nothing Nixonian about Clinton, before urging all good men and women to support the "censure" compromise dreamed up by the Nixon-pardoning Gerald Ford?)

It may be worth noting that Mr. Clinton took federal matching funds from the taxpayers to keep pace with his exorbitant spending, and never pretended to be "out of the loop." One video of a high-tab feast at the Hay-Adams Hotel, on December 7, 1995, has him gloating to his contributors: "We realized we could run these ads through the Democratic Party, which means we could raise [soft] money in twenty, fifty, and one-hundred thousand-dollar blocks. We didn't have to do it all in thousand-dollar contributions and run down what I can spend, which is limited by law. So that is what we have done." A video of another Lucullan repast at this hotel, on February 19, 1996, has him thanking his benefactors in the same fulsome way: "In the last quarter of last year...we spent about $1 million per week to advertise our point of view to somewhere between 26 and 42 percent of the American electorate...The lead that I enjoy today in public opinion polls is about one-third due to that advertising...I cannot overstate to you the impact that these paid ads have had." Since soft money is by definition not to be lawfully spent in promoting a candidate, Mr. Clinton appears to have been more unbuttoned and candid to his bankrollers than he ever was with the target voters. But that's populism for you. Dick Morris did not lie when he said that "Every line of every ad came under his informed, critical and often meddlesome gaze. Every ad was *his* ad." In other words, Clinton's the one.

So much so, as it happens, that somebody managed

to move large sums of the soft money raised by the agile internationalist Charlie Trie, and transfer them from the coffers of the Democratic Party to the account of the Clinton Legal Defense Fund. Here is the perfect paradox of public and private: where the Democrats are a public and accountable party dealing in deniable and surreptitious funds, while the president in his legal capacity is a private citizen subject to audit and disclosure. Even so, the two wires became inextricably crossed. That could have been embarrassing, if anyone had cared to make anything of it. Generally speaking, though, the Clinton forces have always been able to count upon Republican discretion—even understanding—when it comes to difficulties about political money.

For all that, the 4,878 pages of the report by the House Committee on Government Oversight may be reduced to one single sentence: "Because of the unprecedented lack of cooperation of witnesses, including 120 relevant individuals who either asserted Fifth Amendment privileges or fled the country, both the House and Senate investigations were severely hampered." By February 1999, this number had risen to 121. The Committee's indispensable report provides partial but illuminating accounts of covert donations by the Chinese military-industrial complex and its Indonesian surrogates, of favors returned to those who could produce brown bags of funny money (Charlie Trie was appointed to the Commission on U.S.–Pacific Trade and Investment Policy), and of mutual stroking between the Clinton administration and a number of foreign dictatorships. And it makes one thing piercingly clear. Those *one hundred and twenty one* potential witnesses who either left town or took the Fifth, who either "fled or pled," had as urgent a need as the President to assert their right to privacy.

On September 18, 1997, the Senate inquiry called Roger Tamraz, who revealed that he had paid $300,000 for his coffee at the White House and— showing the contempt which the "donor community" manifested throughout—added that next time he'd make it $600,000. Dick Morris was not called to testify, but did submit a 500-page deposition in which he proudly recalled his delight at finding a way through the legally imposed spending limits. By using "soft money" for "issue ads," and dumping a fortune into early TV spots, and by the not-unrelated tactic of stealing the Republicans' clothes (because big donors don't show up for campaign breakfasts to "keep welfare as we know it"), Morris was able to buy a commanding lead in the polls. Mr. Clinton evidently regarded Mr. Morris's covert control over policy, and his personal "cut" of the take amounting to almost $1.5 million, as a price well worth paying. I remember George Stephanopoulos ruefully reminiscing: "For eight months of 1995 and 1996, Morris was the president." And the scandal is not so much that nobody voted for Morris. It's the fact that, for much of that time, he operated under a Clinton-assigned code name and *nobody knew he was there.* By the time the stolen and bought and staged election was over, and the Democrats were hastily paying back the millions they had accepted from crepuscular overseas sources, the damage was done, and the entire electorate had been triangulated by a man whose only mistake was to be caught having illicit sex. (I allude, of course, to Mr. Morris.)

In the critical days of his impeachment struggle, Mr. Clinton was often said to be worried sick about his place in history. That place, however, is already secure. He will be remembered as the man who used the rhetoric of the New Democrat to undo the New Deal. He will also be remembered as a man who offered a groaning board of incentives for the rich and draconian admonitions to the poor.

The centerpiece of his legacy was "welfare reform." The passage of a timely pre-election bill, removing federal guarantees from impoverished children for the first time in sixty years, became essential not only to President Morris but to President Clinton as well. Not only did it annex the main "issue" from the Republicans, it also provided background and depth to the unending Clintonian homilies about moral continence, thrift, and family values. It signaled, to approving audiences among the better fed, that for the indigent, "the party was over." The many who had never been invited to this supposed party were less inclined to vote, and less able to register. And the children among them, of course, did not vote at all. Nor were their opinions solicited by Mr. Morris's expensive pollsters.

As Peter Edelman, the most dedicated and expert worker in the field of welfare and family, pointed out to me:

> There is a submerged class question here. I always get at it in my speeches by pointing out the hypocrisy in the rhetoric as to who should stay at home with their children. Many on the right (and elsewhere) are saying mothers should stay at home with their small children because the new research data on brain development shows that small children need that stimulation. These same people then turn around and say poor moms have to go out and work immediately. (Many states have work requirements beginning when an infant is twelve weeks old, and the vast majority of the remainder require work

when the child is a year old.) That's a pretty clear class distinction.

But, as we are endlessly instructed, while rich people will *not* work unless they are given money, poor people will *only* work if they are not. (These are the two modern meanings of the term "incentive": a tax break on the one hand and the threat of the workhouse on the other.) And, once the Democratic Party had adopted this theology, the poor had no one to whom they could turn. The immediate consequence of this was probably an intended one: the creation of a large helot underclass disciplined by fear and scarcity, subject to endless surveillance, and used as a weapon against any American worker lucky enough to hold a steady or unionized job.

The evidence lies all around us, and will be around us for some time to come. Whether it is gleaned from the most evenhanded and "responsible" reporting, such as that of Jason DeParle atop the great rampart of the *New York Times*, or from writers like Christopher Cook in the *Progressive*, we shall have to accustom ourselves to stories like this. In Missouri, under the Direct Job Placement scheme (such schemes are always known officially as "initiatives"), the state bureaucracy mutates itself into a hiring hall for cheap labor in junk-nutrition conglomerates such as Tyson Foods. Welfare recipients are told to sign on and gut fifty chickens a minute, or be wiped from the rolls of the new Poor Law. They are directed to an industry which is well used to turnover among employees:

> As one woman on welfare discovered never mind her name, even having a newborn baby and no means of transportation is no excuse. When the thirty-year-old mother informed her case managers of these extenuating circumstances, they were not sympathetic. "They told her she had to work at Tyson's even if she had to walk to get there—a six-mile trek," says Helen Chewning, a former family advocate with the Missouri Valley Human Resource Center in Sedalia. "They sanctioned her while she was pregnant," and then ordered her to work at Tyson's when her baby was just eleven days old. She hasn't had any income for six months. How are they supposed to live?"

The process of "sanctioning"—the new state euphemism for coercion via the threat of cut-off—involves facing defenseless people with the rather old choice between "work or starve." It is the tactic by which welfare rolls are being "trimmed," if you will allow another Clintonian euphemism. You can be "sanctioned" if you refuse any job, or miss any interview.

I did not select Missouri because it's a famously

unsentimental state. I selected it because President Clinton, in an August 1997 address to businessmen in St. Louis, touted it as the model laboratory for his welfare reform. It's useful only for dialectical purposes to mention that Tyson Foods uses the Direct Job Placement scheme as its taxpayer-funded recruiting sergeant. The first shock of recognition, experienced by those who are supposed to be grateful for a dose of nonalienated and dignified labor, is the "puller job." This involves gutting birds—later to provide tasteless nourishment at the tables of the badly off—at a rapid rate. The fingernails of the inexperienced are likely to be the first to go; dissolved in bacteria and chicken fat. Of Missouri's 103,000 poultry workers, according to the Bureau of Labor Statistics, almost one-third endured an injury or an illness in 1995 alone. That this may be an undercounting is suggested by the experience of one hard-pressed toiler on the Tyson chicken-thigh assembly line named Jason Wolfe: "They want you to hang forty or fifty of these birds in a minute, for four to six hours straight, without a break. If you miss any, they threaten to fire you." He himself was fired because of too many "sick days."

Supplied by the state with a fearful, docile labor force, the workhouse masters are relatively untroubled by unions, or by any back-talk from the staff. Those who have been thus "trimmed" from the wel-

fare rolls have often done no more than disappear
into a twilight zone of casual employment, uninsured illness, intermittent education for their children, and unsafe or temporary accommodation. Only
thus—by their disappearance from society—can they
be counted as a "success story" by ambitious gover-
nors, and used in order to qualify tightfisted states
for "caseload-reduction credits" from the federal government. The women among them, not infrequently
pressed for sexual favors as the price of the ticket,
can be asked at random about the number of tooth-
brushes found in the trailer, and are required by law
to name the overnight guest or the father of the child
if asked. Failure or refusal to name the father can lead
to termination of "benefits" or (an even better word)
"entitlements." We were once told from the bought-
and-sold Oval Office itself, that "even presidents are
entitled to privacy": it seems now that *only* presidents
and their wealthy backers can claim this entitlement.
I pause again to note that Tyson Foods, which is
based in Arkansas, has spread a banquet of donations
before Bill Clinton ever since his boyhood as a candidate, and that its famously colorful chairman Don
Tyson sits in a corporate sanctum modeled to scale
on the Oval Office itself, with the doorknobs shaped
in ovals to resemble chicken eggs. Truly was it said
that the poor have such people always with them.

In the great city and state of New York, once the

redoubt of Democratic liberalism, a federal audit in January 1999 found that "city officials routinely violate the law by denying poor people the right to apply promptly for food stamps, fail to screen families for emergency food needs, require the poor to search for jobs before receiving help, and cut off food stamps to needy families who were still eligible for those benefits." As for those who had—in Mayor Giuliani's boastful words—"left" the welfare rolls for gainful employment, a state survey of those dropped between July 1996 and March 1997 found that only 29 percent of those dismissed from welfare had found employment—"employment" being defined as earning $100 over three months. Many of the rest, as in even more exacting states like Wisconsin, had simply gone missing. So had their children, because as already noted children don't vote while—as nobody understands better than Clinton—retired people do. These vanished Americans had merged into a ballooning underclass which is not even head-counted in the age of cheerful statistics, and which will show up only on the other side of the shining span of bridge that beckoned us to the 21st century.

Should all else fail, the poor of Missouri or any other of the fifty states could enlist in the employer of last resort, the military, where they could be subjected at random to mandatory drug tests (which are well on their way to becoming a craze in private industry as well) and legally prohibited from committing adultery. Should their personal tastes have ripened to warmth in the embrace of their own gender, they could be hounded and prosecuted by the Navy Investigative Service or its equivalent. If they were ostensibly male and wed and heterosexual and even suspected of deviance, their wives could also be visited without warning by the NIS and asked such leading questions as: "Did he ever fuck you up the ass?" (This question and others like it were documented by the late Randy Shilts, a real hero among the chroniclers of gay history and experience.) Failure to cooperate, or to incriminate others, could lead at once to unemployment or to disgrace—or both at once—and, in not a few cases, to incarceration. Such persecutions markedly increased during the Clinton era, with discharges for sexual incorrectness touching an all-time high in 1998. Mr. Clinton can also claim credit for warrantless searches of public housing and the innovation of the "roving wiretap." If any successor to Arthur Miller wanted to depict a modern Salem, he would do better to investigate the hysteria of the war on drugs, where to be suspected is to be guilty. In 1995, arrests for drug offenses that involved no violence were numbered at 1.5 million per annum, having climbed 31 percent in Mr. Clinton's first three years of tenure. The crime and terrorism statutes enacted in the same period caused even his most dogmatic apologists—Anthony Lewis, most notably—to wince.

An early and demagogic adoption of mandatory sentences, of the moronic chant of "three strikes and you're out," and of the need for speedy capital sentences was, of course, part of the Dick Morris strategy. But it was also an element in Clinton's attempt to distance himself from the bleeding hearts of the Democratic Party and to recast himself as a Southern sheriff. As a direct and intended result of this make-over, minors and the mentally ill are arraigned for the death penalty in America, the appeals procedure from Death Row has been abruptly and arbitrarily curtailed, and there is an execution every five days. The protection of habeas corpus has been withdrawn from immigrants, life sentences may be mandated for stunned defendants and imposed by shocked judges for the possession of cannabis alone, and sentences for possession of "crack" cocaine, a poor people's drug, are ten times harsher than those for possession of the powder cocaine consumed by the rich. The prison economy outperforms the college economy even in states like California, and the incarceration rate for American citizens is many multiples higher than that of any European nation, and barely trails behind that of Russia.

By 1997, all economic analysts were showing an abrupt and widening gap in income distribution in the United States, with many more super-rich and many more abjectly poor, and an astonishing increase in the number of "working poor" who, even with tough and unrewarding jobs, are unable to earn enough to transcend officially defined poverty. (Income distribution is often compared by classical economists to a diamond diagram, with an upper and lower apex and a thinner or fatter middle. A diamond diagram, of course, is two triangles piled on top of one another.) In softer and apparently less coercive tones, meanwhile, the First Lady appeared on platforms to tell people what was in their own best interests, and to demand a tobacco-free and "buckle-up" society as well. For millions of people living in the Clinton epoch, "the era of big government" was by no means "over." It had, in fact, just begun.

All of the above had to be endured, in order that gay and feminist and civil rights and civil libertarian forces could "come together" in the midterm elections of November 1998, and exclaim almost with one voice that racism and oligarchy threatened their president and his spouse, and that government should be kept out of the bedroom.

A single expression, culled from that bizarre period and kept (at least by this reviewer) like a fragrant petal pressed between the leaves of an old and cherished book, will do duty for the entire period of hysterical illusion. I shall preserve it lovingly, until long after those who uttered it have pretended with embarrassment that they never did. That expression is "the coup." Which Clintonoid columnist or propagandist did not employ this dramatic phrase, as their hero found himself at the mercy, not of a law 'n' order Democrat on the approved model, but of a law 'n' order Republican? (The most the Republican leadership could have hoped to achieve was the confirmation of Al Gore as President two years before his time—some coup.) The term *coup* refers, properly as well as metaphorically, to an abrupt seizure of power by unelected forces, along the lines of the *pronunciamenti* so well remembered by our southern neighbors. It is sometimes given its full dignity in French as *coup d'état*, or "blow at the state," and was in that form employed by many of the outraged Democrats who took the floor of the House on December 19, 1998. Their outrage was directed not at any action of their commander in chief but at any motion to depose him or even to impugn his character.

On that day, Clinton ordered the smiting of Mesopotamia. At the time, this decision seemed to complete his adoption of the military-industrial worldview, though in fact his full and absolute conversion to that theology lay two weeks ahead. One may also find the origins of his conversion in his past. Clinton's relationship with the unelected and unaccountable uniformed para-state is, in some ways, an old story. It is known that he opposed the war on Vietnam, and it is also known that he dodged, rather than resisted, the draft. The distinction is not without a difference. Looking back, George Stephanopoulos shudders to recall the moment in 1992 when a reporter handed him a Xeroxed copy of Clinton's draft notice. This, after candidate Clinton assured him that no such summons had ever been issued, and instructed him to say as much. It was later to emerge that candidate Clinton believed that all known copies of the document had been weeded from the files. In other words, Clinton borrowed the moral prestige of the antiwar movement in order to shield his own skin.

I myself recall reading with keen interest Clinton's 1969 letter to his draft board when news of it broke. Obviously wasted on the colonel to whom it was addressed, it breathes with much of the spirit of those most defensible of days. Clinton had written of "working every day with a depth of feeling I had reserved solely for racism in America before Vietnam." And he had protested having to "fight and kill and die" in such a war, with the verbs not only in the morally correct order but repeated as "fight, kill and maybe die" lower down. Anyone who believes that the objection of antiwar activists was to personal danger rather than to complicity in atrocity and aggression just wasn't there at the time. Also redolent of the period was Clinton writing in the same letter, "I decided to accept the draft in spite of my beliefs for one reason: to maintain my political viability within the system." "Within the system" is vintage 1960s, but now I wonder. Who else of that band of brave and cheerful young Americans, so apparently selfless in their opposition to their country's disgrace, was asking, "How will this play in New Hampshire in around 1992?" The thought gave me the creeps, though perhaps it shouldn't have. Someone had to be thinking about the long haul, I suppose. But I would bet a goodly sum that most of those concerned were not planning much beyond the downfall of Richard Nixon. A calculating young man this Clinton, in any event.

Once elected, he never even pretended that civilian control was the operative principle. Harry Truman, no friend of the white feather or the conscientious objector, fired General Douglas MacArthur without overmuch hesitation when he challenged presidential authority, and withstood the subsequent opinion-poll and populist riot, and probably lost no more shut-eye than he did when incinerating Hiroshima and Nagasaki. ("New Democrats" in that epoch knew how to be tough.) Bill Clinton was no sooner elected than, bullied by the Joint Chiefs, he broke his election promise to open the ranks to gays. He then allowed Colin Powell, the hero of Panama and My Lai, to dictate a policy of capitulation to the junta in Haiti and the national socialists in Belgrade. And he catered faithfully to military-industrial constituencies, supporting exorbitant weapons-building projects like the Seawolf submarine, in which even the Pentagon had lost interest. No matter how fanciful or budget-busting the concept, from the B-1 bomber upward, Clinton always relaxed his commitment to trimming government spending and invariably advocated not only a welfare "safety net" for the likes of General Dynamics and Boeing, but a handout free and clear.

This had been standard practice among Democratic aspirants during the haunted years of the contest with Soviet Russia, where "softness" was at an understandable discount among sophisticated and ambitious liberals. However, Mr. Clinton was the first postwar and post–Cold War president. His "watch" occurred during a unique and unprecedented period of military and political relaxation, when the totalitarian codes of "launch on warning" and "balance of terror" had been abandoned even by many of their former advocates. Let the record show, then, that the Clinton White House took no step of any kind to acknowledge, much less take advantage of this new reality, and always acted as if the most paranoid predictions of John Foster Dulles were about to be fulfilled. With the help of a tremendous lobbying effort from the aerospace and other defense conglomerates, the NATO alliance was "enlarged," at least partly to furnish a sales market for those in "the contractor community" who would otherwise have had to close production lines. The budget of the Central Intelligence Agency was increased, while Democratic "oversight" of its activity was held to a myopic level and even the records of its past activities in Guatemala, Chile, and Iran were shrouded or shredded (illegally at that) without demur. The Clinton administration contrived the feat of being the only major government in the West to make no comment on the arrest of General Pinochet, despite the existence of outstanding cases of American citizens murdered on his direct instructions. The promiscuous sale of arms and technology to other countries, including existing dictatorships as well as potential ones, was enthusiastically pursued. Not an eyebrow was raised when the "special forces" of the Indonesian army, trained and equipped for the sole purpose of combating malcontent Indonesian civilians, were found to have been supervised by United States authorities in open defiance of a supposed congressional ban.

Conducting relations with the bankrupt and humiliated "former superpower," Clinton and his understrappers Strobe Talbott and Sandy Berger followed a policy which history may well remember, of always covering up for their diseased autocratic marionette Boris Yeltsin when he was wrong (in Chechnya and in Bosnia and in Mafia matters) and always weakening him when he was in the right (as in their breaches of promise about the expansion of NATO and the demolition of the ABM treaty). No doubt they considered his bleary, raging, oafish conduct to be a "private" issue, kept as it was from being investigated by any legal authority in the new Russia.

In a manner which actually mirrors rather than contradicts the above, Bill Clinton sometimes did find the strength and the nerve to disagree with his military chiefs. He overruled them when they expressed doubts on the rocketing of Khartoum and Afghanistan in August 1998. But on that occasion, he had urgent political reasons of his own to wish to "stand tall." All was made whole on January 6, 1999, when the president announced, even as the Senate was convening on his impeachment, that the dearest wish of the Joint Chiefs and the Republican Right would be granted after all. After twenty years and $55 billion spent on a series of completely unsuccessful "tests," he promised that an actual $7 billion would be set aside to build a "Star Wars" missile system. The figure, much understated, was in a sense irrelevant, because the promise to "build," rather than to experiment, was the threshold which neither Reagan nor Bush had crossed. But Clinton claimed, in his State of the Union address in January 1999, that there had been a terrible shortfall in military expenditure since the middle of 1985—high noon of the Reagan era. Triangulation could go no further.

A September report in the *New York Times* completes the picture. Leaked by someone close to the Joint Chiefs, it shows the president—a king of shreds and patches—summoned to a uniformed conclave at the National Defense University in Fort McNair and there informed that he has lost his moral standing as commander in chief, because laws enforceable on officers and other ranks have been flouted by himself. Within weeks, he was proffering a hitherto unbudgeted increase in military spending of $110 billion over six years—another boost to big government for the rich and another reminder of good government for the poor. Along with the mooted handover of Social Security funds to Wall Street, this was the fabled "agenda" from which, according to solemn Democratic commentators, the country was being distracted by a distressing focus on the president's personal crookery. The cover-up and the "agenda," however, soon became indistinguishable as Clinton played out the bipartisan hand to the end.

*　　*　　*

In the Clinton administration's relationship with the international community, the policy of triangulation almost satirizes itself. Thanks to an unusually warm and fetid relationship between Senator Jesse Helms on the one hand—he being chairman of the Senate Foreign Relations Committee—and Ms. Madeleine Albright on the other, the Clinton administration was and is the only important negative vote on the establishment of a land mines treaty, and on the setting up of an international body to try war criminals. (The other noteworthy "contras" are Saddam Hussein's Iraq and Colonel Qaddafi's Libya.) The same administration also uses the UN as a ditto for U.S. unilateralism, all the time contemptuously refusing to pay its dues to the world body.

"Globalization," usually the company song of the American corporate strategy, stops at the water's edge and turns prickly and isolationist when it comes to the rights of others to judge American actions. This dualism was seen to perfect effect when Clinton supported the Jesse Helms and Dan Burton legislation, which not merely intensified the stupid embargo on Cuba but presumptuously extended it into an attack on trade with Havana conducted by third countries like Canada, France, or Great Britain. This covert understanding is arrived at by means of a sweetheart deal with Dick Morris's former boss in North Carolina.

Over the course of seven precious and irrecoverable years of potential peace and disarmament, then, Clinton has squandered every conceivable opportunity for a renegotiated world order. He has been the front-man for a silent coup rather than the victim of one, and has learned, for a bad combination of private and public motives, to stop worrying and to love all bombs.

FOUR

A Question of Character

At the initial moment of the Clinton campaign in 1992, there was much pompous talk about the question of "character." This was relatively easily deflected by those who maintained, and also by those who were paid to maintain, that "issues" should weigh more than "personalities." And, at that same initial moment, the line that favored issues over personalities seemed to many people the more serious one—the one for the high-minded to take. One can still hear this echo, like the last squeak from a dying planet, in the automatic response of those poll respondents and other loyalists who say that they care more about health insurance than about Monica Lewinsky.

Well, I could sign my own name to *that* proposition. But could Clinton? And wasn't that the point to begin with? In 1992, it seemed to many people that the late Paul Tsongas, a man of probity and competence and fiscal integrity, was the authentic "New Democrat." A bit bloodless perhaps, and a bit low on compassion, but an efficient technocrat and a modernizer. Mr. Clinton had nothing substantial to put against Tsongas's program. He just thought that he, and not Mr. Tsongas, should be the nominee and the one who enjoyed the fruits of office. So "personality" came into it from the start, and all denials of that fact are idle. Not one—I repeat, not one—of Clinton's team in 1992 did not harbor the fear that a "flaw" might embarrass and even humiliate everybody. Was this not a recognition of the character issue, however oblique? Some thought it would be funny money, some thought it would be "bimbo eruptions," a few guessed that it would be a sordid combination of the two. All were prepared to gloss it over in favor of the big picture, of getting the job done, or of getting a job for themselves.

The Establishment injunction—to focus on "issues" and "concerns" and "agendas" rather than mere "personalities"—is overripe for the garbage heap. The whole apparatus of professionalized and privatized political management is devoted to the idea of "the candidate," and it is to a person with a memory for names and faces, rather than to any computer-generated manifesto, that donors at home and abroad give large sums of money that the newspapers don't discover until it's too late. Moreover, the judgment of "character" is one of the few remaining decisions that an otherwise powerless and unconsulted voter is able to make for himself (or, and here I defer to Ann Lewis, for herself). Simply put, a candidate can change his/her campaign platform when in office, but he/she cannot change his/her nature. Even more simply put, the honest and the powerless have a vested interest in a politician who cannot be bought, whereas the powerful and the dishonest have already begun to haggle over the tab while the acceptance speech is still being written. And, even in a political system renowned worldwide for its venality, Bill Clinton seemed anxious to be bought, and willing if not indeed eager to advertise the fact in advance.

Venturing, then, onto the territory of sociopathy, one can notice some other filiations between the public and private Clinton. There is, clearly, something very distraught in his family background. Our physicians tell us that that thirst for approval is often the outcome of a lonely or insecure childhood (and Clinton's entire menu of initiatives, from provincial governor to provincial president, betrays a preoccupation with the small and wheedling and ingratiating effect), but what about this, from Hillary Clinton's book *It Takes a Village*? In 1986, Chelsea Clinton was six:

> One night at the dinner table, I told her, "You know, Daddy is going to run for governor again. If he wins, we would keep living in this house, and he would

keep trying to help people. But first we have to have an election. And that means other people will try and convince voters to vote for them instead of for Daddy. One of the ways they may do this is by saying terrible things about him." Chelsea's eyes went wide, and she asked, "What do you mean?" We explained that in election campaigns, people might even tell lies about her father in order to win, and we wanted her to be ready for that. Like most parents, we had taught her that it was wrong to lie, and she struggled with the idea, saying over and over, "Why would people do that?" I didn't have an answer for that one. (I still don't.) Instead, we asked her to pretend she was her dad and was making a speech about why people should vote for her. She said something like, "I'm Bill Clinton. I've done a good job and I've helped a lot of people. Please vote for me." We praised her and explained that now her daddy was going to pretend to be one of the men running against him. So Bill said terrible things about himself, like how he was really mean to people and didn't try to help them. Chelsea got tears in her eyes and said, "Why would anybody say things like that?"

According to the First Lady, it took several repeats of this "role-playing" exercise before the kid stopped crying. Heaven knows what things are like now, with the daddy president having used the same child as a prop to gull the public between January and August 1998. He's not much better with the more mature females, either. Mr. Clinton held precisely two Cabinet meetings—count them—in 1998. At the first one, immediately after the first Lewinsky revelation in January, he convened his team and asked them to step outside in the street and echo his falsehoods, which many of them did. At the second one, in August, he told them that he was moving to Plan B, and telling some part of the truth. Donna Shalala thereupon asked him if he had not, perhaps, put his own interests above those of his colleagues and even—heaven forbid—his agenda. At once, and according to eyewitnesses, the supposedly contrite chief executive whirled upon her. "If it was up to you, Nixon would have been better than Kennedy in 1960." There was a craven silence in the room—anyone who had lasted that long with Clinton must already have had a self-respect deficit that a lifetime won't requite—but afterward someone was heard to murmur thoughtfully: "He'll say *anything*."

I have known a number of people who work for and with, or who worked for and with, this man. They act like cult members while they are still under the spell, and talk like ex–cult members as soon as they have broken away. Even the disgraced Webster Hubbell, whose loyalty to Clinton is based on cronyism and on the old requirement of knowing what to do for the boss without having to be told, has had his moments of anxiety. Promoted from the revolving-door back-slappery of the Arkansas "business community" to the halls of the Justice Department, he was taken to one side by the new president and "tasked" with two occult inquiries. "Find out who killed Kennedy, and tell me whether there are UFOs or not." At other moments, staff have been asked to Camp David to meet with "enablers" and other shamans of the New Age. The vacuous language of uplift and therapy, commingled with the tawdry pieties of Baptist and Methodist hypocrisy, clings to both Clintons like B.O. It was suggested by the First Lady herself that her husband's off-the-record meetings with a female intern were a form of "ministry."

This obtuse righteousness is inscribed in every move, physical or political, that the Clintons make. Neither ever offers—for all their tin-roof "humility"—a word of self-criticism. The president has been told for many years, by advisers who in some cases adore him, that he must not speak for too long when given the podium. His prolixity remains stubborn and incurable, yet it remains a fact that in all his decades of logorrhea Clinton has failed to make a single remark (absent some lame catch phrases like "New Covenant" and of course the imperishable "It all depends on what the meaning of 'is' is") that could possibly adhere to the cortex of a thinking human being. The Oval Office may have presented itself to him as a potentially therapeutic location, but once he arrived there he half realized that he had no big plans, no grand thoughts, no noble dreams. He also realized that he might have to give up one of the few things that did bring him release from his demons. He lost little time in substituting the one for the other, and reacted with extreme indignation when confronted with the disclosure of the fact. This was the empty rage of Caliban glimpsing his visage in the glass. It was not the first such instance, or even the most revealing. The driveling idiom of therapy was his only alternative to red-faced self-righteousness, as when he was interviewed in September 1998:

> You know some people say to me, "I feel so terrible for you. It's been so awful what has been publicized to the whole country; the whole world." Believe it or not, and I know it's hard for people to believe, that has not bothered me very much because of the opportunity I've had to seek spiritual counseling and advice and to think through this and to try to focus much more on how I can properly atone, how I can be forgiven, and then how I can go back to healing with my family.

A month later he was to describe his short-lived public-relations triumph at the disastrous Wye agreement with Benjamin Netanyahu and Yasir Arafat, as a step on his own "path of atonement." And two months after that, it was bombs away again over Baghdad. Mrs. Ceausescu must have had days of ministry like this.

As early as April 1993, according to an eyewitness account given to Bob Woodward for his book *The Agenda*, Clinton found himself with nothing to propose, and nothing to give away. He had been told that the bond market and its managers had boxed him in. He lost his temper to an operatic degree. "I hope you're all aware we're all Eisenhower Republicans," he bellowed to his team. "We're Eisenhower Republicans here, and we are fighting with Reagan Republicans. We stand for lower deficits and free trade and the bond market. Isn't that great?...We must have something for the common man. It won't hurt me in 1994, and I can put enough into '95 and '96 to crawl through to reelection. At least we'll have health care to give them, if we can't give them anything else."

I cannot guess what it's like for a Democratic loyalist to read that bombast now. The Republicanism of Clinton's presidency has not, in fact, risen to the Eisenhower level. He has entrusted policy to much more extreme Republicans like Alan Greenspan and Dick Morris, without manifesting any of the old general's robust suspicion of the military-industrial complex. (And it's impossible to imagine Eisenhower, who always showed contempt for his venal vice president, making the spectacle of himself that Clinton made at Nixon's graveside.)

In 1996 I wrote an attack on the "lesser evil" theory of political choice, which was printed in *Dissent* magazine and discussed at its editorial board. There the editor, Michael Walzer, inquired plaintively: "Why is it that some people on the Left seem to *hate* Bill Clinton?" I thought then, and I think even more now, that the mystery lies elsewhere. Why do so many people on the *Right* hate Bill Clinton?

Of course, there's an element of the stupid party involved: the conservatives thought Franklin Roosevelt was a communist even as he saved capital from itself by means of the National Recovery Act. But Bill Clinton, who has gone further than Reagan ever dared in repealing the New Deal and seconding the social Darwinist ethic at home and abroad, is nonetheless detested on the Right. The old slogan, "draft-dodging, pot-smoking, lying, womanizing sonofabitch" still resonates. As why should it not, given that a person of such qualities has been able to annex and even anticipate the Republican platform, thereby demonstrating conclusively that there is no sufficient or necessary connection between the said platform and personal honor, or political honesty? At least Trent Lott and Newt Gingrich and the Christian Coalition got something for their frustration: the sight of Bomber Bill carrying a large Bible from prayer breakfast to prayer breakfast while ordering the downtrodden to shape up, and the war planes to discipline the wogs, and the military production lines to restart.

Walzer's question, at least in its inverted form, remains. It's become tiring to hear people on the Left say that Clinton should perhaps be arraigned, but not for anything he's actually been charged with. A vast number of liberal academics and intellectuals wouldn't even go that far, preferring to place themselves under the leadership of Arthur Schlesinger, Jr., as he instructed the Congress that a gentleman was obliged to lie, under any duress, in matters of sex. (Also that: "Only a cad tells the truth about his love affairs.") This polka-dotted popinjay has been himself permitted to lie, these many years, about the record of the Kennedy gang. But not until now had he been called as a witness on who is, or is not, a gentleman, let alone about what is, or is not, a "love affair." (On caddishness he perhaps does possess real historical expertise that was, alas, not sought by the House Judiciary Committee.) His nominee for the title of gentleman, however, was certainly in keeping with the standards he has upheld until now. Gentlemen are indeed supposed to be discreet about affairs, at any hazard to themselves, in order to protect the honor and modesty of the ladies involved. This doesn't quite track with Clinton's policy of maintaining a semi-official staff for the defamation and bullying of inconvenient but truthful former girlfriends: "the politics of personal destruction" elevated into an annex of the state machine. It is not "philandering"—a term of some dash and gaiety that has been much abused—to hit on the help and then threaten dire reprisals. A gentleman, having once implied that Gennifer Flowers was a lying gold digger, does not make it up to her, or to those he misled, by agreeing in a surly manner years later that perhaps he did sleep with her "once." All other considerations to one side, doesn't he know that it's the height of bad manners to make love to somebody only once? Those who claim to detect, in the widespread loathing of Clinton, an aggressive "culture war" against the freedom-loving sixties should be forced to ask themselves if Clinton, with his almost sexless conquests and his eerie affectless claim that the female felt no pleasure, represents the erotic freedom that they had in mind. (After the Juanita Broaddrick revelations, Schlesinger was not given the opportunity to say that a gentleman is obliged, if only from gallantry, to lie about rape.)

There remains the irony of Amendments 413 and

415 of Clinton's own crime bill, signed into law in September 1994, which permit a defendant in a sexual harassment lawsuit to be asked under oath about his other sexual entanglements. Lobbied by certain feminists for the inclusion of these amendments, Clinton had professed himself shocked that such a law was not already on the books. Thus when caught in his own law, and required by a Supreme Court vote of 9–0 to answer the questions, Clinton would commit various common law crimes if he decided to do other than tell the truth, let alone if he decided to recruit subordinates to lie. He would also be committing a crime that it is only in his power to commit—a direct violation of the presidential oath of office.

Gore Vidal was perhaps more honest than Schlesinger, and certainly more accurate, when he explained that: "Boys are meant to squirt as often as possible with as many different partners as possible. Girls are designed to take nine months to lay an egg...Clinton doesn't much care for Warm Mature Relationships with Warm Caring Women. Hence an addiction to the impersonal blowjob." When he wrote this, Mr. Vidal was emerging as a defender of the president and a friend of the First Lady. I echo the desire of my friend Geoffrey Wheatcroft to see Hillary Clinton sitting next to Vidal "nodding gravely while he says that."

*   *   *

Is it not in fact rather clear that Clinton's conduct in
the Lewinsky and Jones and Willey cases represents
a microcosm of Clintonism itself? There is, first and
most saliently, the use of public office for private
ends and gratification. The bodyguards bring the
chick to the room, just as in any banana republic, and
the witnesses can be taken care of in the usual way,
and the man who later uses the Lincoln Bedroom
as an off-the-record rental for fat cats thinks nothing of claiming the Oval Office as a *chambre particu-
lier.* There is, again, the fact that Monica Lewinsky
was originally supplied to the White House on
the recommendation of Walter Kaye, a bored and
wealthy nonentity who later testified that he could
not remember how much he had donated to Clintonian funds. (The relationship between the Kathleen
Willey cover-up and Nathan Landow makes a similar point in a slightly different way.) There is, in a
recurring pattern, the use of that other fund-raiser
and influence-peddler Vernon Jordan to arrange soft
landings and "deniability." There is, very conspicu-
ously, the automatic resort to the use of publicly paid
officials (some with their consent but most without)
as liars and hacks for a supposedly "private and personal" matter. And where they fail, lawyers from the
school of Cochran and Dershowitz—loophole artists

for rich thugs—are flung into the breach. Scarcely worth noticing, as being too predictable for words, is the employment of White House full-timers to spread the idea that Ms. Lewinsky was "a stalker"— as if a president, who surrounded the executive mansion with ugly concrete barriers out of concern for his personal safety, and who is protected night and day by men who are paid to take a bullet for him, could be unsafe from harassment in his "own" Oval Office.

Most telling, in a way, was the smearing of Ms. Jones as a woman so common and dirty that she might even have enjoyed an encounter with Clinton or, depending on which cover story was which, might have been actuated by the sort of greed only found in trailer parks. Here is the real contempt with which Clinton and his circle view the gullible rubes who make up their voting base: "those people whose toil and sweat sends us here and pays our way," as Clinton oleaginously phrased it in his banal first inaugural address. Since that speech, he has never voluntarily spent any time in the company of anyone who earns money rather than makes it. And, when told by the United States Supreme Court that he had to answer questions from an apparent female nobody, under the terms of a statute on sexual harassment that he had himself caused to be made law, he decided that he could lie his way out as he always had. It's not much of a riposte, at this point, for Clinton's people to say that the unfashionable nobody had some shady right-wing friends. However shady they were, they didn't fall to the standard of Dick Morris.

When I look out of my window in Washington, D.C., I am forced to confront the statue of General McClellan, which stands isolated in traffic at the confluence of Connecticut Avenue and Columbia Road. The worst commander on either side in the Civil War, he was rightly suspected of surreptitious pro-slavery political ambitions and indeed ran against Lincoln as a Democrat for the Presidency. His equestrian figure, whether by accident or design, still has him pointing his horse away from the enemy and toward the White House. Accepting the Democratic Party's nomination on July 16, 1992, Clinton made the most of his Dixie drawl as he said: "I know how President Lincoln felt when General McClellan wouldn't attack in the Civil War. He asked him, 'If you're not going to use your army, may I borrow it?' And so I say: 'George Bush, if you won't use your power to help people, step aside. I will.'"

Karl Marx predicted McClellan's firing by Lincoln, and accused the supposedly timorous general of an ill-concealed sympathy for the other side. In demanding that Bush hand him the reins, Clinton pretended that government would and should still be "activist" for the powerless. But he was, in fact, a stealthy envoy from the enemy camp. In power, he has completed the Reagan counter-revolution and made the state into a personal friend of those who are already rich and secure. He has used his armed forces in fits of pique, chiefly against the far-off and the unpopular, and on dates which suit his own court calendar. The draft dodger has mutated into a pliant serf of the Pentagon, the pot smoker into the chief inquisitor in the "war on drugs," and the womanizer into a boss who uses subordinates as masturbatory dolls. But the liar and the sonofabitch remain, and who will say that these qualities played no part in the mutation?

FIVE

Clinton's War Crimes

Toward the end of the amputated and perfunctory impeachment process, a small bleat was set up on the Internet and in the pages of America's half-dead Left and liberal press. "Impeach President Clinton," said the appeal, "But For the Right Reasons." The signatories had noticed that Clinton used unbridled executive power to make war in what used to be called the Third World. But they thought that this ought to be sharply distinguished from his other promiscuities.

Reality, however, did not admit of any such distinction. In this instance, perhaps more than any other, Clinton's private vileness meshed exactly with his brutal and opportunistic public style. In idle moments, I used to amuse myself with the defining slogan of the herbivorous Left: "Think globally, act locally." It always seemed to me just as persuasive, and just about as inspiring, if phrased the other way around. How satisfying, then, that when Clinton acted globally, and did so for the most "localized" and provincial motives, it should have been the Left who were the last to see it.

This essay of mine, slightly adapted from its original form, appeared in *Vanity Fair* just as the predetermined vote on impeachment was coming up in the Senate. It shows the failure of all political forces to examine the most crucial, and the least scrutinized, of the failed counts of impeachment. That count is Abuse of Power.

✳   ✳   ✳

This is an essay about canines. It concerns, first, the president of the United States and commander in chief of the U.S. armed forces, whose character was once memorably caught by a commentator in his native Arkansas who called him "a hard dog to keep on the porch." It concerns, second, the dog or dogs which did not bark in the nighttime. (In the Sherlock Holmes tale "Silver Blaze," the failure of such a beast to give tongue—you should pardon the expression—was the giveaway that exposed his master as the intruder.) And it concerns, third, the most famous dog of 1998: the dog that was wagged by its own tail. Finally, it concerns the dogs of war, and the circumstances of their unleashing.

Not once but three times last year, Bill Clinton ordered the use of cruise missiles against remote and unpopular countries. On each occasion, the dispatch of the missiles coincided with bad moments in the calendar of his long and unsuccessful struggle to avoid impeachment. Just before the Lewinsky affair became public in January 1998, there was a New York prescreening party for Barry Levinson's movie *Wag the Dog*, written by Hilary Henkin and David Mamet. By depicting a phony president starting a phony war in order to distract attention from his filthy lunge at a beret-wearing cupcake, this film became the political and celluloid equivalent of a Clintonian roman à clef. Thrown by Jane Rosenthal and Robert DeNiro, whose Tribeca Productions produced the movie, the party featured Dick Morris and an especially pleased and excited Richard Butler, who was described by an eyewitness as "glistening." Mr. Morris was Mr. Clinton's fabled and unscrupulous adviser on matters of public opinion. Mr. Butler was the supervisor of United Nations efforts to disarm Saddam Hussein's despotism. In February 1998, faced with a threatened bombing attack that never came, Iraqi state TV prophylactically played a pirated copy of *Wag the Dog* in prime time. By Christmastime 1998, Washington police officers were giving the shove to demonstrators outside the White House who protested the December 16–19 bombing of Iraq with chants of "Killing children's what they teach—that's the crime they should impeach" and a "No blood for blow jobs" placard.

Is it possible—is it even thinkable—that these factors are in any way related? "In order that he might rob a neighbor whom he had promised to defend," wrote Macaulay in 1846 of Frederick the Great, "black men fought on the coast of Coromandel, and red men scalped each other by the Great Lakes of North America." Did, then, a dirtied blue dress from the Gap cause widows and orphans to set up grieving howls in the passes of Afghanistan, the outer precincts of Khartoum, and the wastes of Mesopotamia? Is there only a Hollywood link between Clinton's carnality and Clinton's carnage? Was our culture hit by weapons of mass distraction? Let us begin with the best-studied case, which is Khartoum.

On August 20, 1998, the night of Monica Lewinsky's return to the grand jury and just three days after his dismal and self-pitying nonapology had "bombed" on prime-time TV, Clinton personally ordered missile strikes against the El Shifa Pharmaceutical Industries Company on the outskirts of Sudan's capital city. The Clinton administration made three allegations about the El Shifa plant:

- That it did not make, as it claimed, medicines and veterinary products.
- That it did use the chemical EMPTA (O-ethyl methylphosphonothioic acid), which is a "precur-

sor," or building block, in the manufacture of VX nerve gas.

- That it was financed by Osama bin Laden—the sinister and fanatical Saudi entrepreneur wanted in connection with lethal attacks on U.S. embassies in Africa—or by his shadowy business empire.

These three claims evaporated with astonishing speed. It was conceded within days, by Defense Secretary William Cohen, that the factory did make medicines, vials of which were filmed as they lay in the rubble. It was further conceded that there was no "direct" financial connection between the plant and bin Laden's holdings. Later came the humbling admission that a local CIA informer in Sudan had been fired for the fabrication of evidence. Later still came the even more humbling refusal to produce the "soil sample," taken from outside the factory, which the Clinton administration claimed contained traces of EMPTA. In the end, the United States was placed in the agonizing position, at the United Nations, of opposing a call for on-site inspection that had been put forward by the Sudanese.

Bad enough, you might think. But this was only the beginning. The British engineer who was technical manager at the time of El Shifa's construction, Mr. Tom Carnaffin, came forward to say that it contained no space for clandestine procedures or experiments. The German ambassador to Khartoum, Werner Daum, sent a report to Bonn saying that he was familiar with the factory—often used as a showcase for foreign visitors—and that it could not be adapted for lethal purposes. R.J.P. Williams, professor emeritus at Oxford University, who has been called the grandfather of bio-inorganic chemistry, told me that even if the soil sample could be produced it would prove nothing. EMPTA can be used to make nerve gas, just as fertilizer can be used to make explosives, but it is also employed in compounds for dealing with agricultural pests. "'Trace' elements in adjacent soil are of no use," Williams said. "We must be told where the compound was found, and in what quantity it is known to have been produced. Either the Clinton administration has something to hide or for some reason is withholding evidence." It was a rout.

Seeking to reassure people, Clinton made a husky speech on Martha's Vineyard eight days after the attack. He looked the audience in the eye and spoke as follows: "I was here on this island up till 2:30 in the morning, trying to make absolutely sure that at that chemical plant there was no night shift. I believed I had to take the action I did, but I didn't want some person who was a nobody to me—but who may have a family to feed and a life to live and probably had no earthly idea what else was going on there—to die needlessly."

At the time, I thought it odd that such a great statesman and general could persuade himself, and attempt to persuade others, that the more deadly the factory, the smaller the chance of its having a night watchman. Silly me. I had forgotten the scene in Rob Reiner's *The American President*, where a widower First Citizen played by Michael Douglas has a manly affair with a woman lobbyist of his own age played by Annette Bening. While trying to impress us with his combination of determination and compassion, this character says, "Somewhere in Libya right now, a janitor is working the night shift at Libyan intelligence headquarters. And he's going about doing his job because he has no idea that in about an hour he's going to die in a massive explosion."

In the event, only one person was killed in the rocketing of Sudan. But many more have died, and will die, because an impoverished country has lost its chief source of medicines and pesticides. (El Shifa made over 60 percent of the human and veterinary medicine in Sudan.) We know that Clinton picked the target, from a "menu" of options, himself. He seems to have had an additional motive of political opportunism, beyond the obvious one, for selecting this particular underdeveloped country. Many Americans know little about Sudan, but some know a great deal. With its ramshackle fundamentalist regime, the Khartoum government is almost number one on the hate list of Southern Christian activists in the United States, who were at this very time loudly demanding an Act of Congress, prohibiting economic intercourse with countries that discriminated against variant monotheisms, especially of the Christian variety. The Clinton administration, which strongly prefers less sentimental trade policies (and which was then on the verge of "de-linking" human rights from its trade and military relationship with China) was nonetheless willing to compromise on this bill. So by choosing a Sudanese target, Clinton was sending a "message" (to use his argot) at least as much to the biblical sectarians among his own voting base as to the Koranic sectarians of the upper Nile. Triangulation could go no further.

The rout continues. In fact, it becomes a shambles. Let us suppose that everything the administration alleged about El Shifa was—instead of embarrassingly untrue—absolutely verifiable. The Sudanese regime has diplomatic relations with Washington. Why not give it a warning or notice of, say, one day to open the plant to inspection? A factory making deadly gas cannot be folded like a tent and stealthily moved away. Such a demand, made publicly, would give pause to any regime that sheltered Mr. bin Laden or his assets. (Of course, his best-known holdings

have been in Saudi Arabia, but a surprise Clintonian cruise-missile attack on that country, with the
princes finding out the news only when they fiddle
with the remote and get CNN, seems improbable, to say the least.) It is this question which has
led me to the Ritz-Carlton Hotel on the edge of the
Beltway—the non-Monica Ritz-Carlton located
within brunching distance of Langley, Virginia—to
meet with Milt Bearden.

Mr. Bearden is one of the Central Intelligence
Agency's most decorated ex-officers, having retired
in 1994 without any stain from assassination plots,
black-bag jobs, or the like. During his long service,
he was chief of station in Sudan, where he arranged
the famous airlift of Ethiopian Jews to Israel. He
also directed the CIA effort in Afghanistan. (His
excellent new thriller, *The Black Tulip*, carries a 1991
photograph of him standing at the Russian end of
the Friendship Bridge, across which the Red Army
had marched in defeat.) Nobody knows clandestine
Sudan and clandestine Afghanistan in the way he
does. We speak on background, but after some fine-
tuning he agrees to be quoted in exactly these words:
"Having spent thirty years in the CIA being familiar
with soil and environmental sampling across a number of countries, I cannot imagine a single sample,
collected by third-country nationals and especially

by third-country nationals whose country has a common border, serving as a pretext for an act of war against a sovereign state with which we have both diplomatic relations and functioning back channels."

This bald statement contains a lot of toxic material. The local "agents" who collected that discredited soil sample were almost certainly Egyptians, who have a Nilotic interest in keeping Sudan off balance because, as Bearden pungently says, "their river runs through it." Moreover, when the United States wanted Mr. bin Laden to leave the territory of Sudan, Washington contacted Khartoum and requested his deportation, which followed immediately. (He went to Afghanistan.) When the French government learned that Carlos "the Jackal" was lurking in Sudan, they requested and got his extradition. Business can be done with the Sudanese regime. What, then, was the hurry last August 20? No threat, no demand, no diplomatic démarche...just a flight of cruise missiles hitting the wrong target. Take away every exploded hypothesis, says Sherlock Holmes—this time in "The Adventures of the Beryl Coronet"—and the one you are left with, however unlikely, will be true. Take away all the exploded claims about Sudan, and the question "What was the hurry?" practically answers itself.

Can the implication—of lawless and capricious presidential violence—be taken any further? Oh yes, amazingly enough, it can. On more than one occasion, I have argued the case across Washington dinner tables with Philip Bobbitt of the National Security Council. He's a nephew of LBJ, and he tries to trump me by saying that the U.S. does possess evidence of nerve-gas production at El Shifa and "human and signals intelligence" about a bin Laden connection to the Sudanese. But this evidence cannot be disclosed without endangering "sources and methods"—and the lives of agents.

Bearden has forgotten more about "sources and methods" than most people will ever know, and snorts when I mention this objection. "We don't like to reveal sources and methods, true enough. But we always do so if we have to, or if we are challenged. To justify bombing [Colonel Qaddafi] in 1986, Reagan released the cables we intercepted between Tripoli and the Libyan Embassy in East Berlin. Same with Bush and Iraq. Do you imagine that the current administration is sitting on evidence that would prove it right? It's the dogs that don't bark that you have to listen to." And so my canine theme resumes.

In a slightly noticed article in the *New Yorker* of October 12, 1998 (almost the only essay in that journal in the course of the entire twelve months which was not a strenuous, knee-padded defense of the president), Seymour Hersh revealed that the four service chiefs of the Joint Chiefs of Staff had been deliberately kept in the dark about the Sudan and Afghanistan bombings because if they had been consulted they would have argued against them. He further disclosed that Louis Freeh, head of the FBI, was kept "out of the loop." Mr. Freeh, who has clashed with Clinton and with Attorney General Janet Reno over the issue of a special prosecutor for campaign finance, was not delighted to hear of the raids. For one thing, he and many of his agents were already in the field in East Africa, somewhat exposed as to their own security, and were in the course of securing important arrests. They would have greatly appreciated what they did not in fact get: adequate warning of a strike that would enrage many neighboring societies and governments. It's now possible to extend the list of senior intelligence personnel who disapproved both of the bombings and of their timing. At the CIA, I gather, both Jack Downing, the deputy director for operations, and the chief for the Africa Division told colleagues in private that they were opposed. It is customarily very hard to get intelligence professionals to murmur dissent about an operation that involves American credibility. However, it is also quite rare for a cruise-missile strike to occur on an apparent whim, against an essentially powerless country, at a time when presidential credibility is a foremost thought in people's minds.

The Afghanistan attack, which took place on the same night as the Sudan fiasco, is more easily disposed of. In that instance, the Clinton administration announced that Osama bin Laden and his viciously bearded associates were all meeting in one spot, and that there was only one "window" through which to hit them. This claim is unfalsifiable to the same extent that it is unprovable. Grant that, on the run after the embassy bombings, bin Laden and his gang decided it would be smart to foregather in one place, on territory extremely well known to American intelligence.

All that requires explaining is how a shower of cruise missiles did not manage to hit even one of the suspects. The only casualties occurred among regular Pakistani intelligence officers, who were using the "training camps" to equip guerrillas for Kashmir. As a result, indignant Pakistani authorities released two just-arrested suspects in the American Embassy bombings—one Saudi and one Sudanese. (The Saudi citizen, some American sources say, was a crucial figure in the planning for those outrages in Nairobi and Dar es Salaam.) Not great, in other words. One might add that a stray cruise missile didn't even hit Afghanistan but fell on Pakistani territory, thus handing the Pakistani military a free sample just months after it had defied Clinton's feeble appeals to refrain from joining the "nuclear club." All in all, a fine day's work. Pressed to come up with something to show for this expensive farce, the Clintonoids spoke of damage to bin Laden's "infrastructure." Again, to quote Milt Bearden, who knows Afghanistan by moonlight: "What 'infrastructure'? They knocked over a lean-to? If the administration had anything—anything at all—the high-resolution satellite images would have been released by now." Another nonbarking canine, for a president half in and half out of the doghouse.

Speaking of the doghouse, last fall the president's lawyer Bob Bennett gave a speech to the National Press Club in Washington. On a single day—so he informed an openmouthed audience—he had had four substantial conversations with Clinton about the Paula Jones case and, feeling this excessive, "I had to cut it short and the president said, 'Yeah, I've got to get back to Saddam Hussein,' and I said, 'My God, this is lunacy that I'm taking his time on this stuff.'" Well, I hope Mr. Bennett didn't charge for that day, or for the other time-wasting day when he naively introduced Lewinsky's false affidavit on Clinton's behalf. But, if he hoped to persuade his audience that Clinton should be left alone to conduct a well-meditated Iraq policy, his words achieved the opposite effect. Policy toward Baghdad has been without pulse or direction or principle ever since

Mr. Clinton took office. As one who spent some horrible days in Halabja, the Kurdish city that was ethnically cleansed by Saddam's chemical bombs, I have followed Washington's recent maneuvers with great attention. The only moment when this president showed a glimmer of interest in the matter was when his own interests were involved as well.

And thus we come to the embarrassing moment last December when Clinton played field marshal for four days, and destroyed the UN inspection program in order to save it. By November 14, 1998, Saddam Hussein had exhausted everybody's patience by his limitless arrogance over inspections of weapon sites, and by his capricious treatment of the United Nations Special Commission (UNSCOM) inspectorate. In a rare show of Security Council solidarity, Russia, China, and France withdrew criticism of a punitive strike. The Republican leadership in both houses of Congress, which had criticized the Clinton administration for inaction, was ready to rock 'n' roll with Iraq. The case had been made, and the airplanes were already in the air when the president called them back. No commander in chief has ever done this before. Various explanations were offered as to why Clinton, and his close political crony Sandy Berger, had made such a wan decision. It was clearly understood that the swing vote had been the president's, and that Madeleine Albright and William Cohen had argued the other way.

But in mid-November the president was still flushed with the slight gain made by his party in the midterm elections. Impeachment seemed a world away, with Republican "moderates" becoming the favorite of headline writers and op-ed performers alike. This theme persisted in the news and in the polls until after the pre-Hanukkah weekend of December 12–13, when, having been rebuffed by Benjamin Netanyahu at a post-Wye visit in Israel, Clinton had to fly home empty-handed. This must have been galling for him, since he had only imposed himself on the original Wye agreement, just before the November elections, as a high-profile/high-risk electoral ploy. (He had carried with him to Tel Aviv, on Air Force One, Rick Lazio and Jon Fox, two Republican congressmen widely hailed as fence-sitters regarding impeachment. So it can't easily be said that he wasn't thinking about the domestic implications of foreign policy.) But by Tuesday, December 15, after Clinton's last-ditch nonapology had "bombed" like all its predecessors, every headline had every waverer deciding for impeachment after all. On Wednesday afternoon, the president announced that Saddam Hussein was, shockingly enough, not complying with the UN inspectorate. And the cruise missiles took wing again. Within hours the House Republicans had met and, "furious and fractured," according to the *New York Times*, had announced the postponement of the impeachment debate, due to begin Thursday morning.

This was not quite like the preceding dramas. For one thing, it could and probably would have happened—unlike Sudan and Afghanistan—at any time. For another thing, the president was careful to say that he had the support of his whole "national security team," which he wouldn't have been able to say of his cop-out decision in November. Presidents don't normally list the number of their own employees and appointees who agree with them about national-security questions, but then, most presidents don't feel they have to. (Though most presidents have avoided making their Cabinet members back them in public on falsehoods about "private" and "inappropriate" conduct.) Having gone on slightly too long about the endorsements he'd won from his own much-bamboozled team, Clinton was faced with only a few remaining questions. These included:

- Why, since Saddam Hussein has been in constant noncompliance, must bombing start tonight?
- Why has there been no open consultation with either Congress or the United Nations?
- When did you find out about the Richard Butler report on Saddam Hussein's violations?

The last question, apparently a simple one, was the most difficult to answer. It emerged that Clinton had known the contents of the Butler report at least two days before it was supposed to be handed to the UN secretary-general, Kofi Annan. It was Kofi Annan's job, furthermore, to present it to the world body for action. Members of the National Security Council in Washington, however, were leaking the report (which "discovered" Saddam Hussein's violations) to friends of mine in Washington by Tuesday, December 15. This timeline simply means that Clinton knew well in advance that he was going to be handed a free pretext in case of need. Mr. Butler might care to explain why he hurriedly withdrew his inspectors without Security Council permission—leaving some 400 United Nations humanitarian aid workers to face the music— at least a day before the bombs began to drop.

Once again the question: What was the rush? It must have meant a lot to Clinton to begin the strikes when he did, because he forfeited the support of the UN, of Russia, of China, of France, and of much of the congressional leadership—all of which he had enjoyed in varying degrees in November. (The Russians, whose volatile stock of "weapons of mass destruction" is far more of a menace than Iraq's actually withdrew their ambassador from Washington for the first time in history, and threatened again to freeze talks on strategic-arms limitation.)

To the "rush" question, Clinton at first answered that the weekend of December 19–20 marked the start of the Muslim holy month of Ramadan, and one would not want to be bombing an Islamic people while they were beginning their devotions. However, the postponed impeachment debate continued well into Saturday, December 19, and so did the bombardment, which concluded a few hours after the impeachment vote itself. Muslim susceptibilities were therefore even more outraged, even in morally friendly countries such as Kuwait, by the suspicious coincidence of timing. During the debate, the House Democratic leadership took the position, openly encouraged by the White House, that a president should not be embarrassed at home while American troops were "in harm's way" abroad. Again, it is made clear by Clinton's own conduct and arguments that, for him, foreign policy and domestic policy do not exist in parallel universes, but are one and the same.

And, again, I found myself talking to someone who is normally more hawkish than I am. Scott Ritter, who served with UNSCOM from 1991 until August 1998 and who was the chief of its Concealment Investigations Unit, had been warning for months that Saddam Hussein was evading compliance inspections. This warning entailed a further accusation, which was that UNSCOM in general, and Richard Butler in particular, were too much

under the day-to-day control of the Clinton administration. (An Australian career diplomat who, according to some of his colleagues, was relinquished with
relief by his masters Down Under, Butler owes his
job to Madeleine Albright in the first place.) Thus,
when the United States did not want a confrontation
with Iraq, over the summer and into the fall, Butler
and the leadership acted like pussycats and caused
Ritter to resign over their lack of seriousness. But
then, when a confrontation was urgently desired in
December, the slightest pretext would suffice. And
that, Ritter says, is the bitterest irony of all. The
December strikes had no real military value, because
the provocation was too obviously staged.

"They sent inspectors to the Baath Party HQ in
Baghdad in the week before the raids," Ritter told
me. "UNSCOM then leaves in a huff, claiming to
have been denied access. There was nothing inside
that facility anyway. The stuff was moved before they
got there. The United States knew there was nothing in that site. And then a few days later, there are
reports that cruise missiles hit the Baath Party HQ!
It's completely useless. Butler knew that I'd resign if
the U.S. continued to jerk UNSCOM around, and
he even came to my leaving party and bought me a
drink. But now he's utterly lost his objectivity and
impartiality, and UNSCOM inspections have been
destroyed in the process, and one day he'll be hung

out to dry. Ask your colleagues in Washington when they got his report."

From the *Washington Post* account by Barton Gellman, on Wednesday, December 16, written the day before the bombing began and on the day that Kofi Annan saw the Butler report for the first time:

> Butler's conclusions were welcome in Washington, which helped orchestrate the terms of the Australian diplomat's report. Sources in New York and Washington said Clinton-administration officials played a direct role in shaping Butler's text during multiple conversations with him Monday at secure facilities in the U.S. mission to the United Nations.

"Of course," Ritter told me almost conversationally, "though this is *Wag the Dog*, it isn't quite like Sudan and Afghanistan in August, which were *Wag the Dog* pure and simple."

Well, indeed, nothing is exactly like *Wag the Dog*. In the movie, the whole war is invented and run out of a studio, and nobody actually dies, whereas in Sudan and Afghanistan and Iraq, real corpses were lying about and blood spilled. You might argue, as Clinton's defenders have argued in my hearing, that if there was such a "conspiracy" it didn't work. To this there are three replies. First, no Clinton apologist can dare, after the victim cult sponsored by both the president and the First Lady, to ridicule the idea of "conspiracy," vast or otherwise. Second, the bombings helped to raise Clinton's poll numbers and to keep them high, and who will say that this is not a permanent White House concern? Third, the subject was temporarily changed from Clinton's thing to Clinton's face, and doubtless that came as some species of relief. But now we understand what in November was a mystery. A much less questionable air strike was canceled because, at that time, Clinton needed to keep an "option" in his breast pocket.

On January 6, two weeks after I spoke to Scott Ritter, UN secretary-general Kofi Annan's office angrily announced that, under Richard Butler's leadership, UNSCOM had in effect become a wholly owned subsidiary of the Clinton administration. The specific disclosure concerned the organization's spying activities, which had not been revealed to the UN. But Ritter's essential point about UNSCOM's and Butler's subservient client role was also underscored. This introduces two more canines—the UN inspectors being metamorphosed from watchdogs into lapdogs.

The staged bombing of Iraq in December was in reality the mother of all pinpricks. It was even explained that nerve-gas sites had not been hit, lest the gas be released. (Odd that this didn't apply in the case of the El Shifa plant, which is located in a suburb of Khartoum.) The Saddam Hussein regime survived with contemptuous ease, while its civilian hostages suffered yet again. During the prematurely triumphant official briefings from Washington, a new bureaucratic euphemism made its appearance. We were incessantly told that Iraq's capacities were being "degraded." This is not much of a target to set oneself, and it also leads to facile claims of success, since every bomb that falls has by definition a "degrading" effect on the system or the society. By acting and speaking as he did, not just in August but also in December, Clinton opened himself, and the United States, to a charge of which a serious country cannot afford even to be suspected. The tin pots and yahoos of Khartoum and Kabul and Baghdad are micro-megalomaniacs who think of their banana republics as potential superpowers. It took this president to "degrade" a superpower into a potential banana republic.

So overwhelming was the evidence in the case of the Sudanese atrocity that by January 1999 it had become a serious embarrassment to the Clinton administration. The true owner of the El Shifa plant, a well-known Sudanese entrepreneur named Saleh Idris, approached Dr. Thomas Tullius, head of the chemistry department at Boston University, and asked him to conduct a forensic examination of the site. Samples taken from all levels, and submitted to three different laboratories in different world capitals, yielded the same result. There were no traces of any kind of toxicity, or indeed of anything but standard pharmaceutical material. Armed with this and other evidence, Mr. Idris demanded compensation for his destroyed property and initiated proceedings for a lawsuit. His case in Washington was taken up by the law firm of Akin, Gump, Strauss, Hauer and Feld—perhaps best known for the prominence with which Vernon Jordan adorns its board of partners.

As a capitalist and holder of private property, Mr. Idris was always likely to receive due consideration if he was prepared to hire the sorts of help that are understood in the Clintonoid world of soft money and discreet law firms. The worker killed at the plant, the workers whose livelihood depended upon it, and those further down the stream whose analgesics and antibiotics never arrived, and whose names are not recorded, will not be present when the recompenses are agreed. They were expendable objects of Clinton's ruthless vanity.

Note

On 27 October 1999, the *New York Times* finally published an entire page of reportage, under the byline of James Risen, disclosing extensive official misgiving about the Al-Shifa atrocity. Under the subheading "After the Attack, Albright and Top Aide Killed Critical Report," it was revealed that a report from the State Department's Bureau of Intelligence and Research, which cast serious doubt on any connection between the plant and either bin Laden or the manufacture of chemical weapons, had been suppressed by Ms. Albright and her Under Secretary of State Thomas Pickering. Several highly placed diplomatic and intelligence chieftains were quoted by name as sharing in the view that Al-Shifa was not a legitimate target. The *New York Times* did not, however, see fit to ask what the urgency had been, or to discompose its readers by mentioning what else had been on the presidential mind that week.

SIX

Is There a Rapist in the Oval Office?

Some years ago, after the disappearance of civil rights workers Chaney, Goodman, and Schwirner in Mississippi, some friends of mine were dragging the rivers for their bodies. This one wasn't Schwirner. This one wasn't Goodman. This one wasn't Chaney. Then, as Dave Dennis tells it, "It suddenly struck us—what difference did it make that it wasn't them? What are these bodies doing in the river?"

That was nineteen years ago. The questions has not been answered, and I dare you to go digging in the bayou.

—James Baldwin,
The Evidence of Things Not Seen, 1985

On 14 December 1999, quite uncarried by the networks (though it was filmed and televised locally) and almost unreported in the so-called "pencil press" or print media, there occurred the following astonishing moment. Vice President Albert Gore Jr. was holding a "town meeting" in Derry, New Hampshire, when a woman named Katherine Prudhomme stood up to ask:

When Juanita Broaddrick made the claim, which I found to be quite credible, that she was raped by Bill Clinton, did that change your opinion about him being one of the best presidents in history? And do you believe Juanita Broaddrick's claim? And what did you tell your son about this?

THE VICE PRESIDENT (with a nervous giggle): Well, I don't know what to make of her claim, because I don't know how to evaluate that story, I really don't.

MS. PRUDHOMME Did you see the interview?

THE VICE PRESIDENT No, I didn't see the interview. No. Uh-uh.

MS. PRUDHOMME I'm very surprised that you didn't watch the interview.

THE VICE PRESIDENT Well, which show was it on?

MS. PRUDHOMME ABC, I believe.

THE VICE PRESIDENT I didn't see it. There have been so many personal allegations and such a non-stop series of attacks, I guess I'm like a lot of people in that I think enough is enough. I do not know how to evaluate each one of these individual stories. I just don't know. I would never violate the privacy of my communication with one of my children, a member of my family, as for that part of your question. But—

MS. PRUDHOMME So you didn't believe Juanita Broaddrick's claim?

THE VICE PRESIDENT No I didn't say that. I said I don't know how to evaluate that, and I didn't see the interview. But I must say something else to you about this. Why don't you just stand back up; I'd like to look you in the eye. I think that whatever mistakes [Clinton] made in his personal life are in the minds of most Americans balanced against what he has done in his public life as president. My philosophy, since you asked about my religious faith, I'm taught in my religious tradition to hate the sin and love the sinner. I'm taught that all of us are heir to the mistakes that—are prone to the mistakes that flesh is heir to. And I think that, in judging his performance as a president, I think that most people are anxious to stop talking about all the personal attacks against him. And trying to sort out all of the allegations, and want to, instead, move on and focus on the future. Now I'll say this to you, he is my friend, and that friendship is important, and if you've ever had a friend who made a serious mistake and then you repaired the friendship and moved on, then you know what that relationship has been like for me.

Secondly, I felt the same disappointment and anger at him during the period when all this was going on that most people did. You may have felt a different kind of emotion, I don't know. I sense that maybe you did. I certainly felt what most Americans did.

Third, I have been involved in a lot of battles where he and I have fought together on behalf of the American people, and I think we've made a good, positive difference for this country.

Number four, I'm running for president on my own. I want to take my own values of faith and family to the presidency, and I want you to evaluate me on the basis of who I am and what you believe I can do for this country as president. Thank you.

And thank *you*, too, Mr. Vice President. Innumerable grotesqueries strike the eye, even as it glides over this inert expanse of boilerplate evasion and unction. Mr. Gore is evidently seeking to identify himself painlessly with "most" (four repetitions) of the public. Yet he also feels a vague need to assert courage and principle and thus asks his lone lady questioner (who has properly resumed her seat) to stand up and be looked in the eye. Such gallantry! He then tells

her that "since you asked about my religious faith"—
which she had not—she is entitled to some pieties,
in which he proceeds to misremember *Hamlet* rather
than the Sermon on the Mount.

But all of this is paltry detail when set against the
one arresting, flabbergasting, inescapable realization. For the first time in American history, a sitting Vice President has been asked whether or not
there is a rapist in the Oval Office. A Vice President with "access" to boot, and a likely nominee for
the same high position. A Vice President who has
described the incumbent as a close friend. And he
replies, at inhuman length, that he doesn't really
know! The despicable euphemisms he deploys only
serve to emphasize the echoing moral emptiness: if
Clinton made the "mistake" with Ms. Broaddrick
that the lady questioner alleges, it was an intervention in *her* "personal life," not his. This is where
we live now, in the room-temperature ethics of the
2000 election. But more astonishing still is what is
not said. In the course of a lengthy, drivelling, and
alternately obsequious and blustering response, the
President's eight-year understudy, close colleague,
self-confessed friend, and would-be successor will
not say that he disbelieves this foulest of all allegations. He twice mumbles that he cannot "evaluate"
the charge of rape. Most of the male readers of this
article, I hope and believe, would expect even their

nodding acquaintances to do better than that for them. The question of "which show was it on?" is, in the circumstances, rather beside the point. Most politicians in any case either do watch NBC's *Dateline* (Ms. Prudhomme was in error about the network) or have their researchers watch it for them. It's a popular and respected and well-produced show. "Most Americans" who did watch it, in March 1999, concluded that Juanita Broaddrick was unlikely to be lying. Mr. Gore must have read at least that much in the press; his arranging to be adequately uninformed about the story—his positively freakish lack of curiosity—must therefore have taken him some trouble. An open mind need not be an empty mind—though in some cases one is compelled to wonder.

And one can often tell a good deal from an initial reaction, in which the affectation of innocence is present, yet present in such a way as to arouse or confirm suspicion. Take the following excerpt from Roger Morris's book *Partners in Power: The Clintons and Their America*, published in 1996. On page 238 appears the following story:

> A young woman lawyer in Little Rock claimed that she was accosted by Clinton when he was attorney general and that when she recoiled he forced himself on her, biting and bruising her. Deeply affected by the assault, the woman decided to keep it all

quiet for the sake of her hardwon career and that of her husband. When the husband later saw Clinton at the 1980 Democratic Convention, he delivered a warning. "If you ever approach her," he told the governor, "I'll kill you." Not even seeing fit to deny the incident, Bill Clinton sheepishly apologized and duly promised never to bother her again.

Roger Morris, who resigned from the National Security Council in protest at the Vietnam war, and who has since authored an acclaimed and garlanded critical biography of Richard Nixon, is not from the ranks of the traditional Clinton-haters or right-wing sleuths. (Not that one would exactly relish being called a Clinton-*lover*, either.) He invites us to notice what Clinton did *not* say when accosted. Most male readers of these pages, I again hope and trust, would react differently if approached by an irate man and threatened with deadly force if they so much as approached his wife again. Normal, human reaction? "I don't know what you're talking about" or "Are you sure you know who you're addressing?" Clinton reaction: "OK, OK, I'll stay away from her…"

I've talked to Morris at length about the incident, and he agreed to relay messages to and from the couple concerned, to go over his real-time notes with me, to put his own reputation behind the story and to do everything, in short, except reveal the identity of the woman. (Keep your eye on that last point, which will recur.) Here's what happened. In the summer of 1993 he had been commissioned by Henry Holt, one of America's most liberal publishers, to do a book on Clinton's first hundred days:

> I went down to Little Rock and started cold: most of my friends were liberal lawyers from Common Cause and I started with the local contacts they gave me. A young attorney from Hot Springs took me aside one evening and said that, for all the jokes and rumors about Clinton's sex life, not all the encounters had been consensual. He gave me the name of one young woman in particular. When I called her at her office she stonewalled me completely but then her husband telephoned me at the Camelot Hotel and said: "We'll talk; but it's off the record."

At that time, Arkansas had a freshly-anointed President to boast of; the well-to-do in Little Rock were not anxious to be making disagreeable waves. Morris went to a family home in the upscale part of the town and found two prosperous and well-educated lawyers, the woman from Arkansas and the husband from a neighboring Southern state.

She was still frightened while he, I would say, was still furious. The incident had occurred about the time when they were getting married, and they'd since had children. From the photos on the mantelpiece and around the place, I could see that they were well-connected locally, and they talked as if social as well as family embarrassment might be involved in any publicity. I thought they might be taking themselves much too seriously; even over-dramatizing things. And I also thought—come on. Clinton may be sleazy but he's not an *ogre* for Christ's sake.

Morris asked the woman the mandatory questions: Did he think you were coming on to him? Were there mixed signals? Was this just a bad date, or a misunderstanding? However, the woman later called him and arranged to meet in a roadhouse barbeque joint on the far outskirts of town. She still wished, she said, that no one had ever found out. But she'd had to tell one or two people the following:

She told me it took place in "a work situation," but after work. She'd been working on his campaign, not in his Arkansas government office. When I asked her "were you interested or were you attracted?" she said definitely not, she already had a man and was on the cusp of marriage. At a party in a campaign supporter's home they were left alone after the main crowd had departed and he suddenly got very nasty—threw her down, forced her, bit her hard on the mouth and face... She told me she felt more disgraced than violated.

Professional investigators on police rape squads learn to recognize an MO in these matters, and the biting of the lip or the face was also the specialized, distinctive feature in the case of Juanita Broaddrick. It is important to stress, here, that neither Ms. Broaddrick nor the woman in the Morris biography can possibly have known of each other's existence, or in any way concerted their separate stories, at the time they told them. Here, in its extensively corroborated detail, is the testimony of Juanita Broaddrick:

In the spring of 1978 Juanita Hickey (as she was then known during her first marriage) was a registered nurse running a nursing home in the town of Van Buren, Arkansas. Clinton was the state's attorney general, and much engaged in his first run for the governorship. Impressed by his candidacy, Juanita (as I'll now call her) volunteered to hand out bumper stickers and signs, and first met the aspiring governor when he made a campaign stop at her nursing home. "While he was there visiting, he said, 'If you're ever in the Little Rock area, please drop by our campaign office... be sure and call me when you come in.'" (A photograph of this first meeting exists: it shows a personable Juanita and a young Clinton

CHRISTOPHER HITCHENS

looking like someone auditioning for a Bee Gees
look-a-like contest.) On 25 April 1978 Juanita was
in Little Rock for a nursing home convention held
at the Camelot Hotel, and she did call him. He said
that after all he wouldn't be at the campaign office so
"Why don't I just meet you for coffee in the Camelot
coffee shop?" She agreed to this, and also to a later
call from him which proposed, since he said there
were reporters in the coffee shop, that they meet
instead in her hotel room.

I had coffee sitting on a little table over there by
the window. And it was a real pretty window view
that looked down at the river. And he came around
me and sort of put his arm over my shoulder to point
to this little building. And he said that he was real
interested, if he became governor, to restore that
little building, and then all of a sudden, he turned
me around and started kissing me...I first pushed
him away...Then he tries to kiss me again. And the
second time he tries to kiss me, he starts biting on
my lip...He starts to bite on my top lip, and I try to
pull away from him. And then he forces me down
on the bed. And I just was very frightened...It was
a real panicky, panicky situation. And I was even to
the point where I was getting very noisy, you know,
yelling to—you know—to please stop. But that's

when he would press down on my right shoulder
and he would bite on my lip.

Her skirt was torn at the waist, her pantyhose ripped
at the crotch, and the attorney general of Arkansas
forced an entry.

When everything was over with and he got up
and straightened himself, and I was crying at the
moment, and he walks to the door and calmly puts
on his sunglasses. And before he goes out the door
he says "You'd better get some ice on that." And he
turned and went out the door.

The advice about ice turned out to be sound, according to Juanita's friend Norma Kelsey who had come
along for the trip, who knew that a meeting with
Clinton was planned, and who found Juanita in tears
with a badly swollen lip and ripped pantyhose. She is
one of five real-time witnesses to whom Juanita told
the story while her injuries were still visible, the others (all of whom have testified to this effect) being
Susan Lewis, Louise Mah, Jean Darby (the sister of
Norma Kelsey) and her husband-to-be, David Broaddrick. At the time, it is important to mention, she
was carrying on a love affair with Mr. Broaddrick
and hoped to escape her first marriage and become

his wife. This supplied (a.) a disincentive for casual dalliance with the candidate, of the sort his less tasteful supporters have been known to suggest, and (b.) an additional incentive to keep quiet and avoid scandal. All of her friends also urged her to maintain silence because nobody, in the Arkansas of the time, would believe her.

NBC News possesses great fact-checking resources, and did not air its interview with the highly-convincing Juanita until after an exhaustive process of inquiry. It established her whereabouts on the day in question, even confirming that the view from the hotel bedroom would have been as she described it. There should have been no difficulty in establishing the whereabouts of a state attorney general on any given day: records and appointment books are kept and of course the presumption of innocence suggests that a politician will be eager to help establish an alibi. But according to Lisa Myers, the much-respected correspondent on the story:

> Was Bill Clinton even in Little Rock on April 25, 1978? *Despite our repeated requests, the White House would not answer that question and declined to release any information about his schedule.* So we checked 45 Arkansas newspapers and talked to a dozen former Clinton staffers. We found no evidence that Clinton had any public appearances on the morning in

question. Articles in Arkansas newspapers suggest
he was in Little Rock that day. (Italics added.)

There's one grace-note, to set beside the biting as a
kind of Clintonian signature. In 1991, Juanita was at
another nursing-home meeting in Little Rock, and
was suddenly called out into the hallway to meet the
Governor. At least one witness remembers seeing
them together, and wondering what they could be
talking about. According to Juanita:

> He immediately began this profuse apology, saying
> "Juanita, I'm so sorry for what I did." He would say
> things like "I'm not the man that I used to be. Can
> you ever forgive me? What can I do to make things
> up to you?" And I'm standing there in absolute
> shock and I told him to go to hell and I walked off.

She wondered why he had made this clumsy bid for
contrition, until, a short while afterward, she heard
him announce publicly that he was beginning a
campaign for the Democratic nomination for the
Presidency. For this, of course, and on many future
occasions, a "new Clinton" would be required.

By the time that NBC aired its Broaddrick
interview—which it withheld until the impeachment
trial was over—the President's defenders had become
hardened to dealing with accusations from outraged

females. They were usually able to imply either that the woman in question was an ally of the political Right, or on a gold-digging expedition, or a slut of low character who had probably asked for it, or eager to cash in on a memoir. None of these tactics would work with Juanita, because she had been a political supporter of Clinton's, had not asked for or received any money for her story, did not wish to market a book and had, since her divorce and remarriage, lived a highly respectable life owning and operating a horse-farm with her husband. Indeed, she had not in the ordinary sense "gone public" at all. Rather, she had been "outed" by one of the very few people she had told who was a Republican. Having at one point gone to the length of denying the story under oath in order to protect her privacy and that of her new family, she saw that this was futile and determined that if the story were to be told it should be told fully and by her. (The lie under oath resulted from a subpoena from Paula Jones's lawyers, in a case in which she did not wish to involve herself.)

No forensic or medical or contemporary evidence exists and there were no direct witnesses, even though the number of immediate aftermath witnesses is impressive and their evidence consistent. This does not mean that the matter dissolves into the traditional moral neutrality of "he said, she said."

For one thing, "she" did not wish to say anything.
For another—and here again we are in the eerie
territory of the Clintonian psyche—"he" has not
denied it. I repeat for emphasis; the President of
the United States, plausibly accused of rape by a
reputable woman whose story has been minutely
scrutinized by a skeptical television network, offers
no denial. His private lawyer David Kendall, a man
who did not even know Clinton at the time (and a
man who had publicly denied that fellatio is a sexual
act) issued the following statement on 19 February
1999:

> Any allegation that the President assaulted Mrs.
> Broaddrick more than twenty years ago is absolutely
> false. Beyond that, we're not going to go.

And beyond that, they haven't gone. Of course the
statement is open to Clintonian parsing. *Any* allegation? Oh, you mean *this* allegation? In 1978 the
President was Jimmy Carter, who certainly didn't
"assault" any woman that year. And in 1978, Juanita
was Mrs. Hickey. So—did Bill Clinton rape Mrs.
Hickey that year? The question, under White
House rules of evidence, has not even been posed
yet. (The President has since paid a fine of $90,000
for lying under oath in a Federal Court, and made a
payment of $850,000 to settle an allegation of sexual

harassment, and has been cited by a DC judge for a criminal violation of the Privacy Act in the matter of Kathleen Willey, so the "he said" element would be weaker than usual in any event.)

The next month, on 19 March, Sam Donaldson of ABC News raised the matter at a press conference and was referred by Clinton to the above lawyer's statement. The President would not even deny the allegation in the first person, or in his own voice. "Can you not simply deny it, sir?" asked Donaldson plaintively. And answer came there none.

It is just possible that the Broaddrick scandal, despite having been dropped by a generally compliant press, is not yet over. On 16 December 1999, Lanny Davis, one of the President's more sinuous apologists, was asked on an MSNBC chat show to address the issue and replied that Ms. Broaddrick had been adjudged unreliable by the FBI. "How do you know, Lanny?" he was asked, and had no immediately very convincing answer, since her FBI file, if any, would be none of his business. On 20 December, Juanita Broaddrick filed a suit in Federal District Court seeking any files on her kept by the White House or the Justice Department. The White House responds that "there will be no comment" from them on this legal initiative by a private citizen who might be said to have suffered enough.

If Juanita Broaddrick is not telling the truth, then she is either an especially cruel and malicious liar, who should at a minimum be sued for defamation, or a delusional woman who should be seeking professional help. Nobody who has met or spoken with her believes that these necessary corollaries obtain even in the slightest way. And on this occasion, we can't just lazily say that it's her (not unsupported) word against that of a proven liar, because the proven liar hasn't even cared, or do I mean dared, to open his mouth.

For mentioning this squalid subject on TV and radio, I have once or twice been accused of being "obsessed" by Clinton's rape victims. That's neat of course, and typical of his political bodyguards; in their minds nothing is his fault and it's only his accusers who have any explaining to do. But in the third case I know about, which is so far unpublished anywhere, the story came to me without my asking, let alone soliciting. I was in San Francisco, and got a call and later a visit from a very well-known Bay Area journalist and editor. He's a veteran radical and was once quite a Clinton fan; we'd argued about the man before. He wanted, he said, to disburden himself of the following information.

He (I can't give his name without identifying her) had once employed a young female assistant. In the early 1970s, Bill Clinton had come out to the Bay Area to see his fiancée, Hillary, who was then working, for some other friends of mine as it happens, as a legal intern in Oakland. An introduction occurred between young Bill and my friend's aforementioned assistant. He asked her out for lunch; she accepted. He proposed a walk in Golden Gate Park; she accepted that too. He made a lunge at her; she declined the advance and was rammed, very hard indeed, against a tree trunk before being rolled in the bushes and badly set-upon. She's a tall and strong woman, and got away without submitting. She told my friend the same day, and he'd kept the secret for almost thirty years. In those days, girls on the Left were proud of being the equals of men, and took the rough, so to speak, with the smooth. It wasn't done to whine or complain, let alone to go to the forces of law and order, or of repression as they were then known.

Years later, the woman was sitting at her desk when she got a telephone call from Brooke Shearer, who is also Mrs. Strobe Talbott and a veteran of the Clinton kitchen-cabinet. "Bill is thinking of running for office," said Ms. Shearer. "He wanted to know if that was all right with you." My subject was annoyed, but she had retained her old liberal allegiances. She also—see how this keeps coming up?—was thinking of getting engaged and becoming a mother. She replied that she wouldn't stand in the way of a Clinton candidacy. But I have since talked to two further very respectable San Francisco citizens, who have heard her relate the identical story at their own dinner table, and who have neither met nor heard of my original informant (nor he of them). I know the woman's name; I know that she has married well; I know her maiden name at the time of the assault; I know the high-powered Bay Area foundation where she works on good causes; I have communicated with her by Federal Express and by voicemail. I have excellent witnesses who have heard her say that if the story ever breaks she'll deny it under oath. I don't blame her—though in our present unshockable moral atmosphere it's very unlikely that reporters, let alone prosecutors, would even turn over in bed before consigning the whole thing to the memory hole. It is time, as we keep hearing, to put the country behind us and move this forward. (At least, I *think* I've got that right.)

There are several other documented or partly-sourced allegations of rape against this President, and many more allegations of biting and of brutish sexual conduct. Some of these seem to me to be scurrilous, and some that are not scurrilous could be the result of copycat publicity. But the three stories above are untainted in this way, and they seem to leave Juanita Broaddrick, for the moment, with a very strong *prima facie* case.

Circumstantial evidence, as Justice Holmes once phrased it, is often very powerful (and can be used for an indictment or a conviction) precisely because *it is the hardest to arrange.* What are the chances that three socially and personally respectable women, all three of them political supporters of Mr. Clinton and none of them known to each other, would confect or invent almost identical experiences which they did not desire to make public? And how possible would it be for a network of anti-Clinton rumor-mongers to create, let alone ventilate, such a coincidence? The odds that any of these ladies is lying seem to me to approach zero; their reasons for reticence are all perfectly intelligible.

Reticence and feminine discretion, sometimes used to discredit women who don't come forward in time, or at all, are in fact the ally of the perp, as the feminist movement used to instruct us. Indeed, voting against the confirmation of Clarence Thomas to the Supreme Court in 1991, Senator Albert Gore said with almost pompous gravity: "Every woman who has ever struggled to be heard over a society that too often ignores even their most painful calls for justice—we simply cannot take for granted that the victim, or the woman, is always wrong." *Even* their *most* painful? Judge Thomas's accuser said that he had talked dirty to her; no more, even while (if you remember) she'd continued to work for and support him. That didn't stop then-Governor Clinton from denouncing President Bush as "anti-woman" for his disbelief in Professor Hill's charges.

If it was "time to speak out" then, as Hillary Clinton said in presenting Anita Hill with an award, then it's time to speak out now. The same Al Gore has been unable to repress a feeling that there might be something in what Juanita Broaddrick told us. And she tells me that she still cries every time she sees Clinton's gloating face on the TV. The official feminist leadership has forgotten what it used to affirm—which is how seldom decent women lie about rape and how often they bite their lips and keep silent for fear of being defamed or disbelieved. Biting their own lips is still better than having them furiously and lovelessly bitten; is our society so dulled that we simply pass the ice-bag and turn to other things?

Taken together with his silence on the legal lynching of Rickey Ray Rector, and the numb acceptance of the criminal Strangelove bombings of Sudan and Iraq, the mute reception of Juanita Broaddrick's charges illuminates the expiring, decadent phase of American liberalism.

SEVEN

The Shadow of the Con Man

Rodham's Last Hurrah

"When you come right down to it, there are only two points that really count."

"Such as?"

Skeffington held up two fingers. "One," he said, ticking the first, "all Ireland must be free. Two," he said, ticking the second, "Trieste belongs to Italy." They count. At the moment the first counts more than the second, but that's only because the Italians were a little slow in getting to the boat."

—Edwin O'Connor, *The Last Hurrah*

CYRIL: *Lying! I should have thought that our politicians kept up that habit.*

VIVIAN: *I assure you that they do not. They never rise beyond the level of misrepresentation, and actually condescend to prove, to discuss, to argue. How different from the true liar, with his frank, fearless statements, his superb irresponsibility, his healthy, natural disdain of proof of any kind! After all, what*

*is a fine lie? Simply that which is its own evidence.
If a man is sufficiently unimaginative to produce
evidence in support of a lie, he might just as well
speak the truth at once. No, the politicians won't
do. Something may, perhaps, be urged on behalf of
the Bar. The mantle of the Sophist has fallen on its
members. Their feigned ardors and unreal rhetoric
are delightful.*

—Oscar Wilde, *The Decay of Lying*

Two full terms of Clintonism and of "triangulation," and of loveless but dogged bipartisanship, reduced the American scene to the point where politicians had become to politics what lawyers had become to the law: professionalized parasites battening on an exhausted system that had lost any relationship to its original purpose (democracy or popular sovereignty in the first instance; justice or equity in the second). The permanent political class and its ancillaries held all the cards by the 2000 campaign, controlled all the money, decided on all the predigested questions in all the manipulated polls. They did their job almost too well, leaving insufficient room for illusion and inadequate grounds for maintaining any steady or principled party allegiance. As a result, the only realists were the cynics.

And this in turn permitted some alarming honesties to be committed in public.

Toward the opening of the campaign season, and on the cusp of an anticlimactic and apathetic millennium, Norman Podhoretz wrote a very striking cover essay for *National Review*. In this article, the former editor of *Commentary* sought to persuade the fans of William F. Buckley that Bill Clinton was not really all that bad. Mr. Podhoretz of course had made his name as a campaigner for the "neo-conservative" opinion that the origins of all moral rot lie in "The Sixties." With his wife, Midge Decter, and his gifted polemicist son, John, and by means of a nexus of other family and political filiations on the Right, he had inveighed against antiwar and anti-imperialist groups, against homosexuals and feminists, against cultural pluralism and anything smacking of the dreaded "correctness." He was one of the many prominent conservative Jews willing to countenance a pact with the Christian Coalition.

Staying at least partly in character, Podhoretz stipulated rather matter-of-factly that Clinton was of course a liar, a crook, a traitor to friends and family alike, a drug-user, a perjurer, a hypocrite, and all the rest of it. However, he argued, this could be set against his one great and unarguable achievement, which was the destruction of "McGovernism" in the

Democratic Party. Clinton might, said Podhoretz, have wavered occasionally on matters like the sellout to China. But he had forever defeated the liberal, union-minded, bleeding heart and environmentalist faction, of the sort that had once stuck up for Vietnamese or Nicaraguans or (worst of all) Palestinians:

> Bill Clinton is a scoundrel and a perjurer and a disgrace to the office he has held. Yet it is this scoundrel, this perjurer, this disgrace to the presidency of the United States who has pushed and pulled his party into moving in a healthier direction than it had been heading in since its unconditional surrender to the Left nearly thirty years ago. As if this were not extraordinary enough in itself, the explanation for it can be found in the very defects of Clinton's character I have just listed.

> In my experience, very few politicians have solid principles that they are unwilling to sell out for the sake of winning elections. They are, most of them, "the hollow men, the stuffed men" of whom T. S. Eliot wrote, and in Clinton we have perhaps as extreme an embodiment of this professional deformation as can be unearthed. If he had been a man of any principles at all, a man with something inside him besides the lust for power (and the other lusts that power contributes to satisfying) he would have been incapable of betraying the people and the ideas

he was supposed to represent. If he had not been so great a liar, he would have been unable to get away not only with his own private sins but with the political insults he was administering to some of his core constituencies. And if he had not been such a disgrace to the presidency, he would not have been impeached, and would not thereby have forced even the intransigent McGovernites of his party, who had every reason to hate him, into mobilizing on his behalf for fear of the right-wing conspiracy they fantasied would succeed him.

The admission that Clinton is a political conservative, who has moved the Democratic Party to the right while relying on rather prostituted "correctness" constituencies, is one that few authentic conservatives allow themselves. The concession does, however, show an understanding of "triangulation" and it does possess some explanatory power. By the spring of 2000, it was clear that the liberal pulse of the party was to all intents and purposes undetectable. Even former Senator Bill Bradley, returning to the hustings after marinating for a while in the casks of Wall Street, looked discountenanced by the utter failure of the patient to respond. And he was only seeking to awaken the liberal reformist instinct in its mildest and most manageable form. He didn't even brush the G-spot.

Indeed, in what had begun as a rather stilted and fixed campaign, the only outlet for insurgent feeling was that offered in a Republican primary by the eccentric Senator from Arizona. John McCain achieved at least an initial burst of speed by his proclaimed dislike of the system, by his professed distaste for campaign-finance racketeering and by his (apparently) unscripted and unspun style. It was puerile anti-politics but it worked for a space, and drew for its effect on many voters who had registered as Democrats or independents. Nowhere within the echoing emptiness of the Democratic fold was there any hint of a live dialogue. And McCain, of course, had voted to impeach and to convict Clinton, and had gravely upset Governor Bush of Texas, in the course of the South Carolina primary, by comparing him to the incumbent President. ("You don't," said Bush in a tone of outrage, "you just don't say that of a man.")

Meanwhile Vice President Gore rather noticeably did not ask his boss to campaign for him, and was often ridiculed for the campaign-finance fiascos and lies in which Clinton had involved him, and discovered that he had all along been very downcast by the President's selfish and thoughtless conduct—never exactly specified, but wincingly hinted at. Looking somewhat like (and very much resembling) a dog being washed, Mr. Gore also feigned excitement at the local campaign he and his backers liked the least: the decision by Hillary Rodham Clinton—the other half of a "buy one, get one free" sleazy lawyer couple—to try and succeed to the vacant Senatorship from the great state of New York.

Everything about this campaign, and everything about this candidate, was rotten from the very start. Mrs. Clinton has the most unappetizing combination of qualities to be met in many days' march: she is a tyrant and a bully when she can dare to be, and an ingratiating populist when that will serve. She will sometimes appear in the guise of a "strong woman" and sometimes in the softer garb of a winsome and vulnerable female. She is entirely un-self-critical and quite devoid of reflective capacity, and has never found that any of her numerous misfortunes or embarrassments are her own fault, because the fault invariably lies with others. And, speaking of where things lie, she can in a close contest keep up with her husband for mendacity. Like him, she is not just a liar but a lie; a phoney construct of shreds and patches and hysterical, self-pitying, demagogic improvisations.

In the early days of her campaign, and just before (this following a clumsy fan-dance of inordinate length) its formal announcement, even her staunchest backers at the *New Yorker* were manifesting alarm. Her kind of slithery rhetoric, wrote the devoted Elizabeth Kolbert, would not quite do. An instance from an address to the Democrats of Westchester County:

What's important to me are the issues. I mean, who, at the end of the day, is going to improve education for the children of New York? Who's going to improve health care for the people of New York? Who's going to bring people together? And that's what I'm going to be talking about.

Mrs. Clinton's standards were not set high ("improve" instead of the once-bold "reform"? And a Senator "bringing people together," instead of vigorously representing them?). But Ms. Kolbert's standards were not high, either. (Given the chance to ask her candidate a question, she managed to inquire courageously about the difficulty of running as someone from out-of-state, and this as late as January 2000.) But even she had to cringe at the following, delivered to a solidly sympathetic yet bored audience at Riverside Church on the Upper West Side:

I think it's appropriate to take a few minutes to reflect on some of the issues that people of faith have in common, and from my perspective, as I have traveled extensively through New York and been in the company of New Yorkers from so many different walks of life, I agree that the challenges before us, as individuals, as members and leaders of the community of faith, as those who already hold positions of public responsibility and those who seek them, that we do all share and should be committed to an understanding of how we make progress, but we define that progress, deeply and profoundly.

This, in a prepared text, where even the bored annotators didn't bother to notice that progress was defined as both deep and profound. (Not unlike Vice President Gore's robotic assurance that his use of marijuana had been "infrequent and rare.") Liars can often be detected in that latter way, brashly asserting more than has been asked of them: Mrs. Clinton's chloroform rhetoric is an indication of another kind of falsity; one that is so congested with past lies and evasions—and exposures—that it can only hope to stay alive on the podium by quacking out the clock, ducking or stunning the "question period" and saying nothing testable or original or courageous. This is not, as the *New Yorker* would have us believe, a problem of dynamism or a lapse in the all-important "presentation." And the once-proud New York Democratic Party had actually asked for all this. In the clumsy, sycophantic words of Representative Charles Rangel, whose original idea it was, the Party "pulled together an offer that the First Lady can't refuse": the offer of a coronated nomination without any primary contest. "You can always promise no primary to an 800-pound gorilla," said the Congressman stupidly to the *New York Times*, as if the short-circuiting of voter choice was an achievement to beam about. (We don't have the First Lady's reaction to the primate or the weight comparison: a mirthless grin probably covered it.)

The "Hillary" campaign was inaugurated by a positive Niagara of dishonesty and deceit, much of it related to that most base and obvious pander of the New York politico—the conscription of ethnic politics. New York Jews are hardened by now to the most shameless promises; New York Puerto Ricans perhaps somewhat less so: both constituencies were to receive double-barreled insults to their intelligence almost before the bandwagon had begun to roll. Mr. Clinton had decided to pardon and release some Puerto Rican nationalists, imprisoned for placing indiscriminate bombs in lower Manhattan; the cause was popular among Puerto Ricans but less favored by other communities. Mrs. Clinton, who almost certainly solicited the favor from a President who almost never employs his power of pardon—and who slew the helpless Rickey Ray Rector—then denounced the clemency when it proved to play badly, and then claimed that she had never discussed any stage of the process with her husband. (On other occasions, she slyly lets on that they have no secrets from each other: the classic alternation of ditsy "little me" housewife and "strong woman.") But "we talk," she had told Tina Brown's *Talk* magazine already.

"We talk in the solarium, in the bedroom, in the kitchen—it's just constant conversation." Hard to keep Puerto Rico out of it.

Then, if I may quote myself writing in *The Nation* of May Day 2000, there was the open scandal of the Pakistanian connection:

> Remember when every liberal knew how to sneer at George W. Bush, not only for forgetting the name of Pakistan's new dictator but for saying that he seemed like a good guy? Well, General Musharraf's regime has now hired, at a retainer of $22,500 per month, the DC law firm of Patton Boggs, for which Lanny Davis, one of the First Family's chief apologists, toils. Perhaps for reasons having to do with the separation of powers, Patton Boggs also collects $10,000 monthly from Pak-Pac, the Pakistani lobby in America, for Davis's services in its behalf. Suddenly, no more Dem jokes about ignorance of Pakistan.
>
> Last December, after Clinton announced that Pakistan would not be on his itinerary when he visited the subcontinent, his former White House "special counsel" arranged a fundraiser in Washington at which lawyers from Patton Boggs made contributions to the First Lady's Senate campaign that now total $25,500. So, not very indirectly, Pakistani military money was washed into her coffers from

the very start. Then, in February, another Pak-Pac event, in New York, was brought forward so as to occur before the arrangements for the President's passage to India had been finalized. Having been told that the First Lady did not grace any event for less than $50,000 upfront, the Pakistanis came up with the dough and were handsomely rewarded for their trouble by the presence of Lanny Davis and by a statement from Mrs. Clinton that she hoped her spouse would stop off in Pakistan after all. And a few days later, he announced that, after much cogitation, he would favor General Musharraf with a drop-by.

How does this look to you? One way of deciding it is to try the cover stories on for size. "I wish I could say I had the influence and had applied the right pressure for the President to visit Pakistan, but I didn't, so I can't." That's Lanny Davis. Is this what he tells the Pakistanis in return for his large stipend? "If anybody thinks they can influence the President by making a contribution to me, they are dead wrong." That's Hillary Clinton. Is that what she said at the Pak-Pac fundraiser?

One thing that strikes the eye immediately is how *cheap* this is. And inexpensive, too. The Pakistani nuclear junta must be rubbing its eyes: For such a relatively small outlay of effort it can get the First Family to perform public political somersaults.

The problem with Pakistan is that it is a banana republic with nuclear weapons, run by ambitious and greedy politicians who are scared of their own military-industrial complex. Aren't you glad you don't live there?

As for the Holy Land (the third "I" in the Last Hurrah trilogy of Ireland, Italy, and Israel), Mrs. Clinton came to New York with the uneasy memory of an unscripted remark about the desirability of a Palestinian state. Eager to live down this momentary embrace of a matter of principle—where else, one wonders, are the Palestinian people to live? Under occupation? In camps? In exile? Even Shimon Peres is for a state by now—she rushed to contradict her husband again, and demand that the United States embassy in Israel be moved forthwith to Jerusalem, before the status of that city has been determined by continuing negotiations. This well-worn pander proposal, set out in a letter to an Orthodox congregation, was somewhat eclipsed by a highly incautious visit to Israel and the occupied territories, in which she sat mutely through a poorly-phrased and paranoid attack on Zionism by Chairman Arafat's first lady. There was therefore nothing for it but the announcement, in August 1999, that Hillary Rodham Clinton had made the joyous discovery of a Jewish step-grandfather on (I hope) her mother's side. For abject currying, this easily outdid the witless and obvious donning of the New York Yankees cap. Gail Sheehy, not her most critical biographer, tells us that the First Lady has had numerous tucks and lifts and has deployed the magic of liposuction on her thighs and rear end. This is clearly not designed to please her husband; we shall see if it pleases New Yorkers. It may work. More than artifice is involved in the claim made at her 1999 Thanksgiving press conference that: "I don't pay attention to polls." Not long afterward, a poll was taken about whether Mrs. Clinton should make an appearance on the *Late Show with David Letterman*, an invitation to which had been languishing on her mantelpiece for many months. The poll showed that New Yorkers wished she would appear: she duly turned up accompanied by none other than her pollster. Mr. Letterman—as preoccupied as Ms. Kolbert with the "carpet-bagging" non-issue—asked her to name the New York state bird, the state flower and so forth. She answered all the questions correctly; it took a few days before Mr. Letterman admitted that he'd shown her the quiz in advance. Small dishonesties are the reflection of big ones; every trip Mrs. Clinton takes, with sirens blaring and New York traffic brought to a stop, is underwritten by the taxpayer.

*   *   *

That at least cannot be said for the mansion the Clintons bought for themselves in the upscale suburb of Chappaqua. "Bought for themselves" is, in any case, a euphemism: the First Couple is somewhat cleaned out by legal expenses—despite having made use of the Justice Department as private firm—and the $850,000 paid to Paula Jones had to be extracted from the First Lady's blind trust and cattle-futures fund. (One wonders what the "constant conversation" in the family home was like on *that* special morning.) Thus the job of financing the mortgage and closing the deal fell on one single opulent fund-raiser, the egregious Terry McAuliffe. Here again, the entire business was infected with duplicity from the very start. Mr. McAuliffe, who posted the $1.35 million necessary to secure the house in the first place, was at the time facing a grand jury in the matter of some extremely dubious business involving the Teamsters Union. His role in franchising the public rooms of the White House for fund-raisers during the 1996 election (see page 55) almost certainly resulted in the aborting of his nomination as secretary of commerce in Clinton's second term. Never before had a sitting President made himself so beholden to an active money-man and influence-peddler. Yet when questions were finally asked, both Clintons stuck mechanically to the line that the Office of Government Ethics had reviewed

the deal and found it unobjectionable. Not everybody knows that the Office of Government Ethics is forbidden to answer questions from the press
until its report is completed: the brazen lie got the
Clintons through the news cycle of house-purchase
and, by the time the Office of Government Ethics
had announced that it had said no such thing, the
story was well down-page. By that time, also, Mr.
McAuliffe's good offices had given way to a bank
loan offered on much more favorable terms than
any average citizen can hope to command. And still
the drizzle of tiny lies continued: on 16 November
1999, the First Lady's media flack, Howard Wolfson,
announced on *Larry King Live* that the President
himself would be moving to the Chappaqua home
in the New Year. For a sitting President to quit the
Executive Mansion is likewise news: Ms. Hillary
when asked about this said blandly, "I haven't really
talked to him about that." She claimed also that she
had not told the President about the announcement
of her candidacy—even as that announcement contained the boast that he would be campaigning for
her. Only those who are totally habituated to falsehood will so easily and naturally lie when the truth
would have done just as well.

It's possible to speculate about whether the First Lady
has become such a mistress of mendacity by a sort

of osmosis from her husband, and the many levels of "denial" he has imposed upon her, or whether she had the same original talent that he did. (Some objective biographers describe her early shock and alarm at Arkansas Tammany practices, at the discovery of what was considered legal.) Whatever may be the case here, there's no doubt that her single-mindedness, combined with a natural authoritarian self-discipline, have become political phenomena in themselves. Mrs. Clinton may now find it opportune to present herself as a survivor or even a victim, but the plain facts remain that:

- The hiring of the squalid and unscrupulous Dick Morris, as adviser both at state and national level, was her idea. Mr. Morris has boasted of being a procurer for her husband as part of his package of political skills.
- The hiring of private detectives for the investigation and defamation of inconvenient women was also her idea.
- The dubious use of a powerful law firm as an engine of political patronage was principally her scheme.
- The firing of non-client White House staff, the amassing of files on political opponents, and the magical vanishing and reappearance of subpoenaed documents, all took place in her wing of the White House, and on her apparent instructions.

- A check for $50,000, written by a donor with intimate ties to the Chinese military-industrial complex, was hand-delivered to her chief of staff in the White House.
- On a notable occasion, she urged investigative journalists to pursue the rumor that President George Bush had kept a mistress on his payroll.
- She allowed the exploitation of her daughter in the crudest and most painful photo-ops in living memory.
- She regarded the allegation of a sexual arrangement with Monica Lewinsky as proof positive of "a vast right-wing conspiracy."
- She further accused those who pursued that allegation of harboring a prejudice against people from Arkansas, while hailing herself from Illinois, and readying a campaign to represent New York.
- On a visit to New Zealand, she claimed to have been named for Sir Edmund Hillary's ascent of Everest; a triumph that occurred some years after her birth and christening. (I insert this true story partly for comic relief, as showing an especially fantastic sense of self-reinvention as well as a desperate, mysterious willingness to pander for the Kiwi vote.)

A whole chapter could be written under any of these separate headings. Mrs. Clinton, of course, is to be pitied in a way that her husband cannot be. Desperately keen to run him for the nomination in 1988 after the implosion of Gary Hart, she had to debase herself by listening to Betsey Wright's recitation of the roster of outraged women who made that impossible. But this revelation never inhibited her from blaming the female victims; from announcing for example that she would "crucify" Gennifer Flowers, or from helping her spouse to lie his way through that difficulty, and through all the subsequent ones, up to and including believable accusations of rape and molestation.

Her role model, according to herself, is that of Eleanor Roosevelt. She has even claimed, during her remarkably frank admissions of traffic with enablers and facilitators and other modern voodoo-artists, to have "channeled" the former First Lady. Mrs. Roosevelt, who also suffered "pain in her marriage," was constantly urging her husband to be more brave about civil rights, about the threat of fascism, about the plight of the dispossessed. She often shamed him into using some of his credit, with Congress and public opinion, for unpopular causes. There is not one shard of evidence that Mrs. Clinton has ever done any such thing. To the contrary: Dick Morris was her preferred consigliere, and according to him, in 1995 she said:

Our liberal friends are just going to understand that we have to go for welfare reform—for eliminating the welfare entitlement. They are just going to have to get used to it. I'm not going to listen to them or be sympathetic to them.

At every stage of the fund-raising bonanzas and the stone-walling of special investigators, Mrs. Clinton was at the forefront of the action and found to be urging a more ruthless style. Her reward was to hear Dick Morris say, when he had been fired, that "Bill loves Bill, and Hillary loves Bill, and so that gives them something in common." A sadder dysfunctional bonding would be hard to find: the most bitter and reproachful element being the open and cynical use, in the lying campaign against Jones, Lewinsky, and the other "Jane Does," of Mrs. Clinton's only worthwhile achievement in the shape of her daughter, Chelsea. A speck of pity, here, perhaps.

It comes down, though, to the exploitation of mammalian sentiments by reptilian people. When caught making a gigantic profit on cattle-future trades in which she was "carried" by clients of her husband, Mrs. Clinton abandoned the pose of the strong businesswoman perusing the stock pages of the *Wall Street Journal*, and simperingly claimed that her hormones were all out of whack because she was pregnant with Chelsea. How could she be expected to remember details? When the 1996 election looked to be a bit more close-fought than it turned out to be, she artfully told my friend Walter Isaacson, editor of *Time* magazine, that she and "Bill" were "talking" (that word again) about having or adopting a new baby. We are "talking about it more now," she breathed. "I must say we're hoping to have another child." Duly reproduced—if you allow the expression—in print, the revelation pointed up the difference in child-bearing or even child-adopting age between her husband and the creaking Senator Bob Dole, later to be a talking, if not exactly walking, advertisement for the wonder-working properties of Viagra. None of the supposed "attack dogs" of the self-regarding New York press has yet asked what happened to that unborn or unconceived or unadopted child. Evidently, it took a different kind of village.

In the same way, a woman whose main claim to sympathy is the supposed violation of her intimate privacy, and that of her notorious husband, made an on-the-record incitement to journalists in 1992, telling my *Vanity Fair* colleague Gail Sheehy: "I don't understand why nothing's ever been said about a George Bush girlfriend. I understand he has a Jennifer, too." Especially outrageous was the "too," in view of the fact that she had hysterically denied that Clinton had a "Jennifer" at all. Or perhaps it all depends on what the spelling of "Gennifer" is. (For the record, I myself investigated and ventilated the Jennifer Fitzgerald story in 1988: it seemed at least plausible that there had been an affair but not that Ms. Fitzgerald had (a.) been awarded her government job in return for sexual favors, or (b.) been denounced as either a nut or a slut by her former lover when embarrassed, or (c.) been asked to perform sexual acts while Bush was on the telephone in the Oval Office, or (d.) been overheard by a foreign embassy's electronic eavesdroppers while in the course of a phone-sex session linking the White House and the Watergate building, or (e.) been farmed out to a job in the Pentagon or the United Nations, or (f.) been bitten on the mouth, or (g.) been raped. If there was an affair, it was strictly consensual. And even Bushes are allowed some privacy, and can be expected to lie about sex.) Mrs. Clinton went on to help hire sordid private dicks like Terry Lenzner and Jack Palladino; a banana-republic auxiliary police for a White House who lied and lied and lied—not just about the sex, but about the women.

It's possible to feel a certain sympathy for the poor old American Right when confronted with this most protean and professional antagonist. They wish— how they wish—to convict her as the secular humanist, feminist, subversive schoolmarm they need her to be. And she goes on evading their net. Her main crimes have been the ones alleged by Jerry Brown and Ralph Nader in 1992—the transmutation of public office into private interest and vice versa, via a nexus of shady property deals and Savings and Loans. (Not a nexus that Reagan fans show any special willingness to unravel.) She is a dogged attender at church and a frequent waffler at Prayer Breakfasts and similar spectacles. She is for sexual abstinence, law and order, and the war on drugs. She stands by her man. She is for a woman's right to "choose," but then so are most Republican ladies these days. She used to be a Goldwater girl and a preachy miss, and it shows. She once assured Larry King that "there is no Left in the Clinton White House."

In 1992, the GOP's "opposition research" people thought they had her. It emerged that twenty years before, she had worked as a summer intern from Yale Law School in the deep-Red law firm of Bob Treuhaft, husband of Jessica Mitford. This firm had long handled all the radical labor cases in the Bay Area—leading Jessica or "Decca" to discover the scandal of the American funeral industry and its annexation of the death benefit, and to write the imperishable exposé *The American Way of Death*. In 1972, the same firm was heavily engaged in providing legal defense to the Black Panther Party, which for all its crimes and depredations was in physical danger from the Oakland police department.

Here was an actual and potential "gotcha." But by the time the Bush-Quayle team found it out, their private polls showed that American voters recoiled in principle from any attacks on the wife of candidate Clinton. So the material was reluctantly laid aside, to resurface every now and then in books and pamphlets written by rancorous conservatives who can't believe, even today, that Mr. and Mrs. Clinton escaped the nemesis of the law. I can scarcely believe it either but I can clear up a point or two.

Decca Mitford was a dear friend of mine; an honorable and brave ex-Communist, and a foe of all bores and all bigots. In the carrying tones of her class, she once described the experience of knowing the young Hillary Rodham.

A nice enough girl if a bit intense…married this young chap who later became the governor of Arkansas. We had a client on Death Row there, extradited from California. Turned out to be innocent, by the way, no thanks to Jerry Brown who let him be extradited. Anyway I thought I'd pop across to Little Rock and look up Miss Hillary. Got asked to tea on the strength of an old acquaintance, made my pitch for the poor defendant, got a flea in my ear. Situation all changed; big political prospects for the happy couple; not interested in reopening the case.

Realism, I think she said. The real world. Perfectly *ghastly* if you ask me.

She went on to express herself forcefully about the corporate Clintons, and about the slimy speech that Bill had made at Nixon's funeral.

Returning from California, and from seeing the splendid Ms. Mitford in the fall of 1994, I met Hillary Clinton one-on-one for the first and last time. Wondering what she'd say, I brought her the greetings of Decca and Bob. Even in a roomful of liberals—this was Sidney Blumenthal's birthday party, on the eve of Newt Gingrich's clean midterm sweep—she could not disown the connection fast enough. "Oh yes, I think I was there for a very short period." She had put that behind her and moved on.

At whose expense is this irony, if it is indeed an irony at all? Partly at the expense of the Right, which clings to its necessary myth of a diabolic liberal who will stop at nothing. Yet surely more at the expense of the liberals, especially the liberals of New York, willing to immolate themselves once again for a woman who has proved over and over that she cares nothing for their cherished "causes" but will risk anything, say anything, pay any price, bear any burden, to get her family a big house and secure herself a high-profile job. She is owed this, after all, for

NO ONE LEFT TO LIE TO

everything she has suffered on our behalf. Where do we find such women? And how shall we be worthy? Passing through its decadent phase, American liberalism enters the moment of the purely amnesiac.

On the morning of their inauguration in January 1993, the Clintons were observed standing on the steps of Blair House, official hospitality headquarters of L'Enfant's grand and dignified federal city. "Fucking bitch," the President-elect screamed at his newly-minted First Lady. "Stupid mother-fucker," she riposted. We may never know what hideous story of "enabling" and betrayal lay behind this poisoning of their big day, but we can fix it in time as the one moment when both were totally candid in public, and both were utterly right on the facts. Those who would vote to prolong the presence of this partnership in public life are not doing so with the excuse of innocence or gullibility that might have obtained in 1992.

The figure of Mrs. Clinton was anticipated by Henry Adams in his tremendous novel *Democracy*, published as an anonymous satire on Washington corruption in 1880. Here we encounter Mrs. Lightfoot Lee, female manipulator extraordinaire:

> In her own mind, however, she frowned on the idea of seeking for men. What she wished to see, she

thought, was the clash of interests, the interests
of forty millions of people and a whole continent,
centering at Washington: guided, restrained, controlled, or unrestrained and uncontrollable, by men
of ordinary mold; the tremendous forces of government, and the machinery of society, at work. What
she wanted was POWER.

The capitals were Adams's. Mrs. Lee in the end
found the Senate a disappointment; in any case the
condition of her making any headway was that she
was a widow.

Afterword

*"Then, Patrick, you do feel it too? You do feel…
something? It would be so bleak if you felt nothing.
That's what scares women, you know."*

*"I do know, and you needn't be scared. I feel
something all right."*

"Promise me you'll always treat me as a person."

"I promise."

"Promises are so easily given."

"I'll fulfil this one. Let me show you."

*After a shaky start he was comfortably into the
swing of it, having recognised he was on familiar
ground after all. Experience had brought him to
see that this kind of thing was nothing more than
the levying of cock-tax, was reasonable and normal,
in fact, even though some other parts of experience
strongly suggested that what he had shelled out so far
was only a down payment.*

—Kingsley Amis, *Difficulties With Girls*

*"I asked him why he doesn't ask me any questions
about myself, and…is this just about sex, or do*

you have some interest in getting to know me as a person?" The President laughed and said, according to Ms. Lewinsky, that "he cherishes the time he had with me." She considered it "a little bit odd" for him to speak of cherishing their time together "when I felt like he didn't really even know me yet."
—Judge Kenneth Starr, *Official Report of the Independent Counsel's Investigation of the President* (entry for January 21, 1996)

The abysmal finale of the Clinton folly was enacted, for every practical purpose, as if the President had a natural right to pass on his cock-tax costs to the consumer. At no point were any political or constitutional or even legal considerations permitted to "rise to the level," in the canting phrase of the day, where they might disturb the orderly running and management of the consensus and the stock market. Most bizarre of all was the manner in which this priority appeared under its own name.

The United States Senate, before which the final hearing of the first impeachment of an elected president took place, is perhaps the world's most deliberately conservative political body. Owing in part to Article V of the Constitution, it is impossible to amend the provision that grants two senators to each state of the union, regardless of population. Thus—in an arrangement aptly described by Daniel Lazare as one of "rotten boroughs"—unpopulous white and rural states such as Montana and Wyoming have the same representation as do vast and all-American and ethnically diverse states like New York and California. (Lazare gives a ratio of twelve to one between most populated and least populated state in 1790; today the ratio would be sixty-seven to one—an imbalance about which opinion has not yet been tested by polling.)

Moreover, the Senate is bound by arcana, procedural and historical, which are designed to limit not just public pressure but even public understanding. How often was it written, in the opening stages of the impeachment trial, that only one senator (and he the somewhat "unpredictable" veteran member from West Virginia, Robert Byrd) even comprehended the rule book. Like the Schleswig-Holstein question, or Bagehot's evocation of the British monarchy, the United States Senate is supposed to be immune from rational scrutiny and unintelligible to the ordinary gaze.

The decent conservative defense of such an institution would be, quite simply, that this evident flummery also furnishes a rampart against sudden gusts of demotic emotion. Such was certainly the intent of the Framers. So it was most fascinating, in the early weeks of the century's closing year, to witness the open collusion between constitutional obscurantism and the hucksterism of the polls; between antique ritual and shrewdly calculated advice on short-term media advantage; between, to go back to my beginning, the elitist style and the populist style. The clear winners in this cynical charade were the Clintonoid Democrats, who (as well as being hardened to switching and shifting between elitism and populism) could supply the most cobwebbed rules-monger on one hand—the aforementioned Senator Byrd—and the most sinuous arguments of the short-term general will on the other. Senator Daniel Patrick Moynihan, as so often, provided the fluid pivot and axis on which such a strategy could be made to turn, according to need, or according to the needs of New York's lumpen intellectuals.

During the Reagan era, the White House managers more than once managed to attain to the very nirvana of modern elitist populism—namely, they got a good press for getting a good press. I don't remember seeing the trick pulled again until the late decadence of the Clinton era, when journalists considered it their job to ridicule the very idea of a Senate trial, and when certain of the more savvy senators understood what was needful to attract a favorable story. (Reading *Sports Illustrated* on the floor of the Senate, with his back artfully turned to the press gallery, was the tactic successfully adopted

by Democratic Senator Herbert Kohl of Wisconsin.)
More distressing still was the open declaration that
evidence would make, or could make, no difference.
Since impeachment was not liked by the electorate,
in either its actual or virtual forms, and not desired
by Wall Street, and since conviction could only result
in removal from office, it followed that no conviction
was possible. From this reverse reasoning, the exclu-
sion of witnesses was but a short step. As Hilaire
Belloc put it: "The stocks were sold. The press was
squared. The middle class was quite prepared."

I shall not forget the telephone call I received at
home, on the Sunday before the final vote (February 7) from a Democratic senator not known for his
political caution. He was, he said, now minded to vote
for conviction on the obstruction of justice point. He
also said that he felt the House of Representatives
should have impeached Clinton for abuse of power:
the one count that did not involve the cock-tax fall-
out, and that would have raised evident matters of the
public interest. I was encouraged by something in his
tone, and then discouraged again. "They haven't presented the case very well," he offered, as if the Republicans had really been allowed to present their case
at all. "And they seem so partisan..." As soon as the
keyword of the moment had escaped his lips, I knew
all I needed to know. I asked him whether it wouldn't

seem "partisan" if not a single Democrat voted to
convict. I suggested that, if power had been abused
and justice obstructed, as he thought, it might have
been nice if more people on the Left had troubled to
notice it. To overlook the matter, and to leave it to the
conservatives to call attention to it, and then to speak
of a right-wing conspiracy, appeared to me in the light
of the grossest casuistry. (There was something tri-
angular about it.) "Anyway," I closed by saying, "now
I know what you think, and you know I know, and
if you end up voting with the bloc, then only I will
know." And then we ended—we really did end—with
mutual expressions of esteem. He did his duty by the
party on the following Friday.

The words "only I will know" had by then acquired
a special "resonance," as people tend to say in Washington, in my own head. On January 23, Clinton's
chief defense counsel, Mr. Charles Ruff, had told the
Senate in rotund terms:

> Let me be very clear about one proposition which
> has been a subtheme running through some of the
> comments of the [House] managers over the last
> many days. The White House, the President, the
> President's agents, the President's spokespersons,
> no one has ever trashed, threatened, maligned, or
> done anything else to Monica Lewinsky. *No one.*
> (My italics.)

No knowledgeable person witnessing that statement—and there were many such witnesses—could be unaware of its complete falsity. To take one example: James Warren, the redoubtable bureau chief of the *Chicago Tribune*, commented later on CNN:

> I can tell you one thing, having listened to Mr. Ruff yesterday or the day before talk about the injustice done to the White House by reports that they were bad-mouthing her, and that they were calling her a stalker. That comment by Ruff was so palpably untrue. If I had a buck for every person at the White House who bad-mouthed her to me last January I could leave the set now and head off to Antigua.

This direct contradiction, on an apparently small matter, had momentous implications. One of Mr. Ruff's deputy counsels, Ms. Cheryl Mills, had earlier instructed the Senate that in order to prove obstruction of justice it was necessary to show that a witness had been offered inducements *and* subjected to threats. This is actually untrue: it is sufficient to prove that a potential witness has been exposed to *either* sort of pressure. However, after Clinton had involved the White House, the Pentagon, the U.S. mission to the UN, and his soft-money chief whip Vernon Jordan in trying to find Ms. Lewinsky a job, the "inducement" business required no further demonstration. With the spreading of allegations about stalking and blackmail, one could hear the other shoe dropping. Lewinsky was being warned of what might happen to her if she did not stay perjured. The House managers in the trial had become aware of this fact, and had made a good deal of it in the trial. There was thus a salient difference, on an important point of evidence.

At this point, I became the hostage of a piece of information that I possessed. Returning to Washington from the University of California, where I had been teaching the previous spring, I had gone with my wife for a "catch-up" lunch with our old friend Sidney Blumenthal. Filling us in on what we had missed by being out of town when the scandal broke, he said that what people didn't understand, and needed to know, was the following: Monica Lewinsky had been threatening the president. Sidney had firsthand knowledge of the truth of this story (which I later discovered he also related, along with its original Presidential authorship, to the grand jury). Perhaps to spare my feelings or to avoid any too-obvious insult to my intelligence or our friendship, he did not include Clinton's portrayal of himself as the prisoner Rubashov in *Darkness at Noon*. But otherwise, his account of the Chief Magistrate's sufferings was as it later appeared in the Starr Report.

*   *   *

At the time, I remember thinking—but not saying—
that the story seemed axiomatically untrue. Even if
Ms. Lewinsky had stalking and blackmailing tendencies, it remains the case that a president cannot
be interrupted—except conceivably by his wife—in
his "own" Oval Office. Apart from anything else, the
suggestion also sat ill with Clinton's repeated claim,
sometimes when under oath, that he and Ms. Lewinsky had never been alone together. Also at the time, I
was more struck by the tone Sidney adopted in speaking about Kathleen Willey, whose allegations of a
direct sexual lunge by Clinton had been aired on the
program *60 Minutes* the previous weekend. "Her poll
numbers look good now," he said rather coldly, "but
you watch. They'll be down by the end of the week."
As indeed they were. The White House, which when
subpoenaed in the Jones case had been unable to locate
them, rapidly unearthed all of Ms. Willey's private
notes to Clinton and made them public in one day.*

The "stalker" story had appeared extensively in print
by then, immediately following the president's false
claim to Sidney (a claim which he later, in his Senate
testimony, truthfully described as a lie). I believe that
clippings to this effect were in a folder of material that

---

* In April 2000, a Federal Judge found Clinton guilty of a criminal violation of the Privacy Act for this piece of squalor, which was concocted
with the First Lady and Sidney Blumenthal.

he brought along to give me, and which I no longer possess. I also believe that at least two other senior White House aides were involved in spreading the smear against a defenseless and vulnerable young woman, who was not known at the time to possess any "forensic" evidence. One may imagine what would have been said about her, and done to her, if her garments had not once been flecked with DNA. Again at the time, the worst thing about the allegation was that Sidney seemed to believe it. It did not, for some months, acquire the significance that it assumed at trial.

In different formats and forums, including once in print, I passed the story along as an instance of what people have to believe, and how they have to think and speak, if they work for Clinton. I was readying another column on the subject when I was contacted by the chief investigative counsel of the House Judiciary Committee, on the Friday before the last day of Clinton's trial, and asked if I would put my name to it again. Had I decided not to cooperate (and on the assumption that no attempt to compel my testimony would have been made), then only I need have known. The door marked "insider" would have shut noiselessly behind me. My decision, to carry on saying what I knew to be true, was in one way very easy. Having made it plain that I would not testify against anyone but Clinton, and only in his Senate trial (an option I would have forfeited by any delaying tactics), and having understood that I had lodged this point with my interlocutors, I signed an affidavit confirming my authorship of the story, and the President's authorship of a vulgar and menacing slander. The consequences in my own life have made a literal truth out of what I had once written only metaphorically: Clintonism poisons everything it touches.

I had not known, when I met Sidney Blumenthal that day, that Kathleen Willey had already begun to experience harassment at her home, and that on the Monday after our lunch, she would receive a call from private investigator Jarrett Stern, who had sickened of his work. He warned her to be careful. It hasn't even crossed my mind, at any time since, that Sidney would have or could have had anything to do with any sleazy tactics, or even possess any knowledge of them. But I do have to say that I didn't like the tone he had acquired since we last met, and that in my memory it came to symbolize a certain *mens rea* in the Clinton White House.

There's been a certain amount made of the subject of journalistic etiquette in these matters. Suppose, then, that I had lunched with some George Bush flack in 1986, who had apologized for being late because the vice president had been delayed by the prolixity of Oliver North. The information would have been trivial at the time. But then suppose that I saw the same George Bush raise his hand a year later, to swear that he had never even met Oliver North. I would then be in possession of evidence. And it would be too easy (as a matter of fact, it already is much too easy) for any administration to make journalists into accomplices by telling them things, often unasked for, and then holding them to the privileges of confidentiality. Had such an occasion arisen in 1986 or 1987, I would certainly have made public what I knew. (I would have told Sidney, among others.) The pact which a journalist makes is, finally, with the public. I did not move to Washington in order to keep quiet and, as a matter of fact, nobody has yet asked me to do so. Nor am I usually given inadvertent glimpses of obstruction of justice, even by the sincerest apologists.

There's a simple proof of what I mean here. The House Committee staff never asked me about Kathleen Willey. I voluntarily cited her only as part of the material of the conversation, and included the mention of her in the final affidavit because I had later come to believe that she was the victim of an injustice. Not one reporter or commentator dwelt on this for more than an instant: I suppose because it involved no conflict of evidence between Sidney Blumenthal and myself, and thus it didn't help the "story" about fratricide at Washington dinner tables. But I knew or suspected by then that Clinton would "walk," as they say, and I wanted to reproach those who had voted for his acquittal in the hope of a quick disposal of all charges about his exploitation of women and his use of the soft-money world to cover it up. They did not deserve to be able to say that they had not been told in time. (I made the same point, to no effect, in a *Washington Post* column published amid a pelting calumny on February 9, 1999.) By then, too, I knew about Juanita Broaddrick, and a few other things.

Hannah Arendt once wrote that the great success of Stalinism among the intellectuals could be attributed to one annihilating tactic. Stalinism replaced all debate about the merit of an argument, or a position, or even a person, with an inquiry about motive. I can attest, in a minor key, to the effect of this tactic in smaller matters. It was instantly said of me that I did what I did in order to promote this very book— still then uncompleted. Other allegations against me failed to rise to this elevated level. The truth or otherwise of what I had said was not disputed so much as ignored. When the finger points at the moon, the Chinese say, the idiot looks at the finger. As a much-scrutinized digit, I can attest to the effect of that, too.

The acquittal of Clinton, and the forgiving by implication of his abuses of public power and private resources, has placed future crooked presidents in a strong position. They will no longer be troubled by the independent counsel statute. They will, if

they are fortunate, be able to employ "the popular-
ity defense" that was rehearsed by Ronald Reagan
and brought to a dull polish by Clinton. They will
be able to resort to "the privacy defense" also, especially if they are inventive enough to include, among
their abuses, the abuse of the opposite sex. And they
will only be impeachable by their own congressional
supporters, since criticism from across the aisle will
be automatically subjected to reverse impeachment
as "partisan." This is the tawdry legacy of a sub-
Camelot court, where unchecked greed, thuggery,
and egotism were allowed to operate just above the
law, and well beneath contempt.

I composed the title of this book, and had written
most of its opening passages, before I was asked to
repeat under oath what I had already attested. I regret
very much that the only piece of exposed flank, in a
sadly successful Clintonian defense based exclusively
on Clintonian lies, was offered by the confused testimony of an old friend, who was wrongly placed in
the seat where the president should have sat. I had
my chance to lie to the House counsel (and to lie
transparently at that) or to affect amnesia, or to run
out the clock and perhaps later be required to testify against an underling. I decided that in the latter
case I would sooner be held in contempt, but it took
no time to make up my mind that I wouldn't protect

Clinton's lies, or help pass them along. I wasn't going to be the last one left to lie to.

Anyway, it was a pleasure and a privilege to be hated and despised in Clinton's Washington, and also to discover that those who preached everlasting lenience and the gospel of the "non-judgmental" could at last summon the energy to cast a stone, even if only at myself.

A year or so later, it sometimes seemed as if the whole scandal had never been. By forcing an informal plebiscite not on his own personal and political morality, but on the morality of everybody *except* himself, Clinton had achieved the acme of corruption that comes with the enlistment of wide and deep complicity. Most politicians can only dream of such an outcome: Huey Long was one. By chance during that bizarre and shame-faced closure I heard a zoologist talking in Georgetown about the relationship between mammals and reptiles. "The reptile," she said, "can break into the mammal's nest and destroy and eat all the young, and be burrowed into the still-warm and living flank of the mother, before any reaction is evident. Our anthropomorphic verdict would be that reptiles don't even know that they are lucky, while mammals don't really believe that reptiles can exist."

*   *   *

The impression has been allowed to solidify that there was no price to be paid for all this; that the very definition of political skill was an ability to act without conscience. Appalled by the sheer raw ruthlessness of the President and his defenders, the Republicans and the conservative churches decided to call it a day. Marvin Olasky, the born-again Rightist who had originated the idea of "welfare reform" and been at Newt Gingrich's elbow, wrote a book on Presidential morality in which he said that if only Clinton had been a more regular churchgoer, and would even now ask for God's mercy, all might be well. It was not only liberals who failed the test set by Clintonism: the world of the "prayer breakfast" was his ally as surely as were the boardrooms and the Dow Jones. But millions of Americans still realized that something had been lost in the eight years of reptilian rule. The embarrassing emptiness of the 2000 election, especially the loss by the Democratic Party of even the slightest claim to any moral or ethical advantage, is one small symptom of what has been so casually thrown away. Meanwhile, the warm-blooded and the thin-blooded could only discuss the scaly and the remorseless in hushed tones, as the ensuing chapter will demonstrate. Perhaps one day the hot-blooded will have their revenge...

Index

Bobbitt, Philip, 105
Bradley, Bill, 146
Breslin, Jimmy, 25
bribes. *See* hush money; rewards
Broaddrick, David, 131–32
Broaddrick, Juanita (Hickey)
 lying under oath by, 134
 rape and biting charges made by,
  89, 121–26, 130–31, 135–36
 witnesses for, 131–32
Brown, Gerry, 163–64, 165
Brown, Ron, 29
Brown, Tina, 151
Buckley, William F., 144
Bureau of Intelligence and
 Research (INR), 119
Burton, Dan, 77
Bush, George W.
 alleged mistress of, 159, 162–63
 capital punishment and, 25
 Los Angeles unrest and, 29
 reaction to impeachment
  trial, 147
 Yitzhak Shamir and, 18
Butler, Richard, 97, 111
Butler report, 111, 112, 115

campaign ads, 47, 48, 57, 59
campaign donations/fund-raisers.
 See also rewards
 international, 55, 58–59, 159
 racketeering, 147, 158
 soft money, 57, 118, 181
 White House used for, 51–53, 54,
  55, 156
campaign finance laws, 54. *See also*
 soft money
capital punishment, 24–28, 68, 151
Carnaffin, Tom, 99
Carter, Jimmy, 12, 22, 135
Carville, James, 41
Casse, Daniel, 12, 13
Center for Public Integrity, 52
Central Intelligence Agency (CIA),
 74, 103, 106

Chicago Tribune, 175
chicken gutting, 63, 64
children, 36–37, 61–62, 63. *See
 also It Takes a Village* (H. R.
 Clinton)
Chinese campaign donations, 55,
 58–59
Christian Coalition, 88, 144
Cigna, 47, 49
Civil Rights Division. *See* U.S.
 Department of Justice
civil rights movement, 20, 30–31, 35
Clinton, Bill. *See also* Clinton, Bill/
 Hillary Rodham marriage;
 impeachment debate/trial
 Al Gore support for, 121–26
 as attorney general of Arkansas,
  125, 129–33
 biting/bruising allegations
  against, 42, 125–26, 129,
  130–31, 139, 141
 criminal violation of Privacy Act
  by, 136, 177
 DNA testing of, 42–43, 177
 draft notice denial, 71–72
 as governor of Arkansas, 21, 22,
  81–82
 legacy as president, 60–61, 144–45
 lying by, 71–72, 79–81, 83
 presidential nomination
  acceptance, 93
 rape allegations against, 121–26,
  130–31, 135, 137–39
 relationship with blacks, 23, 29,
  34–35, 43, 44–45
 Richard Nixon funeral speech
  by, 166
 Rickey Ray Rector execution
  and, 24, 26–28
 sexual harassment allegations
  against, 92, 135–36, 179
 60 Minutes appearance, 28
 subordinates lying for and
  supporting, 71–72, 83, 90, 134,
  144–45

INDEX

INDEX

New Deal, 16, 60, 87
New Democrats, 60, 79
New York, New York, 65–66,
147–51, 155, 172
New York Democratic Party, 150
New Yorker
   article on withholding of
   intelligence, 105–7
   essay on Rector last days, 25–26
   Hillary Clinton Senate campaign
   and, 147–51
   profile on Al Gore, 13
   review of *The President We
   Deserve* (Walker), 21
New York Times, 7, 62, 76, 111,
118–19, 150
Nixon, Richard, 56, 72, 87, 166
North, Oliver, 179–80
Norton Utilities, 53

occult, 84, 160
Olasky, Marvin, 184
O'Neil, Tip, 12
Osama bin Laden. *See* bin Laden,
Osama
Oval Office. *See also* White House
   coffee meetings, 54
   Don Tyson office modeled on, 65
   as public-business space, 55
   sexual encounters in, 92, 163, 177

PAC (Democrats for the Eighties),
30
Pakistan
   bombing of, 107–8
   indirect donations to H. R.
   Clinton campaign, 152–53
   nuclear weapons threat of,
   153–54
Palladino, Jack, 163
Panetta, Leon, 38
Partners in Power (Morris), 125–29
Patrick, Derval, 33–34
Patton Boggs, 152
payoffs. *See* rewards

Pearson, Rodney, 26
Physicians for a National Health
   Program, 48, 49
Pigman, Dennis, 26
Pinochet, Augusto, 74
Podhoretz, John, 144
Podhoretz, Norman, 144–46
polling. *See* public opinion polls
portable healthcare coverage, 50
poultry workers, 62–65. *See also*
   Tyson Foods
poverty, 68–69. *See also* children;
   welfare reform
Powell, Colin, 73
prayer breakfasts, 88, 164, 184
President We Deserve, The (Walker),
21–23
Primary Colors (Klein), 13
Privacy Act, 136, 177
privacy as shield, 17, 51–52
Progressive, 62
Prudential, 47, 49
Public Citizen, 49
public opinion polls, 17, 57, 59, 72,
79, 155
puller job. *See* chicken gutting
"Putting People First," 2

Qaddafi, Muammar, 77
Queen Bedroom, 52–53. *See also*
   Lincoln Bedroom
quotas. *See* affirmative action

"race card," 40, 44–45
Rainbow Coalition conference,
23–24
Rangel, Charles, 150–51
Reagan, Ronald, 12, 43–44
Reagan administration, 172
Reagan Republicans, 86, 94
Rector, Rickey Ray, 24–28, 151
Reich, Robert, 7–8, 9–10
Reiner, Rob, 101
Reno, Janet, 38, 42, 54–55, 106
Republican Moderates, 110

About the Author

Christopher Hitchens (1949-2011) was a contributing editor to *Vanity Fair* and a columnist for *Slate*. He was the author of numerous books, including works on Thomas Jefferson, Thomas Paine, George Orwell, Mother Teresa, Henry Kissinger and Bill and Hillary Clinton, as well as his international bestseller and National Book Award nominee, *god Is Not Great*. His memoir, *Hitch-22*, was nominated for the Orwell Prize and was a finalist for the National Book Critics Circle Award. His last collection of essays, *Arguably* (Atlantic, 2011), was a *Sunday Times* bestseller. In 2012, Hitchens was awarded a memorial by the Orwell Prize.

THE TRIAL OF HENRY KISSINGER

THE TRIAL OF HENRY KISSINGER

Foreword by Ariel Dorfman

Christopher Hitchens

Atlantic Books
London

First published in 2002 by Verso, an imprint of New Left Books.

Published in hardback and e-book in Great Britain in 2012 by Atlantic Books, an imprint of Atlantic Books Ltd.

10 9 8 7 6 5 4 3 2 1

A CIP catalogue record for this book is available from the British Library.

E-book ISBN: 978-0-85789-836-4
Hardback ISBN: 978-0-85789-835-7

Printed in Great Britain by the MPG Books Group

Atlantic Books
An imprint of Atlantic Books Ltd
Ormond House
26–27 Boswell Street
London
WC1N 3JZ

www.atlantic-books.co.uk

For the brave victims of Henry Kissinger,
whose example will easily outlive him,
and his "reputation."

And for Joseph Heller, who saw it early
and saw it whole:

*In Gold's conservative opinion, Kissinger
would not be recalled in history as a Bismarck,
Metternich or Castlereagh but as an odious* schlump
who made war gladly. (Good as Gold, 1976)

Contents

CONTENTS

Foreword to the Twelve Edition

It was not long into our first conversation with Hitch—can it be thirty years ago?—that the unctuous presence of Henry Kissinger made itself felt. The year must have been 1981, and my wife, Angélica, and I were in exile from a Chile terrorized by General Augusto Pinochet and Christopher had just arrived in Washington, DC, to write for *The Nation*, after a recent stint as a foreign correspondent on the luckless island of Cyprus. Cyprus and Chile, two countries joined in misfortune and sorrow and betrayal, hounded by the same man, the same "statesman," the same war criminal who had been Nixon's secretary of state.

I can't recall exactly the place where Angélica and I met Hitch—it may have been Barbara Ehrenreich's apartment or at the always welcoming house of Saul Landau—nor can I recollect the exact contours of our almost simultaneous diatribe against Kissinger that evening, but I like to think that in some glorious recess of Christopher's febrile and extraordinary brain, he was already planning this book, starting to put on trial the despoiler of Chile and Cyprus. And let's not forget Cambodia and Vietnam and East Timor and the Kurds—the Kurds, above all let us not ever forget the Kurds, because Christopher never did.

Over the years, more indictments like those of that first evening were sprinkled through our long and plentiful and often contentious friendship. Like true friends, we did not agree on everything, but Kissinger was always there to remind us of how deep our desire for justice ran; our conviction, his and mine, that if one could not physically bring a man responsible for genocide before a tribunal, there was always the written word to pin him to the wall and eviscerate his impunity. Neither of us thought—at least I didn't—that such a trial in the world of realpolitik and fawning media and obsequious politicians would ever be possible.

General Pinochet's arrest in London in 1998 changed that. That a former head of state could be subjected to universal jurisdiction (a term that Christopher highlights in his opening remarks of this book) for crimes against humanity, that the decision to find sufficient reasons to extradite the former Chilean dictator to Spain had been approved by the several courts in London and confirmed by the Law Lords (an equivalent to the US Supreme Court), was undoubtedly the trigger that led to *The Trial of Henry Kissinger* being written. If Pinochet, then why not

Kissinger? Why not anyone whose dossier proved a conscious and systematic involvement in egregious human rights violations, no matter how influential that person might be? Or should the law only be applied to a land like Chile, with no nuclear weapons or bases strewn around the world, and not the United States, flexing its power and muscle?

The book itself is vintage Hitchens, in the tradition of Thomas Paine, one of his heroes: incisive, ironic, chock full of information, contemptuous of what the pundits might think, redolent with indignation and choice adjectives. But most crucial, what I now read behind the rant, many years later, is the same thing that struck me about Christopher in that very first conversation we had.

A topic that Hitch kept coming back to on that night in 1981, as he would often during the years ahead, was that of the missing of Chile, the *desaparecidos*, men and women abducted from the streets or their homes by the secret police and never heard of again, absent from the world as if they had never been born. We discussed at some length (it was my obsession then and still is) how this atrocity, along with affecting the bodies of those who had been kidnapped, devastated the lives of the relatives who could not find their beloved, who could not even bury their corpses or mourn an uncertain death.

Hitch's interest in this tragedy was motivated,

naturally, by something that would define a life crusading for the rights of those who were neglected and forgotten and postponed. Especially by the mainstream media. And it was Cyprus, which Christopher mentioned to me and Angélica during that first interminable and deep conversation, gesturing toward his own then wife, Eleni, a Greek Cypriot whom Hitch had met while covering the Turkish invasion of the island. "Eleni's people also have *desaparecidos*," was, if I am not mistaken, the stark way in which he introduced the theme. And not long thereafter, he called me up at our home and invited us to the opening of an exhibition of photographs about the plight of the Cypriot refugees, which emphasized in particular the calamity of those who were still missing after the war. When Angélica and I arrived for the inauguration (it was at an out-of-the-way place, a small gallery, I think), there was hardly a soul there—an instance of inattention that outraged Hitch and made him even more determined to highlight the invisible sorrow that was visiting a people he had fallen in love with. Years later he would recall, both publicly and privately, how moved he was that we had taken the time to share that experience of exile and sorrow and struggle when so many others simply didn't give a damn.

But he got that one wrong. I wasn't the one to be thanked for having been present at that exhibition.

Hitch was the one to be thanked for caring enough, for helping me understand (as he does in this book) how the catastrophe of Chile was linked in so many ways to the disasters assailing other areas of the earth, how we need to hold those who inflicted the damage accountable in as many ways as we possibly can. In that invitation to see the photos, as in this book that now sees the light of day again, as in a variety of other instances, he expanded the universe, he made the connections. He was always ready to open doors and windows that nobody else dared to even notice, and he did so, invariably with unfailing wit and grace and a sort of penetrating lyricism, provoking us till we paid attention. He simply refused to remain silent.

That is what really pulses through this book.

The victims. So many who have not lived to see Kissinger and others like him put on trial. So many who are represented in the sweet tirade against a war criminal who walks in freedom but who is always, thanks to books like these, looking over his shoulder.

Wondering if the Hitch will get him.

Because a year after this book was published, the heroic Kissinger was sojourning at (where else?) the Ritz Hotel in Paris when he was summoned to appear before French judge Roger Le Loire, who wanted to question the "elder statesman" about his involvement in Operation Condor (and whether he knew anything about five French nationals who had been "disappeared" during the Pinochet dictatorship). Rather than take the occasion to clear his name, Kissinger fled that very night. And he has never been able to sleep abroad with any semblance of serenity ever since: more indictments followed, from Spain, from Argentina and Uruguay, and even a civil suit in Washington, DC.

Oh yes, maybe the Hitch will indeed get him.

True, Christopher did not believe in ghosts or spirits or the afterlife.

But indulge me, comrade. Accept that while books like these are alive, and while your innumerable allies continue the quest for justice, well, perhaps you can smile at the thought that we will refuse to let you become one more *desaparecido*.

ARIEL DORFMAN
February 2012

Foreword

It was not long into our first conversation with
Hitch—can it be thirty years ago?—that the unctuous presence of Henry Kissinger made itself felt.
The year must have been 1981, and my wife, Angélica, and I were in exile from a Chile terrorized by
General Augusto Pinochet and Christopher had
just arrived in Washington, DC, to write for *The
Nation*, after a recent stint as a foreign correspondent on the luckless island of Cyprus. Cyprus and
Chile, two countries joined in misfortune and sorrow and betrayal, hounded by the same man, the
same "statesman," the same war criminal who had
been Nixon's secretary of state.

I can't recall exactly the place where Angélica and
I met Hitch—it may have been Barbara Ehrenreich's
apartment or at the always welcoming house of Saul
Landau—nor can I recollect the exact contours of
our almost simultaneous diatribe against Kissinger
that evening, but I like to think that in some glorious recess of Christopher's febrile and extraordinary
brain, he was already planning this book, starting to

boast if I say that most of these disclosures and initiatives were foreshadowed in the first version of this book. At any rate, they now appear below and any reader may judge by comparison with the unaltered original text.

Indochina

Further material has come to light about both the origins and the conclusion of this terrible episode in American and Asian history. The publication of Larry Berman's *No Peace, No Honor: Nixon, Kissinger and Betrayal in Vietnam* in early 2001 provided further evidence of the secret and illegal diplomacy conducted by Nixon and his associates in the fall of 1968, and discussed on pages 1–21 here as well as in my appendix on page 205. Indeed, it can now be safely said that the record of this disgusting scandal has become, so to speak, a part of the official and recognized record, rather as President Johnson's original provocation in the Gulf of Tonkin is now generally called by its right name. (In his edition of President Johnson's private papers and conversations in the fall of 2001, Professor Michael Beschloss produced first-hand and direct proof that Johnson himself knew at the time that he was lying to the Congress and the world about the episode.)

As for the expiring moments of that hideous war, the month of May 2001 saw the publication of an extraordinary book, *The Last Battle: The Mayaguez*

Incident and the End of the Vietnam War. Written
by Ralph Wetterhahn, a Vietnam veteran who had
decided to stay with the subject, the book establishes
beyond doubt by the use of contemporary documents and later interviews that:

a) The crew of the *Mayaguez* were never held on Koh
   Tang island, the island that was invaded by the
   United States Marine Corps.

b) The Cambodians had announced that they intended
   to return the vessel, and had indeed done so even as
   the bombardment of Cambodian territory was continuing. During that time, the crew was being held
   on quite another island, named Rong Sam Lem. The
   statements of Ford and Kissinger, claiming credit for
   the eventual release and attributing it to the intervention on the wrong island, were knowingly false.

c) American casualties were larger than has ever been
   admitted: twenty-three men were pointlessly sacrificed in a helicopter crash in Thailand that was
   never acknowledged as part of the operation. Thus,
   a total of sixty-four servicemen were sacrificed to
   "free" forty sailors who had already been let go, and
   who were not and had never been at the advertised
   location.

d) As a result of the official panic and confusion, three
   Marines were left behind alive on Koh Tang island,
   and later captured and murdered by the Khmer

Rouge. The names of Lance Corporal Joseph Hargrove, Pfc Gary Hall and Pvt Danny Marshall do not appear on any memorial, let alone the Vietnam Veterans' wall (see my page 31). For a long time, their names had no official existence at all, and this "denial" might have succeeded indefinitely were it not for Mr. Wetterhahn's efforts.

Kissinger was the crucial figure at all stages of this crime and cover-up, arguing at the onset of the crisis that B-52 bombers should at once (and again) be launched against Cambodia and arguing, too, for the dropping of the BLU-82 bomb—a 15,000-pound device—on the center of Koh Tang island. He must also have been crucial in the following hair-raising episode, made public by William Triplett in the official publication of the Vietnam Veterans of America. Mr. Triplett interviewed then-Secretary of Defense James Schlesinger, who recalled two cabinet meetings during the crisis. The first was the one at which Kissinger demanded the use of B-52s. The second was the one—no less alarming to Secretary Schlesinger—at which it was decided to sink *all ships* spotted in the vicinity of Koh Tang island. As Schlesinger recalled it:

When I got [back] to the Pentagon...I said that before any ships are sunk, our pilots should fly low

over the ships and see what they could see, particularly if there were any [*Mayaguez*] crew members
aboard. If they did see them, they were to report
back immediately before doing anything. In the
course of flying over the area, one of our Navy pilots
called back saying that he saw "Caucasians" aboard
a ship.... Or he thought he saw that. It later turned
out that every member of the *Mayaguez* crew was on
that ship.

Q: Did you apprise the White House of this ship
with the Caucasians aboard?
A: Yes, indeed.
Q: And it was then that the White House said to
sink it?
A: Yes, the White House said, "We told you to sink
all ships, so sink it!"

By stalling for three hours, the Secretary of Defense
managed to avoid committing this atrocity. And by
"the White House" he clearly does not mean the
President, or he would have said so. In any case, we
know who was managing the *Mayaguez* "rescue,"
and who took credit for it at the time. We are sure to
learn even more about Kissinger's "hands-on" policy
in Indochina as still more officials write their memoirs or make their confessions.

Latin America

The documentary record on Chile is now more or less complete, but much remains to be discovered about Kissinger's role in Operation Condor (see my pages 101–4), and in the nexus of dictatorship and repression which gave it birth. Recent published work by Martin Edwin Andersen and John Dinges, in the conservative Washington magazine *Insight* in January 2002, has presented us with incontrovertible proof of high-level approval for Argentina's "dirty war" of death and "disappearance" in the mid-1970s.

The evidence here might be described as unimpeachable, since it originates with a senior member of the Argentine dictatorship and an ultra-conservative United States diplomat. The first man, Admiral Cesar Guzzetti, foreign minister of the Videla dictatorship, had a dispute about both means and ends with the second man, US Ambassador Robert Hill. Ambassador Hill was a Cold-War veteran with tight family connections to the business oligarchy in Latin America. A Nixon appointee to the Buenos Aires post, he had also served contentedly as envoy to a number of despotic right-wing regimes. However, he was appalled by the campaign of murder unleashed in Argentina after the 1976 military coup, and became distressed by the way in which Kissinger, from Washington, undercut his representations on the matter.

To those familiar with the Chile investigation, in which a "two-track" policy was pursued and the officially accredited ambassador is not *supposed* to know of the real or covert policy, this may seem unsurprising. But not to Hill, an old-school type, the declassification of whose cables furnishes much of the new material. Before Admiral Guzzetti traveled to Washington to see Kissinger in October 1976, Hill had met him and told him that "murdering priests and dumping forty-seven bodies in the street in one day could not be seen in the context of defeating the terrorists quickly; on the contrary such acts were probably counterproductive. What the USG [United States Government] hoped was that the GOA [Government of Argentina] could soon defeat terrorists, yes, but as nearly as possible within the law."

Even this admonition, which might be seen by some as containing a loophole or two, was considered too harsh by Kissinger. Guzzetti set off for Washington, Hill subsequently minuted, "fully expecting to hear some strong, firm, direct warnings on his government's human rights practices." However, having met Guzzetti on his return to Buenos Aires, he concluded:

Rather than that, he [Guzzetti] has returned in a state of jubilation, convinced that there is no real problem with the United States over this issue. Based on what Guzzetti is doubtless reporting to the GOA, it must now believe that if it has any problems with the US over human rights, they are confined to certain elements of Congress and what it regards as biased and/or uninformed minor segments of public opinion.... While this conviction exists, it will be unrealistic and ineffective for this Embassy to press representations to the GOA over human rights violations.

This is even more grave in its implications than may at first appear. In October 1976 the rate of state-sponsored kidnapping and "disappearance" was relatively slow and could, Ambassador Hill believed, be made slower still. But the declassified documents show Kissinger advising Guzzetti, in effect, to speed up the pace. He told him that "if the terrorist problem was over by December or January, he [Kissinger] believed that serious problems could be avoided in the United States." These and other reassurances were, according to Hill—and in a phrase that has since become obscenely familiar—"the green light" for intensified repression. When Kissinger and Guzzetti first met, the number of "disappeared" was estimated at 1,022. By the time that Argentina had become an international byword for torture, for anti-Semitism, for death-squads and for the concept of the *desaparecido*, a minimum of 15,000 victims had been registered by reliable international and local monitors. In 1978, when the situation was notorious, Kissinger (by then out of office) accepted a personal invitation from the dictator General Videla to be his guest during Argentina's hosting of the soccer World Cup. The former Secretary of State made use of the occasion to lecture the Carter administration for its excessive tenderness concerning human rights. General Videla, with whom I had a horrifying interview at about this time in the Casa Rosada in Buenos Aires, has since been imprisoned for life. One of the more specific charges on which he was convicted was the sale of the children of rape victims held in his secret jails. His patron and protector, meanwhile, is enjoying a patriarchal autumn that may still (see below) be disturbed by the memory of what he permitted and indeed encouraged.

East Timor

On more than one occasion (see my pages 138–66) Henry Kissinger has absolutely and publicly denied that he had any foreknowledge of the Indonesian invasion of East Timor, any interest in the subject, or even any awareness of its importance. That this is a huge falsehood, or perhaps a series of interlocking falsehoods, has long been apparent from independent evidence. What might be called conclusive or "smoking gun" proof, however, only became available in December 2001, when a fresh document became available. Declassified by the State Department, and publicized by the National Security Archive, it is the official record of a conversation that took place in the Indonesian capital of Jakarta on 6 December 1975. Present were Henry Kissinger and Gerald Ford, and the Indonesian dictator Suharto with a group of his military advisers.

Since Kissinger himself had received a cable from Washington two days before, informing him that the Indonesian junta had "plans" to invade East Timor, he cannot have been very much surprised to be told exactly that. Nor can he have been startled to hear from Suharto that: "We want your understanding if we deem it necessary to take rapid or drastic action." President Ford did not attempt to mask his endorsement in any ambiguity. "We will understand and will not press you on the issue," he said. "We understand the problem and the intentions you have." Kissinger, more experienced in the spin-problems that could result from unleashing extremist dictatorships, employed language similar to that which he had (see above) lavished upon Admiral Guzzetti of Argentina. "The use of US-made arms could create problems," he mused, adding that "it depends on how we construe it; whether it is in self-defense or a foreign operation." This was an absolute untruth, since (see my page 159) Kissinger knew perfectly well that the use of American-*supplied* (not "American made") weaponry would violate international law and United States law as well. Brightening somewhat, he assured Suharto that: "We would be able to influence the reaction in America if whatever happens happens after we return....If you have made plans, we will do our best to keep everyone quiet until the President returns home." As ever, he was willing to act as errand-boy for an unelected foreign dictatorship and to consider only Congress as his enemy.

It was therefore agreed, in an early instance of the now-famous pseudoscience of "deniability," that the aggression be timed to suit the fact that "The President will be back on Monday at 2.00 pm Jakarta time. We understand your problem and the need to move quickly but I am only saying that it would be better if it were done after we returned." With these words, Kissinger made himself directly complicit in the letter and the spirit of Indonesia's attack. A certain nervousness prompted him to ask Suharto if he anticipated "a long guerrilla war"; proof in itself that he did not believe Suharto's claim of popular support in East Timor. The dictator was reassuring, predicting that there would "probably be a short guerrilla

war," while refusing to be drawn on its actual duration. The announced imperative of speed, as in
Argentina above, was a spur to ruthless methods that
had in effect been demanded by Washington. "It is
important," said Kissinger coldly, "that whatever
you do succeeds quickly." The consequences of this
deadly injunction are discussed on my pages 140–42.

The same memorandum shows that the talk
then turned to Indonesia's oil policy, and to Suharto's complaint that major petroleum corporations
shared more of the wealth with their Middle Eastern partners than they did with Indonesia. Expressing sympathy for his attempt to negotiate a better
deal, Kissinger found time to warn the despot that,
whatever he did, he should "not create a climate that
discourages investment." This was a case of pushing at an open door: to the very end of his regime
Suharto maintained an investment-friendly climate,
at least for a certain class of cronies of whom, perhaps coincidentally (see my pages 194–96), Kissinger
eventually became one. Indeed, Indonesian "crony
capitalism" and its practitioners became a major
element in the scandal of United States campaign
finance, and of the Congressional investigation into
it, that marked the Clinton years. Kissinger even
hired Clinton's former White House Chief of Staff
Mack McLarty as a partner in Kissinger Associates, and it may not be fanciful to suppose that the

Indonesian connection played a role in this beautiful piece of bipartisanship.

The Suharto regime collapsed and imploded between the years 2000 and 2001. East Timor won its independence, and Indonesia formally withdrew its claim to the territory. Suharto himself was indicted by the Indonesian courts for corruption and only escaped the verdict by resorting, as had General Pinochet, to the claim of mental and physical incompetence. Once again, though, the senior partner in the massacres and in the corruption managed to escape condemnation.

Washington

As I was preparing to publish the original version of this book, I received a call from William Rogers. Mr. Rogers is a partner in the distinguished Washington law firm of Arnold and Porter and was, during Kissinger's period as Secretary of State, the Deputy Assistant Secretary for Inter-American Affairs. He is also a cog in the wheel of Kissinger Associates (for the activities of which, see chapter 10). Someone had leaked the advance news of publication to a New York newspaper and Mr. Rogers, on first contact, was all friendliness. Could he help? he wanted to know. I told him that I had already forwarded a request for an interview to his boss, and had mentioned the headings—Chile, Timor, Bangladesh and the Demetracopoulos affair—which I hoped to discuss with him. Mr. Rogers professed astonishment at the fourth of these topics. "Who is this guy Demetra-whatsisname?" he inquired. "We've never heard of him." He then asked me to send a list of all my questions, in order that he might be more "helpful" still. Recognizing a fishing expedition when I saw one, I instead wrote again to Kissinger offering to pay him for his trouble and proposing that, if he would give me and *Harper's* magazine half an hour on the record, we would pay him at the same rate offered by ABC News *Nightline*. (I did not add that, for this honorarium, we would ask him all the questions he has never been asked by Mr. Ted Koppel.)

Mr. Rogers then dropped the mask of pretended if inquisitive politeness and sent me a savage e-mail, in which he said that he had never heard of such a disgraceful proposal. How could I, he demanded to know, propose to pay a source? Quite obviously I was morally unfit for further conversation. His indignation got the better of him. I was only making an ironic reference to Kissinger's habit of charging immense fees for his time (and at no period did I think of him as a "source"). I wrote back to Rogers, saying that he seemed to be the same man who had attended the Kissinger-Pinochet private discussion on 8 June 1976 (see my pages 105–9) during which Pinochet had threatened a Chilean exile then living in Washington. On that occasion, I pointed out, the record showed that Mr. Rogers had sat in silence. It was therefore good to know what did, and what did not, touch his nerve of outrage. Mr. Rogers, it now turns out, also played a role in facilitating the Kissinger-Guzzetti conversations in 1976, and later in trying to put a positive shine upon them. Such men are always, it seems, with us.

The absurdity of the official pretense, that Elias Demetracopoulos was beneath Kissinger's notice, is even further exposed by a recently declassified letter from Kissinger to Nixon, sent on 22 March 1971. It is headed "SECRET: The Demetracopoulos Affair." It begins by saying to the President: "You may have heard some repercussions from the recent flap over a request by Greek 'journalist' and resistance leader, Elias Demetracopoulos, to return to Greece to see his sick father." (It's rather flattering that Kissinger should have put "journalist" in sarcastic quotes, but left the definition of resistance leader unamended.) The letter goes on to say:

> Since Demetracopoulos has such a following in Congress and has an outlet in Rowland Evans [then a senior Washington columnist] I thought you might be interested in knowing that he has long been an irritant in US-Greek relations. Among his intrigues—which have included selling himself

as a trusted US agent to anyone and everyone—he has touched off a record number of controversies and embarrassments between Greek and American officials. Through various journalistic enterprises, he has somehow managed to gain access to press and government circles. CIA, State, Defense and USIA have repeatedly warned officials about Demetracopoulos…

It would appear safe to say, then, that Demetracopoulos was taken with sufficient seriousness by Kissinger to warrant a slanderous and paranoid memorandum for the President's desk. This only strengthens the argument made in my chapter 9, that Kissinger was attempting to represent his Greek critic as a person dangerous and sinister enough to be dealt with.

Another declassified secret document, this time of a "Secretary's Analytical Staff Meeting" at the State Department on 20 March 1974, shows Kissinger's obsession at work again. Irritated by talk of a return to constitutional rule in Greece, he said: "My question is: Why is it in the American interest to do in Greece what we apparently don't do anywhere else—of requiring them to give a commitment to the President to move to representative government?"

This was only a few months after the existing right-wing dictatorship in Athens had been overthrown from the extreme right by the psychopath Brigadier Ioannidis. Even Henry Tasca, then United States Ambassador to Athens and a trusted friend of the regime, was moved to reply:

> Well, I think because Greece and the Greek people—in terms of their position and public opinion in Western Europe—are quite unique. You can go back to the constitutional Greece or the Greek lobby—whatever you want to call it—and they've got a position in Western Europe and the United States that Brazil and Chile and these other countries don't have. None of these countries has a Demetracopoulos—a Greek refugee who's been activated and who for four years has been leading a very vigorous fight on our policy in Greece.

To this Kissinger made the glacial reply that "That just means we're letting Demetracopoulos's particular group make policy." But he was clearly nettled that some of his own deputies found it difficult to treat Greece as a banana republic.

This was a high-level meeting. The minutes record the attendance of such policy heavyweights as Joseph Sisco, Helmut Sonnenfeld, Lawrence Eagleburger and Arthur Hartman. It is clear that the dangerous activity of a single dissident was not beneath official attention.

Once again, I note that the Greek government, for which Kissinger was acting as proxy here, was a murderous and torturing dictatorship, with aggressive designs upon its Cypriot neighbor, and that its then leaders are now in prison for life. And once again, I note that their senior partner and patron is still at liberty, and still lying about his part in all this.

Legal Consequences

Just as this book was being published, Kissinger produced a volume of his own with the pseudo-solemn title *Does America Need a Foreign Policy?* It contained an anxious chapter on the perils of the new legal doctrine of "universal jurisdiction," and this same chapter was reprinted as a separate essay in the Establishment's house-organ, *Foreign Affairs*. There was a certain amount of public laughter at the sheer disingenuousness of this: Kissinger wrote as if he was cogitating the subject with absolute disinterest.

Events, however, were to give independent validation of his professed concern. In May 2001, Judge Rodolfo Corral, a senior magistrate in Argentina, issued a summons to Kissinger to answer questions about his knowledge of Operation Condor (see my pages 101–4). Judge Corral's investigation, like many similar human rights inquiries in the southern hemisphere of the Americas, could proceed no further without disclosure of what the United States knew and when it knew it, and Kissinger was the chief material witness at all material times.

Only a few days later, on 28 May 2001, Kissinger was visited in his suite at the Ritz Hotel in Paris by the criminal division of the French *gendarmerie*. They brought him a summons, issued by Judge Roger Le Loire, to appear at the Palais de Justice the following morning and answer questions about the "disappearance" of five French citizens in Chile during the early days of the Pinochet regime. Kissinger might reasonably have thought himself safe in the hotel owned by Mohammed al-Fayed, but chose the path of prudence and left Paris at once. (The summons remains valid if he should ever choose to return; I should like to boast briefly that the European press attributed this judicial move in part to the then-recent appearance of this book in its French translation.)

Since then, the Chilean courts—including the judge who is deciding the Pinochet case itself—have written to Kissinger asking for his cooperation as a witness in the case of Charles Horman, an American reporter murdered during Pinochet's coup, and in the general matter of "Condor"-related crime. This means that duly constituted magistrates in three democratic nations are seeking—and are being refused—his testimony on grave crimes against humanity. As predicted in my introduction (see pages *xliii–li*) he can no longer make travel plans without consulting his expensive attorneys.

Most serious of all, though, was the suit filed in Federal Court in Washington, DC, on 10 September 2001. This suit is brought by the surviving members of the family of General Rene Schneider of Chile (see my pages 84–101 and 203). It charges Kissinger and others with "summary execution" of the General; in other words, but in a civil case, with murder and international terrorism. The date of the lawsuit may seem unpropitious to some, but in fact the hideous aggression against American civil society that occurred the following day has laid greater emphasis than ever on the need for a single standard, and one day a single international court, for the hearing of crimes against humanity, state-sponsored murder and international nihilism.

In the same period, the National Security Archive and others compelled Kissinger to return 50,000 pages of the public documents he had illegally abstracted when he left office (see my page 116–17) and to have these returned to the scrutiny of scholars and historians (and victims). It is an empirically safe bet that Kissinger did not seek to conceal or bury material that put him in a good light. We may therefore expect the coming years to be as full of appalling disclosure, of official crime and official lying on his part, as the last year has been. And there is just a chance that some of the victims may secure some justice on their own account, by means of American and other courts. It seems to me deplorable, though, and even shameful, that those who have already suffered enough should have to volunteer for the performance of a task that properly lies on the shoulders of Congress and the Justice Department.

To leave a personal note to the very last, I had myself rather hoped to be engaged in litigation with Kissinger. Had he sued me over this book (as the London *Literary Review* said that he was in honor bound to do, if he valued his reputation) I had dreamed of producing witnesses, and subpoenaing documents, that would accelerate the process of discovery. It was not to be: Kissinger's reticence remained his best counsel. I did, however, find myself threatening to sue him when he publicly accused me of being an anti-Semite and a denier of the Holocaust. In very grudging and graceless terms, he did through his lawyers offer me a swift retraction. In other words, he admitted that he had no basis for this especially foul accusation, but had thought it worth trying. Those who are curious to learn the background and to follow the correspondence may direct their trusty search engines and browsers.

CHRISTOPHER HITCHENS
Washington, DC, 15 February 2002

Preface

It will become clear, and may as well be stated at the outset, that this book is written by a political opponent of Henry Kissinger. Nonetheless, I have found myself continually amazed at how much hostile and discreditable material I have felt compelled to omit. I am concerned only with those Kissingerian offenses that might or should form the basis of a legal prosecution: for war crimes, for crimes against humanity, and for offenses against common or customary or international law, including conspiracy to commit murder, kidnap and torture.

Thus, in my capacity as a political opponent I might have mentioned Kissinger's recruitment and betrayal of the Iraqi Kurds, who were falsely encouraged by him to take up arms against Saddam Hussein in 1974–75, and who were then abandoned to extermination on their hillsides when Saddam Hussein made a diplomatic deal with the Shah of Iran, and who were deliberately lied to as well as abandoned. The conclusions of the report by Congressman Otis Pike still make shocking reading, and reveal on

Kissinger's part a callous indifference to human life and human rights. But they fall into the category of depraved realpolitik, and do not seem to have violated any known law.

In the same way, Kissinger's orchestration of political and military and diplomatic cover for apartheid in South Africa and the South African destabilization of Angola, with its appalling consequences, presents us with a morally repulsive record. Again, though, one is looking at a sordid period of Cold War and imperial history, and an exercise of irresponsible power, rather than an episode of organized crime. Additionally, one must take into account the institutional nature of this policy, which might in outline have been followed under any administration, national security advisor or secretary of state.

Similar reservations can be held about Kissinger's chairmanship of the Presidential Commission on Central America in the early 1980s, which was staffed by Oliver North and which whitewashed death squad activity in the isthmus. Or about the political protection provided by Kissinger, while in office, for the Pahlavi dynasty in Iran and its machinery of torture and repression. The list, it is sobering to say, could be protracted very much further. But it will not do to blame the whole exorbitant cruelty and cynicism of decades on one man. (Occasionally one gets an intriguing glimpse, as when Kissinger urges President Ford not to receive the inconvenient Alexander Solzhenitsyn, while all the time he poses as Communism's most daring and principled foe.)

No, I have confined myself to the identifiable crimes that can and should be placed on a proper bill of indictment, whether the actions taken were in line with general "policy" or not. These include:

1. The deliberate mass killing of civilian populations in Indochina.
2. Deliberate collusion in mass murder, and later in assassination, in Bangladesh.
3. The personal suborning and planning of murder, of a senior constitutional officer in a democratic nation—Chile—with which the United States was not at war.
4. Personal involvement in a plan to murder the head of state in the democratic nation of Cyprus.
5. The incitement and enabling of genocide in East Timor.
6. Personal involvement in a plan to kidnap and murder a journalist living in Washington, DC.

The above allegations are not exhaustive. And some of them can only be constructed *prima facie*, since Mr. Kissinger—in what may also amount to a deliberate and premeditated obstruction of justice—has caused large tranches of evidence to be withheld or destroyed.

However, we now enter upon the age when the defense of "sovereign immunity" for state crimes has been held to be void. As I demonstrate below, Kissinger has understood this decisive change even if many of his critics have not. The Pinochet verdict in London, the splendid activism of the Spanish magistracy, and the verdicts of the International Tribunal at The Hague have destroyed the shield that immunized crimes committed under the justification of *raison d'état*. There is now no reason why a warrant for the trial of Kissinger may not be issued, in any one of a number of jurisdictions, and why he may not be compelled to answer it. Indeed, and as I write, there are a number of jurisdictions where the law is at long last beginning to catch up with the evidence. And we have before us in any case the Nuremberg precedent, by which the United States solemnly undertook to be bound.

A failure to proceed will constitute a double or triple offense to justice. First, it will violate the essential and now uncontested principle that not even the most powerful are above the law. Second, it will suggest that prosecutions for war crimes and crimes against humanity are reserved for losers, or for minor despots in relatively negligible countries. This in turn will lead to the paltry politicization of what could have been a noble process, and to the justifiable suspicion of double standards.

Many if not most of Kissinger's partners in crime are now in jail, or are awaiting trial, or have been otherwise punished or discredited. His own lonely impunity is rank; it smells to heaven. If it is allowed to persist then we shall shamefully vindicate the ancient philosopher Anacharsis, who maintained that laws were like cobwebs: strong enough to detain only the weak, and too weak to hold the strong. In the name of innumerable victims known and unknown, it is time for justice to take a hand.

Introduction

On 2 December 1998, Mr. Michael Korda was being interviewed on camera in his office at Simon & Schuster. As one of the reigning magnates of New York publishing, he had edited and "produced" the work of authors as various as Tennessee Williams, Richard Nixon, Joan Crawford and Jo Bonanno. On this particular day, he was talking about the life and thoughts of Cher, whose portrait adorned the wall behind him. And then the telephone rang and there was a message to call "Dr." Henry Kissinger as soon as possible. A polymath like Mr. Korda knows—what with the exigencies of publishing in these vertiginous days—how to switch in an instant between Cher and high statecraft. The camera kept running, and recorded the following scene for a tape which I possess.

Asking his secretary to get the number (759-7919—the digits of Kissinger Associates) Mr. Korda quips drily, to general laughter in the office, that it "should be 1-800-CAMBODIA ... 1-800-BOMB-CAMBODIA." After

a pause of nicely calibrated duration (no senior editor likes to be put on hold while he's receiving company, especially media company), it's "Henry—Hi,
how are you?...You're getting all the publicity you
could want in the *New York Times*, but not the *kind*
you want....I also think it's very, very dubious for
the administration to simply say yes, they'll release
these papers...no...no, absolutely...no...no...well,
hmmm, yeah. We did it until quite recently, frankly,
and he did prevail....Well, I don't think there's any
question about that, as uncomfortable as it may be....
Henry, this is totally outrageous...yeah....Also the
jurisdiction. This is a Spanish judge appealing to
an English court about a Chilean head of state. So
it's, it...Also Spain has no rational jurisdiction over
events in Chile anyway so that makes absolutely no
sense....Well, that's probably true....If you would.
I think that would be by far and away the best....
Right, yeah, no I think it's exactly what you should
do and I think it should be long and I think it should
end with your father's letter. I think it's a very important document....Yes, but I think the letter is won-
derful, and central to the entire book. Can you let
me read the Lebanon chapter over the weekend?" At
this point the conversation ends, with some jocular
observations by Mr. Korda about his upcoming colo-
noscopy: "a totally repulsive procedure."

By means of the same tiny internal camera, or its

forensic equivalent, one could deduce not a little about the world of Henry Kissinger from this microcosmic exchange. The first and most important thing is this. Sitting in his office at Kissinger Associates, with its tentacles of business and consultancy stretching from Belgrade to Beijing, and cushioned by innumerable other directorships and boards, he still shudders when he hears of the arrest of a dictator. Syncopated the conversation with Mr. Korda may be, but it's clear that the keyword is "jurisdiction." What had the *New York Times* been reporting that fine morning? On that 2 December 1998, its front page carried the following report from Tim Weiner, the paper's national security correspondent in Washington. Under the headline "U.S. Will Release Files on Crimes Under Pinochet," he wrote:

> Treading into a political and diplomatic confrontation it tried to avoid, the United States decided today to declassify some secret government documents on the killings and torture committed during the dictatorship of Augusto Pinochet in Chile.... The decision to release such documents is the first sign that the United States will cooperate in the case against General Pinochet. Clinton Administration officials said they believed the benefits of openness in human rights cases outweighed the risks to national security in this case.

But the decision could open "a can of worms," in the words of a former Central Intelligence Agency official stationed in Chile, exposing the depth of the knowledge that the United States had about crimes charged against the Pinochet Government....

While some European government officials have supported bringing the former dictator to court, United States officials have stayed largely silent, reflecting skepticism about the Spanish court's power, doubts about international tribunals aimed at former foreign rulers, *and worries over the implications for American leaders who might someday also be accused in foreign countries.* [italics added]

President Richard M. Nixon and Henry A. Kissinger, who served as his national security advisor and Secretary of State, supported a right-wing coup in Chile in the early 1970s, previously declassified documents show.

But many of the actions of the United States during the 1973 coup, and much of what American leaders and intelligence services did in liaison with the Pinochet government after it seized power, remain under the seal of national security. The secret files on the Pinochet regime are held by the CIA, the Defense Intelligence Agency, the State Department, the Pentagon, the National Security Council, the National Archives, the Presidential libraries of

Gerald R. Ford and Jimmy Carter, and other Government agencies.

According to Justice Department records, these files contain a history of human rights abuses and international terrorism:

- In 1975 State Department officials in Chile protested the Pinochet regime's record of killing and torture, filing dissents to American foreign policy with their superiors in Washington.
- The CIA has files on assassinations by the regime and the Chilean secret police. The intelligence agency also has records on Chile's attempts to establish an international right-wing covert-action squad.
- The Ford Library contains many of Mr. Kissinger's secret files on Chile, which have never been made public. Through a secretary, Mr. Kissinger declined a request for an interview today.

One must credit Kissinger with grasping what so many other people did not: that if the Pinochet precedent became established, then he himself was in some danger. The United States believes that it alone pursues and indicts war criminals and "international terrorists"; nothing in its political or journalistic culture yet allows for the thought that it might be harboring and sheltering such a senior one.

Yet the thought had very obliquely surfaced in Mr. Weiner's story, and Kissinger was a worried man when he called his editor that day to discuss a memoir (eventually published under the unbearably dull and self-regarding title *Years of Renewal*) that was still in progress.

"Harboring and sheltering," though, are understatements for the lavishness of Henry Kissinger's circumstances. His advice is sought, at $25,000 an appearance, by audiences of businessmen and academics and policymakers. His turgid newspaper column is syndicated by the *Los Angeles Times*. His first volume of memoirs was part written and also edited by Harold Evans, who with Tina Brown is among the many hosts and hostesses who solicit Kissinger's company, or perhaps one should say society, for those telling New York soirées. At different times, he has been a consultant to ABC News and CBS; his most successful diplomacy, indeed, has probably been conducted with the media (and his single greatest achievement has been to get almost everybody to call him "Doctor"). Fawned on by Ted Koppel, sought out by corporations and despots with "image" problems or "failures of communication," and given respectful attention by presidential candidates and those whose task it is to "mold" their global vision, this man wants for little in the pathetic universe that the "self-esteem" industry exists to serve. Of whom else would Norman Podhoretz write, in a bended-knee encomium to *Years of Upheaval*:

> What we have here is writing of the very highest order. It is writing that is equally at ease in portraiture and abstract analysis; that can shape a narrative as skillfully as it can paint a scene; that can achieve marvels of compression while moving at an expansive and leisurely pace. It is writing that can shift without strain or falsity of tone from the *gravitas* befitting a book about great historical events to the humor and irony dictated by an unfailing sense of human proportion.

A critic who can suck like that, as was once drily said by one of my moral tutors, need never dine alone. And nor need his subject. Except that, every now and then, the recipient (and donor) of so much sycophancy feels a tremor of anxiety. He leaves the well-furnished table and scurries to the bathroom. Is it perhaps another disclosure on a newly released Nixon tape? Some stray news from Indonesia, portending the fall or imprisonment of another patron (and perhaps the escape of an awkward document or two)? The arrest or indictment of a torturer or assassin, the expiry of the statute of secrecy for some obscure cabinet papers in a faraway country—any one of these can instantly spoil his day. As we see

xlix

from the Korda tape, Kissinger cannot open the morning paper with the assurance of tranquility. Because he knows what others can only suspect, or guess at. He knows. And he is a prisoner of the knowledge as, to some extent, are we.

Notice the likable way in which Mr. Korda demonstrates his broadmindedness with the Cambodia jest. Everybody "knows," after all, that Kissinger inflicted terror and misery and mass death on that country, and great injury to the United States Constitution at the same time. (Everybody also "knows" that other vulnerable nations can lay claim to the same melancholy and hateful distinction, with incremental or "collateral" damage to American democracy keeping pace.) Yet the pudgy man standing in black tie at the *Vogue* party is not, surely, the man who ordered and sanctioned the destruction of civilian populations, the assassination of inconvenient politicians, the kidnapping and disappearance of soldiers and journalists and clerics who got in his way? Oh, but he *is*. It's exactly the same man. And that may be among the most nauseating reflections of all. Kissinger is not invited and feted because of his exquisite manners or his mordant wit (his manners are in any case rather gross, and his wit consists of a quiver of borrowed and secondhand darts). No, he is sought after because his presence supplies a *frisson*: the authentic touch of raw and unapologetic power.

There's a slight guilty nervousness on the edge of Mr. Korda's gag about the indescribable sufferings of Indochina. And I've noticed, time and again standing at the back of the audience during Kissinger speeches, that laughter of the nervous, uneasy kind is the sort of laughter he likes to provoke. In exacting this tribute, he flaunts not the "aphrodisiac" of power (another of his plagiarized *bons mots*) but its pornography.

1

Curtain-Raiser: The Secret of '68

There exists, within the political class of Washington, DC, an open secret that is too momentous and too awful to tell. Though it is well known to academic historians, senior reporters, former cabinet members and ex-diplomats, it has never been summarized all at one time in any one place. The reason for this is, on first viewing, paradoxical. The open secret is in the possession of both major political parties, and it directly implicates the past statecraft of at least three former presidencies. Thus, its full disclosure would be in the interest of no particular faction. Its truth is therefore the guarantee of its obscurity; it lies like Poe's "purloined letter" across the very aisle that signifies bipartisanship.

Here is the secret in plain words. In the fall of 1968, Richard Nixon and some of his emissaries and underlings set out to sabotage the Paris peace negotiations on Vietnam. The means they chose were simple: they privately assured the South Vietnamese military rulers that an incoming Republican regime would offer them a better deal than would a Democratic one. In this way, they undercut both the talks themselves and the electoral strategy of Vice President Hubert Humphrey. The tactic "worked," in that the South Vietnamese junta withdrew from the talks on the eve of the election, thereby destroying the "peace plank" on which the Democrats had contested it. In another way, it did not "work," because four years later the Nixon administration concluded the war on the same terms that had been on offer in Paris. The reason for the dead silence that still surrounds the question is that, in those intervening four years, some twenty thousand Americans and an uncalculated number of Vietnamese, Cambodians and Laotians lost their lives. Lost them, that is to say, even more pointlessly than had those slain up to that point. The impact of those four years on Indochinese society, and on American democracy, is beyond computation. The chief beneficiary of the covert action, and of the subsequent slaughter, was Henry Kissinger.

I can already hear the guardians of consensus scraping their blunted quills to describe this as a "conspiracy theory." I happily accept the challenge. Let us take, first, the White House journal of that renowned conspirator (and theorist of conspiracy) H.R. Haldeman, published in May 1994. I choose to start with this for two reasons. First, because, on the logical inference of "evidence against interest," it is improbable that Mr. Haldeman would supply evidence of his knowledge of a crime unless he was (posthumously) telling the truth. Second, because it is possible to trace back each of his entries to its origin in other documented sources.

In January 1973, the Nixon-Kissinger administration—for which Mr. Haldeman took the minutes—was heavily engaged on two fronts. In Paris, Henry Kissinger was striving to negotiate "peace with honor" in Vietnam. In Washington, DC, the web of evidence against the Watergate burglars and buggers was beginning to tighten. On 8 January 1973, Haldeman records:

> John Dean called to report on the Watergate trials, says that if we can prove in any way by hard evidence that our [campaign] plane was bugged in '68, he thinks that we could use that as a basis to say we're going to force Congress to go back and investigate '68 as well as '72, and thus turn them off.

Three days later, on 11 January 1973, Haldeman hears from Nixon ("The P," as the *Diaries* call him):

> On the Watergate question, he wanted me to talk to [Attorney General John] Mitchell and have him find

out from [Deke] De Loach [of the FBI] if the guy who did the bugging on us in 1968 is still at the FBI, and then [FBI acting director Patrick] Gray should nail him with a lie detector and get it settled, which would give us the evidence we need. He also thinks I ought to move with George Christian [President Johnson's former press secretary, then working with Democrats for Nixon], get LBJ to use his influence to turn off the Hill investigation with Califano, Hubert, and so on. Later in the day, he decided that wasn't such a good idea, and told me not to do it, which I fortunately hadn't done.

On the same day, Haldeman reports Henry Kissinger calling excitedly from Paris, saying "he'll do the signing in Paris rather than Hanoi, which is the key thing." He speaks also of getting South Vietnam's President Thieu to "go along." On the following day:

The P also got back on the Watergate thing today, making the point that I should talk to Connally about the Johnson bugging process to get his judgment as to how to handle it. He wonders if we shouldn't just have Andreas go in and scare Hubert. The problem in going at LBJ is how he'd react, and we need to find out from De Loach who did it, and then run a lie detector on him. I talked to Mitchell

on the phone on this subject and he said De Loach
had told him he was up to date on the thing because
he had a call from Texas. A *Star* reporter was making an inquiry in the last week or so, and LBJ got
very hot and called Deke [De Loach] and said to
him that if the Nixon people are going to play with
this, that he would release [*deleted material—national
security*], saying that our side was asking that certain things be done. By our side, I assume he means
the Nixon campaign organization. De Loach took
this as a direct threat from Johnson.... As he recalls
it, bugging was requested on the planes, but was
turned down, and all they did was check the phone
calls, and put a tap on the Dragon Lady [Mrs. Anna
Chennault].

This bureaucratic prose may be hard to read, but it
needs no cipher to decode itself. Under intense pressure about the bugging of the Watergate building,
Nixon instructed his chief of staff Haldeman, and
his FBI contact Deke De Loach, to unmask the bugging to which his own campaign had been subjected
in 1968. He also sounded out former President Johnson, through former senior Democrats like Governor John Connally, to gauge what his reaction to
the disclosure might be. The aim was to show that
"everybody does it." (By another bipartisan paradox,
in Washington the slogan "they all do it" is used as

a slogan for the defense rather than, as one might hope, for the prosecution.)

However, a problem presented itself at once. How to reveal the 1968 bugging without at the same time revealing what that bugging had been about? Hence the second thoughts ("that wasn't such a good idea..."). In his excellent introduction to *The Haldeman Diaries*, Nixon's biographer Professor Stephen Ambrose characterizes the 1973 approach to Lyndon Johnson as "prospective blackmail," designed to exert backstairs pressure to close down a congressional inquiry. But he also suggests that Johnson, himself no pushover, had some blackmail ammunition of his own. As Professor Ambrose phrases it, the Haldeman *Diaries* had been vetted by the National Security Council (NSC), and the bracketed deletion cited above is "the only place in the book where an example is given of a deletion by the NSC during the Carter administration. Eight days later Nixon was inaugurated for his second term. Ten days later Johnson died of a heart attack. What Johnson had on Nixon I suppose we'll never know."

The professor's conclusion here is arguably too tentative. There is a well-understood principle known as "Mutual Assured Destruction," whereby both sides possess more than enough material with which to annihilate the other. The answer to the question of what the Johnson administration "had" on Nixon is a relatively easy one. It was given in a book entitled *Counsel to the President*, published in 1991. Its author was Clark Clifford, the quintessential blue-chip Washington insider, who was assisted in the writing by Richard Holbrooke, the former Assistant Secretary of State and Ambassador to the United Nations. In 1968, Clark Clifford was Secretary of Defense and Richard Holbrooke was a member of the United States negotiating team at the Vietnam peace talks in Paris.

From his seat in the Pentagon, Clifford had actually been able to read the intelligence transcripts that picked up and recorded what he terms a "secret personal channel" between President Thieu in Saigon and the Nixon campaign. The chief interlocutor at the American end was John Mitchell, then Nixon's campaign manager and subsequently Attorney General (and subsequently Prisoner Number 24171-157 in the Alabama correctional system). He was actively assisted by Madame Anna Chennault, known to all as The Dragon Lady. A fierce veteran of the Taiwan lobby, and all-purpose right-wing intriguer, she was a social and political force in the Washington of her day and would rate a biography on her own.

Clifford describes a private meeting at which he, President Johnson, Secretary of State Dean Rusk, and National Security Advisor Walt Rostow were present. Hawkish to a man, they kept Vice President

Humphrey out of the loop. But, hawkish as they were, they were appalled at the evidence of Nixon's treachery. They nonetheless decided not to go public with what they knew. Clifford says that this was because the disclosure would have ruined the Paris talks altogether. He could have added that it would have created a crisis of public confidence in United States institutions. There are some things that the voters can't be trusted to know. And, even though the bugging had been legal, it might not have looked like fair play. (The Logan Act prohibits any American from conducting private diplomacy with a foreign power, but it is not very rigorously or consistently enforced.)

In the event, Thieu pulled out of the negotiations anyway, ruining them just two days before the election. Clifford is in no doubt of the advice on which he did so:

> The activities of the Nixon team went far beyond the bounds of justifiable political combat. It constituted direct interference in the activities of the executive branch and the responsibilities of the Chief Executive, the only people with authority to negotiate on behalf of the nation. The activities of the Nixon campaign constituted a gross, even potentially illegal, interference in the security affairs of the nation by private individuals.

Perhaps aware of the slight feebleness of his lawyerly prose, and perhaps a little ashamed of keeping the secret for his memoirs rather than sharing it with the electorate, Clifford adds in a footnote:

> It should be remembered that the public was considerably more innocent in such matters in the days before the Watergate hearings and the 1975 Senate investigation of the CIA.

Perhaps the public was indeed more innocent, if only because of the insider reticence of white-shoe lawyers like Clifford, who thought there were some things too profane to be made known. He claims now that he was in favor either of confronting Nixon privately with the information and forcing him to desist, or else of making it public. Perhaps this was indeed his view.

A more wised-up age of investigative reporting has brought us several updates on this appalling episode. And so has the very guarded memoir of Richard Nixon himself. More than one "back channel" was required for the Republican destabilization of the Paris peace talks. There had to be secret communications between Nixon and the South Vietnamese, as we have seen. But there also had to be an informant inside the incumbent administration's camp—a source of hints and tips and early warnings

of official intentions. That informant was Henry
Kissinger. In Nixon's own account, *RN: The Memoirs
of Richard Nixon*, the disgraced elder statesman tells
us that, in mid-September 1968, he received private
word of a planned "bombing halt." In other words,
the Johnson administration would, for the sake
of the negotiations, consider suspending its aerial
bombardment of North Vietnam. This most useful
advance intelligence, Nixon tells us, came "through
a highly unusual channel." It was more unusual even
than he acknowledged. Kissinger had until then been
a devoted partisan of Nelson Rockefeller, the match-
lessly wealthy prince of liberal Republicanism. His
contempt for the person and the policies of Richard
Nixon was undisguised. Indeed, President Johnson's
Paris negotiators, led by Averell Harriman, considered Kissinger to be almost one of themselves. He
had made himself helpful, as Rockefeller's chief foreign policy advisor, by supplying French intermediaries with their own contacts in Hanoi. "Henry
was the only person outside of the government we
were authorized to discuss the negotiations with,"
says Richard Holbrooke. "We trusted him. It is not
stretching the truth to say that the Nixon campaign
had a secret source within the US negotiating team."

So the likelihood of a bombing halt, wrote Nixon,
"came as no real surprise to me." He added: "I told
Haldeman that Mitchell should continue as liaison

with Kissinger and that we should honor his desire to keep his role completely confidential." It is impossible that Nixon was unaware of his campaign manager's parallel role in colluding with a foreign power. Thus began what was effectively a domestic covert operation, directed simultaneously at the thwarting of the talks and the embarrassment of the Hubert Humphrey campaign.

Later in the month, on 26 September to be precise, and as recorded by Nixon in his memoirs, "Kissinger called again. He said that he had just returned from Paris, where he had picked up word that something big was afoot regarding Vietnam. He advised that if I had anything to say about Vietnam during the following week, I should avoid any new ideas or proposals." On the same day, Nixon declined a challenge from Humphrey for a direct debate. On 12 October, Kissinger once again made contact, suggesting that a bombing halt might be announced as soon as 23 October. *And so it might have been.* Except that for some reason, every time the North Vietnamese side came closer to agreement, the South Vietnamese increased their own demands. We now know why and how that was, and how the two halves of the strategy were knit together. As far back as July, Nixon had met quietly in New York with the South Vietnamese ambassador, Bui Diem. The contact had been arranged by Anna Chennault. Bugging of the South

Vietnamese offices in Washington, and surveillance of the Dragon Lady, showed how the ratchet operated. An intercepted cable from Diem to President Thieu on the fateful day of 23 October had him saying: "Many Republican friends have contacted me and encouraged us to stand firm. They were alarmed by press reports to the effect that you had already softened your position." The wiretapping instructions went to one Cartha De Loach, known as Deke to his associates, who was J. Edgar Hoover's FBI liaison officer to the White House. We met him, you may recall, in H.R. Haldeman's *Diaries*.

In 1999 the author Anthony Summers was finally able to gain access to the closed FBI file of intercepts of the Nixon campaign, which he published in his 2000 book *The Arrogance of Power: The Secret World of Richard Nixon*. He was also able to interview Anna Chennault. These two breakthroughs furnished him with what is vulgarly termed a "smoking gun" on the 1968 conspiracy. By the end of October 1968, John Mitchell had become so nervous about official surveillance that he ceased taking calls from Chennault. And President Johnson, in a conference call to the three candidates, Nixon, Humphrey and Wallace (allegedly to brief them on the bombing halt), had strongly implied that he knew about the covert efforts to stymie his Vietnam diplomacy. This call created near-panic in Nixon's inner circle and caused Mitchell to telephone Chennault at the Sheraton Park Hotel. He then asked her to call him back on a more secure line. "Anna," he told her, "I'm speaking on behalf of Mr. Nixon. It's very important that our Vietnamese friends understand our Republican position, and I hope you made that clear to them.... Do you think they really have decided not to go to Paris?"

The reproduced FBI original document shows what happened next. On 2 November 1968, the agent reported as follows:

MRS ANNA CHENNAULT CONTACTED VIET-NAMESE AMBASSADOR BUI DIEM, AND ADVISED HIM THAT SHE HAD RECEIVED A MESSAGE PROM HER BOSS (NOT FURTHER IDENTIFIED), WHICH HER BOSS WANTED HER TO GIVE PERSONALLY TO THE AMBASSADOR. SHE SAID THAT THE MESSAGE WAS THAT THE AMBASSADOR IS TO "HOLD ON, WE ARE GONNA WIN" AND THAT HER BOSS ALSO SAID "HOLD ON, HE UNDERSTANDS ALL OF IT." SHE REPEATED THAT THIS IS THE ONLY MESSAGE. "HE SAID PLEASE TELL YOUR BOSS TO HOLD ON." SHE ADVISED THAT HER BOSS HAD JUST CALLED FROM NEW MEXICO.

Nixon's running mate, Spiro Agnew, had been campaigning in Albuquerque, New Mexico, that day, and subsequent intelligence analysis revealed that he, and another member of his staff (the one principally concerned with Vietnam), had indeed been in touch with the Chennault camp.

The beauty of having Kissinger leaking from one side, and Anna Chennault and John Mitchell conducting a private foreign policy for Nixon on the other, was this. It enabled him to avoid being drawn into the argument over a bombing halt. And it further enabled him to suggest that it was the Democrats who were playing politics with the issue. On 25 October in New York, Nixon used his tried-and-tested tactic of circulating an innuendo while purporting to disown it. Of LBJ's Paris diplomacy he said, "I am told that this spurt of activity is a cynical, last-minute attempt by President Johnson to salvage the candidacy of Mr. Humphrey. This I do not believe."

Kissinger himself showed a similar ability to play both ends against the middle. In the late summer of 1968, on Martha's Vineyard, he had offered Nelson Rockefeller's files on Nixon to Professor Samuel Huntington, a close adviser to Hubert Humphrey. But when Huntington's colleague and friend Zbigniew Brzezinski tried to get him to make good on the offer, Kissinger became shy. "I've hated Nixon for years," he told Brzezinski. But the time wasn't quite ripe for the handover. Indeed, it was a very close-run election, turning in the end on a difference of a few hundred thousand votes, and many hardened observers believe that the final difference was made when Johnson ordered a bombing halt on 31 October and the South Vietnamese made him look a fool by boycotting the peace talks the very next day. But had things gone the other way, Kissinger was a near-certainty for a senior job in a Humphrey administration.

With slight differences of emphasis, the larger pieces of this story appear in Haldeman's work as cited, and in Clifford's memoir. They are also partially rehearsed in President Johnson's autobiography *The Vantage Point*, and in a long reflection on Indochina by William Bundy (one of the architects of the war) entitled rather tritely *The Tangled Web*. Senior members of the press corps, among them Jules Witcover in his history of 1968, Seymour Hersh in his study of Kissinger, and Walter Isaacson, editor of *Time* magazine, in his admiring but critical biography, have produced almost congruent accounts of the same abysmal episode. I myself parsed *The Haldeman Diaries* in *The Nation* in 1994. The only mention of it that is completely and utterly false, and false by any literary or historical standard, appears in the memoirs of Henry Kissinger himself. He writes just this:

Several Nixon emissaries—some self-appointed—telephoned me for counsel. I took the position that I would answer specific questions on foreign policy, but that I would not offer general advice or volunteer suggestions. This was the same response I made to inquiries from the Humphrey staff.

This contradicts even the self-serving memoir of the man who, having won the 1968 election by these underhand means, made *as his very first appointment* Henry Kissinger as National Security Advisor. One might not want to arbitrate a mendacity competition between the two men, but when he made this choice Richard Nixon had only once, briefly and awkwardly, met Henry Kissinger in person. He clearly formed his estimate of the man's abilities from more persuasive experience than that. "One factor that had most convinced me of Kissinger's credibility," Nixon wrote later in his own delicious prose, "was the length to which he went to protect his secrecy."

But that ghastly secret is now out. In the December 1968 issue of the establishment house organ *Foreign Affairs*, written months earlier but published a few days after his gazetting as Nixon's right-hand man, there appeared Henry Kissinger's own evaluation of the Vietnam negotiations. On every point of substance, he agreed with the line taken in Paris by the Johnson-Humphrey negotiators. One has to pause for an instant to comprehend the enormity of this. Kissinger had helped elect a man who had surreptitiously promised the South Vietnamese junta a better deal than they would get from the Democrats. The Saigon authorities then acted, as Bundy ruefully confirms, as if they did indeed have a deal. This meant, in the words of a later Nixon slogan, "Four More Years." But four more years of an unwinnable and undeclared and murderous war, which was to spread before it burned out, and was to end on the same terms and conditions as had been on the table in the fall of 1968.

This was what it took to promote Henry Kissinger. To promote him from being a mediocre and opportunist academic to becoming an international potentate. The signature qualities were there from the inaugural moment: the sycophancy and the duplicity; the power worship and the absence of scruple; the empty trading of old non-friends for new non-friends. And the distinctive effects were also present: the uncounted and expendable corpses; the official and unofficial lying about the cost; the heavy and pompous pseudo-indignation when unwelcome questions were asked. Kissinger's global career started as it meant to go on. It debauched the

American republic and American democracy, and it levied a hideous toll of casualties on weaker and more vulnerable societies.

By Way of Warning:
A Brief Note on the 40 Committee

In many of the ensuing pages and episodes, I've found it essential to allude to the "40 Committee" or the "Forty Committee," the semi-clandestine body of which Henry Kissinger was the chairman between 1969 and 1976. One does not need to picture some giant, octopuslike organization at the center of a web of conspiracy: however, it is important to know that there was a committee which maintained ultimate supervision over United States covert actions overseas (and, possibly, at home) during this period.

The CIA was originally set up by President Harry Truman at the beginning of the Cold War. In the first Eisenhower administration, it was felt necessary to establish a monitoring or watchdog body to oversee covert operations. This panel was known as the Special Group, and sometimes also referred to as the 54/12 Group, after the number of the National Security Council directive which set it up. By the time of President Johnson it was called the 303 Committee and during the Nixon and Ford administrations it was called the 40 Committee. Some believe that these changes of name reflect the numbers of later NSC directives; in fact the committee was known by the numbers of the successive rooms in the handsome Old Executive Office Building (now annexed to the neighboring White House) which used to shelter the three departments of "State, War and Navy," in which it met. No mystery there.

If any fantastic rumors shroud the work of the committee, this may be the outcome of the absurd cult of secrecy that at one point surrounded it. At Senate hearings in 1973, Senator Stuart Symington was questioning William Colby, then Director of Central Intelligence, about the origins and evolution of the supervisory group:

SENATOR SYMINGTON: Very well. What is the name of the latest committee of this character?

MR. COLBY: Forty Committee.

SENATOR SYMINGTON: Who is the chairman?

MR. COLBY: Well, again, I would prefer to go into executive session on the description of the Forty Committee, Mr. Chairman.

SENATOR SYMINGTON: As to who is the chairman, you would prefer an executive session?

MR. COLBY: The chairman—all right, Mr. Chairman—Dr. Kissinger is the chairman, as the Assistant to the President for National Security Affairs.

Kissinger held this position *ex officio,* in other words. His colleagues at the time were Air Force General George Brown, chairman of the Joint Chiefs of Staff; William P. Clements, Jr., the Deputy Secretary of Defense; Joseph Sisco, the Under-Secretary of State for Political Affairs; and the Director of Central Intelligence, William Colby.

With slight variations, those holding these positions have been the permanent members of the Forty Committee which, as President Ford phrased it in the first public reference by a president to the group's existence, "reviews every covert operation undertaken by our government." An important variation was added by President Nixon, who appointed his former campaign manager and attorney general, John Mitchell, to sit on the committee, the only attorney general to have done so. The founding charter of the CIA prohibits it from taking any part in domestic operations: in January 1975 Attorney General Mitchell was convicted of numerous counts of perjury, obstruction and conspiracy to cover up the Watergate burglary, which was carried out in part by former CIA operatives. He became the first attorney general to serve time in jail.

We have met Mr. Mitchell, in concert with Mr. Kissinger, before. The usefulness of this note, I hope and believe, is that it supplies a thread which will be found throughout this narrative. Whenever any major US covert undertaking occurred between the years 1969 and 1976, Henry Kissinger may be at least presumed to have had direct knowledge of, and responsibility for, it. If he claims that he did not, then he is claiming not to have been doing a job to which he clung with great bureaucratic tenacity. And, whether or not he cares to accept the responsibility, the accountability is his in any case.

2

Indochina

Even while compelled to concentrate on brute
realities, one must never lose sight of that
element of the surreal that surrounds Henry Kissinger. Paying a visit to Vietnam in the middle 1960s,
when many technocratic opportunists were still convinced that the war was worth fighting and could be
won, the young Henry reserved judgment on the
first point but developed considerable private doubts
on the second. Empowered by Nelson Rockefeller
with a virtual free hand to develop contacts of his
own, he had gone so far as to involve himself with
an initiative that extended to direct personal contact
with Hanoi. He became friendly with two French-
men who had a direct line to the Communist leadership in North Vietnam's capital. Raymond Aubrac,
a French civil servant who was a friend of Ho Chi
Minh, made common cause with Herbert Marco-
vich, a French biochemist, and began a series of trips
to North Vietnam. On their return, they briefed

Kissinger in Paris. He in his turn parlayed their information into high-level conversations in Washington, relaying the actual or potential negotiating positions of Pham Van Dong and other Communist statesmen to Robert McNamara. (In the result, the relentless bombing of the North made any "bridge-building" impracticable. In particular, the now-forgotten American destruction of the Paul Doumer bridge outraged the Vietnamese side.)

This weightless mid-position, which ultimately helped enable his double act in 1968, allowed Kissinger to ventriloquize Governor Rockefeller and to propose, by indirect means, a future détente with America's chief rivals. In his first major address as a candidate for the Republican nomination in 1968, Rockefeller spoke ringingly of how "in a subtle triangle with Communist China and the Soviet Union, we can ultimately improve our relations with *each*— as we test the will for peace of *both*." This foreshadowing of a later Kissinger strategy might appear at first reading to illustrate prescience. But Governor Rockefeller had no more reason than Vice President Humphrey to suppose that his ambitious staffer would defect to the Nixon camp, risking and postponing this same détente in order later to take credit for a debased simulacrum of it.

Morally speaking, Kissinger treated the concept of superpower rapprochement in the same way as he treated the concept of a negotiated settlement in Vietnam: as something contingent to his own needs. There was a time to feign support of it, and a time to denounce it as weak-minded and treacherous. And there was a time to take credit for it. Some of those who "followed orders" in Indochina may lay a claim to that notoriously weak defense. Some who even issued the orders may now tell us that they were acting sincerely at the time. But Kissinger cannot avail himself of this alibi. He always knew what he was doing, and he embarked upon a second round of protracted warfare having knowingly helped to destroy an alternative which he always understood was possible. This increases the gravity of the charge against him. It also prepares us for his improvised and retrospective defense against that charge—that his immense depredations eventually led to "peace." When he falsely and prematurely announced that "peace is now at hand" in October 1972, he made a boastful claim that could have been genuinely (and much less bloodily) made in 1967. And when he claimed credit for subsequent superpower contacts, he was announcing the result of a secret and corrupt diplomacy that had originally been proposed as an open and democratic one. In the meantime, he had illegally eavesdropped on and shadowed American citizens and public servants whose misgivings about the war, and about unconstitutional authority, were mild compared to those of Messieurs Aubrac and Marc-ovich. In establishing what lawyers call the *mens rea*, we can say that in Kissinger's case he was fully aware of, and is entirely accountable for, his own actions.

Upon taking office at Richard Nixon's side in the winter of 1968, it was Kissinger's task to be *plus roy-aliste que le roi* in two respects. He had to confect a rationale of "credibility" for punitive action in an already devastated Vietnamese theater, and he had to second his principal's wish that he form part of a "wall" between the Nixon White House and the Department of State. The term "two-track" was later to become commonplace. Kissinger's position on both tracks, of promiscuous violence abroad and flagrant illegality at home, was decided from the start. He does not seem to have lacked relish for either commitment; one hopes faintly that this was not the first twinge of the "aphrodisiac."

President Johnson's "bombing halt" had not lasted long by any standards, even if one remembers that its original conciliatory purpose had been sordidly undercut. Averell Harriman, who had been LBJ's chief negotiator in Paris, later testified to Congress that the North Vietnamese had withdrawn 90 per-cent of their forces from the northern two prov-inces of South Vietnam, in October–November 1968, in accordance with the agreement of which the halt might have formed a part. In the new context, however, this withdrawal could be interpreted as a sign of weakness, or even as a "light at the end of the tunnel."

The historical record of the Indochina war is voluminous, and the resulting controversy no less so. However, this does not prevent the following of a consistent thread. Once the war had been unnaturally and undemocratically prolonged, more exorbitant methods were required to fight it and more fantastic excuses had to be fabricated to justify it. Let us take four separate but connected cases in which the civilian population was deliberately exposed to indiscriminate lethal force, in which the customary laws of war and neutrality were violated, and in which conscious lies had to be told in order to conceal these facts, and others.

The first such case is an example of what Vietnam might have been spared had not the 1968 Paris peace talks been sabotaged. In December 1968, during the "transition" period between the Johnson and Nixon administrations, the United States military command turned to what General Creighton Abrams termed "total war" against the "infrastructure" of the Vietcong/NLF insurgency. The chief exhibit in this campaign was a six-month clearance of the Mekong Delta province of Kien Hoa. The code name for the sweep was Operation Speedy Express. (See pages 41–46.)

It might, in some realm of theory, be remotely conceivable that such tactics could be justified under the international laws and charters governing the sovereign rights of self-defense. But no nation capable of deploying the overwhelming and annihilating force described below would be likely to find itself on the defensive. And it would be least of all likely to find itself on the defensive on its own soil. So the Nixon-Kissinger administration was not, except in one unusual sense, fighting for survival. The unusual sense in which its survival *was* at stake is set out, yet again, in the stark posthumous testimony of H.R. Haldeman. From his roost at Nixon's side he describes a Kissingerian moment on 15 December 1970:

> K[issinger] came in and the discussion covered some of the general thinking about Vietnam and the P's big peace plan for next year, which K later told me he does not favor. He thinks that any pullout next year would be a serious mistake because the adverse reaction to it could set in well before the '72 elections. He favors instead a continued winding down and then a pullout right at the fall of '72 so that if any bad results follow they will be too late to affect the election.

One could hardly wish for it to be more plainly put than that. (And put, furthermore, by one of

Nixon's chief partisans with no wish to discredit the re-election.) But in point of fact Kissinger himself admits to almost as much in his own first volume of memoirs, *The White House Years*. The context is a meeting with General de Gaulle in which the old warrior demanded to know by what right the Nixon administration subjected Indochina to devastating bombardment. In his own account, Kissinger replies that "a sudden withdrawal might give us a credibility problem." (When asked "Where?" Kissinger hazily proposed the Middle East.) It is important to bear in mind that the future flatterer of Brezhnev and Mao, and the proponent of the manipulative "triangle" between them, was in no real position to claim that he made war in Indochina to thwart either. He certainly did not dare try such a callow excuse on Charles de Gaulle. And indeed, the proponent of secret deals with China was in no very strong position to claim that he was combating Stalinism in general. No, it all came down to "credibility," and to the saving of face. It is known that 20,492 American servicemen lost their lives in Indochina between the day that Nixon and Kissinger took office and the day in 1972 that they withdrew United States forces and accepted the logic of 1968. What if the families and survivors of these victims have to confront the fact that the "face" at risk was Kissinger's own?

Thus the colloquially entitled "Christmas bombing"

of North Vietnam, begun during the same election campaign that Haldeman and Kissinger had so tenderly foreseen two years previously, and continued after that election had been won, must be counted as a war crime by any standard. The bombing was not conducted for anything that could be described as "military reasons," but for twofold political reasons. The first of these was domestic: to make a show of strength to extremists in Congress and to put the Democratic Party on the defensive. The second reason was to persuade the South Vietnamese leaders like President Thieu—still intransigent after all those years—that their objections to a United States withdrawal were too nervous. This, again, was the mortgage on the initial secret payment of 1968.

When the unpreventable collapse occurred, in Vietnam and in Cambodia, in April and May 1975, the cost was infinitely higher than it would have been seven years previously. These locust years ended as they had begun—with a display of bravado and deceit. On 12 May 1975, Cambodian gunboats detained an American merchant vessel named the *Mayaguez*. In the immediate aftermath of the Khmer Rouge seizure of power, the situation was a distraught one. The ship had been stopped in international waters claimed by Cambodia and then taken to the Cambodian island of Koh Tang. In spite of reports that the crew had been released, Kissinger pressed for an immediate face-saving and "credibility"-enhancing strike. He persuaded President Gerald Ford, the untried and undistinguished successor to his deposed former boss, to send in the Marines and the Air Force. Out of a Marine force of 110, 18 were killed and 50 wounded. Some 23 Air Force men died in a crash. The United States used a 15,000-pound bomb on the island, the most powerful non-nuclear device that it possessed. Nobody has the figures for Cambodian deaths. The casualties were pointless because the ship's company of the *Mayaguez* were nowhere on Koh Tang, having been released some hours earlier. A subsequent congressional inquiry found that Kissinger could have known of this by listening to Cambodian Broadcasting or by paying attention to a third-party government which had been negotiating a deal for the restitution of the crew and the ship. It was not as if any Cambodians doubted, by that month of 1975, the willingness of the US government to employ deadly force.

In Washington, DC, there is a famous and hallowed memorial to the American dead of the Vietnam War. Known as the Vietnam Veterans' Memorial, it bears a name that is slightly misleading. I was present for the extremely affecting moment of its dedication in 1982, and noticed that the list of nearly 60,000 names is incised in the wall not by alphabet but by date. The first few names appear in 1954, and the last few in 1975. The more historically minded visitors can sometimes be heard to say that they didn't know the United States was engaged in Vietnam as early or as late as that. Nor were the public supposed to know. The first names are of the covert operatives sent in by Colonel Lansdale without congressional approval to support French colonialism before Dien Bien Phu. The last names are of those thrown away in the *Mayaguez* fiasco. It took Henry Kissinger to ensure that a war of atrocity, which he had helped prolong, should end as furtively and ignominiously as it had begun.

3

A Sample of Cases: Kissinger's War Crimes In Indochina

Some statements are too blunt for everyday, consensual discourse. In national "debate," it is the smoother pebbles that are customarily gathered from the stream, and used as projectiles. They leave less of a scar, even when they hit. Occasionally, however, a single hard-edged remark will inflict a deep and jagged wound, a gash so ugly that it must be cauterized at once. In January 1971, General Telford Taylor, who had been chief prosecuting counsel at the Nuremberg trials, made a considered statement. Reviewing the legal and moral basis of those hearings, and also the Tokyo trials of Japanese war criminals and the Manila trial of Emperor Hirohito's chief militarist, General Tomoyuki Yamashita, Taylor said that if the standards of Nuremberg and Manila were applied evenly, and applied to the

American statesmen and bureaucrats who designed the war in Vietnam, then "there would be a very strong possibility that they would come to the same end he [Yamashita] did." It is not every day that a senior American soldier and jurist delivers the opinion that a large portion of his country's political class should probably be hooded and blindfolded and dropped through a trapdoor on the end of a rope.

In his book *Nuremberg and Vietnam*, General Taylor also anticipated one of the possible objections to this legal and moral conclusion. It might be argued for the defense, he said, that those arraigned did not really know what they were doing; in other words had achieved the foulest results but from the highest and most innocent motives. The notion of Indochina as some *Heart of Darkness* "quagmire" of ignorant armies has been sedulously propagated, then and since, but Taylor had no patience with such a view. American military and intelligence and economic and political missions and teams had been in Vietnam, he wrote, for much too long to attribute anything they did "to lack of information." It might have been possible for soldiers and diplomats to pose as innocents until the middle of the 1960s, but after that time, and especially after the My Lai massacre of 16 March 1968, when serving veterans reported to their superior officers a number of major atrocities, nobody could reasonably claim to have been uninformed and of those who could, the least believable would be those who—far from the confusion of battle—read and discussed and approved the panoptic reports of the war that were delivered to Washington.

General Taylor's book was being written while many of the most reprehensible events of the Indochina war were still taking place, or were still to come. He was unaware of the intensity and extent of, for example, the bombing of Laos and Cambodia. However, enough was known about the conduct of the war, and about the existing matrix of legal and criminal responsibility, for him to arrive at some indisputable conclusions. The first of these concerned the particular obligation of the United States to be aware of, and to respect, the Nuremberg principles:

> Military courts and commissions have customarily rendered their judgments stark and unsupported by opinions giving the reason for their decision. The Nuremberg and Tokyo judgments, in contrast, were all based on extensive opinions detailing the evidence and analyzing the factual and legal issues, in the fashion of appellate tribunals generally. Needless to say they were not of uniform quality, and often reflected the logical shortcomings of compromise, the marks of which commonly mar the opinions of multi-member tribunals. But the process

was *professional* in a way seldom achieved in military courts, and the records and judgments in these trials provided a much-needed foundation for a corpus of judge-made international penal law. The results of the trials commended themselves to the newly-formed United Nations, and on December 11, 1946, the General Assembly adopted a resolution affirming "the principles of international law recognized by the Charter of the Nuremberg Tribunal and the judgment of the Tribunal."

However history may ultimately assess the wisdom or unwisdom of the war crimes trials, one thing is indisputable. At their conclusion, the United States Government stood legally, politically and morally committed to the principles enunciated in the charters and judgments of the tribunals. The President of the United States, on the recommendations of the Departments of State, War and Justice, approved the war crimes programs. Thirty or more American judges, drawn from the appellate benches of the states from Massachusetts to Oregon, and Minnesota to Georgia, conducted the later Nuremberg trials and wrote the opinions. General Douglas MacArthur, under authority of the Far Eastern Commission, established the Tokyo tribunal and confirmed the sentences it imposed, and it was under his authority as the highest American military officer in the Far East that the Yamashita and other such proceedings were held. The United States delegation to the United Nations presented the resolution by which the General Assembly endorsed the Nuremberg principles. Thus the integrity of the nation is staked on those principles, and today the question is how they apply to our conduct of the war in Vietnam, and whether the United States Government is prepared to face the consequences of their application.

Facing and cogitating these consequences himself, General Telford Taylor took issue with another United States officer, Colonel William Corson, who had written that "Regardless of the outcome of... the My Lai courts-martial and other legal actions, the point remains that American judgment as to the effective prosecution of the war was faulty from beginning to end and that the atrocities, alleged or otherwise, are a result of failure of judgment, not criminal behavior." To this Telford responded thus:

Colonel Corson overlooks, I fear, that negligent homicide is generally a crime of bad judgment rather than evil intent. Perhaps he is right in the strictly causal sense that if there had been no failure of judgment, the occasion for criminal conduct would not have arisen. The Germans in occupied Europe made gross errors of judgment which no doubt created the conditions in which the slaughter

of the inhabitants of Klissura [a Greek village anni-
hilated during the Occupation] occurred, but that
did not make the killings any the less criminal.

Referring this question to the chain of command
in the field, General Taylor noted further that the
senior officer corps had been:

more or less constantly in Vietnam, and splendidly
equipped with helicopters and other aircraft, which
gave them a degree of mobility unprecedented in
earlier wars, and consequently endowed them with
every opportunity to keep the course of the fighting and its consequences under close and constant
observation. Communications were generally rapid
and efficient, so that the flow of information and
orders was unimpeded.

These circumstances are in sharp contrast to
those that confronted General Yamashita in 1944
and 1945, with his troops reeling back in disar-
ray before the oncoming American military pow-
erhouse. For failure to control his troops so as to
prevent the atrocities they committed, Brigadier
Generals Egbert F. Bullene and Morris Handwerk
and Major Generals James A. Lester, Leo Donovan
and Russel B. Reynolds found him guilty of violating the laws of war and sentenced him to death by
hanging.

Nor did General Taylor omit the crucial link between the military command and its political supervision; this was again a much closer and more immediate relation in the American-Vietnamese instance than in the Japanese-Filipino one, as the regular contact between, say, General Creighton Abrams and Henry Kissinger makes clear:

> How much the President and his close advisers in the White House, Pentagon and Foggy Bottom knew about the volume and cause of civilian casualties in Vietnam, and the physical devastation of the countryside, is speculative. Something was known, for the late John Naughton (then Assistant Secretary of Defense) returned from the White House one day in 1967 with the message that "We seem to be proceeding on the assumption that the way to eradicate the Vietcong is to destroy all the village structures, defoliate all the jungles, and then cover the entire surface of South Vietnam with asphalt."

This remark had been reported (by Townsend Hoopes, a political antagonist of General Taylor) before that metaphor had been extended into two new countries, Laos and Cambodia, without a declaration of war, a notification to Congress or a warning to civilians to evacuate. But Taylor anticipated the Kissinger case in many ways when he recalled the trial of the Japanese statesman Koki Hirota:

> who served briefly as Prime Minister and for several years as Foreign Minister between 1933 and May 1938, after which he held no office whatever. The so-called "Rape of Nanking" by Japanese forces occurred during the winter of 1937–38, when Hirota was Foreign Minister. Upon receiving early reports of the atrocities, he demanded and received assurances from the War Ministry that they would be stopped. But they continued, and the Tokyo tribunal found Hirota guilty because he was "derelict in his duty in not insisting before the Cabinet that immediate action be taken to put an end to the atrocities," and "was content to rely on assurances which he knew were not being implemented." On this basis, coupled with his conviction on the aggressive war charge, Hirota was sentenced to be hanged.

Melvin Laird, as Secretary of Defense during the first Nixon administration, was queasy enough about the early bombings of Cambodia, and dubious enough about the legality or prudence of the intervention, to send a memo to the Joint Chiefs of Staff, asking, "Are steps being taken, on a continuing basis, to minimize the risk of striking Cambodian peoples and structures? If so, what are the steps? Are we reasonably sure such steps are effective?" There is no evidence of Henry Kissinger, as National Security Advisor or Secretary of State, ever seeking even such modest assurances. Indeed, there is much evidence of his deceiving Congress about the true extent to which such assurances as were offered were deliberately false. Others involved, like Robert McNamara, McGeorge Bundy and William Colby, have since offered varieties of apology or contrition or at least explanation: Henry Kissinger never. General Taylor described the practice of air strikes against hamlets suspected of "harboring" Vietnamese guerrillas as "flagrant violations of the Geneva Convention on Civilian Protection, which prohibits 'collective penalties' and 'reprisals against protected persons' and equally in violation of the Rules of Land Warfare." He was writing before this atrocious precedent had been extended to "reprisal raids" that treated two whole countries—Laos and Cambodia—as if they were disposable hamlets.

For Henry Kissinger, no great believer in the boastful claims of the war-makers in the first place, a special degree of responsibility attaches. Not only did he have good reason to know that field commanders were exaggerating successes and claiming all dead bodies as enemy soldiers—a commonplace piece of knowledge after the spring of 1968—but he also knew that the issue of the war had been settled politically and diplomatically, for all intents and purposes, before he became National Security Advisor. Thus he had to know that every additional casualty, on either side, was not just a death but an avoidable death. And with this knowledge, and with a strong sense of the domestic and personal political profit, he urged the expansion of the war into two neutral countries—violating international law—while persisting in a breathtakingly high level of attrition in Vietnam itself.

From a huge range of possible examples, I have chosen cases which involve Kissinger directly and in which I have myself been able to interview surviving witnesses. The first, as foreshadowed above, is Operation Speedy Express.

My friend and colleague Kevin Buckley, then a much-admired correspondent and Saigon bureau chief for *Newsweek*, became interested in the "pacification" campaign which bore this breezy code name. Designed in the closing days of the Johnson-Humphrey administration, it was put into full effect in the first six months of 1969, when Henry Kissinger had assumed much authority over the conduct of the war. The objective was the disciplining, on behalf of the Thieu government, of the turbulent Mekong Delta province of Kien Hoa.

CHRISTOPHER HITCHENS

On 22 January 1968, Defense Secretary Robert McNamara had told the Senate that "no regular North Vietnamese units" were deployed in the
Mekong Delta, and no military intelligence documents have surfaced to undermine his claim, so that
the cleansing of the area cannot be understood as
part of the general argument about resisting Hanoi's
unsleeping will to conquest. The announced purpose of the Ninth Division's sweep, indeed, was to
redeem many thousands of villagers from political
control by the National Liberation Front (NLF) or
Viet Cong (VC). As Buckley found, and as his magazine *Newsweek* partially disclosed at the rather late
date of 19 June 1972:

All the evidence I gathered pointed to a clear conclusion: a staggering number of noncombatant
civilians—perhaps as many as 5,000 according to
one official—were killed by US firepower to "pac-
ify" Kien Hoa. The death toll there made the My
Lai massacre look trifling by comparison....

The Ninth Division put all it had into the operation. Eight thousand infantrymen scoured the heavily populated countryside, but contact with the
elusive enemy was rare. Thus, in its pursuit of pacification, the division relied heavily on its 50 artillery pieces, 50 helicopters (many armed with rockets

and mini-guns) and the deadly support lent by the Air Force. There were 3,381 tactical air strikes by fighter bombers during "Speedy Express."...

"Death is our business and business is good," was the slogan painted on one helicopter unit's quarters during the operation. And so it was. Cumulative statistics for "Speedy Express" show that 10,899 "enemy" were killed. In the month of March alone, "over 3,000 enemy troops were killed... which is the largest monthly total for any American division in the Vietnam War," said the division's official magazine. When asked to account for the enormous body counts, a division senior officer explained that helicopter gun crews often caught unarmed "enemy" in open fields....

There is overwhelming evidence that virtually all the Viet Cong were well armed. Simple civilians were, of course, not armed. And the enormous discrepancy between the body count (11,000) and the number of captured weapons (748) is hard to explain—except by the conclusion that many victims were unarmed innocent civilians....

The people who still live in pacified Kien Hoa all have vivid recollections of the devastation that American firepower brought to their lives in early 1969. Virtually every person to whom I spoke had suffered in some way. "There were 5,000 people in our village before 1969, but there were none in 1970," one village elder told me. "The Americans destroyed every house with artillery, air strikes, or by burning them down with cigarette lighters. About 100 people were killed by bombing, others were wounded and others became refugees. Many were children killed by concussion from the bombs which their small bodies could not withstand, even if they were hiding underground."

Other officials, including the village police chief, corroborated the man's testimony. I could not, of course, reach every village. But in each of the many places where I went, the testimony was the same: 100 killed here, 200 killed there.

Other notes by Buckley and his friend and collaborator Alex Shimkin (a worker for International Voluntary Services who was later killed in the war) discovered the same telltale evidence in hospital statistics. In March 1969, the hospital at Ben Tre reported 343 patients injured by "friendly fire" and 25 by "the enemy," an astonishing statistic for a government facility to record in a guerrilla war where suspected membership of the Viet Cong could mean death. And Buckley's own citation for his magazine—of "perhaps as many as 5,000 deaths" among civilians in this one sweep—is an almost deliberate understatement of what he was told by a

United States official, who actually said that *"at least 5,000"* of the dead "were what we refer to as non-combatants": a not-too-exacting distinction, as we have already seen, and as was by then well understood. [italics mine]

Well understood, that is to say, not just by those who opposed the war but by those who were conducting it. As one United States official put it to Buckley:

> The actions of the Ninth Division in inflicting civilian casualties were worse [than My Lai]. The sum total of what the Ninth did was overwhelming. In sum, the horror was worse than My Lai. But with the Ninth, the civilian casualties came in dribbles and were pieced out over a long time. And most of them were inflicted from the air and at night. Also, they were sanctioned by the command's insistence on high body-counts.... The result was an inevitable outcome of the unit's command policy.

The earlier sweep which had mopped up My Lai—during Operation Wheeler Wallawa—had also at the time counted all corpses as those of enemy soldiers, including the civilian population of the village, who were casually included in the mind-bending overall total of 10,000.

Confronted with this evidence, Buckley and Shimkin abandoned a lazy and customary usage and replaced it, in a cable to *Newsweek* headquarters in New York, with a more telling and scrupulous one. The problem was not "indiscriminate use of fire-power," but "charges of quite *discriminating* use—as a matter of policy in populated areas." Even the former is a gross violation of the Geneva Convention; the second charge leads straight to the dock in Nuremberg or The Hague.

Since General Creighton Abrams publicly praised the Ninth Division for its work, and drew attention wherever and whenever he could to the tremendous success of Operation Speedy Express, we can be sure that the political leadership in Washington was not unaware. Indeed, the degree of micro-management revealed in Kissinger's memoirs forbids the idea that anything of importance took place without his knowledge or permission.

Of nothing is this more true than his own individual involvement in the bombing and invasion of neutral Cambodia and Laos. Obsessed with the idea that Vietnamese intransigence could be traced to allies or resources external to Vietnam itself, or could be overcome by tactics of mass destruction, Kissinger at one point contemplated using thermo-nuclear weapons to obliterate the pass through which ran the railway link from North Vietnam to China, and at another stage considered bombing the dikes that prevented North Vietnam's irrigation system from flooding the country. Neither of these measures (reported respectively in Tad Szulc's history of Nixon-era diplomacy and by Kissinger's former aide Roger Morris) was taken, which removes some potential war crimes from our bill of indictment but which also gives an indication of the regnant mentality. There remained Cambodia and Laos, which supposedly concealed or protected North Vietnamese supply lines.

As in the cases postulated by General Telford Taylor, there is the crime of aggressive war and then there is the question of war crimes. (The Koki Hirota case cited above is of importance here.) In the period after the Second World War, or the period governed by the UN Charter and its related and incorporated Conventions, the United States under Democratic and Republican administrations had denied even its closest allies the right to invade countries that allegedly gave shelter to their antagonists. Most famously, President Eisenhower exerted economic and diplomatic pressure at a high level to bring an end to the invasion of Egypt by Britain, France and Israel in October 1956. (The British thought Nasser should not control "their" Suez Canal; the French believed Nasser to be the inspiration and source of their troubles in Algeria; and the Israelis claimed that he played the same role in fomenting their difficulties with the Palestinians. The United States maintained that even if these propaganda fantasies were true, they would not retrospectively legalize an invasion of Egypt.) During the Algerian war of independence, also, the United States had repudiated France's claimed right to attack a town in neighboring Tunisia that succored Algerian guerrillas, and in 1964 Ambassador Adlai Stevenson at the United Nations had condemned the United Kingdom for attacking a town in Yemen that allegedly provided a rear guard for rebels operating in its then colony of Aden.

All this law and precedent was to be thrown to the winds when Nixon and Kissinger decided to aggrandize the notion of "hot pursuit" across the borders of Laos and Cambodia. Even before the actual territorial invasion of Cambodia, for example, and very soon after the accession of Nixon and Kissinger to power, a program of heavy bombardment of the country was prepared and executed in secret. One might with some revulsion call it a "menu" of bombardment, since the code names for the raids were "Breakfast," "Lunch," "Snack," "Dinner," and "Dessert." The raids were flown by B-52 bombers which, it is important to note at the outset, fly at an altitude too high to be observed from the ground and carry immense tonnages of high explosive: they give no warning of approach and are incapable of accuracy or discrimination because of both their altitude and the mass of their shells. Between 18 March 1969 and May 1970, 3,630 such raids were flown across the Cambodian frontier. The bombing campaign began as it was to go on—with full knowledge of its effect on civilians, and with flagrant deceit by Mr. Kissinger in this precise respect.

For example, a memorandum prepared by the Joint Chiefs of Staff and sent to the Defense Department and the White House said plainly that "some Cambodian casualties would be sustained in the operation" and "the surprise effect of attack could tend to increase casualties." The target district for Breakfast (Base Area 35) was inhabited, said the memo, by about 1,640 Cambodian civilians. Lunch (Base Area 609) was inhabited by 198 of them, Snack (Base Area 351) by 383, Dinner (Base Area 352) by 770, and Dessert (Base Area 350) by about 120 Cambodian peasants. These oddly exact figures are enough in themselves to demonstrate that Kissinger was lying when he later told the Senate Foreign Relations Committee that areas of Cambodia selected for bombing were "unpopulated."

As a result of the expanded and intensified bombing campaigns, it has been estimated that as many as 350,000 civilians in Laos, and 600,000 in Cambodia, lost their lives. (These are not the highest estimates.) Figures for refugees are several multiples of that. In addition, the widespread use of toxic chemical defoliants created a massive health crisis which naturally fell most heavily on children, nursing mothers, the aged and the already infirm, and which persists to this day.

Though this appalling war, and its appalling consequences, can and should be taken as a moral and political crisis for American institutions, for at least five United States presidents, and for American society, there is little difficulty in identifying individual responsibility during this, its most atrocious and indiscriminate stage. Richard Nixon as Commander in Chief bears ultimate responsibility, and only narrowly escaped a congressional move to include his crimes and deceptions in Indochina in the articles of impeachment, the promulgation of which eventually compelled his resignation. But his deputy and closest advisor, Henry Kissinger, was sometimes forced, and sometimes forced himself, into a position of virtual co-presidency where Indochina was concerned.

For example, in the preparations for the invasion of Cambodia in 1970, Kissinger was caught between the views of his staff—several of whom resigned in protest when the invasion began—and his need to please his President. His President listened more to his two criminal associates—John Mitchell and Bebe Rebozo—than he did to his Secretaries of State and Defense, William Rogers and Melvin Laird, both of whom were highly skeptical about widening the war.

On one especially charming occasion, a drunken Nixon telephoned Kissinger to discuss the invasion plans. He then put Bebe Rebozo on the line. "The President wants you to know if this doesn't work, Henry, it's your ass." "Ain't that right, Bebe?" slurred the Commander in Chief. (The conversation was monitored and transcribed by one of Kissinger's soon-to-resign staffers, William Watts.*) It could be said that in this instance the National Security Advisor was under pressure; nevertheless he took the side of the pro-invasion faction and, according to the memoirs of General William Westmoreland, actually lobbied for that invasion to go ahead.

A somewhat harder picture is presented by former Chief of Staff H.R. Haldeman in his *Diaries*. On 22 December 1970, he records:

> Henry came up with the need to meet with the P[resident] today with Al Haig and then tomorrow with Laird and Moorer because he has to use the P[resident] to force Laird and the military to go ahead with the P[resident]'s plans, which they won't carry out without direct orders. The plans in question, involved...attacking enemy forces in Laos.

---

*According to Woodward and Bernstein, Watts then had a word with General Alexander Haig, who told him: "You've just had an order from your Commander in Chief. You can't resign." "Fuck you, Al," said Watts. "I just did."

In his own memoirs, *White House Years*, Kissinger claims that he usurped the customary chain of command whereby commanders in the field receive, or believe that they receive, their orders from the President and then the Secretary of Defense. He boasts that he, together with Haldeman, Alexander Haig and Colonel Ray Sitton, evolved "both a military and a diplomatic schedule" for the secret bombing of Cambodia. On board Air Force One, which was on the tarmac at Brussels airport on 24 February 1969, he writes, "we worked out the guidelines for the bombing of the enemy's sanctuaries." Air Force Colonel Sitton, the reigning expert on B-52 tactics at the Joint Chiefs of Staff, noted that the President was not at the meeting but had said that he would be discussing the subject with Kissinger. A few weeks later, Haldeman's *Diaries* for 17 March record:

Historic day. K[issinger]'s "Operation Breakfast" finally came off at 2.00 PM our time. K[issinger] really excited, as was P[resident].

The next day's entry reads:

K[issinger]'s "Operation Breakfast" a great success. He came beaming in with the report, very productive.

It only got better. On 22 April 1970, Haldeman reports that Nixon, following Kissinger into a National Security Council meeting on Cambodia, "turned back to me with a big smile and said 'K[issinger]'s really having fun today, he's playing Bismarck.'"

The above is an insult to the Iron Chancellor. When Kissinger was finally exposed in Congress and the press for conducting unauthorized bombings, he weakly pleaded that the raids were not all that secret, really, because Prince Sihanouk of Cambodia had known of them. He had to be reminded that a foreign princeling cannot give permission to an American bureaucrat to violate the United States Constitution. Nor, for the matter of that, can he give permission to an American bureaucrat to slaughter large numbers of his "own" civilians. It's difficult to imagine Bismarck cowering behind such a contemptible excuse. (Prince Sihanouk, it is worth remembering, later became an abject puppet of the Khmer Rouge.)

Colonel Sitton began to notice that by late 1969 his own office was being regularly overruled in the matter of selecting targets. "Not only was Henry carefully screening the raids," said Sitton, "he was reading the raw intelligence" and fiddling with the mission patterns and bombing runs. In other departments of Washington insiderdom, it was also noticed that Kissinger was becoming a Stakhanovite committeeman. Aside from the crucial Forty Committee, which planned and oversaw all foreign covert actions, he chaired the Washington Special Action Group (WSAG), the Verification Panel, which was concerned with arms control, the Vietnam Special Studies Group, which oversaw the day-to-day conduct of the war, and the Defense Program Review Committee, which supervised the budget of the Defense Department.

It is therefore impossible for him to claim that he was unaware of the consequences of the bombings of Cambodia and Laos; he knew more about them, and in more intimate detail, than any other individual. Nor was he imprisoned in a culture of obedience that gave him no alternative, or no rival arguments. Several senior members of his own staff, most notably Anthony Lake and Roger Morris, resigned over the invasion of Cambodia, and more than two hundred State Department employees signed a protest addressed to Secretary of State William Rogers. Indeed, as has been noted, both Rogers and Secretary of Defense Melvin Laird were opposed to the B-52 bombing policy, as Kissinger himself records with some disgust in his own memoirs. Congress was also opposed to an extension of the bombing (once it had agreed to become informed of it) but, even after the Nixon-Kissinger administration had undertaken on Capitol Hill not to intensify the raids, there was a 21 percent increase of the bombing of Cambodia in the months July–August 1973. The Air Force maps of the targeted areas show them to be, or to have been, densely populated.

Colonel Sitton does recall, it must be admitted, that Kissinger requested that bombing avoid civilian casualties. His explicit motive in making this request was to avoid or forestall complaints from the government of Prince Sihanouk. But this does no more in itself than demonstrate that Kissinger was aware of the possibility of civilian deaths. If he knew enough to know of their likelihood, and was director of the policy that inflicted them, and neither enforced any actual precautions nor reprimanded any violators, then the case against him is legally and morally complete.

As early as the fall of 1970, an independent investigator named Fred Branfman, who spoke Lao and knew the country as a civilian volunteer, had gone to Bangkok and interviewed Jerome Brown, a former targeting officer for the United States embassy in the Laotian capital of Vientiane. The man had retired from the Air Force because of his disillusionment at the futility of the bombing and his consternation at the damage done to civilians and society. The speed and height of the planes, he said, meant that targets were virtually indistinguishable from the air. Pilots would often decide to drop bombs where craters already existed, and chose villages as targets because they could be more readily identified than alleged Pathet Lao guerrillas hiding in the jungle. Branfman, whom I interviewed in San Francisco in the summer of 2000, went on to provide this and other information to Henry Kamm and Sydney Schanberg of the *New York Times*, to Ted Koppel of ABC, and to many others. He also wrote up and published his findings in *Harper's* magazine, where they were not controverted by any authority. Under pressure from the US embassy, the Laotian authorities had Branfman deported back to the United States, which was probably, from their point of view, a mistake. He was able to make a dramatic appearance on Capitol Hill on 22 April 1971, at a hearing held by Senator Edward Kennedy's Senate Subcommittee on Refugees. His antagonist was the State Department's envoy William Sullivan, a former ambassador to Laos. Branfman accused him in front of the cameras of helping to conceal evidence that Laotian society was being mutilated by ferocious aerial bombardment.

Partly as a consequence, Congressman Pete McCloskey of California (a much-decorated veteran of the war in Korea) paid a visit to Laos and acquired a copy of an internal US embassy study of the bombing. He also prevailed on the US Air Force to furnish him with aerial photographs of the dramatic damage. Ambassador Sullivan was so disturbed by these pictures, some of them taken in areas known to him, that his first reaction was to establish to his own satisfaction that the raids had occurred after he left his post in Vientiane. (He was later to learn that, for his pains, his own telephone was being tapped at Henry Kissinger's instigation, one of the many such violations of American law that were to eventuate in the Watergate tapping-and-burglary scandal: a scandal that Kissinger was furthermore to plead— in an astounding outburst of vanity, deceit and self-deceit—as his own alibi for inattention in the Cyprus crisis.)

Having done what he could to bring the Laotian nightmare to the attention of those whose con-stitutional job it was to supervise such questions, Branfman went back to Thailand and from there to Phnom Penh, capital of Cambodia. Having gained access to a pilot's radio, he tape-recorded the con-versations between pilots on bombing missions over the Cambodian interior. On no occasion did they run any checks designed to reassure themselves and others that they were not bombing civilian targets. It had been definitely asserted, by named US govern-ment spokesmen, that such checks were run. Branf-man handed the tapes to Sydney Schanberg, whose *New York Times* report on them was printed just before the Senate met to prohibit further blitzing of Cambodia (the very resolution that was flouted by Kissinger the following month).

From there Branfman went back to Thailand and traveled north to Nakhorn Phanom, the new headquarters of the US Seventh Air Force. Here, a war room code-named "Blue Chip" served as the command and control center of the bombing campaign. Branfman, who is tall and well built, was able to pose as a new recruit just up from Saigon, and ultimately to gain access to the war room itself. Here, consoles and maps and screens plotted the progress of the bombardment. In conversation with the "bombing officer" on duty, he asked if pilots ever made contact before dropping their enormous loads of ordnance. Oh, yes, he was assured, they did. Worried about hitting the innocent? Oh, no—merely concerned about the whereabouts of CIA "ground teams" infiltrated into the area. Branfman's report on this, which was carried by Jack Anderson's syndicated column and also in the *Washington Monthly*, was likewise uncontroverted by any official denial.

One reason that the United States command in Southeast Asia finally ceased employing the crude and horrific tally of "body count" was that, as in the relatively small but specific case of Speedy Express cited above, the figures began to look ominous when they were counted up. Sometimes, totals of "enemy"

dead would turn out, when computed, to be suspiciously larger than the number of claimed "enemy"
in the field. Yet the war would somehow drag on,
with new quantitative goals being set and enforced.
Thus, according to the Pentagon, the following are
the casualty figures between the first Lyndon Johnson bombing halt in March 1968 and the same date
in 1972:

Americans	31,205
South Vietnamese regulars	86,101
"Enemy"	475,609

The US Senate Subcommittee on Refugees estimated that in the same four-year period rather more
than three million civilians were killed, injured or
rendered homeless. In the same four-year period, the
United States dropped almost 4,500,000 tons of high
explosive on Indochina. (The Pentagon's estimated
total for the tonnage dropped in the entire Second
World War is 2,044,000.) This total does not include
massive sprayings of chemical defoliants and pesticides, the effects of which are still being registered
by the region's ecology. Nor does it include the land-
mines which detonate to this day.

It is unclear how we count the murder or abduction of 35,708 Vietnamese civilians by the CIA's
counter-guerrilla "Phoenix program" during the

first two and a half years of the Nixon-Kissinger administration. There may be some "overlap." There is also some overlap with the actions of previous administrations in all cases. But the truly exorbitant death tolls all occurred on Henry Kissinger's watch, were known and understood by him, were concealed from Congress, the press and the public by him—at any rate to the best of his ability—and were, when questioned, the subject of political and bureaucratic vendettas ordered by him. They were also partly the outcome of a secretive and illegal process in Washington, unknown even to most cabinet members, of which Henry Kissinger stood to be, and became, a prime beneficiary.

On that closing point one may once again cite H.R. Haldeman, who had no further reason to lie and who had, by the time of his writing, paid for his crimes by serving a sentence in prison. Haldeman describes the moment in Florida when Kissinger was enraged by a *New York Times* story telling some part of the truth about Indochina:

> Henry telephoned J. Edgar Hoover in Washington from Key Biscayne on the May morning the *Times* story appeared.
>
> According to Hoover's memo of the call, Henry said the story used "secret information which was extraordinarily damaging." Henry went on to tell

Hoover that he "wondered whether I could make a major effort to find out where that came from . . . and to put whatever resources I need to find out who did this. I told him I would take care of this right away."

Henry was no fool, of course. He telephoned Hoover a few hours later to remind him that the investigation be handled discreetly "so no stories will get out." Hoover must have smiled, but said all right. And by five o'clock he was back on the telephone to Henry with the report that the *Times* reporter "may have gotten some of his information from the Southeast Asian desk of the Department of Defense's Public Affairs Office." More specifically, Hoover suggested the source could be a man named Mort Halperin (a Kissinger staffer) and another man who worked in the Systems Analysis Agency. . . . According to Hoover's memo, Kissinger hoped "I would follow it up as far as we can take it and they will destroy whoever did this if we can find him, no matter where he is."

The last line of that memo gives an accurate reflection of Henry's rage, as I remember it.

Nevertheless, Nixon was one hundred percent behind the wiretaps. And I was, too. And so the program started, inspired by Henry's rage but ordered by Nixon, who soon broadened it even further to include newsmen. Eventually, seventeen people were wiretapped by the FBI including seven on Kissinger's NSC staff and three on the White House staff.

And thus occurred the birth of the "plumbers" and of the assault on American law and democracy that they inaugurated. Commenting on the lamentable end of this process, Haldeman wrote that he still believed that ex-President Nixon (who was then still alive) should agree to the release of the remaining tapes. But:

> This time my view is apparently not shared by the man who was one reason for the original decision to start the taping process. Henry Kissinger is determined to stop the tapes from reaching the public....
>
> Nixon made the point that Kissinger was really the one who had the most to lose from the tapes becoming public. Henry apparently felt that the tapes would expose a lot of things he had said that would be very disadvantageous to him publicly.
>
> Nixon said that in making the deal for custody of his Presidential papers, which was originally announced after his pardon but then was shot down by Congress, it was Henry who called him and insisted on Nixon's right to destroy the tapes. That was, of course, the thing that destroyed the deal.

A society that has been "plumbed" has the right to demand that its plumbers be compelled to make some restitution by way of full disclosure. The litigation to put the Nixon tapes in the public trust is only partially complete; no truthful account of the Vietnam years will be complete until Kissinger's part in what we already know has been made fully transparent.

Until that time, Kissinger's role in the violation of American law at the close of the Vietnam war makes the perfect counterpart to the 1968 covert action that helped him to power in the first place. The two parentheses enclose a series of premeditated war crimes which still have power to stun the imagination.

4

Bangladesh: One Genocide, One Coup and One Assassination

The annals of American diplomacy contain many imperishable pages of humanism, which may, and should, be set against some of the squalid and dispiriting traffic recorded in these pages. One might cite the extraordinary 1915 dispatches of Ambassador Henry Morgenthau from his post in Ottoman Turkey, in which he employed consular and intelligence reports to give a picture of the deliberate state massacre of the Armenian minority, the first genocide of the twentieth century. (The word "genocide" having not then been coined, Ambassador Morgenthau had recourse to the—in some ways more expressive—term "race murder.")

By 1971, the word "genocide" was all too easily understood. It surfaced in a cable of protest from the United States consulate in what was then East

Pakistan—the Bengali "wing" of the Muslim state of
Pakistan, known to its restive nationalist inhabitants
by the name Bangladesh. The cable was written on 6
April 1971 and its senior signatory, the Consul General in Dacca, was named Archer Blood. But it might
have become known as the Blood Telegram in any
case. Also sent directly to Washington, it differed
from Morgenthau's document in one respect. It was
not so much reporting on genocide as denouncing
the complicity of the United States government in
genocide. Its main section read thus:

> Our government has failed to denounce the sup-
> pression of democracy. Our government has failed
> to denounce atrocities. Our government has failed
> to take forceful measures to protect its citizens
> while at the same time bending over backward to
> placate the West Pak[istan] dominated government
> and to lessen any deservedly negative international
> public relations impact against them. Our govern-
> ment has evidenced what many will consider moral
> bankruptcy, ironically at a time when the USSR
> sent President Yahya Khan a message defending
> democracy, condemning the arrest of a leader of a
> democratically elected majority party, incidentally
> pro-West, and calling for an end to repressive mea-
> sures and bloodshed.... But we have chosen not to
> intervene, even morally, on the grounds that the

Awami conflict, *in which unfortunately the overworked term genocide is applicable*, is purely an internal matter of a sovereign state. Private Americans have expressed disgust. We, as professional civil servants, express our dissent with current policy and fervently hope that our true and lasting interests here can be defined and our policies redirected.

This was signed by twenty members of the United States diplomatic team in Bangladesh and, on its arrival at the State Department, by a further nine senior officers in the South Asia division. It was the most public and the most strongly worded demarche from State Department servants to the State Department that has ever been recorded.

The circumstances fully warranted the protest. In December 1970, the Pakistani military elite had permitted the first open elections for a decade. The vote was easily won by Sheik Mujibur Rahman, the leader of the Bengali-based Awami League, who gained a large overall majority in the proposed National Assembly. (In the East alone, it won 167 out of 169 seats.) This, among other things, meant a challenge to the political and military and economic hegemony of the Western "wing." The National Assembly had been scheduled to meet on 3 March 1971. On 1 March, General Yahya Khan, head of the supposedly outgoing military regime, postponed its convening.

This resulted in mass protests and nonviolent civil disobedience in the East.

On 25 March, the Pakistani army struck at the Bengali capital of Dacca. Having arrested and kidnapped Rahman, and taken him to West Pakistan, it set about massacring his supporters. The foreign press had been preemptively expelled from the city, but much of the direct evidence of what then happened was provided via a radio transmitter operated by the United States consulate. Archer Blood himself supplied an account of one episode directly to the State Department and to Henry Kissinger's National Security Council. Having readied the ambush, Pakistani regular soldiers set fire to the women's dormitory at the university, and then mowed the occupants down with machine guns as they sought to escape. (The guns, along with all the other weaponry, had been furnished under United States military assistance programs.)

Other reports, since amply vindicated, were supplied to the London *Times* and *Sunday Times* by the courageous reporter Anthony Mascarenhas, and flashed around a horrified world. Rape, murder, dismemberment and the state murder of children were employed as deliberate methods of repression and intimidation. At least ten thousand civilians were butchered in the first three days. The eventual civilian death toll has never been placed at less than

half a million and has been put as high as three million. Since almost all Hindu citizens were at risk by
definition from Pakistani military chauvinism (not
that Pakistan's Muslim coreligionists were spared),
a vast movement of millions of refugees—perhaps
as many as ten million—began to cross the Indian
frontier. To summarize, then: first, the direct negation of a democratic election; second, the unleashing of a genocidal policy; third, the creation of a very
dangerous international crisis. Within a short time,
Ambassador Kenneth Keating, the ranking United
States diplomat in New Delhi, had added his voice to
those of the dissenters. It was a time, he told Washington, when a principled stand against the authors
of this aggression and atrocity would also make the
best pragmatic sense. Keating, a former senator
from New York, used a very suggestive phrase in his
cable of 29 March 1971, calling on the administration to "promptly, publicly, and prominently deplore
this brutality." It was "most important these actions
be taken now," he warned, "prior to inevitable and
imminent emergence of horrible truths."

Nixon and Kissinger acted quickly. That is to
say, Archer Blood was immediately recalled from
his post, and Ambassador Keating was described
by the President to Kissinger, with some contempt,
as having been "taken over by the Indians." In late
April 1971, at the very height of the mass murder,

Kissinger sent a message to General Yahya Khan, thanking him for his "delicacy and tact."

We now know of one reason why the general was so favored, at a time when he had made himself—and his patrons—responsible for the grossest war crimes and crimes against humanity. In April 1971, a United States ping-pong team had accepted a surprise invitation to compete in Beijing and by the end of that month, using the Pakistani ambassador as an intermediary, the Chinese authorities had forwarded a letter inviting Nixon to send an envoy. Thus there was one motive of realpolitik for the shame that Nixon and Kissinger were to visit on their own country for its complicity in the extermination of the Bengalis.

Those who like to plead realpolitik, however, might wish to consider some further circumstances. There already was, and had been for some time, a back channel between Washington and Beijing. It ran through Nicolae Ceausescu's Romania—not a much more decorative choice but not, at that stage, a positively criminal one. There was no reason to confine approaches, to a serious person like Chou En Lai, to the narrow channel afforded by a blood-soaked (and short-lived, as it turned out) despot like the "delicate and tactful" Yahya Khan. Either Chou En Lai wanted contact, in other words, or he did not. As Lawrence Lifschultz, the primary historian of this period, has put it:

Winston Lord, Kissinger's deputy at the National
Security Council, stressed to investigators the internal rationalization developed within the upper ech-
elons of the Administration. Lord told [the staff of
the Carnegie Endowment for International Peace]
"We had to demonstrate to China we were a reliable
government to deal with. We had to show China
that we respect a mutual friend." How, after two
decades of belligerent animosity with the People's
Republic, mere support for Pakistan in its bloody
civil war was supposed to demonstrate to China that
the US "was a reliable government to deal with"
was a mystifying proposition which more cynical observers of the events, both in and outside the
US government, consider to have been an excuse
justifying the simple convenience of the Islamabad
link—a link which Washington had no overriding
desire to shift.

Second, the knowledge of this secret diplomacy
and its accompanying privileges obviously freed the
Pakistani general of such restraints as might have
inhibited him. He told his closest associates, including his minister of information, G.W. Choudhury,
that his private understanding with Washington and
Beijing would protect him. Choudhury later wrote:
"If Nixon and Kissinger had not given him that
false hope, he'd have been more realistic." Thus, the

collusion with him in the matter of China *increases* the direct complicity of Nixon and Kissinger in the massacres. (There is another consideration outside the scope of this book, which involves the question: why did Kissinger confine his China diplomacy to channels provided by authoritarian or totalitarian regimes? Why was an open diplomacy not just as easy, if not easier? The answer—which also lies outside the scope of this book—is apparently that surreptitiousness, while not essential in itself, was essential if Nixon and Kissinger were going to be able to take the credit for it.)

It cannot possibly be argued, in any case, that the saving of Kissinger's private correspondence with China was worth the deliberate sacrifice of hundreds of thousands of Bengali civilians. And—which is worse still—later and fuller disclosures now allow us to doubt that this was indeed the whole motive. The Kissinger policy toward Bangladesh may well have been largely conducted for its own sake, as a means of gratifying his boss's animus against India and as a means of preventing the emergence of Bangladesh as a self-determining state in any case.

The diplomatic commonplace term "tilt"—signifying that mixture of signals and nuances and codes that describe a foreign policy preference that is often too embarrassing to be openly avowed—actually originates in this dire episode. On 6 March 1971,

Kissinger summoned a meeting at the National Security Council and—*in advance of* the crisis in East–West Pakistan relations that was by then palpable and predictable to those attending—insisted that no preemptive action be taken. Those present who suggested that a warning to General Yahya Khan be issued, essentially advising him to honor the election results, he strongly opposed. His subsequent policy was as noted above. After returning from China in July, he began to speak in almost Maoist phrases about a Soviet-Indian plot to dismember and even annex part of Pakistan, which would compel China to intervene on Pakistan's side. (In pursuit of this fantasy of confrontation, he annoyed Admiral Elmo Zumwalt by ordering him to dispatch the aircraft carrier USS *Enterprise* from the coast of Vietnam to the Bay of Bengal, while giving it no stated mission.) But no analyst in the State Department or the CIA could be found to underwrite such a bizarre prediction and, at a meeting of the Senior Review Group, Kissinger lost his temper with this insubordination. "The President always says to tilt toward Pakistan, but every proposal I get is in the opposite direction. Sometimes I think I'm in a nuthouse." The Nixon White House was, as it happens, in the process of becoming exactly that, but his hearers only had time to notice that a new power-term had entered Washington's vernacular of crisis and conspiracy.

"The President always says to tilt toward Pakistan." That at least was true. Long before any conception of his "China diplomacy," indeed even during the years when he was inveighing against "Red China" and its sympathizers, Nixon detested the government of India and expressed warm sympathy for Pakistan. Many of his biographers and intimates, including Kissinger, have recorded the particular dislike he felt (more justifiably, perhaps) for the person of Indira Gandhi. He always referred to her as "that bitch" and on one occasion kept her waiting for an unprecedented forty-five minutes outside his White House door. However, the dislike originated with Nixon's loathing for her father Pandit Nehru, and with his more general loathing for Nehru's sponsorship—along with Makarios, Tito and Soekarno—of the Non-Aligned Movement. There can be no doubt that, with or without an occluded "China card," General Yahya Khan would have enjoyed a sympathetic hearing, and treatment, from this president, and thus from this national security advisor.

This is also strongly suggested by Kissinger's subsequent conduct, as Secretary of State, toward Bangladesh as a country and toward Sheik Mujib, leader of the Awami League and later the father of Bangladeshi independence, as a politician. Unremitting hostility and contempt were the signature elements in both cases. Kissinger had received some very bad and even mocking press for his handling of the Bangladesh crisis, and it had somewhat spoiled his supposedly finest hour in China. He came to resent the Bangladeshis and their leader, and even compared (this according to his then aide Roger Morris) Mujib to Allende.

As soon as Kissinger became Secretary of State in 1973, he downgraded all those who had signed the genocide protest in 1971. In the fall of the next year, 1974, he inflicted a series of snubs on Mujib, then on his first visit to the United States as head of state. In Washington, Kissinger boycotted the fifteen-minute meeting that Mujib was allowed by President Ford. He also opposed Mujib's main request, which was for emergency United States grain shipments, and some help with debt relief, in order to recuperate the country so ravaged by Kissinger's friend and ally. To cite Roger Morris again: "In Kissinger's view there was very much a distant hands-off attitude toward them. Since they had the audacity to become independent of one of my client states, they will damn well float on their own for a while." It was at about this time that Kissinger was heard to pronounce Bangladesh "an international basket case," a judgment which, to the extent that it was true, was also self-fulfilling.

In November 1974, on a brief face-saving tour of the region, Kissinger made an eight-hour stop in Bangladesh and gave a three-minute press conference in which he refused to say why he had sent the USS *Enterprise* into the Bay of Bengal three years before. Within a few weeks of his departure, we now know, a faction at the US embassy in Dacca began covertly meeting with a group of Bangladeshi officers who were planning a coup against Mujib. On 14 August 1975, Mujib and forty members of his family were murdered in a military takeover. His closest former political associates were bayoneted to death in their prison cells a few months after that.*

The Senate Foreign Relations Committee was at that time conducting its sensational inquiries into CIA involvement with assassinations and subversion in the Third World. The "two-track" concept, whereby an American ambassador like Ed Korry in Chile could find that his intelligence officers and military attachés were going behind his back and over his head, with secret authorizations from Washington, and running their own show, had not become a familiar one. However, exhaustive research by Lawrence Lifschultz of Yale University now strongly suggests that a "two-track" scheme was implemented in Bangladesh as well.

---

*In December 2000 those responsible were convicted by a Bangladeshi court and (wrongly, in my opinion) sentenced to death. Some of the accused were unavailable for sentencing because they had taken refuge in the United States: a feat not achievable by the average Bengali immigrant.

The man installed as Bangladesh's president by the young officers who had slain Rahman was Khondakar Mustaque, generally identified as the leader of the right-wing element within the Awami League. He was at pains to say that the coup had come to him as a complete surprise, and that the young majors who had led it—Major Farooq, Major Rashid and four others, at the head of a detachment numbering just three hundred men—had "acted on their own." He added that he had never met the mutinous officers before. Such denials are of course customary, almost matters of etiquette. So are the ensuing statements from Washington, which invariably claim that this or that political upheaval has taken the world's largest and most powerful intelligence-gathering system completely off guard. That expected statement, too, was made in the aftermath of the assassination in Dacca.

The cover story (one might term it the coincidence version) leaks at every joint and comes apart at the most cursory inspection. Major Rashid was interviewed by Anthony Mascarenhas, the journalistic hero of the Bangladesh war, on the anniversary of the coup. He confirmed that he had met Mustaque before the coup, and again on the days immediately preceding it. In fact, a senior Bangladeshi officer has dated meetings between Mustaque and the mutineers more than six months before Mujib's overthrow.

The United States ambassador in Dacca, Davis Eugene Boster, was aware that a coup was being discussed. He was also aware of the highly controversial congressional hearings in Washington, which had unveiled high-level official wrongdoing and ruined the career of many a careless foreign service officer. He ordered that all contact between his embassy and the mutinous officers be terminated. Thus his alarm and annoyance, on 14 August 1975, was great. The men who had seized power were the very ones with whom he had ordered a cessation of contact. Embassy sources have since confirmed to Lifschultz (a) that United States officials had been approached by, and had by no means discouraged, the officers who intended a coup and (b) that Ambassador Boster became convinced that his CIA station was operating a back channel without his knowledge. Such an operation would be meaningless, and also pointlessly risky, if it did not extend homeward to Washington where, as is now notorious, the threads of the Forty Committee and the National Security Council were very closely held in one fist.

Philip Cherry, the then head of the CIA station in Bangladesh, was interviewed by Lifschultz in September 1978. He was vague and evasive even about having held the job but did say, "There is one thing. There are politicians who frequently approach embassies, and perhaps have contacts there. They

think they may have contacts." The shift from officer to politician is suggestive. And, of course, those
who think they may have contacts may even act as if
they do, unless they are otherwise advised.

Not only did Khondakar Mustaque *think* he had
contacts with the United States government, including with Henry Kissinger himself, but he did indeed
have such contacts, and had had since 1971. In 1973
in Washington, and in the aftermath of the unprecedented revolt of professional diplomats against
the Kissinger policy in Bangladesh, the Carnegie
Endowment for International Peace (publisher of the
magazine *Foreign Policy*) conducted a full-dress study
of the "tilt" that had put the United States on the
same side as those committing genocide. More than
150 senior officials from the State Department and
the CIA agreed to be interviewed. The study was
coordinated by Kissinger's former aide Roger Morris. The result of the nine-month inquiry was never
made public, due to internal differences at Carnegie,
but the material was made available to Lifschultz and
it does establish one conclusion beyond doubt.

In 1971 Henry Kissinger had attempted the
impossible by trying to divide the electorally victo-
rious Awami League, and to dilute its demand for
independence. In pursuit of this favor to General
Yahya Khan, he had initiated a covert approach to
Khondakar Mustaque, who led the tiny minority

who were willing to compromise on the main principle. A recently unearthed "Memorandum for the Record" gives us details of a White House meeting between Nixon, Kissinger and others on 11 August 1971, at which Under Secretary of State John Irwin reported: "We have had reports in recent days of the possibility that some Awami League leaders in Calcutta want to negotiate with Yahya on the basis of giving up their claim for the independence of East Pakistan." This can only have been a reference to the Provisional Government of Bangladesh, set up in exile in Calcutta after the massacres, and could only have been an attempt to circumvent its leadership. The consequences of this clumsy approach were that Mustaque was exposed and placed under house arrest in October 1971, and that the American political officer who contacted him, George Griffin, was declared *persona non grata* when gazetted to the US embassy in New Delhi a decade later.

Those involved in the military preparations for the coup have told Lifschultz that they, too, had a "two-track" policy. There were junior officers ready to mutiny and there was a senior officer—the future dictator General Zia—who was ready but more hesitant. Both factions say that they naturally checked with their United States contacts in advance, and were told that the overthrow of Mujib was "no problem." This is at least partially confirmed by a signed letter from Congressman Stephen J. Solarz of the House Foreign Affairs Committee, who undertook to investigate the matter for Lifschultz in 1980 and who on 3 June of that year wrote to him: "With respect to the Embassy meetings in the November 1974–January 1975 period with opponents of the Rahman regime, the State Department once again does not deny that the meetings took place." This would appear to be a rebuff to the evidence of Mr. Cherry of the CIA, even if the letter goes on to say: "The Department does claim that it notified Rahman about the meetings, including the possibility of a coup." If true, that "claim" is being made for the first time, and in the name of the man who was murdered during the coup and cannot refute it. The admission is stronger than the claim in any case.

Congressman Solarz forwarded the questions about CIA involvement to the office of Congressman Les Aspin of the Permanent Select Committee on Intelligence, which committee, as he said, "has the best chance of obtaining access both to CIA cable traffic and to the relevant figures in the intelligence community." But the letter he sent was somehow lost along the way, and was never received by the relevant inquiring committee, and shortly afterward the balance of power in Washington shifted from Carter to Reagan.

Only a reopened congressional inquiry with subpoena power could determine whether there was any direct connection, apart from the self-evident ones of consistent statecraft attested by recurring reliable testimony, between the secret genocidal diplomacy of 1971 and the secret destabilizing diplomacy of 1975. The task of disproving such a connection, meanwhile, would appear to rest on those who believe that everything is an accident.

5

Chile

In a famous expression of his contempt for democracy, Kissinger once observed that he saw no reason why a certain country should be allowed to "go Marxist" merely because "its people are irresponsible." The country concerned was Chile, which at the time of this remark had a justified reputation as the most highly evolved pluralistic democracy in the southern hemisphere of the Americas. The pluralism translated, in the years of the Cold War, into an electorate that voted about one-third conservative, one-third socialist and communist, and one-third Christian Democratic and centrist. This had made it relatively easy to keep the Marxist element from having its turn in government, and ever since 1962 the CIA had—as it had in Italy and other comparable nations—largely contented itself with funding the reliable elements. In September 1970, however, the Left's candidate actually gained a slight plurality of 36.2 percent in the presidential elections.

Divisions on the Right, and the adherence of some smaller radical and Christian parties to the Left, made it a moral certainty that the Chilean Congress would, after the traditional sixty-day interregnum, confirm Dr. Salvador Allende as the next president. But the very name of Allende was anathema to the extreme Right in Chile, to certain powerful corporations (notably ITT, Pepsi Cola and the Chase Manhattan Bank) which did business in Chile and the United States, and to the CIA.

This loathing quickly communicated itself to President Nixon. He was personally beholden to Donald Kendall, the President of Pepsi Cola, who had given him his first corporate account when, as a young lawyer, he had joined John Mitchell's New York firm. A series of Washington meetings, held within eleven days of Allende's electoral victory, essentially settled the fate of Chilean democracy. After discussions with Kendall and with David Rockefeller of Chase Manhattan, and with CIA director Richard Helms, Kissinger went with Helms to the Oval Office. Helms's notes of the meeting show that Nixon wasted little breath in making his wishes known. Allende was not to assume office. "Not concerned risks involved. No involvement of embassy. $10,000,000 available, more if necessary. Full-time job—best men we have....Make the economy scream. 48 hours for plan of action."

Declassified documents show that Kissinger—who had previously neither known nor cared about Chile, describing it offhandedly as "a dagger pointed at the heart of Antarctica"—took seriously this chance to impress his boss. A group was set up in Langley, Virginia, with the express purpose of running a "two-track" policy for Chile: one the ostensible diplomatic one and the other—unknown to the State Department or the US ambassador to Chile, Edward Korry—a strategy of destabilization, kidnap and assassination, designed to provoke a military coup.

There were long- and short-term obstacles to the incubation of such an intervention, especially in the brief interval available before Allende took his oath of office. The long-term obstacle was the tradition of military abstention from politics in Chile, a tradition which marked off the country from its neighbors. Such a military culture was not to be degraded overnight. The short-term obstacle lay in the person of one man—General René Schneider. As chief of the Chilean General Staff, he was adamantly opposed to any military meddling in the electoral process. Accordingly, it was decided at a meeting on 18 September 1970 that General Schneider had to go.

The plan was to have him kidnapped by extremist officers, in such a way as to make it appear that leftist and pro-Allende elements were behind the plot. The resulting confusion, it was hoped, would panic the Chilean Congress into denying Allende the presidency. A sum of $50,000 was offered around the Chilean capital, Santiago, for any officer or officers enterprising enough to take on this task. Richard Helms and his director of covert operations, Thomas Karamessines, told Kissinger that they were not optimistic. Military circles were hesitant and divided, or else loyal to General Schneider and the Chilean constitution. As Helms put it in a later account of the conversation, "We tried to make clear to Kissinger how small the possibility of success was." Kissinger firmly told Helms and Karamessines to press on in any case.

Here one must pause for a recapitulation. An unelected official in the United States is meeting with others, without the knowledge or authorization of Congress, to plan the kidnapping of a constitution-minded senior officer in a democratic country with which the United States is not at war, and with which it maintains cordial diplomatic relations. The minutes of the meetings may have an official look to them (though they were hidden from the light of day for long enough) but what we are reviewing is a "hit"—a piece of state-supported terrorism.

Ambassador Korry has testified that he told his embassy staff to have nothing to do with a group styling itself *Patria y Libertad* (Fatherland and Free-dom), a quasi-fascist group intent on defying the election results. He sent three cables to Washington warning his superiors to have nothing to do with them either. He was unaware that his own military attachés had been told to contact the group and keep the fact from him. And when the outgoing presi-dent of Chile, the Christian Democrat Eduardo Frei, announced that he was opposed to any US interven-tion and would vote to confirm the legally elected Allende, it was precisely to this gang that Kissinger turned. On 15 October 1970, Kissinger was told of an extremist right-wing officer named General Roberto Viaux, who had ties to *Patria y Libertad* and who was willing to accept the secret US commission to remove General Schneider from the chessboard. The term "kidnap" was still being employed at this point, and is often employed still. However, Kissinger's Track Two group authorized the supply of machine guns as well as tear gas grenades to Viaux's associates, and never seems to have asked what they would do with the general once they had kidnapped him.

Let the documents tell the story. A CIA cable to Kissinger's Track Two group from Santiago dated 18 October 1970 reads (with the names still blacked out for "security" purposes and cover identities written in by hand—in my square brackets—by the ever-thoughtful redaction service):

1. [Station cooptee] met clandestinely evening 17 Oct with [two Chilean armed forces officers] who told him their plans were moving along better than had thought possible. They asked that by evening 18 Oct [cooptee] arrange furnish them with eight to ten tear gas grenades. Within 48 hours they need three 45 calibre machine guns ("grease guns") with 500 rounds ammo each. [One officer] commented has three machine guns himself but can be identified by serial numbers as having been issued to him therefore unable use them.

2. [Officers] said they have to move because they believe they now under suspicion and being watched by Allende supporters. [One officer] was late to meeting having taken evasive action to shake possible surveillance by one or two taxi cabs with dual antennas which he believed being used by opposition against him.

3. [Cooptee] asked if [officers] had Air Force contacts. They answered they did not but would welcome one. [Cooptee] separately has since tried contact [a Chilean Air Force General] and will keep trying until established. Will urge [Air Force General] meet with [other two officers] a.s.a.p. [Cooptee] commented to station that [Air Force General] has not tried contact him since ref a talk.

4. [Cooptee] comment: cannot tell who is leader of this movement but strongly suspects it is

Admiral [Deleted]. It would appear from [his contact's] actions and alleged Allende suspicions about them that unless they act now they are lost. Trying get more info from them evening 18 Oct about support they believe they have.

5. Station plans give six tear gas grenades (arriving noon 18 Oct by special courier) to [cooptee] for delivery to [armed forces officers] instead of having [false flag officer] deliver them to Viaux group. Our reasoning is that [cooptee] dealing with active duty officers. Also [false flag officer] leaving evening 18 Oct and will not be replaced but [cooptee] will stay here. Hence important that [cooptee] credibility with [armed forces officers] be strengthened by prompt delivery what they requesting. Request headquarters agreement by 1500 hours local time 18 Oct on decision delivery of tear gas to [cooptee] vice [false flag officer].

6. Request prompt shipment three sterile 45 calibre machine guns and ammo per para 1 above, by special courier if necessary. Please confirm by 2000 hours local time 18 Oct that this can be done so [cooptee] may inform his contacts accordingly.

The reply, which is headed "IMMEDIATE SANTIAGO (EYES ONLY [DELETED])" is dated 18 October and reads:

Sub-machine guns and ammo being sent by regular [deleted] courier leaving Washington 0700 hours 19 October due arrive Santiago late evening 20 October or early morning 21 October. Preferred use regular [deleted] courier to avoid bringing undue attention to op.

A companion message, also addressed to "Santiago 562," went like this:

1. Depending how [cooptee] conversation goes evening 18 October you may wish submit Intel report [deleted] so we can decide whether should be dissemed.

2. New subject. If [cooptee] plans lead coup, or be actively and publicly involved, we puzzled why it should bother him if machine guns can be traced to him. Can we develop rationale on why guns must be sterile? Will continue make effort provide them but find our credulity stretched by Navy [officer] leading his troops with sterile guns? What is special purpose for these guns? We will try send them whether you can provide explanation or not.

The full beauty of this cable traffic cannot be appreciated without a reading of another message, dated 16 October. (It must be borne in mind that the

Chilean Congress was to meet to confirm Allende as president on the 24th of that month.)

1. [Deleted/handwritten code name Trickturn] policy, objectives and actions were reviewed at high USG [United States Government] level afternoon 15 October. Conclusions, which are to be your operational guide, follow:

2. It is firm and continuing policy that Allende be overthrown by a coup. It would be much preferable to have this transpire prior to 24 October but efforts in this regard will continue vigorously beyond this date. We are to continue to generate maximum pressure toward this end utilizing every appropriate resource. *It is imperative that these actions be implemented clandestinely and securely so that the USG and American hand be well hidden.* [italics added] While this imposes on us a high degree of selectivity in making military contacts and dictates that these contacts be made in the most secure manner it definitely does not preclude contacts such as reported in Santiago 544 which was a masterful piece of work.

3. After the most careful consideration it was determined that a Viaux coup attempt carried out by him alone with the forces now at his disposal would fail. Thus, it would be counterproductive to our [deleted; handwritten insert "Track Two"]

objectives. It was decided that [deleted; handwritten insert "CIA"] get a message to Viaux warning him against precipitate action. In essence our message is to state, "We have reviewed your plans, and based on your information and ours, we come to the conclusion that your plans for a coup at this time cannot succeed. Failing, they may reduce your capabilities for the future. Preserve your assets. We will stay in touch. The time will come when you together with all your other friends can do something. You will continue to have our support." You are requested to deliver the message to Viaux essentially as noted above. Our objectives are as follows: (A) To advise him of our opinion and discourage him from acting alone; (B) Continue to encourage him to amplify his planning; (C) Encourage him to join forces with other coup planners so that they may act in concert either before or after 24 October. (N.B. Six gas masks and six CS cannisters [*sic*] are being carried to Santiago by special [deleted] courier ETD Washington 1100 hours 16 October.)

4. There is great and continuing interest in the activities of Tirado, Canales, Valenzuela et al and we wish them maximum good fortune.

5. The above is your operating guidance. No other policy guidance you may receive from [indecipherable: State?] or its maximum exponent in Santiago, on his return, are to sway you from your course.

6. Please review all your present and possibly new activities to include propaganda, black operations, surfacing of intelligence or disinformation, personal contacts, or anything else your imagination can conjure which will permit you to press forward our [deleted] objective in a secure manner.

Finally, it is essential to read the White House "memorandum of conversation," dated 15 October 1970, to which the above cable directly refers and of which it is a more honest summary. Present for the "high USG level" meeting were, as noted in the heading: "Dr. Kissinger, Mr. Karamessines, Gen. Haig." The first paragraph of their deliberations has been entirely blacked out, with not so much as a scribble in the margin from the redaction service. (Given what has since been admitted, this twenty-line deletion must be well worth reading.) Picking up at paragraph two, we find the following:

2. Then Mr. Karamessines provided a run-down on Viaux, the Canales meeting with Tirado, the latter's new position [after Porta was relieved of command "for health reasons"] and, in some detail, the general situation in Chile from the coup possibility viewpoint.
3. A certain amount of information was available to us concerning Viaux's alleged support throughout

the Chilean military. We had assessed Viaux's claims carefully, basing our analysis on good intelligence from a number of sources. Our conclusion was clear: Viaux did not have more than one chance in twenty—perhaps less—to launch a successful coup.

4. The unfortunate repercussions, in Chile and internationally, of an unsuccessful coup were discussed. Dr. Kissinger ticked off his list of these negative possibilities. His items were remarkably similar to the ones Mr. Karamessines had prepared.

5. It was decided by those present that the Agency must get a message to Viaux warning him against any precipitate action. In essence our message was to state: "We have reviewed your plans, and based on your information and ours, we come to the conclusion that your plans for a coup at this time cannot succeed. Failing, they may reduce your capabilities for the future. Preserve your assets. We will stay in touch. The time will come when you with all your other friends can do something. You will continue to have our support."

6. After the decision to de-fuse the Viaux coup plot, *at least temporarily*, Dr. Kissinger instructed Mr. Karamessines to preserve Agency assets in Chile, working clandestinely and securely to maintain the capability for Agency operations against Allende in the future.

7. Dr. Kissinger discussed his desire that the word of our encouragement to the Chilean military in recent weeks be kept as secret as possible. Mr Karamessines stated emphatically that we had been doing everything possible in this connection, including the use of false flag officers, car meetings and every conceivable precaution. But we and others had done a great deal of talking recently with a number of persons. For example, Ambassador Korry's wideranging discussions with numerous people urging a coup "cannot be put back into the bottle". [Three lines of deletion follow.] (Dr. Kissinger requested that copy of the message be sent to him on 16 October.)

8. The meeting concluded on Dr. Kissinger's note that the Agency should continue keeping the pressure on every Allende weak spot in sight: - now, after the 24th of October, after 5 November, and into the future until such time as new marching orders are given. Mr. Karamessines stated that the Agency would comply.

So Track Two contained two tracks of its own. Track Two/One was the group of ultras led by General Roberto Viaux and his sidekick Captain Arturo Marshal. These men had tried to bring off a coup in 1969 against the Christian Democrats; they had been cashiered and were disliked even by conservatives in the officer corps. "Track Two/Two" was a more ostensibly "respectable" faction headed by General Camilo Valenzuela, the chief of the garrison in the capital city, whose name occurs in the cables above and whose identity is concealed by some of the deletions. Several of the CIA operatives in Chile felt that Viaux was too much of a mad-dog to be trusted. And Ambassador Korry's repeated admonitions also had their effect. As shown in the 15 October memo cited above, Kissinger and Karamessines developed last-minute second thoughts about Viaux, who as late as 13 October had been given $20,000 in cash from the CIA station and promised a life insurance policy of $250,000. This offer was authorized direct from the White House. However, with only days to go before Allende was inaugurated, and with Nixon repeating that "it was absolutely essential that the election of Mr. Allende to the Presidency be thwarted," the pressure on the Valenzuela group became intense. As a direct consequence, especially after the warm words of encouragement he had been given, General Roberto Viaux felt himself under some obligation to deliver also, and to disprove those who had doubted him.

On the evening of 19 October 1970, the Valenzuela group, aided by some of Viaux's gang, and equipped with the tear gas grenades delivered by the CIA, attempted to grab General Schneider as he left an official dinner. The attempt failed because he left in a private car and not the expected official vehicle.

The failure produced an extremely significant cable from CIA headquarters in Washington to the local station, asking for urgent action because "Headquarters must respond during morning 20 October to queries from high levels." Payments of $50,000 each to General Viaux and his chief associate were then authorized on condition that they made another attempt. On the evening of 20 October, they did. But again there was only failure to report. On 22 October, the "sterile" machine guns above-mentioned were handed to Valenzuela's group for another try. Later that same day, General Roberto Viaux's gang finally murdered General René Schneider.

According to the later verdict of the Chilean military courts, this atrocity partook of elements of both tracks of Track Two. In other words, Valenzuela was not himself on the scene but the assassination squad, led by Viaux, contained men who had participated in the preceding two attempts. Viaux was convicted on charges of kidnapping and of conspiring to cause a coup. Valenzuela was convicted of the charge of conspiracy to cause a coup. So any subsequent attempt to distinguish the two plots from each other, except in point of degree, is an attempt to confect a distinction without a difference.

It scarcely matters whether Schneider was slain because of a kidnapping scheme that went awry (he was said, but only by the assassins, to have had the temerity to resist) or whether his assassination was the objective in the first place. The Chilean military police report, as it happens, describes a straightforward murder. Under the law of every law-bound country (including the United States), a crime committed in the pursuit of a kidnapping is thereby aggravated, not mitigated. You may not say, with a corpse at your feet, "I was only trying to kidnap him." At least, you may not say so if you hope to plead extenuating circumstances.

Yet a version of "extenuating circumstances" has become the paper-thin cover story with which Kissinger has since protected himself from the charge of being an accomplice, before and after the fact, in kidnap and murder. And this sorry cover story has even found a refuge in the written record. The Senate Intelligence Committee, in its investigation of the matter, concluded that since the machine guns supplied to Valenzuela had not actually been employed in the killing, and since General Viaux had been officially discouraged by the CIA a few days before the murder, there was therefore "no evidence of a plan to kill Schneider or that United States officials specifically anticipated that Schneider would be shot during the abduction."

Walter Isaacson, one of Kissinger's biographers, takes at face value a memo from Kissinger to Nixon after his meeting on 15 October with Karamessines, in which he reports to the President that he had "turned off" the Viaux plot. He also takes at face value the claim that Viaux's successful hit was essentially unauthorized.

These excuses and apologies are as logically feeble as they are morally contemptible. Henry Kissinger bears direct responsibility for the Schneider murder, as the following points demonstrate.

1. Brian MacMaster, one of the "false flag" agents mentioned in the cable traffic above, a career CIA man carrying a forged Colombian passport and claiming to represent American business interests in Chile, has told of his efforts to get "hush money" to jailed members of the Viaux group, *after* the assassination and before they could implicate the Agency.
2. Colonel Paul M. Wimert, a military attaché in Santiago and chief CIA liaison with the Valenzuela faction, has testified that after the Schneider killing he hastily retrieved the two payments of $50,000 that had been paid to Valenzuela and his partner, and also the three "sterile" machine guns. He then drove rapidly to the Chilean seaside town of Vina del Mar and hurled the guns into the ocean. His accomplice in this action, CIA station chief Henry Hecksher, had assured Washington only days before that *either* Viaux or Valenzuela would be able to eliminate Schneider and thereby trigger a coup.

3. Look again at the White House/Kissinger memo of 15 October, and at the doggedly literal way it is retransmitted to Chile. In no sense of the term does it "turn off" Viaux. If anything, it incites him—a well-known and boastful fanatic—to redouble his efforts. "Preserve your assets. We will stay in touch. The time will come when you together with all your other friends can do something. You will continue to have our support." This is not exactly the language of standing him down. The remainder of the memo speaks plainly of the intention to "discourage him from acting *alone*," to "continue to *encourage* him to amplify his planning" and to "*encourage* him to join forces with other coup planners so that they may act in concert either before or after 24 October" (italics added). The last three stipulations are an entirely accurate, not to say prescient, description of what Viaux actually did.

4. Consult again the cable received by Henry Hecksher on 20 October, referring to anxious queries "from high levels" about the first of the failed attacks on Schneider. Thomas Karamessines, when questioned by the Senate Intelligence Committee about this cable, testified of his certainty that the words "high levels" referred directly to Kissinger. In all previous communications from Washington, as a glance above will show, that had indeed been the case. This on its own is enough to demolish

Kissinger's claim to have "turned off" Track Two (and its interior tracks) on 15 October.

5. Ambassador Korry later made the obvious point that Kissinger was attempting to build a paper alibi in the event of a failure by the Viaux group. "His interest was not in Chile but in who was going to be blamed for what. He wanted me to be the one who took the heat. Henry didn't want to be associated with a failure and he was setting up a record to blame the State Department. He brought me in to the President because he wanted me to say what I had to say about Viaux; he wanted me to be the soft man."

The concept of "deniability" was not as well understood in Washington in 1970 as it has since become. But it is clear that Henry Kissinger wanted two things simultaneously. He wanted the removal of General Schneider, by any means and employing any proxy. (No instruction from Washington to leave Schneider unharmed was ever given; deadly weapons were sent by diplomatic pouch, and men of violence were carefully selected to receive them.) And he wanted to be out of the picture in case such an attempt might fail, or be uncovered. These are the normal motives of anyone who solicits or suborns murder. However, Kissinger needed the crime very slightly more than he needed, or was able to design, the deniability. Without waiting for his many hidden papers to be released or subpoenaed, we can say with safety that he is *prima facie* guilty of direct collusion in the murder of a democratic officer in a democratic and peaceful country.

There is no particular need to rehearse the continuing role of the Nixon-Kissinger administration in the later economic and political subversion and destabilization of the Allende government, and in the creation of favorable conditions for the military coup that occurred on 11 September 1973. Kissinger himself was perhaps no more and no less involved in this effort than any other high official in Nixon's national-security orbit. On 9 November 1970 he authored the National Security Council's "Decision Memorandum 93," reviewing policy toward Chile in the immediate wake of Allende's confirmation as President. Various routine measures of economic harassment were proposed (recall Nixon's instruction to "make the economy scream") with cutoffs in aid and investment. More significantly, Kissinger advocated that "close relations" be maintained with military leaders in neighboring countries, in order to facilitate both the coordination of pressure against Chile and the incubation of opposition within the country. In outline, this prefigures the disclosures that have since been made about Operation Condor, a secret collusion between military dictatorships across the hemisphere, operated with United States knowledge and indulgence.

The actual overthrow of the Allende government in a bloody *coup d'état* took place while Kissinger was going through his own Senate confirmation process as Secretary of State. He falsely assured the Foreign Relations Committee that the United States government had played no part in the coup. From a thesaurus of hard information to the contrary, one might select Situation Report #2, from the Navy Section of the United States Military Group in Chile, and written by the US Naval Attaché, Patrick Ryan. Ryan describes his close relationship with the officers engaged in overthrowing the government, hails 11 September 1973 as "our D-Day" and observes with satisfaction that "Chile's coup de etat [*sic*] was close to perfect." Or one may peruse the declassified files on Project FUBELT—the code name under which the CIA, in frequent contact with Kissinger and the Forty Committee, conducted covert operations against the legal and elected government of Chile.

What is striking, and what points to a much more direct complicity in individual crimes against humanity, is the microcosmic detail in which Kissinger kept himself informed of Pinochet's atrocities.

On 16 November, Assistant Secretary of State Jack B. Kubisch delivered a detailed report on the Chilean junta's execution policy which, as he notes to the new secretary of state, "you requested by cable from Tokyo." The memo goes on to enlighten Kissinger in various ways about the first nineteen days of Pinochet's rule. Summary executions during that period, we are told, total 320. (This contrasts with the publicly announced total of 100, and is based on "an internal, confidential report prepared for the junta" to which US officials are evidently privy.) Looking on the bright side, "On November 14, we announced our second CCC credit to Chile—$24 million for feed corn. Our longstanding commitment to sell two surplus destroyers to the Chilean navy has met a reasonably sympathetic response in Senate consultations. The Chileans, meanwhile, have sent us several new requests for controversial military equipment." Kubisch then raises the awkward question of two US citizens murdered by the junta—Frank Teruggi and Charles Horman—details of whose precise fate are still, more than a quarter-century later, being sought by their families. The reason for the length of the search may be inferred from a later comment by Mr. Kubisch, dated 11 February 1974, in which he reports on a meeting with the junta's foreign minister, and notes that he raises the matter of the missing Americans "in the context of the need to be careful to keep relatively small issues in our relationship from making our cooperation more difficult."

To return, via this detour, to Operation Condor.

This was a machinery of cross-border assassination, abduction, torture and intimidation, coordinated between the secret police forces of Pinochet's Chile, Stroessner's Paraguay, Videla's Argentina and other regional *caudillos*. This internationalization of the death-squad principle is now known to have been responsible, to name only the most salient victims, for the murder of the dissident general Carlos Prats of Chile (and his wife) in Buenos Aires, the murder of the Bolivian general Juan Jose Torres, and the maiming of a Chilean Christian Democrat senator, Bernardo Leighton, in Italy. A Condor team also detonated a car bomb in downtown Washington, DC, in September 1976, killing the former Chilean foreign minister Orlando Letelier and his aide Ronni Moffitt. United States Government complicity has been uncovered at every level of this network. It has been established, for example, that the FBI aided Pinochet in capturing Jorge Isaac Fuentes de Alarcón, who was detained and tortured in Paraguay, then turned over to the Chilean secret police, and "disappeared." Astonishingly, the surveillance of Latin US dissident refugees in the United States was promised to Condor figures by US intelligence.

These and other facts have been established by the work of "truth and reconciliation" commissions set up by post-dictatorship forces in the countries of the southern hemisphere. Stroessner has been overthrown, Videla is in prison, Pinochet and his henchmen are being or have been brought to account in Chile. The United States has not so far found it convenient to establish a truth and reconciliation commission of its own, which means that it is less ready at present to face its historical responsibility than are the countries once derided as "banana republics."

All of the above-cited crimes, and many more besides, were committed on Kissinger's "watch" as secretary of state. And all of them were and are punishable, under local or international law, or both. It can hardly be argued, by himself or by his defenders, that he was indifferent to, or unaware of, the true situation. In 1999 a secret memorandum was declassified, giving excruciating details of a private conversation between Kissinger and Pinochet in Santiago, Chile, on 8 June 1976. The meeting took place the day before Kissinger was due to address the Organization of American States. The subject was human rights. Kissinger was at some pains to explain to Pinochet that the few *pro forma* remarks he was to make on that topic were by no means to be taken seriously. My friend Peter Kornbluh has performed the service of comparing the "Memcon" (Memorandum of Conversation) with the account of the meeting given by Kissinger himself in his third volume of apologia, *Years of Renewal*:

THE MEMOIR: "A considerable amount of time in my dialogue with Pinochet was devoted to human rights, which were, in fact, the principal obstacle to close United States relations with Chile. I outlined the main points in my speech to the OAS which I would deliver the next day. Pinochet made no comment."

THE MEMCON: "I will treat human rights in general terms, and human rights in a world context. I will refer in two paragraphs to the report on Chile of the OAS Human Rights Commission. I will say that the human rights issue has impaired relations between the US and Chile. This is partly the result of Congressional actions. I will add that I hope you will shortly remove these obstacles....I can do no less, without producing a reaction in the US which would lead to legislative restrictions. The speech is not aimed at Chile. I wanted to tell you about this. My evaluation is that you are a victim of all left-wing groups around the world and that your greatest sin was that you overthrew a government that was going Communist."

THE MEMOIR: "As Secretary of State, I felt I had the responsibility to encourage the Chilean government in the direction of greater democracy through a policy of understanding Pinochet's concerns....Pinochet reminded me that 'Russia supports their people 100 percent. We are behind you. You are the leader. But you have a punitive system for your friends.' I returned to my underlying theme that any major help from us would realistically depend on progress on human rights."

THE MEMCON: "There is merit in what you say. It is a curious time in the US....It is unfortunate. We have been through Vietnam and Watergate. We have to wait until the [1976] elections. We welcomed the overthrow of the Communist-inclined government here. We are not out to weaken your position."

In an unpleasant way, Pinochet twice mentioned the name of Orlando Letelier, the exiled Chilean opposition leader, accusing him of misleading the United States Congress. Kissinger's response, as can be seen, was to apologize for the Congress and (in a minor replay of his 1968 Paris tactic over Vietnam) to suggest that the dictator should hope for better days after the upcoming elections. Three months later, a car bomb in Washington killed Letelier; today still it remains the only such outrage ever committed in the nation's capital by agents of a foreign regime. (This notable incident is completely absent from Kissinger's memoirs.) The man responsible for arranging the crime, the Chilean secret policeman General Manuel Contreras, has since testified at trial that he took no action without specific and personal orders from Pinochet. He remains in prison, doubt-less wondering why he trusted his superiors.

"I want to see our relations and friendship improve," Kissinger told Pinochet (but not the readers of his memoirs). "We want to help, not undermine you." In advising a murderer and despot, whose rule he had helped impose, to disregard his upcoming remarks as a sop to Congress, Kissinger insulted democracy in both countries. He also gave the greenest of green lights to further cross-border and internal terrorism, of neither of which he could have been unaware. (In his memoirs, he does mention what he calls Pinochet's "*counterterrorist* intelligence agency.") Further colluding with Pinochet against the United States Congress, which was considering the Kennedy amendment cutting off arms sales to human rights violators, Kissinger obsequiously remarked:

> I don't know if you listen in on my phone, but if you do, you have just heard me issue instructions to Washington to [defeat the Kennedy amendment]. If we defeat it, we will deliver the F-5Es as we agreed to do.

The above passage is worth bearing in mind. It is a good key for decoding the usual relationship between fact and falsehood in Kissinger's ill-crafted memoir. (And it is a huge reproach to his editors at Simon & Schuster and Weidenfeld & Nicolson.) It should also act as an urgent prompting to members of Congress, and to human rights organizations, to reopen the incomplete inquiries and thwarted investigations into the multifarious crimes of this period. Finally, and read in the light of the return to democracy in Chile, and the decision of the Chilean courts to pursue truth and justice, it repudiates Kissinger's patronizing insult concerning the "irresponsibility" of a dignified and humane people, who have suffered very much more than verbal insult at his hands.

6

An Afterword on Chile

A rule of thumb in Washington holds that any late disclosure by officialdom will contain material that is worse than even the cynics suspected. One need not try and turn this maxim into an iron law. However, in September 2000 the CIA disgorged the results of an internal inquiry on Chile, which had been required of it by the Hinchey amendment to the Intelligence Authorization Act for that fiscal year. And the most hardened critics and investigators were reduced to amazement. (The document was handed to me after I had completed the chapter above, and I let it stand so as to preserve the actual order of disclosure.) I reproduce the chief headings below, so as to preserve, also, the Agency's own prose:

Support for Coup in 1970. Under "Track II" of the strategy, CIA sought to instigate a coup to prevent Allende from taking office after he won a plurality

in the 4 September election and before, as Constitu-
tionally required because he did not win an absolute
majority, the Chilean Congress reaffirmed his victory. CIA was working with three different groups
of plotters. All three groups made it clear that any
coup would require the kidnapping of Army Commander René Schneider, who felt deeply that the
Constitution required that the Army allow Allende
to assume power. CIA agreed with that assessment. Although CIA provided weapons to one of
the groups, we have found no information that the
plotters' or CIA's intention was for the general to
be killed. Contact with one group of plotters was
dropped early on because of its extremist tendencies. CIA provided tear gas, submachine guns and
ammunition to the second group, mortally wound-
ing [Schneider] in the attack. CIA had previously
encouraged this group to launch a coup but withdrew support four days before the attack because, in
CIA's assessment, the group could not carry it out
successfully.

This repeats the old canard supposedly distinguish-
ing a kidnap or abduction from a murder, and once
again it raises the intriguing question: what was
the CIA going to do with the general once it had
kidnapped him? (Note, also, the studied passivity
whereby the report "found no information that the

plotters' or CIA's intention was for the general to be killed." What would satisfy this bizarre criterion?) But then we learn, of the supposedly unruly gang that actually took its instructions seriously:

> In November 1970 a member of the Viaux group who avoided capture recontacted the Agency and requested financial assistance on behalf of the group. Although the Agency had no obligation to the group because it acted on its own, in an effort to keep the prior contact secret, maintain the good will of the group, and for humanitarian reasons, $35,000 was passed.

"Humanitarian reasons." One has to admire the sheer inventiveness of this explanation. At 1970 prices, the sum of $35,000 in Chile was a considerable sum to pay. Not the sort of sum that a local station chief could have disbursed on his own. One wants to know how the Forty Committee and its vigilant chairman, Henry Kissinger, decided that the best way to dissociate from a supposedly loose-cannon gang was to pay it a small fortune in cash *after* it had committed a cold-blooded murder.

The same question arises in an even more acute form with another disclosure made by the Agency in the course of the same report. This is headed

"Relationship With Contreras." Manuel Contreras was the head of Pinochet's secret military police, and in that capacity organized the death, torture, and disappearance of innumerable Chileans as well as the use of bombing and assassination techniques as far afield as Washington, DC. The CIA admits early on in the document that it "had liaison relationships in Chile with the primary purpose of securing assistance in gathering intelligence on external targets. The CIA offered these services assistance in internal organization and training to combat subversion and terrorism from abroad, not in combating internal opponents of the government."

Such flat prose, based on a distinction between the "external threat" and the more messy business of internal dictatorial discipline, invites the question—what external threat? Chile had no foreign enemy except Argentina, which disputed some sea lane rights in the Beagle Channel. (In consequence, Chile helped Mrs. Thatcher in the Falklands war of 1982.) And in Argentina, as we know, the CIA was likewise engaged in helping the military regime to survive. No: while Chile had no external enemies to speak of, the Pinochet dictatorship had many, many external foes. They were the numerous Chileans forced to abandon their country. One of the jobs of Manuel Contreras was to hunt them down. As the report puts it:

During a period between 1974 and 1977, CIA maintained contact with Manuel Contreras, who later became notorious for his human rights abuses. The US Government policy community approved CIA's contact with Contreras, given his position as chief of the primary intelligence organization in Chile, as necessary to accomplish the CIA's mission, in spite of concerns that this relationship might lay the CIA open to charges of aiding internal political repression.

After a few bits of back-and-forth about the distinction without a difference (between external and "internal" police tactics) the CIA report states candidly:

By April 1975, intelligence reporting showed that Contreras was the principal obstacle to a reasonable human rights policy within the Junta, but an interagency committee directed the CIA to continue its relationship with Contreras. The US Ambassador to Chile urged Deputy Director of Central Intelligence [General Vernon] Walters to receive Contreras in Washington in the interest of maintaining good relations with Pinochet. In August 1975, with interagency approval, this meeting took place.

In May and June 1975, elements within the CIA recommended establishing a paid relationship with Contreras to obtain intelligence based on his unique position and access to Pinochet. This proposal was overruled, citing the US Government policy on clandestine relations with the head of an intelligence service notorious for human rights abuses. However, given miscommunications in the timing of this exchange, a one-time payment was given to Contreras.

This does not require too much parsing. Sometime *after* it had been concluded, and by the CIA at that, that Manuel Contreras was the "principal obstacle to a reasonable human rights policy," he is given American taxpayers' money and received at a high level in Washington. The CIA's memorandum is careful to state that, where doubts exist, they are stilled by "the US Government policy community" and by "an interagency committee." It also tries to suggest, with unconscious humor, that the head of a murderous foreign secret service was given a large bribe by mistake. One wonders who was reprimanded for this blunder, and how it got past the scrutiny of the Forty Committee.

The report also contradicts itself, stating at one point that Contreras's activities overseas were opaque, and at another that:

Within a year after the coup, the CIA and other US Government agencies were aware of bilateral cooperation among regional intelligence services to track the activities of and, in at least a few cases, kill political opponents. This was the precursor to Operation Condor, an intelligence-sharing arrangement among Chile, Argentina, Brazil, Paraguay and Uruguay established in 1975.

So now we know: the internationalization of the death squad principle was understood and approved by US intelligence and its political masters across two administrations. The senior person concerned in both administrations was Henry Kissinger. Whichever "interagency committee" is meant, and whether it is the Forty Committee or the Interagency Committee on Chile, the traces lead back to the same source.

On leaving the State Department, Kissinger made an extraordinary bargain whereby (having first hastily trucked them for safekeeping on the Rockefeller estate at Pocantico Hills, New York) he gifted his papers to the Library of Congress, on the sole condition that they remained under seal until after his demise. However, Kissinger's friend Manuel Contreras made a mistake when he killed a United States citizen, Ronni Karpen Moffitt, in the Washington car bomb which also murdered Orlando Letelier in 1976. By late 2000, the FBI had finally sought and received subpoena power to review the Library of

Congress papers, a subpoena with which Kissinger dealt only through his attorneys. It was a start, but it was pathetic when compared to the efforts of truth and justice commissions in "Chile, Argentina, Brazil, Paraguay and Uruguay," the nations named above, which have now emerged from years of Kissinger-befriended dictatorship and sought a full accounting. We await the moment when the United States Congress will inaugurate a comparable process, and finally subpoena all the hidden documents that obscure the view of unpunished crimes committed in our names.

7

Cyprus

In the second volume of his trilogy of memoirs, which is entitled *Years of Upheaval*, Henry Kissinger found the subject of the 1974 Cyprus catastrophe so awkward that he decided to postpone consideration of it:

> I must leave a full discussion of the Cyprus episode to another occasion, for it stretched into the Ford presidency and its legacy exists unresolved today.

This argued a certain nervousness on his part, if only because the subjects of Vietnam, Cambodia, the Middle East, Angola, Chile, China and the SALT negotiations all bear legacies that are "unresolved today" and were unresolved then. (To say that these matters "stretched into the Ford administration" is to say, in effect, nothing at all except that this pallid interregnum did, historically speaking, occur.) In most of his writing about himself (and, one presumes, in most of his presentations to his clients) Kissinger projects a strong impression of a man at home in the world and on top of his brief. But there are a number of occasions when it suits him to pose as a sort of Candide: naive, and ill-prepared for and easily unhorsed by events. No doubt this pose costs him something in point of self-esteem. It is a pose, furthermore, which he often adopts at precisely the time when the record shows him to be knowledgeable, and when knowledge or foreknowledge would also confront him with charges of responsibility or complicity.

Cyprus in 1974 is just such a case. Kissinger now argues, in the long-delayed third volume of his memoirs, *Years of Renewal*, that he was prevented and distracted, by Watergate and the deliquescence of the Nixon presidency, from taking a timely or informed interest in the crucial triangle of force between Greece, Turkey and Cyprus. This is a bizarre disclaimer: the phrase "southern flank of NATO" was then a geopolitical commonplace of the first importance, and the proximity of Cyprus to the Middle East was a factor never absent from US strategic thinking. There was no reason of domestic policy to prevent the region from engaging his attention. Furthermore, the very implosion of Nixonian authority, cited as a reason for Kissinger's own absence of mind, in fact bestowed extraordinary powers upon him. To restate the obvious once more: when he became secretary of state in 1973, he took care to retain his post as Special Assistant to the President for National Security Affairs or, as we now say, National Security Advisor. This made him the first and only secretary of state to hold the chairmanship of the elite and secretive Forty Committee, which considered and approved covert actions by the CIA. Meanwhile, as chairman of the National Security Council, he held a position where every important intelligence plan passed across his desk. His former NSC aide, Roger Morris, was not exaggerating by much, if at all, when he said that Kissinger's dual position, plus Nixon's eroded status, made him "no less than acting chief of state for national security."

We know from other sources that Kissinger was not only a micromanager with an eye to detail, but a man with a taste for intervention and rapid response. In the White House memoir of one of his closest associates, Nixon's chief of staff H.R. Haldeman, we learn of an occasion when Kissinger nearly precipitated a crisis because he became excited by some aerial photographs of Cuba. (The pictures showed soccer fields under construction, which he took—believing the Cubans to be exclusively interested in baseball—as the sign of a new and sinister Russian design.) On another occasion, following the downing of a US plane, he was in favor of bombing North

Korea and not excluding the nuclear option. *The Ends of Power* was Haldeman's title; it is only one of many testimonies showing Kissinger's unsleeping attention to potential sources of trouble, and therefore of possible distinction for himself.

This is a necessary preface to a consideration of his self-exculpation in the Cyprus matter, an apologia which depends for its credibility on our willingness to believe that Kissinger was wholly incompetent and impotent and above all uninformed. The energy with which he presses this self-abnegating case is revealing. It is also important, because if Kissinger did have any knowledge of the events he describes, then he is guilty of collusion in an assassination attempt on a foreign head of state, in a fascist military coup, in a serious violation of American law (the Foreign Assistance Act, which prohibits the use of US military aid and *materiel* for non-defensive purposes), in two invasions which flouted international law, and in the murder and dispossession of many thousands of noncombatant civilians.

In seeking to fend off this conclusion, and its implications, Kissinger gives one hostage to fortune in *Years of Upheaval* and another in *Years of Renewal*. In the former volume he says plainly, "I had always taken it for granted that the next intercommunal crisis in Cyprus would provoke Turkish intervention," that is, it would at least risk the prospect of a war within NATO between Greece and Turkey and would certainly involve the partition of the island. That this was indeed common knowledge may not be doubted by any person even lightly acquainted with Cypriot affairs. In the latter volume, where he finally takes up the challenge implicitly refused in the former, he repeatedly asks the reader why anyone (such as himself, so burdened with Watergate) would have sought "a crisis in the Eastern Mediterranean between two NATO allies."

These two disingenuous statements need to be qualified in the light of a third, which appears on page 199 of *Years of Renewal*. Here, President Makarios of Cyprus is described without adornment as "the proximate cause of most of Cyprus's tensions." Makarios was the democratically elected leader of a virtually unarmed republic, which was at the time an associate member of the European Economic Community (EEC), the United Nations and the Commonwealth. His rule was challenged, and the independence of Cyprus was threatened, by a military dictatorship in Athens and a highly militarized government in Turkey, both of which sponsored right-wing gangster organizations on the island, and both of which had plans to annex the greater or lesser part of it. In spite of this, "intercommunal" violence had been on the decline in Cyprus throughout the 1970s. Most killings were in fact "intramural": of Greek and Turkish

democrats or internationalists by their respective
nationalist and authoritarian rivals. Several attempts,
by Greek and Greek-Cypriot fanatics, had been
made on the life of President Makarios himself. To
describe his person as "the proximate cause" of most
of the tensions is to make a wildly aberrant moral
judgment.

This same aberrant judgment, however, supplies
the key that unlocks the lie at the heart of Kissinger's presentation. If the elected civilian authority
(and spiritual leader of the Greek Orthodox community) is the "proximate cause" of the tensions,
then his removal from the scene is self-evidently the
cure for them. If one can demonstrate that there was
such a removal plan, and that Kissinger knew about
it in advance, then it follows logically and naturally
that he was not ostensibly looking for a crisis—as he
self-pityingly asks us to disbelieve—but for a solution. The fact that he got a crisis, which was also a
hideous calamity for Cyprus and the region, does
not change the equation or undo the syllogism. It
is attributable to the other observable fact that the
scheme to remove Makarios, on which the "solution" depended, was in practice a failure. But those
who willed the means and wished the ends are not
absolved from guilt by the refusal of reality to match
their schemes.

It is, from Kissinger's own record and recollection,

as well as from the record of the subsequent official inquiry, quite easy to demonstrate that he did have advance knowledge of the plan to depose and kill Makarios. He admits as much himself, by noting that the Greek dictator Dimitrios Ioannides, head of the secret police, was determined to mount a coup in Cyprus and bring the island under the control of Athens. This was one of the better-known facts of the situation, as was the more embarrassing fact that Brigadier Ioannides was dependent on US military aid and political sympathy. His police state had been expelled from the Council of Europe and blocked from joining the EEC, and it was largely the advantage conferred by his agreement to "home port" the US Sixth Fleet, and host a string of US air and intelligence bases, that kept him in power. This lenient policy was highly controversial in Congress and in the American press, and the argument over it was part of Kissinger's daily bread long before the Watergate drama.

Thus it was understood *in general* that the Greek dictatorship, a US client, wished to see Makarios overthrown and had already tried to kill him or have him killed. (Overthrow and assassination, incidentally, are effectively coterminous in this account; there was no possibility of leaving such a charismatic leader alive, and those who sought his removal invariably intended his death.) This was also understood *in particular.* The most salient proof is this. In May of 1974, two months before the coup in Nicosia which Kissinger later claimed was a shock, he received a memorandum from the head of his State Department Cyprus desk, Thomas Boyatt. Boyatt summarized all the cumulative and persuasive reasons for believing that a Greek junta attack on Cyprus and Makarios was imminent. He further argued that, in the absence of a US demarche to Athens, warning the dictators to desist, it might be assumed that the United States was indifferent to this. And he added what everybody knew—that such a coup, if it went forward, would beyond doubt trigger a Turkish invasion.

Prescient memos are a dime a dozen in Washington after a crisis; they are often then read for the first time, or leaked to the press or Congress in order to enhance (or protect) some bureaucratic reputation. But Kissinger now admits that he saw this document in real time, while engaged in his shuttle between Syria and Israel (both of them within half an hour's flying time of Cyprus). Yet no demarche bearing his name or carrying his authority was issued to the Greek junta.

A short while afterward, on 7 June 1974, the *National Intelligence Daily*, which is the breakfast/bible reading of all senior State Department, Pentagon and national security officials, quoted a US field report dated 3 June which stated the views of the dictator in Athens:

> Ioannides claimed that Greece is capable of removing Makarios and his key supporters from power in twenty-four hours with little if any blood being shed and without EOKA assistance. The Turks would quietly acquiesce to the removal of Makarios, a key enemy.... Ioannides stated that if Makarios decided on some type of extreme provocation against Greece to obtain a tactical advantage, he is not sure whether he should merely pull the Greek troops out of Cyprus and let Makarios fend for himself, or remove Makarios once and for all and have Greece deal directly with Turkey over Cyprus's future.

This report and its contents were later authenticated before Congress by CIA staff who had served in Athens at the relevant time. The fact that it made Brigadier Ioannides seem bombastic and delusional—both of which he was—should have underlined the obvious and imminent danger. (EOKA was a Greek-Cypriot fascist underground, armed and paid by the junta.)

At about the same time, Kissinger received a call from Senator J. William Fulbright, the chairman of the Senate Foreign Relations Committee. Senator Fulbright had been briefed about the impending coup by a senior Greek dissident journalist in Washington named Elias P. Demetracopoulos. He told Kissinger that steps should be taken to avert the planned Greek action, and he gave three reasons. The first was that it would repair some of the moral damage done by the US government's indulgence of the junta. The second was that it would head off a confrontation between Greece and Turkey in the Mediterranean. The third was that it would enhance US prestige on the island. Kissinger declined to take the recommended steps, on the bizarre grounds that he could not intervene in Greek "internal affairs" at a time when the Nixon administration was resisting pressure from Senator Henry Jackson to link US-Soviet trade to the free emigration of Russian Jewry. However odd this line of argument, it still makes it impossible for Kissinger to claim, as he still does, that he had had no warning.

So there was still no high-level US concern registered with Athens. The difficulty is sometimes presented as one of protocol or etiquette, as if Kissinger's regular custom was to whisper and tread lightly. Ioannides was the *de facto* head of the regime but technically only its secret police chief. For the US ambassador, Henry Tasca, it was awkward to make diplomatic approaches to a man he described as "a cop." But again I remind you that Henry Kissinger, in addition to his formal diplomatic eminence, was also head of the Forty Committee, and supervisor of covert action, and was dealing in private with an Athens regime that had long-standing CIA ties. The 1976 House Committee on Intelligence later phrased the problem rather deftly in its report:

> Tasca, assured by the CIA station chief that Ioannides would *continue* to deal only with the CIA, and not sharing the State Department Desk Officer's alarm, was content to pass a message to the Greek leader indirectly....It is clear, however, that the embassy took no steps to underscore for Ioannides the depth of concern over a Cyprus coup attempt. This episode, the exclusive CIA access to Ioannides, Tasca's indications that he may not have seen all important messages to and from the CIA station, Ioannides' suggestions of US acquiescence, and Washington's well-known coolness to Makarios have led to public speculation that either US officials were inattentive to the reports of the developing crisis or simply allowed it to happen.

Thomas Boyatt's memoranda, warning of precisely what was to happen (and echoing the views of several mid-level officials besides himself), were classified as secret and have still never been released. Asked to testify at the above hearings, he was at first forbidden by Kissinger to appear before Congress. He was only finally permitted to do so in order that he might avoid a citation for contempt. His evidence was taken in "executive session," with the hearing-room cleared of staff, reporters, and visitors.

Events continued to gather pace. On 1 July 1974, three senior officials of the Greek foreign ministry, all of them known for their moderate views on the Cyprus question, publicly tendered their resignations. On 3 July President Makarios made public an open letter to the Greek junta, which made the direct accusation of foreign interference and subversion:

> In order to be absolutely clear, I say that the cadres of the military regime of Greece support and direct the activities of the EOKA-B terrorists....I have more than once so far felt, and in some cases I have touched, a hand invisibly extending from Athens and seeking to liquidate my human existence.

He called for the withdrawal from Cyprus of the Greek officers responsible.

Some days after the coup, which eventually occurred on 15 July 1974, and when challenged at a press conference about his apparent failure to foresee or avert it, Kissinger replied that "the information was not lying around in the streets." Actually, it almost was in the streets. But much more important, and much more material to the case, it had been available to him round the clock, in both his diplomatic and his intelligence capacities. His decision to do nothing was therefore a direct decision to do something, or to let something be done.

The argument can be pushed a little further. If we can show that Kissinger is speaking falsely when he says he was surprised by the July coup—and we can show this—and if we assume that foreknowledge accompanied by inaction is evidence for at least passive approval, then we would expect to find the coup, when it came, being received with some show of sympathy or satisfaction. As a matter of fact, that is precisely what we do find.

To the rest of the world, two things were obvious about the coup. The first was that it had been instigated from Athens and carried out with the help of regular Greek forces, and was thus a direct intervention in the internal affairs of one country by another. The second was that it violated all the existing treaties governing the status of Cyprus. The obvious and unsavory illegality was luridly emphasized by the junta itself, which chose a notorious chauvinist gunman named Nicos Sampson to be its proxy "president." Sampson must have been well known to the chairman of the Forty Committee as a long-standing recipient of financial support from the CIA; he also received money for his fanatical Nicosia newspaper *Makhi* (Combat) from a pro-junta

CIA proxy in Athens, Mr. Savvas Constantopoulos, the publisher of the pro-junta organ *Eleftheros Kosmos* (Free World). No European government treated Sampson as anything but a pariah, for the brief nine days in which he held power and launched a campaign of murder against his democratic Greek opponents. But Kissinger told the US envoy in Nicosia to receive Sampson's "foreign minister" *as* foreign minister, thus making the United States the first and only government to extend *de facto* recognition. (At this point, it might be emphasized, the whereabouts of President Makarios were unknown. His palace had been heavily shelled and his death announced on the junta's radio. He had in fact made his escape, and was able to broadcast the fact a few days afterward— to the enormous irritation of certain well-placed persons.) Incidentally, in his memoir *The Truth*, published in Athens in 1986, the then head of the Greek armed forces, General Grigorios Bonanos, records that the junta's attack on Cyprus brought a message of approval and support, delivered to its intelligence service by no less a man than Thomas A. Pappas himself—the chosen intermediary between the junta and the Nixon-Kissinger administration. (We shall hear more about Mr. Pappas in Chapter 9.)

In Washington, Kissinger's press spokesman Robert Anderson flatly denied that the coup—later described by Makarios from the podium of the

United Nations as "an invasion"—constituted foreign intervention. "No," he replied to a direct question on this point. "In our view there has been no
outside intervention." This surreal position was not
contradicted by Kissinger when he met with the
ambassador of Cyprus and failed to offer the customary condolences on the reported death of his
president—the "proximate cause," we now learn
from him, of all the unpleasantness. When asked if
he still recognized the elected Makarios government
as the legal one, Kissinger doggedly and astonishingly refused to answer. When asked if the United
States was moving toward recognition of the Sampson regime, his spokesman declined to deny it. When
Makarios came to Washington on 22 July, the State
Department was asked whether he would be received
by Kissinger "as a private citizen, as Archbishop, or
as President of Cyprus?" The answer? "He [Kiss-
inger] is meeting with *Archbishop* Makarios on Monday [emphasis added]." Every other government in
the world, save the rapidly collapsing Greek dictatorship, recognized Makarios as the legitimate head
of the Cyprus republic. Kissinger's unilateralism
on the point is without diplomatic precedent, and
argues strongly for his collusion and sympathy with
the armed handful of thugs who felt the same way.

It is worth emphasizing that Makarios was invited
to Washington in the first place, as elected and legal

president of Cyprus, by Senator J. William Fulbright of the Senate Foreign Relations Committee and by his counterpart Congressman Thomas Morgan, chairman of the House Foreign Affairs Committee. Credit for this invitation belongs to the above-mentioned Elias Demetracopoulos, who had long warned of the coup and who was a friend of Fulbright. He it was who conveyed the invitation to Makarios, who was by then in London meeting the British Foreign Secretary. This initiative crowned a series of anti-junta activities by this guerrilla journalist and one-man band, who had already profoundly irritated Kissinger and become a special object of his spite. (See Chapter 9.) At the very last moment, and with very poor grace, Kissinger was compelled to announce that he was receiving Makarios in his presidential and not his episcopal capacity.

Since Kissinger himself tells us that he had always known or assumed that another outbreak of violence in Cyprus would trigger a Turkish military intervention, we can assume in our turn that he was not surprised when such an intervention came. Nor does he seem to have been very much disconcerted. While the Greek junta remained in power, his efforts were principally directed to shielding it from retaliation. He was opposed to the return of Makarios to the island, and strongly opposed to Turkish or British use of force (Britain being a guarantor power with a treaty obligation and troops in place on Cyprus) to undo the Greek coup. This same counsel of inertia or inaction—amply testified to in his own memoirs as well as in everyone else's—translated later into equally strict and repeated admonitions against any measures to block a Turkish invasion. Sir Tom McNally, then the chief political advisor to Britain's then Foreign Secretary and future prime minister, James Callaghan, has since disclosed that Kissinger "vetoed" at least one British military action to preempt a Turkish landing. But that was *after* the Greek colonels had collapsed, and democracy had been restored to Athens. There was no longer a client regime to protect.

This may seem paradoxical, but the long-standing sympathy for a partition of Cyprus, repeatedly expressed by the State and Defense departments, make it seem much less so. The demographic composition of the island (82 percent Greek to 18 percent Turkish) made it more logical for the partition to be imposed by Greece. But a second-best was to have it imposed by Turkey. And, once Turkey had conducted two brutal invasions and occupied almost 40 percent of Cypriot territory, Kissinger exerted himself very strongly indeed to protect Ankara from any congressional reprisal for this outright violation of international law, and promiscuous and illegal misuse of US weaponry. He became so pro-Turkish, indeed, that it was if he had never heard of the Greek colonels. (Though his expressed dislike of the returned Greek democratic leaders supplied an occasional reminder.)

Not all the elements of this partitionist policy can be charged to Kissinger personally; he inherited the Greek junta and the official dislike of Makarios. However, even in the dank obfuscatory prose of his own memoirs, he does admit what can otherwise be concluded from independent sources. Using covert channels, and short-circuiting the democratic process in his own country, he made himself an accomplice in a plan of political assassination which, when it went awry, led to the deaths of thousands of civilians, the violent uprooting of almost 200,000 refugees, and the creation of an unjust and unstable amputation of Cyprus which constitutes a serious threat to peace a full quarter-century later. His attempts to keep the record sealed are significant in themselves; when the relevant files are opened they will form part of the longer bill of indictment.

On 10 July 1976, the European Commission on Human Rights adopted a report, prepared by eighteen distinguished jurists and chaired by Professor J.E.S. Fawcett, resulting from a year's research into the consequences of the Turkish invasion. It found that the Turkish army had engaged in the deliberate killing of civilians, in the execution of prisoners, in the torture and ill-treatment of detainees, in the arbitrary collective punishment and mass detention of civilians, and in systematic and unpunished acts of rape, torture, and looting. A large number of "disappeared" persons, both prisoners of war and civilians, are still "missing" from this period. They include a dozen holders of United States passports, which is evidence in itself of an indiscriminate strategy, when conducted by an army dependent on US aid and *materiel*.

Perhaps it was a reluctance to accept his responsibility for these outrages, as well as his responsibility for the original Sampson coup, that led Kissinger to tell a bizarre sequence of lies to his new friends the Chinese. On 2 October 1974, he held a high-level meeting in New York with Qiao Guanhua, Vice Foreign Minister of the People's Republic. It was the first substantive Sino-American meeting since the visit of Deng Xiaoping, and the first order of business was Cyprus. The memorandum, which is headed "TOP SECRET/SENSITIVE/EXCLUSIVELY EYES ONLY," has Kissinger first rejecting China's public claim that he had helped engineer the removal of Makarios. "We did not. We did not oppose Makarios." (This claim is directly belied by his own memoirs.) He says, "When the coup occurred I was in Moscow," which he was not. He says, "my people did not take these intelligence reports [concerning an impending coup] seriously," even though they had. He says that neither did Makarios take them seriously, even though Makarios had gone public in a denunciation of the Athens junta for its coup plans. Kissinger then makes the amazing claim: "We knew the Soviets had told the Turks to invade," which would make this the first Soviet-instigated invasion to be conducted by a NATO army and paid for with US aid.

A good liar must have a good memory: Kissinger is a stupendous liar with a remarkable memory. So perhaps some of this hysterical lying is explained by its context—by the need to enlist China's anti-Soviet instincts. But the total of falsity is so impressive that it suggests something additional, something more like denial or delusion, or even a confession by other means.

8

East Timor

Another small but significant territory has the distinction of being omitted—entirely omitted—from Henry Kissinger's memoirs. And since East Timor is left out of the third and final volume (*Years of Renewal*) it cannot hope, like Cyprus, for a hasty later emendation. It has, in short, been airbrushed. And it is reasonably easy to see why Kissinger hopes to avoid discussion of a country whose destiny he so much affected.

Let me state matters briefly. After the collapse of the Portuguese fascist regime in Lisbon in April 1974, that country's colonial empire deliquesced with extraordinary speed. The metropolitan power retained control only in the enclave of Macau, on the coast of China, and later remitted this territory to Beijing under treaty in 2000. In Africa, after many vicissitudes, power was inherited by the socialist-leaning liberation movements which had, by their tactic of guerrilla warfare, brought about the Portuguese revolution in the first place and established warm relations with its first generation of activists.

In East Timor, situated in the Indonesian archipelago, the postcolonial vacuum was at first also filled by a leftist movement, known as FRETILIN or the Front for the Liberation of East Timor. The popular base of this movement extended from the Catholic Church to the Westernized and sometimes Leninized students who had brought back revolutionary opinions from the "motherland." FRETILIN and its allies were able to form a government but were at once subjected to exorbitant pressure from their gigantic Indonesian neighbor, then led by the dictator (since deposed and disgraced by his own people) General Suharto. Portugal, which had and which retains legal responsibility, was too unstable and too distant to prevent the infiltration of Indonesian regular units into East Timor and the beginning of an obviously expansionist policy of attrition and subversion. This tactic was pursued by the generals in Jakarta for a few months, under the transparent pretext of "aiding" anti-FRETILIN forces which were, in point of fact, deliberately inserted Indonesian ones. All pretense of this sort was abandoned on 7 December 1975, when the armed forces of Indonesia crossed the border of East Timor in strength, eventually proclaiming it (in an act no less lawless than Iraq's proclamation of Kuwait as "our nine-teenth province") a full part of Indonesia proper.

Timorese resistance to this claim was so wide-spread, and the violence required to impose it was so ruthless and generalized, that the figure of 100,000 deaths in the first wave—perhaps one-sixth of the entire population—is reckoned an understatement.

The date of the Indonesian invasion—7 December 1975—is of importance and also of significance. On that date, President Gerald Ford and his secretary of state, Henry Kissinger, concluded an official visit to Jakarta and flew to Hawaii. Since they had come fresh from a meeting with Indonesia's military junta, and since the United States was Indonesia's principal supplier of military hardware (and since Portugal, a NATO ally, broke diplomatic relations with Indo-nesia on the point), it seemed reasonable to inquire whether the two leaders had given the invaders any impression amounting to a "green light." Thus when Ford and Kissinger landed at Hawaii, report-ers asked Mr. Ford for comment on the invasion of Timor. The President was evasive.

> He smiled and said: "We'll talk about that later." But press secretary Ron Nessen later gave report-ers a statement saying: "The United States is always concerned about the use of violence. The President hopes it can be resolved peacefully."

The literal incoherence of this official utterance—the idea of a peaceful resolution to a unilateral use of violence—may perhaps have possessed an inner coherence: the hope of a speedy victory for overwhelming force. Kissinger moved this suspicion a shade nearer to actualization in his own more candid comment, which was offered while he was still on Indonesian soil and "told newsmen in Jakarta that the United States would not recognize the FRETILIN-declared republic and that 'the United States understands Indonesia's position on the question.'"

So gruesome were the subsequent reports of mass slaughter, rape, and deliberate use of starvation that such bluntness fell somewhat out of fashion. The killing of several Australian journalists who had witnessed Indonesia's atrocities, the devastation in the capital city of Dili, and the stubbornness of FRETILIN's hugely outgunned rural resistance made East Timor an embarrassment rather than an advertisement for Jakarta's new order. Kissinger generally attempted to avoid any discussion of his involvement in the extirpation of the Timorese—an ongoing involvement, since he authorized back-door shipments of weapons to those doing the extirpating—and was ably seconded in this by his ambassador to the United Nations, Daniel Patrick Moynihan, who later confided in his memoir *A Dangerous Place* that, in relative terms, the death toll in East Timor during the initial days of the invasion was "almost the toll of casualties experienced by the Soviet Union during the Second World War." Moynihan continued:

> The United States wished things to turn out as they did, and worked to bring this about. The Department of State desired that the United Nations prove utterly ineffective in whatever measures it undertook. This task was given to me, and I carried it forward with no inconsiderable success.

The terms "United States" and "Department of State" are here foully prostituted, by this supposed prose-master, since they are used as synonyms for Henry Kissinger.

Twenty years later, on 11 August 1995, Kissinger was confronted with direct questions on the subject. Publicizing and promoting his then-latest book *Diplomacy*, at an event sponsored by the Learning Annex at the Park Central Hotel in New York, he perhaps (having omitted Timor from his book and from his talk) did not anticipate the first line of questioning that arose from the floor. Constancio Pinto, a former resistance leader in Timor who had been captured and tortured and had escaped to the United States, was first on his feet:

PINTO: I am Timorese. My name is Constancio
Pinto. And I followed your speech today and it's
really interesting. One thing that I know you
didn't mention is this place invaded by Indonesia
in 1975. It is in Southeast Asia. As a result of the
invasion 200,000 people of the Timorese were
killed. As far as I know Dr. Kissinger was in Indonesia the day before the invasion of East Timor.
The United States actually supported Indonesia
in East Timor. So I would like to know what you
were doing at that time.

KISSINGER: What was I doing at that time? The
whole time or just about Timor? First of all, I
want to thank the gentleman for asking the question in a very polite way. The last time somebody
from Timor came after me was at the Oxford
Union and they practically tore the place apart
before they asked the question.

   What most people who deal with government
don't understand is one of the most overwhelming experiences of being in high office. That there
are always more problems than you can possibly
address at any one period. And when you're in
global policy and you're a global power, there are
so many issues.

   Now the Timor issue. First of all you have to
understand what Timor, what Timor, what the

issue of Timor is. Every island that was occupied by the Dutch in the colonial period was constituted as the Republic of Indonesia. In the middle of their archipelago was an island called Timor. Or is an island called Timor. Half of it was Indonesian and the other half of it was Portuguese. This was the situation.

Now I don't want to offend the gentleman who asked the question. We had so many problems to deal with. We had at that time, there was a war going on in Angola. We had just been driven out of Vietnam. We were conducting negotiations in the Middle East, and Lebanon had blown up. We were on a trip to China. Maybe regrettably we weren't even thinking about Timor. I'm telling you what the truth of the matter is. The reason we were in Indonesia was actually accidental. We had originally intended to go to China, we meaning President Ford and myself and some others. We had originally intended to go to China for five days. This was the period when Mao was very sick and there had been an upheaval in China. The so-called Gang of Four was becoming dominant and we had a terrible time agreeing with the Chinese, where to go, what to say. So we cut our trip to China short. We went for two days to China and then we went for a day and a half to the Philippines and a day and a half to Indonesia.

That's how we got to Indonesia in the first place. So this was really at that time to tell the Chinese we were not dependent on them. So that's how we got to Indonesia.

Timor was never discussed with us when we were in Indonesia. At the airport as we were leaving, the Indonesians told us that they were going to occupy the Portuguese colony of Timor. To us that did not look like a very significant event because the Indians had occupied the Portuguese colony of Goa ten years earlier and to us it looked like another process of decolonization. Nobody had the foggiest idea of what would happen afterward, and nobody asked our opinion, and I don't know what we could have said if someone had asked our opinion. It was literally told to us as we were leaving.

Now there's been a terrible human tragedy in Timor afterward. The population of East Timor has resisted and I don't know whether the casualty figures are correct. I just don't know, but they're certainly significant and there's no question that it's a huge tragedy. All I'm telling you is what we knew in 1975. This was not a big thing on our radar screen. Nobody has ever heard again of Goa after the Indians occupied it. And to us, Timor, look at a map, it's a little speck of an island in a huge archipelago, half of which was

Portuguese. We had no reason to say the Portuguese should stay there. And so when the Indonesians informed us, we neither said yes or no. We were literally at the airport. So that was our connection with it, but I grant the questioner the fact that it's been a great tragedy.

ALLAN NAIRN: Mr. Kissinger, my name is Allan Nairn. I'm a journalist in the United States. I'm one of the Americans who survived the massacre in East Timor on November 12, 1991, a massacre during which Indonesian troops armed with American M-16s gunned down at least 271 Timorese civilians in front of the Santa Cruz Catholic cemetery as they were gathered in the act of peaceful mourning and protest. Now you just said that in your meeting with Suharto on the afternoon of December 6, 1975, you did not discuss Timor, you did not discuss it until you came to the airport. Well, I have here the official State Department transcript of your and President Ford's conversation with General Suharto, the dictator of Indonesia. It was obtained through the Freedom of Information Act. It has been edited under the Freedom of Information Act so the whole text isn't there. It's clear from the portion of the text that is here, that in fact you did discuss the impending invasion of Timor with Suharto, a fact which was confirmed to me

by President Ford himself in an interview I had
with him. President Ford told me that in fact you
discussed the impending invasion of Timor with
Suharto and that you gave the US...

KISSINGER: Who? I or he?

NAIRN: That you and President Ford together
gave US approval for the invasion of East Timor.
There is another internal State Department
memo which is printed in an extensive excerpt
here which I'll give to anyone in your audience
that's interested. This is a memo of a December
18, 1975, meeting held at the State Department.
This was held right after your return from that
trip and you were berating your staff for having
put on paper a finding by the State Department
legal adviser Mr. Leigh that the Indonesian invasion was illegal, that it not only violated international law, it violated a treaty with the US because
US weapons were used and it's clear from this
transcript—which I invite anyone in the audience to peruse—that you were angry at them first
because you feared this memo would leak, and
second because you were supporting the Indonesian invasion of East Timor, and you did not want
it known that you were doing this contrary to the
advice of your own people in the State Department. If one looks at the public actions, sixteen
hours after you left that meeting with Suharto the

Indonesian troops began parachuting over Dili, the capital of East Timor. They came ashore and began the massacres that culminated in a third of the Timorese population. You announced an immediate doubling of US military aid to Indonesia at the time, and in the meantime at the United Nations, the instruction given to Ambassador Daniel Patrick Moynihan, as he wrote in his memoirs, was to, as he put it, see to it that the UN be highly ineffective in any actions it might undertake on East Timor... [shouts from the audience]

KISSINGER: Look, I think we all got the point now...

NAIRN: My question, Mr. Kissinger, my question, Dr. Kissinger, is twofold. First, will you give a waiver under the Privacy Act to support full declassification of this memo so we can see exactly what you and President Ford said to Suharto? Secondly, would you support the convening of an international war crimes tribunal under UN supervision on the subject of East Timor and would you agree to abide by its verdict in regard to your own conduct?

KISSINGER: I mean, uh, really, this sort of comment is one of the reasons why the conduct of foreign policy is becoming nearly impossible under these conditions. Here is a fellow who's got one obsession, he's got one problem, he collects a bunch of documents, you don't know what is in these documents...

NAIRN: I invite your audience to read them.

KISSINGER: Well, read them. Uh, the fact is essentially as I described them [thumps podium]. Timor was not a significant American policy problem. If Suharto raised it, if Ford said something that sounded encouraging, it was not a significant American foreign policy problem. It seemed to us to be an anti-colonial problem in which the Indonesians were taking over Timor and we had absolutely no reason at that time to pay any huge attention to it.

Secondly you have to understand these things in the context of the period. Vietnam had just collapsed. Nobody yet knew what effect the domino theory would have. Indonesia was...is a country of a population of 160 million and the key, a key country in Southeast Asia. We were not looking for trouble with Indonesia, and the reason I objected in the State Department to putting this thing on paper; it wasn't that it was put on paper. It was that it was circulated to embassies because it was guaranteed to leak out. It was guaranteed then to lead to some public confrontation and for better or worse our fundamental position on these human rights issues was always to try to see if we could discuss them first, quietly, before they turned into a public confrontation. This was our policy with respect to emigration from Russia, in which we turned out to be right, and this was the policy which we tried to pursue in respect to Indonesia and anybody can go and find some document and take out one sentence and try to prove something fundamental and now I think we've heard enough about Timor. Let's have some questions on some other subject. [applause from audience]

AMY GOODMAN: Dr. Kissinger, you said that the United States has won everything it wanted in the Cold War up to this point. I wanted to go back to the issue of Indonesia and before there's a booing in the audience, just to say as you talk about China and India, Indonesia is the fourth largest country in the world. And so I wanted to ask the question in a current way about East Timor. And that is, given what has happened in the twenty years, the 200,000 people who have been killed, according to Amnesty, according to Asia Watch, even according to the Indonesian military.... Do you see that as a success of the United States?

KISSINGER: No, but I don't think it's an American policy. We cannot be, we're not responsible for everything that happens in every place in the world. [applause from audience]

GOODMAN: Except that 90 percent of the weapons used during the invasion were from the US and it continues to this day. So in that way we are intimately connected to Indonesia, unfortunately. Given that, I was wondering if you think it's a success and whether too, with you on the board of Freeport-McMoRan, which has the largest gold-mining operation in the world in Indonesia, in Irian Jaya, are you putting pressure, since Freeport is such a major lobbyist in Congress on behalf of Indonesia, to change that policy and to support self-determination for the people of East Timor?

KISSINGER: The, uh, the United States as a general proposition cannot fix every problem on the use of American weapons in purely civil conflicts. We should do our best to prevent this. As a private American corporation engaged in private business in an area far removed from Timor but in Indonesia, I do not believe it is their job to get itself involved in that issue because if they do, then no American private enterprise will be welcome there anymore.

GOODMAN: But they do every day, and lobby Congress.

It is interesting to notice, in that final answer, the final decomposition of Kissinger's normally efficient if robotic syntax. (For more material on his involvement with Freeport-McMoRan, and his other holdings in a privatized military-political-commercial complex, see Chapter 10.) It's also fascinating to see, once again, the operations of his denial mechanism. If Kissinger and his patron Nixon were identified with any one core belief, it was that the United States should never be, or even appear to be, a "pitiful, helpless giant." Kissinger's own writings and speeches are heavily larded with rhetoric about "credibility" and the need to impress friend and foe with the mettle of American resolve. Yet, in response to any inquiry that might implicate him in crime and fiasco, he rushes to humiliate his own country and its professional servants, suggesting that they know little, care less, are poorly informed and easily rattled by the pace of events. He also resorts to a demagogic isolationism. In "signaling" terms, this is as much as to claim that the United States is a pushover for any ambitious or irredentist banana republic.

This semi-conscious reversal of rhetoric also leads to renewed episodes of hysterical and improvised lying. (Recall his claim to the Chinese that it was the Soviet Union that had instigated the Turkish invasion of Cyprus.) The idea that Indonesia's annexation of Timor may be compared to India's occupation of Goa is too absurd to have been cited in any apologia before or since. What Kissinger seems to like about the comparison is the rapidity with which Goa was forgotten. What he overlooks is that it was forgotten because (1) it was not a bloodbath and (2) it completed the decolonization of India. The Timor bloodbath represented the *cementing* of colonization by Indonesia. And clearly, an Indonesian invasion that began a few hours after Kissinger had stepped off the tarmac at Jakarta airport must have been planned and readied several days before he arrived. Such plans would have been known by any embassy military attaché worth the name, and certainly by any visiting secretary of state. We have the word of C. Philip Liechty, a former CIA operations officer in Indonesia, that:

> Suharto was given the green light to do what he did. There was discussion in the Embassy and in traffic with the State Department about the problems that would be created for us if the public and Congress became aware of the level and type of military assistance that was going to Indonesia at that time. Without continued heavy US military support the Indonesians might not have been able to pull it off.

Given that legal and international responsibility for East Timor rested with Portugal, a long-term NATO ally of the United States, the decision to disregard this, and at the admitted minimum to

say nothing to the Indonesians about it, must have
been deliberate. Given Kissinger's acute preoccupation with the fate of the Portuguese empire—as we
will see—it may have been even more than that. It
certainly cannot have been the result of inattention,
or of the pressure of other distracting world events
in (to take Kissinger's own cited instance) the other
Portuguese colony of Angola.

The desire to appear to have been uninvolved
may—if we are charitable—have arisen in part
from the fact that even Indonesia's Foreign Minister, Adam Malik, conceded in public a death toll of
between 50,000 and 80,000 Timorese civilians in
the first eighteen months of Indonesia's war of sub-
jugation (in other words on Kissinger's watch) and
inflicted with weapons that he bent American laws to
furnish to the killers. Now that a form of democracy
has returned to Indonesia, which in its first post-
dictatorial act renounced the annexation and—after
a bloody last pogrom by its auxiliaries—withdrew
from the territory, we may be able to learn more
exactly the extent of the genocide.

Kissinger's surreptitious conduct is made very
plain by the State Department cable of December
1975, and the subsequent memorandum concerning it. In point of fact, the essential decisions about
Portugal's ex-colonies had been made during the

preceding July, when Kissinger had secured presidential permission for a covert program of military intervention, coordinated with the South Africans and General Mobutu, to impose a tribalist regime upon Angola. The following month, as a matter of record, he informed the Indonesian generals that he would not oppose their intervention in East Timor. The only bargaining in December involved a request that Indonesia delay the start of its own colonial adventure until after Air Force One, carrying Ford and Kissinger, had left Indonesian airspace.

This "deniable" pattern did not dispose of two matters of legality, both of them in the province of the State Department. The first was the violation of international law by Indonesia, in a case where jurisdiction clearly rested with a Portuguese and NATO government of which Kissinger (partly as a result of its support for "decolonization") did not approve. The second was the violation of American law, which stipulated that weapons supplied to Indonesia were to be employed only for self-defense. State Department officials, bound by law, were likewise bound to conclude that United States aid to the generals in Jakarta would have to be cut off. Their memo summarizing this case was the cause of the tremendous internal row that is minuted below, in a declassified State Department transcript:

SECRET/SENSITIVE
MEMORANDUM OF CONVERSATION

Participants: The Secretary [Henry Kissinger]
Deputy Secretary [Robert]
    Ingersoll
Under Secretary [for Political
    Affairs Joseph] Sisco
Under Secretary [Carlyle] Maw
Deputy Under Secretary
    [Lawrence] Eagleburger
Assistant Secretary [Philip] Habib
Monroe Leigh, Legal Advisor
Jerry Bremer, Notetaker
Date: December 18, 1975
Subject: Department Policy

THE SECRETARY [KISSINGER]: I want to raise a
little bit of hell about the Department's conduct
in my absence. Until last week I thought we had
a disciplined group; now we've gone to pieces
completely. Take this cable on [East] Timor. You
know my mind and attitude and anyone who
knows my position as you do must know that I
would not have approved it. The only consequence is to put yourself on record. It is a disgrace
to treat the Secretary of State this way....

What possible explanation is there for it? I

had told you to stop it quietly. What is your place doing, Phil, to let this happen? It is incomprehensible. It is wrong in substance and procedure. It is a disgrace. Were you here?

HABIB: No.

. . .

HABIB: Our assessment was that if it was going to be trouble, it would come up before your return. And I was told they decided it was desirable to go ahead with the cable.

[KISSINGER]: Nonsense. I said do it for a few weeks and then open up again.

HABIB: The cable will not leak.

[KISSINGER]: Yes it will and it will go to Congress too and then we will have hearings on it.

HABIB: I was away. I was told by cable that it had come up.

[KISSINGER]: That means that there are two cables! And that means twenty guys have seen it.

HABIB: No, I got it back-channel—it was just one paragraph double talk and cryptic so I knew what it was talking about. I was told that Leigh thought that there was a legal requirement to do it.

LEIGH: No, I said it could be done administratively. It was not in our interest to do it on legal grounds.

SISCO: We were told that you had decided we had to stop.

[KISSINGER]: Just a minute, just a minute. You all know my view on this. You must have an FSO-8 [Foreign Service Officer, Class Eight] who knows it well. It will have a devastating impact on Indonesia. There's this masochism in the extreme here. No one has complained that it was aggression.

LEIGH: The Indonesians were violating an agreement with us.

[KISSINGER]: The Israelis when they go into Lebanon—when was the last time we protested that?

LEIGH: That's a different situation.

MAW: It is self-defense.

[KISSINGER]: And we can't construe a Communist government in the middle of Indonesia as self-defense?

LEIGH: Well...

[KISSINGER]: Then you're saying that arms can't be used for defense?

HABIB: No, they can be used for the defense of Indonesia.

[KISSINGER]: Now take a look at this basic theme that is coming out on Angola. These SOBs are leaking all of this stuff to [*New York Times* reporter] Les Gelb.

SISCO: I can tell you who.

[KISSINGER]: Who?

SISCO: [National Security Council member William] Hyland spoke to him.

[KISSINGER]: Wait a minute—Hyland said...

SISCO: He said he briefed Gelb.

[KISSINGER]: I want these people to know that our concern in Angola is not the economic wealth or a naval base. It has to do with the USSR operating 8,000 miles from home when all the surrounding states are asking for our help. This will affect the Europeans, the Soviets, and China.

On the Timor thing, that will leak in three months, and *it will come out that Kissinger overruled his pristine bureaucrats and violated the law.* How many people in L [the Legal Adviser's Office] know about this? [italics added]

LEIGH: Three.

HABIB: There are at least two in my office.

[KISSINGER]: Plus everybody in the meeting so you're talking about not less than 15 or 20. You have a responsibility to recognize that we are living in a revolutionary situation. Everything on paper will be used against me.

HABIB: We do that and take account of that all the time.

. . .

[KISSINGER]: Every day some SOB in the Department is carrying on about Angola but no one is

defending Angola. Find me one quote in the Gelb
article defending our policy in Angola.

HABIB: I think the leaks and dissent are the burden you have to bear.

[KISSINGER]: But the people in charge of this
Department could have lacerated AF [Bureau for
African Affairs].

INGERSOLL: I was told it came from up the river.

EAGLEBURGER: No way.

[KISSINGER]: Don't be ridiculous. It's quoted
there. Read Gelb. Was [Assistant Secretary of
State for African Affairs William] Schaufele
called in and told to get his house under control?
This is not minor league stuff. We are going to
lose big. The President says to the Chinese that
we're going to stand firm in Angola and two
weeks later we get out. I go to a NATO meeting
and meanwhile the Department leaks that we're
worried about a naval base and says it's an exaggeration or aberration of Kissinger's. I don't care
about the oil or the base but I do care about the
African reaction when they see the Soviets pull
it off and we don't do anything. If the Europeans
then say to themselves if they can't hold Luanda,
how can they defend Europe? The Chinese will
say we're a country that was run out of Indochina for 50,000 men and is now being run out

of Angola for less than $50m. Where were the meetings here yesterday? Were there any?

. . .

[KISSINGER]: It cannot be that our agreement with Indonesia says that the arms are for internal purposes only. I think you will find that it says that they are legitimately used for self-defense.

There are two problems. The merits of the case which you had a duty to raise with me. The second is how to put these to me. But to put it into a cable 30 hours before I return, knowing how cables are handled in this building, guarantees that it will be a national disaster and that transcends whatever [Deputy Legal Adviser George] Aldrich has in his feverish mind.

I took care of it with the administrative thing by ordering Carlyle [Maw] not to make any new sales. How will the situation get better in six weeks?

HABIB: They may get it cleaned up by then.

[KISSINGER]: The Department is falling apart and has reached the point where it disobeys clear-cut orders.

HABIB: We sent the cable because we thought it was needed and we thought it needed your attention. This was ten days ago.

[KISSINGER]: Nonsense. When did I get the cable, Jerry?

BREMER: Not before the weekend. I think perhaps on Sunday.

[KISSINGER]: You had to know what my view on this was. *No one who has worked with me in the last two years could not know what my view would be on Timor.* [italics added]

HABIB: Well, let us look at it—talk to Leigh. There are still some legal requirements. I can't understand why it went out if it was not legally required.

[KISSINGER]: Am I wrong in assuming that the Indonesians will go up in smoke if they hear about this?

HABIB: Well, it's better than a cutoff. It could be done at a low level.

[KISSINGER]: We have four weeks before Congress comes back. That's plenty of time.

LEIGH: The way to handle the administrative cut-off would be that we are studying the situation.

[KISSINGER]: And 36 hours was going to be a major problem?

LEIGH: We had a meeting in Sisco's office and decided to send the message.

[KISSINGER]: I know what the law is but how can it be in the US national interest for us to give up on Angola and kick the Indonesians in the teeth? Once it is on paper, there will be a lot of FSO-6s who can make themselves feel good who can write for the Open Forum Panel on the thing even though I will turn out to be right in the end.

HABIB: The second problem on leaking of cables is different.

[KISSINGER]: No it's an empirical fact.

EAGLEBURGER: Phil, it's a fact. You can't say that any NODIS ["No Distribution": most restricted level of classification] cable will leak but you can't count on three to six months later someone asking for it [sic] in Congress. If it's part of the written record, it will be dragged out eventually.

[KISSINGER]: You have an obligation to the national interest. I don't care if we sell equipment to Indonesia or not. I get nothing from it, I get no rakeoff. But you have an obligation to figure out how to serve your country. The Foreign Service is not to serve itself. The Service stands for service to the United States and not service to the Foreign Service.

HABIB: I understand that that's what this cable would do.

[KISSINGER]: The minute you put this into the system you cannot resolve it without a finding.

LEIGH: There's only one question. What do we say to Congress if we're asked?

[KISSINGER]: We cut it off while we are studying it. We intend to start again in January.

The delivery of heavy weapons for use against civilian objectives did indeed resume in January 1976, after a short interval in which Congress was misled as advertised. Nobody, it must be said, comes especially well out of this meeting; the Secretary's civil servants were anything but "pristine." Still it can be noted of Kissinger that, in complete contrast to his public statements, he:

1. Forebore from any mention of Goa.
2. Did not trouble to conceal his long-held views on the matter, berating his underlings for being so dense as not to know them.
3. Did not affect to be taken by surprise by events in East Timor.
4. Admitted that he was breaking the law.
5. Felt it necessary to deny that he could profit personally from the arms shipments, a denial for which nobody had asked him.

Evidently, there was a dialectic in Kissinger's mind between Angola and East Timor, both of them many miles from US or Russian borders but both seen as tests of his own dignity. (The "surrounding states" to which he alludes in the Angolan case were apartheid South Africa and General Mobutu's Zaire: the majority of African states, as a matter of record, opposed his intervention on the side of the tribalist and pro–South Africa militias in Angola. His favored regimes have long since collapsed in ignominy; the United States now recognizes the MPLA, with all its deformities, as the legitimate government of Angola. And of course, no European ever felt that the fate of the West hinged on Kissinger's gamble in Luanda.)

That Kissinger understood Portugal's continuing legal sovereignty in East Timor is shown by a NODIS memorandum of a Camp David meeting between himself, General Suharto and President Ford on the preceding 5 July 1975. Almost every line of the text has been deleted by official redaction, and much of the discussion is unilluminating except about the eagerness of the administration to supply naval, air and military equipment to the junta, but at one point, just before Kissinger makes his entrance, President Ford asks his guest, "Have the Portuguese set a date yet for allowing the Timor people to make their choice?" The entire answer is obliterated by deletion, but let it never be said that Kissinger's State Department did not know that Portugal was entitled, indeed mandated, to hold a free election for the Timorese. It is improbable that Suharto, in the excised answer, was assuring his hosts that such an open election would be won by candidates favoring annexation by Indonesia.

On 9 November 1979, Jack Anderson's column in the *Washington Post* published an interview on East Timor with ex-President Ford, and a number of classified US intelligence documents relating to the 1975 aggression. One of the latter papers describes how Indonesia's generals were pressing Suharto "to authorize direct military intervention," while another informs Messrs. Ford and Kissinger that Suharto would raise the East Timor issue at their December 1975 meeting and would "try and elicit a sympathetic attitude." The relatively guileless Ford was happy to tell Anderson that the United States national interest "had to be on the side of Indonesia." He may or may not have been aware that he was thereby giving the lie to everything ever said by Kissinger on the subject.

9

A "Wet Job" in
Washington?

As we have more than once seen, Kissinger has a tendency to personalize his politics. His policies have led directly and deliberately to the deaths of anonymous hundreds of thousands, but have also involved the targeting of certain inconvenient individuals—General Schneider, Archbishop Makarios, Sheik Mujib. And, as we have also more than once glimpsed, Kissinger has an especial relish for the Washington vendetta and the localized revenge.

It seems possible that these two tendencies converge in a single case: a plan to kidnap and murder a man named Elias P. Demetracopoulos. Mr. Demetracopoulos is a distinguished Greek journalist with an unexampled record of opposition to the dictatorship that disfigured his homeland between 1967 and 1974. In the course of those years, he made his home in Washington, supporting himself as a consultant to a respected Wall Street firm. Innumerable senators, congressmen, Hill staffers, diplomats and reporters have testified to the extraordinary one-man campaign of lobbying and information he waged against the military gangsters who had usurped power in Athens. Since that same junta enjoyed the sympathy of powerful interests in Washington, Demetracopoulos was compelled to combat on two fronts, and made (as will shortly appear) some influential enemies.

After the collapse of the Greek dictatorship in 1974—a collapse occasioned by the events I discuss in Chapter 7 on Cyprus above—Demetracopoulos gained access to the secret police files in Athens, and confirmed what he had long suspected. There had been more than one attempt made to kidnap and eliminate him. Files held by the KYP—the Greek equivalent of the CIA—revealed that the then dictator, George Papadopoulos, and his deputy security chief Michael Roufogalis several times contacted the Greek military mission in Washington with precisely this end in view. Stamped with the words "COSMIC: Eyes Only"—the highest security classification— this traffic involved a plethora of schemes. They had in common, it is of interest to note, a desire to see Demetracopoulos snatched from Washington and repatriated. An assassination in Washington might have been embarrassing; moreover there seems to have been a need to interrogate Demetracopoulos before dispatching him. (The Greek junta was in

1970 expelled by the Council of Europe for its systematic use of torture against political opponents,
and a series of public trials held in Athens after 1974
committed the torturers and their political masters
to long terms of imprisonment.) One proposal was to
smuggle Demetracopoulos aboard a Greek civilian
airliner, another was to put him on a Greek military
plane, and still another was to get him aboard a submarine. (If it were not for the proven record of irra-
tionality and mania among the leaders of the junta,
one might be tempted to dismiss at least the third
of these plans as a fantasy.) One sentence stands out
from the COSMIC cables:

> We can rely on the cooperation of the various agen-
> cies of the U.S. Government, but estimate the Con-
> gressional reaction to be fierce.

This was a sober estimate: the CIA and the NSC
in particular were notoriously friendly to the junta,
while Demetracopoulos enjoyed the benefit of many
friendships among senators and members of the
House.

Seeking to discover what kind of "cooperation"
US agencies might have offered, Demetracopoulos
in 1976 engaged an attorney—William A. Dobrovir
of the DC firm of Dobrovir, Oakes & Gebhardt—
and brought suit under the Freedom of Information

Act and the Privacy Act. He was able to obtain many hundreds of documents from the FBI, the CIA and the State Department, as well as the Department of Justice and the Pentagon. A number of these papers indicated that copies had been furnished to the National Security Council, then the domain of Henry Kissinger. But requests for documentation from this source were unavailing. As previously noted, Kissinger had on leaving office made a hostage of his own papers—copying them, classifying them as "personal," and deeding them to the Library of Congress on condition that they be held privately. Thus, Demetracopoulos met with a stone wall when he used the law to try and prise anything from the NSC. In March 1977, however, the NSC finally responded to repeated legal initiatives by releasing the skeletal "computer indices" of the files that had been kept on Demetracopoulos. Paging through these, his attention was not unnaturally caught by the following:

7024513 DOCUMENT=5 OF 5 PAGE = 1 OF 1
KEYWORDS ACKNOWLEDGING SENS MOSS BURDICK
GRAVEL RE MR DEMETRACOPOULOS DEATH IN ATHENS
PRISON DATE 701218

"Well it's not every day," said Demetracopoulos when I interviewed him, "that you read about your own death in a state document." His attorney was bound to agree, and wrote a series of letters to Kissinger asking for copies of the file to which the indices referred. For seven years—I repeat, for seven years—Kissinger declined to favor Demetracopoulos's lawyer with a reply. When he eventually did respond, it was only through his own lawyer, who wrote that:

> Efforts were made to search the collection for copies of documents which meet the description provided.... No such copies could be found.

"Efforts were made" is, of course, a piece of obfuscation that might describe the most perfunctory inquiry. We are therefore left with the question: Did Kissinger know of, or approve, or form a part of, that "cooperation of the various agencies of the U.S. Government" on which foreign despots had been counting for a design of kidnap, torture and execution?

To begin with an obvious question: Why should a figure of Kissinger's stature either know about, or care about, the existence of a lone dissident journalist? This question is easily answered: the record shows that Kissinger knew very well who Demetracopoulos was, and detested him into the bargain. The two men had actually met in Athens in 1956, when Demetracopoulos had hosted a luncheon at the Grande Bretagne Hotel for the visiting professor.

Over the next decade, Demetracopoulos had been prominent among those warning of, and resisting, a military intervention in Greek politics. The CIA generally favored such an intervention and maintained intimate connections with those who were planning it: in November 1963 the director of the CIA, John McCone, signed an internal message asking for "any substantive derogatory data which can be used to deny [Dematracopoulos] subsequent entry to the US." No such derogatory information was in fact available, so that when the coup came, Demetracopoulos was able to settle in Washington, DC, and begin his exile campaign.

He began it auspiciously enough, by supplying "derogatory data" about the Nixon and Agnew campaign of 1968. This campaign—already tainted badly enough by the betrayal of the Vietnam peace negotiations—was also receiving illegal donations from the Greek military dictatorship.

The money came from Michael Roufogalis at the KYP and was handed over, in cash, to John Mitchell by an ultra-conservative Greek-American businessman named Thomas Pappas. The sum involved was $549,000—a considerable amount by the standards of the day. Its receipt was doubly illegal: foreign governments are prohibited from making campaign donations (as are foreigners in general), and given that the KYP was in receipt of CIA subsidies there existed the further danger that American intelligence money was being recycled back into the American political process—in direct violation of the CIA's own charter.

In 1968, Demetracopoulos took his findings to Larry O'Brien, chairman of the Democratic National Committee, who issued a call for an inquiry into the activities of Pappas and the warm relations existing between the Nixon-Agnew campaign and the Athens junta. A number of historians have since speculated as to whether it was evidence for this "Greek connection," with its immense potential for damage, that Nixon's and Mitchell's burglars were seeking when they entered O'Brien's Watergate office under the cover of night. Considerable weight is lent to this view by one salient fact: when the Nixon White House was seeking "hush money" for the burglars, it turned to Thomas Pappas to provide it.

Demetracopoulos's dangerous knowledge of the secret campaign donations, and his incessant lobbying on the Hill and in the press against Nixon's and Kissinger's client regime in Athens, drew unwelcome attention to him. He later sued both the FBI and the CIA—becoming the first person ever to do so successfully—and received written admissions from both agencies that they possessed "no derogatory information" about him. In the course of these suits, he also secured an admission from then FBI director William Webster that he had been under "rather extensive" surveillance on and between the following dates: 9 November 1967 and 2 October 1969; 25 August 1971 and 14 March 1973; and 19 February and 24 October 1974.

Unaware of the precise extent of this surveillance, Demetracopoulos had nonetheless more than once found himself brushed by a heavy hand. On 7 September 1971 he was lunching at Washington's fashionable Jockey Club with Nixon's chief henchman, Murray Chotiner, who told him bluntly, "Lay off Pappas. You can be in trouble. You can be deported. It's not smart politics. You know Tom Pappas is a friend of the President." The next month, on 27 October 1971, Demetracopoulos was lunching with columnist Robert Novak at the Sans Souci and was threatened by Pappas himself, who came over from an adjacent table to tell him and Novak that he could make trouble for anyone who wanted him investigated. On the preceding 12 July, Demetracopoulos had testified before the European subcommittee of the House Foreign Affairs Committee, chaired by Congressman Benjamin Rosenthal of New York, about the influence of Thomas Pappas on US foreign policy and the Athens dictatorship (and vice versa). Before his oral testimony could be printed, a Justice Department agent appeared at the subcommittee's office and demanded a copy of the statement. Demetracopoulos had then, on 17 September, furnished a memorandum on Pappas's activities to the same subcommittee. His written deposition closed thus: "Finally, I have submitted separately to the subcommittee items of documentary evidence which I believe will be useful." This statement, wrote Rowland Evans and Robert Novak in their syndicated column, caused "extreme nervousness in the Nixon White House."

Later disclosures have accustomed us to the part-mafioso and part-banana-republic atmosphere in Washington during those years; it was still very shocking for Demetracopoulos to receive a letter from Ms. Louise Gore. Ms. Gore has since become more celebrated as the cousin of Vice President Albert Gore and the proprietress of the Fairfax Hotel in Washington, DC, where the boy politician grew up. She was then quite celebrated in her own right: as a Republican state Senator from Maryland, and as the woman who introduced Spiro Agnew to Richard Nixon. She was a close friend of Attorney General Mitchell, and had been appointed as Nixon's representative to UNESCO. Demetracopoulos lived, along with many congressmen and political types, as a tenant of an apartment in her hotel. He had also been a friend of hers since 1959. On 24 January 1972 she wrote to him:

Dear Elias—
I went to Perle's [Perle Mesta's] luncheon for Martha Mitchell yesterday and sat next to John. He is
furious at you—and your testimony against Pappas.
He kept threatening to have you deported!!
At first I tried to ask him if he had any reason to
think you could be deported and he didn't have any
answer—But then tried to counter by asking me
what I knew about you and why we were friends.
It really got out of hand. It was all he'd talk
about during lunch and everyone at the table was
listening...

Among those present at the table were George Bush,
then ambassador to the United Nations, and numerous other diplomats. The Attorney General's lack of
restraint and want of tact, on such an occasion and at
the very table of legendary hostess Perle Mesta, were
clearly symptomatic of a considerable irritation, even
rage.

I have related this background in order to show
that Demetracopoulos was under surveillance, that
he possessed information highly damaging to an
important Nixon-Kissinger client regime, and that
his identity was well known to those in power, in
both Washington and Athens. The United States
ambassador in Athens at the time was Henry Tasca,
a Nixon and Kissinger crony with a very lenient

attitude to the dictatorship. (He later testified to
a closed session of Congress that he had known of
the 1968 payments by the Greek secret police to
the Nixon campaign.) In July 1971, shortly after
Demetracopoulos testified before Congressman
Rosenthal's subcommittee, Tasca had sent a four-
page secret cable from Athens. It began:

> For some time I have felt that Elias Demetracopou-
> los is head of a well-organized conspiracy which
> deserves serious investigation. We have seen how
> effective he has been in combatting our present
> policy in Greece. His aim is to damage our rela-
> tions with Greece, loosen our NATO alliance and
> weaken the U.S. security position in the Eastern
> Mediterranean.

This was certainly taking Demetracopoulos seriously. So was the closing paragraph, which read as
follows:

> I am therefore bringing the matter to your personal
> attention in the hope that a way will be found to step
> up an investigation of Demetracopoulos to identify
> his sponsors, his sources of funds, his intentions,
> his methods of work and his fellow conspirators....
> I bring this matter to your attention now, believing
> that as an alien resident in the United States it may

be possible to submit him to the kind of searching and professional FBI investigation which would lift some of the mystery.

The cable was addressed, as is usual from an ambassador, to Secretary of State William Rogers. Yet it was also addressed—highly unusually—to Attorney General John Mitchell. But Mitchell, as we have seen, was the only attorney general ever to serve on Henry Kissinger's supervisory Forty Committee, which oversaw covert operations.

The State Department duly urged that "the Department of Justice do everything possible to see if we can make a Foreign Agent's case, or any kind of a case for that matter" against Demetracopoulos. Of course, as was later admitted, these investigations turned up nothing. The influence wielded by Demetracopoulos did not derive from any sinister source or nexus. But when he said that the Greek dictatorship had trampled its own society, used censorship and torture, threatened Cyprus, and bought itself political influence in Washington, he was uttering potent factual truths. Nixon himself confirmed the connection, between the junta and Pappas and Tasca and the two-way flow of dirty money, on a post-Watergate White House tape dated 23 May 1973. He is talking to his renowned confidential secretary, Rose Mary Woods:

Good old Tom Pappas, as you probably know or heard, if you haven't already heard, it is true, helped, at Mitchell's request, fund-raising for some of the defendants....He came up to see me on March 7, Pappas did. Pappas came to see me about the ambassador to Greece, that he wanted to—he wanted to keep Henry Tasca there.

This same dictatorship had in June 1970 revoked Demetracopoulos's Greek citizenship, so he was a stateless person traveling only on a flimsy document giving him leave to re-enter the United States. This fact assumed its own importance in December 1970, when his blind father was dying of pneumonia, alone, in Athens. Demetracopoulos sought permission to return home under a safe-conduct or *laissez-passer*, and was able to enlist numerous congressional friends in the attempt. Among them were senators Frank E. Moss of Utah, Quentin N. Burdick of North Dakota, and Mike Gravel of Alaska, who signed a letter dated 11 December to the Greek government and to Ambassador Tasca. Senators Edward Kennedy of Massachusetts and William Fulbright of Arkansas also expressed a personal interest.

Neither the Athens regime nor Tasca replied directly, but on 20 December, four days after the old man had died without a visit from his only son, Senators Moss, Burdick, and Gravel received a telegram from the Greek embassy in Washington. This instructed them that Demetracopoulos should have applied in person to the embassy: an odd demand to make of a man whose passport and citizenship had just been canceled by the dictatorship. Meanwhile, Demetracopoulos received a telephone call at his home, from Senator Kennedy in person, advising him not to accept any safe-conduct offer from Greece even if he was offered it. Had Demetracopoulos presented himself at the junta's embassy, he might well have been detained and kidnapped, in accordance with one of the plans we now know had been readied for his "disappearance." Of course, such a scheme would have been extremely difficult to carry out in the absence of some "cooperation"—at least a blind eye—from local US intelligence officials.

Declassified cable traffic between Ambassador Tasca in Athens and Kissinger's deputy Joseph Sisco at the State Department shows that Senator Kennedy's misgivings were amply justified. In a cable dated 14 December from Sisco to Tasca, the ambassador was told: "If GOG [Government of Greece] permits Demetracopoulos to enter, quite clearly we must avoid being put in a position of guaranteeing any assurances that he may have of being able to depart." Concurring with this extraordinary statement, Tasca added that there was a possibility of Senator Gravel attending the funeral of Demetracopoulos senior.

Elias, wrote the ambassador, "undoubtedly hopes to exploit Senator's visit by providing some way of proving that conditions here are as repressive as he has been representing them to be. He could even try to arrange for some manifestation of violence, such as a small bomb."

The absurdity of this—Demetracopoulos had no record whatever of the advocacy or practice of violence, as Tasca subconsciously recognized by making the hypothetical bomb a "small" one—also has its sinister side. Suggested here is just the sort of alibi or provocation or pretext that the junta might need for a frame-up, or to cover up a "disappearance." The entire correspondence reeks of the unspoken priorities of both the embassy and the State Department, which reflect their contempt for elected United States senators, their dislike of dissent, and their need to gratify a group of Greek gangsters who are now rightly serving terms of life imprisonment.

Now look again at the computer index disgorged, after years of litigation, from Kissinger's NSC files. It bears the date of 18 December 1970 and appears to apprise Senators Moss, Burdick and Gravel that Demetracopoulos had met his end in an Athens prison. Was this a contingency plan? A cover story? As long as Dr. Kissinger maintains his stubborn silence, and the control over his "private" state papers, it will be impossible to determine.

The same applies to the second attempt on Mr. Demetracopoulos of which we have knowledge. Having avoided the trap that seems to have been set for him in 1970, Demetracopoulos kept up his fusillade of leaks and disclosures, aimed at discrediting the Greek junta and embarrassing its American friends. He also became an important voice warning of the junta's designs on the independence of Cyprus and of US indifference to (or complicity in) that policy. In this capacity (discussed in detail in Chapter 7) he became a source of annoyance to Henry Kissinger. This can be established without difficulty. In a briefing paper presented to President Gerald Ford in October 1974, there are references to a "trace paper" about Demetracopoulos, to "the derogatory blind memo" about him, and to "the long Kissinger memo" on him. Once again, and despite repeated requests from lawyers, Kissinger has declined to answer any queries about the whereabouts of these papers, or shed any light on their contents. However, his National Security Council asked the FBI to amass any information that might discredit Demetracopoulos, and between 1972 and 1974, according to papers since declassified, the Bureau furnished Kissinger with slanderous and false material concerning, among other things, a romance which Demetracopoulos was allegedly conducting with a woman now dead, and a supposed relationship between him and

Daniel Ellsberg, leaker of the celebrated "Pentagon Papers," a man he has never met.

This might seem trivial, were it not for the memoirs of Constantine Panayotakos, the ambassador of the Greek junta to Washington, DC. Arriving to take up his post in February 1974, as the ambassador wrote in his later memoirs, entitled *In the First Line of Defense*:

> I was informed about some plans to kidnap and transport Elias Demetracopoulos to Greece; plans which reminded me of KGB methods.... On 29 May a document was transmitted to me from Angelos Vlachos, Secretary General of the Foreign Ministry, giving the views of the United States ambassador Henry Tasca, which he agreed with, about the most efficient means of dealing with the conspiracies and the whole activity of Demetracopoulos. Tasca's views are included in a memorandum of conversation with the Foreign Minister Spyridon Tetenes of 27 May.
>
> Finally, another brilliant idea of the most brilliant members of the Foreign Ministry in Athens, transmitted to me on 12 June, was for me to seek useful advice on the *extermination* of Elias Demetracopoulos from George Churchill, director of the Greek desk at the State Department, who was one of his most vitriolic enemies. [italics added]

(In Greek, the italicized word above is *exoudeterosi*. It is pretty strong. It is usually translated as "extermination," though "elimination" might be an alternative rendering. It is not a recipe for inconveniencing or hampering an individual, but for getting rid of him.) Ambassador Panayotakos later wrote a detailed letter, which is in my possession, that he had direct knowledge of a plan to abduct Demetracopoulos from Washington. His testimony is corroborated by an affidavit which I also possess, signed under penalty of perjury by Charalambos Papadopoulos. Papadopoulos was at the time the Political Counsellor to the Greek embassy—the number three position—and was bidden to lunch at the nearby Jockey Club, in late May or early June of 1974, by Ambassador Panayotakos and the assistant military attaché, Lieutenant Colonel Sotiris Yiounis. At the lunch, Yiounis broached the question of the kidnapping of Demetracopoulos, who was to be smuggled aboard a Greek NATO submarine at a harbor in Virginia.

Papadopoulos, who was Greek ambassador to Pakistan at the time he swore his affidavit, has since said that he was assured that Henry Kissinger was fully aware of the proposed operation, and "most probably willing to act as its umbrella." By that stage, the Greek junta had only a few weeks to live because of its crimes in Cyprus. Since the fall of the dictatorship, even more extensive evidence of the junta's assassination plans has been uncovered, if only at the Athenian end of the plot. But this was not a regime which ever acted without Washington's "understanding." Attempts to unearth more detail have also been made in Washington. In 1975, Senators George McGovern and James Abourezk, seconded by Congressman Don Edwards of the House Intelligence Committee, asked Senator Frank Church to include the kidnap plot against Demetracopoulos in the investigative work of his famous committee on US intelligence. As first reported by the *New York Times* and then confirmed by Seymour Hersh, Kissinger intervened personally with Church, citing grave but unspecified matters of national security, to have this aspect of the investigation shut down.

Some of this may seem fantastic, but we do know that Kissinger was conducting a vendetta against Demetracopoulos (as was Ambassador Henry Tasca); we do know that Kissinger was involved in high-level collusion with the Greek junta and had advance knowledge of the plot to assassinate Archbishop Makarios; and we do know that he had used the US embassy in Chile to smuggle weapons for the contract killing of General René Schneider. The cover story in that case, too, was that the hired goons were "only" trying to kidnap him. . . .

We also know that two clients of Kissinger's Forty Committee, General Pinochet and Colonel

Manuel Contreras, made use of the Chilean embassy in Washington to murder the dissident leader Orlando Letelier, not long after being received and flattered and in one case paid by Kissinger and his surrogates.

Thus the Demetracopoulos story, told here in full for the first time, makes a *prima facie* case that Henry Kissinger was at least aware of a plan to abduct and interrogate, and almost certainly kill, a civilian journalist in Washington, DC. In order to be cleared of the suspicion, and to explain the mysterious reference to Demetracopoulos's death in his own archives, Kissinger need only make those same archives at last accessible—or else be subpoenaed to do so.

10

Afterword:
The Profit Margin

In his furious meeting at the State Department on 18 December 1975, shortly after his moment of complicity with the Indonesian generals over East Timor (see pages 156–63), Kissinger makes the following peculiar disavowal:

> "I don't care if we sell equipment to Indonesia or not. I get nothing from it, I get no rakeoff."

One might have taken it for granted that a serving secretary of state had no direct interest in the sale of weapons to a foreign dictatorship; nobody at the meeting had suggested any such thing. How peculiar that Kissinger should deny an allegation that had not been made: answer a question that had not been asked.

It isn't possible to state with certainty when Kissinger began to profit personally from his association with the ruling circles in Indonesia, nor can it be definitely asserted that this profit was part of any "understanding" that originated in 1975. It's just that there is a perfect congruence between Kissinger's foreign policy counsel and his own business connections. One might call it a harmony of interests, rather than a conflict.

Six years after he left office, Kissinger set up a private consulting firm named Kissinger Associates, which exists to smooth and facilitate contact between multinational corporations and foreign governments. The client list is secret, and contracts with "the Associates" contain a clause prohibiting any mention of the arrangement, but corporate clients include or have included American Express, Shearson Lehman, Arco, Daewoo of South Korea, H.J. Heinz, ITT, Lockheed, Anheuser-Busch, the Banca Nazionale del Lavoro, Coca-Cola, Fiat, Revlon, Union Carbide and the Midland Bank. Kissinger's initial fellow "associates" were General Brent Scowcroft and Lawrence Eagleburger, both of whom had worked closely with him in the foreign policy and national security branches of government.

Numerous instances of a harmony between this firm and Kissinger's policy pronouncements can be cited. The best known is probably that of the People's Republic of China. Kissinger assisted several American conglomerates, notably H.J. Heinz, to gain access to the Chinese market. As it was glowingly phrased by Anthony J.F. O'Reilly, CEO of Heinz:

> Kissinger and his associates make a real contribu-
> tion, and we think they are particularly helpful in
> countries with more centrally planned economies,
> where the principal players and the dynamics among
> the principal players are of critical importance. This
> is particularly true in China, where he is a popu-
> lar figure and is viewed with particular respect. On
> China, basically, we were well on our way to estab-
> lishing the baby food presence there before Henry
> got involved. But once we decided to move he had
> practical points to offer, such as on the relationship
> between Taiwan and Beijing. He was helpful in see-
> ing that we did not take steps that would not have
> been helpful in Beijing. His relevance obviously var-
> ies from market to market, but he's probably at his
> best in helping with contacts in that shadowy world
> where that counts.

The Chinese term for this zone of shadowy transactions is *guan-xi*. In less judgmental American speech
it would probably translate as "access," or "influence-
peddling." Selling baby food in China may seem
innocuous enough, but when the Chinese regime
turned its guns and tanks on its own children in
Tiananmen Square in 1989, it had no more staunch

defender than Henry Kissinger. Arguing very strongly against sanctions, he wrote that "China remains too important for America's national security to risk the relationship on the emotions of the moment." Taking the Deng Xiaoping view of the democratic turbulence, and even the view of those we now suppose to have pressed Deng from the Right, he added, "No government in the world would have tolerated having the main square of its capital occupied for eight weeks by tens of thousands of demonstrators." Of course, some governments would have found a way to meet with the leaders of those demonstrators. . . . It is perhaps just as well that Kissinger's services were not retained by the Stalinist regimes of Romania, Czechoslovakia and East Germany, which succumbed to just such public insolence later in the same year.

Nor was Kissinger's influence-peddling confined to Heinz's nutritious products. He assisted Atlantic Richfield/Arco to market oil deposits in China. He helped ITT (a corporation which had once helped him to overthrow the elected government of Chile) to hold a path-breaking board meeting in Beijing, and he performed similar services for David Rockefeller and the Chase Manhattan Bank, which held an international advisory committee meeting in the Chinese capital and met with Deng himself.

Six months before the massacre in Tiananmen

Square, Kissinger set up a limited investment partnership named China Ventures, of which he personally was chairman, CEO and chief partner. Its
brochure helpfully explained that China Ventures
involved itself only with projects that "enjoy the
unquestioned support of the People's Republic of
China." The move proved premature: the climate for
investment on the Chinese mainland soured after
the repression that followed the Tiananmen Square
massacres, and the limited sanctions approved by
Congress. This no doubt contributed to Kissinger's
irritation at the criticism of Deng. But while China
Ventures lasted, it drew large commitments from
American Express, Coca-Cola, Heinz and a large
mining and extraction conglomerate named Freeport-McMoRan, of which more in a moment.

Many of Kissinger's most extreme acts have been
undertaken, at least ostensibly, in the name of anti-
Communism. So it is amusing to find him exerting
himself on behalf of a regime that can guarantee
safe investment by virtue of a ban on trade unions, a
slave-labor prison system and a one-party ideology.
Nor is China the sole example here. When Lawrence Eagleburger left the State Department in 1984,
having been ambassador to Yugoslavia, he became
simultaneously a partner of Kissinger Associates,
a director of a wholly owned banking subsidiary of
the Ljubljanska Banka, a bank then owned by the

Belgrade regime, and the American representative of the Yugo mini-car. Yugo duly became a client of Kissinger Associates, as did a Yugoslav construction concern named Enerjoprojeckt. The Yugo is of particular interest because it was produced by the large state-run conglomerate that also functioned as Yugoslavia's military-industrial and arms-manufacturing complex. This complex was later seized by Slobodan Milosevic, along with the other sinews of what had been the Yugoslav National Army, and used to prosecute wars of aggression against four neighboring republics. At all times during this protracted crisis, and somewhat out of step with many of his usually hawkish colleagues, Henry Kissinger urged a consistent policy of conciliation with the Milosevic regime. (Mr. Eagleburger in due course rejoined the State Department as Deputy Secretary and briefly became Secretary of State. So it goes.)

Another instance of the Kissingerian practice is the dual involvement of "the Associates" with Saddam Hussein. When Saddam was riding high in the late 1980s, and having his way with the departments of Commerce and Agriculture in Washington, and throwing money around like the proverbial drunken sailor (and using poison gas and chemical weapons on his Kurdish population without a murmur from Washington), the US-Iraq Business Forum provided a veritable slot machine of contacts, contracts and opportunities. Kissinger's partner Alan Stoga, who had also been the economist attached to his Reagan-era Commission on Central America, featured noticeably on a Forum junket to Baghdad. At the same time, Kissinger's firm represented the shady Italian Banco Nazionale del Lavoro, which was later shown to have made illegal loans to the Hussein regime. As usual, everything was legal. It always is, when the upper middle class meets the lower Middle East.

In the same year—1989—Kissinger made his lucrative connection with Freeport-McMoRan, a globalized firm based in New Orleans. Its business is the old-fashioned one of extracting oil, gas, and minerals. Its chairman, James Moffett, has probably earned the favorite titles bestowed by the business and financial pages, being beyond any doubt "flamboyant," "buccaneering," and a "venture capitalist."

In 1989, Freeport-McMoRan paid Kissinger Associates a retainer of $200,000 and fees of $600,000, not to mention a promise of a 2 percent commission on future earnings. Freeport-McMoRan also made Kissinger a member of its board of directors, at an annual salary of at least $30,000. In 1990, the two concerns went into business in Burma, the most grimly repressive state in all of South Asia. Freeport-McMoRan would drill for oil and gas, according to the agreement, and Kissinger's other client, Daewoo (which was then itself a venal corporate prop of an unscrupulous Korean regime), would build the plant. However, that year the Burmese generals, under their wonderful collective title of SLORC (State Law and Order Restoration Council), lost a popular election to the democratic opposition led by Daw Aung San Suu Kyi and decided to annul the result. This development—producing yet more irritating calls for the isolation of the Burmese junta—was unfavorable to the Kissinger-Freeport-Daewoo triad, and the proposal lapsed.

But the following year, in March 1991, Kissinger was back in Indonesia with Moffett, closing a deal for a thirty-year license to continue exploiting a gigantic gold and copper mine. The mine is of prime importance for three reasons. First, it was operated as part of a joint venture with the Indonesian military government, and with that government's leader, the now-deposed General Suharto. Second, it is located on the island of Irian Jaya (in an area formerly known as West Irian): a part of the archipelago which—in common with East Timor—is only Indonesian by right of arbitrary conquest. Third, its operations commenced in 1973—two years before Henry Kissinger visited Indonesia and helped unleash the Indonesian bloodbath in East Timor while unlocking a flow of weaponry to his future business partners.

This could mean no more than the "harmony of interest" I suggested above. No more, in other words, than a happy coincidence. What is not coincidental is the following:

- Freeport-McMoRan's enormous Grasberg mine in Irian Jaya stands accused of creating an environmental and social catastrophe. In October 1995 the Overseas Private Investment Corporation (OPIC), a Federal body that exists to help US companies overseas, decided to cancel Freeport-McMoRan's investment insurance for political risk—the very element on which Kissinger had furnished soothing assurances in 1991. OPIC concluded that the Grasberg mine had "created and continues to pose unreasonable or major environmental, health or safety hazards with respect to the rivers that are being impacted by the tailings, the surrounding terrestrial ecosystem, and the local inhabitants."

- The "local inhabitants" who came last on that list are the Amungme people, whose protests at the environmental rape, and at working conditions in the mine, were met by Indonesian regular soldiers at the service of Freeport-McMoRan, and under the orders of Suharto. In March 1996, large-scale rioting nearly closed the mine at a cost of four deaths and many injuries.

Freeport-McMoRan mounted an intense lobbying campaign in Washington, with Kissinger's help, to get its OPIC insurance reinstated. The price was the creation of a trust fund of $100 million for the repair of the Grasberg site after it, and its surrounding ecology, had eventually been picked clean. All of this became moot with the overthrow of the Suharto dictatorship, the detention of Suharto himself, and the unmasking of an enormous nexus of "crony capitalism" involving him, his family, his military colleagues, and certain favored multinational corporations. This political revolution also restored, at incalculable human cost, the independence of East Timor. There was even a suggestion of a war crimes inquiry and a human rights tribunal, to settle some part of the account for the years of genocide and occupation. Once again, Henry Kissinger has had to scan the news with anxiety, and wonder whether even worse revelations are in store for him. It will be a national and international disgrace if the answer to this question is left to the pillaged and misgoverned people of Indonesia, rather than devolving onto a United States Congress that has for so long shirked its proper responsibility.

The subject awaits its magistrate.

11

Law and Justice

Although one could do no more than "deplore" a number of slaughtered children, there was in existence means of preventing one particular aspect of the principle of expediency from doing too much damage. Most international criminals were beyond the reach of man-made laws; Dimitrios happened to be within reach of one law. He had committed at least two murders and had therefore broken the law as surely as if he had been starving and had stolen a loaf of bread.

Eric Ambler, *The Mask of Dimitrios*

As Henry Kissinger now understands, there are increasingly noticeable rents and tears in the cloak of immunity that has shrouded him until now. Recent evolutions in national and international law have made his position an exposed and, indeed, a vulnerable one. For convenience, the distinct areas of law may be grouped under four main headings:

1. International Human Rights Law. This comprises the grand and sonorous covenants on the rights of the individual in relation to the state; it also protects the individual from other actors in the international community who might violate those rights. Following from the French Revolution's "Declaration of the Rights of Man," international human-rights law holds that political associations are legitimate only insofar as they preserve the dignity and well-being of individuals, a view that challenges the realpolitik privilege given to the "national interest." The United States is directly associated with sponsoring many of these covenants and has ratified several others.

2. The Law of Armed Conflict. Somewhat protean and uneven, this represents the gradual emergence of a legal consensus on what is, and what is not, permissible during a state of war. It also comprises the various humanitarian agreements that determine the customary "law of war" and that attempt to reduce the oxymoronic element in this ancient debate.

3. International Criminal Law. This concerns any individual, including an agent of any state, who commits direct and grave atrocities against either his "own" citizens or those of another state; covered here are genocide, crimes against humanity, and other crimes

of war. The Rome Statute, which also establishes an International Criminal Court for the trial of individuals, including governmental offenders, is the codified summa of this law as revised and updated since the Nuremberg precedent. It commands the signatures of most governments as well as, since 31 December 2000, that of the United States.

4. Domestic Law and the Law of Civil Remedies. Most governments have similar laws that govern crimes such as murder, kidnapping, and larceny, and many of them treat any offender from any country as the same. These laws in many cases permit a citizen of any country to seek redress in the courts of the offender's "host" country or country of citizenship. In United States law, one particularly relevant statute is the Alien Tort Claims Act.

The United States is the most generous in granting immunity to itself and partial immunity to its servants, and the most laggard in adhering to international treaties (ratifying the Genocide Convention only in 1988 and signing the Covenant on Civil and Political Rights only in 1992). And the provisions of the Rome Statute, which would expose Kissinger to dire punishment if they had been law from as early as 1968, are not retroactive. The Nuremberg principles, however, were in that year announced by an international convention to have no statute of limitations.

International customary law would allow any signatory country (again exempting the United States) to bring suit against Kissinger for crimes against humanity in Indochina.

More importantly, United States federal courts have been found able to exercise jurisdiction over crimes such as assassination, kidnapping, and terrorism, even when these are supposedly protected by the doctrine of state or sovereign immunity. Of a number of landmark cases, the most salient one is the finding of the DC Circuit Court in 1980, concerning the car-bomb murder, by Pinochet's agents, of Orlando Letelier and Ronni Moffitt. The court held that "[w]hatever policy options may exist for a foreign country," the Pinochet regime "has no 'discretion' to perpetrate conduct designed to result in the assassination of an individual or individuals, action that is clearly contrary to the precepts of humanity as recognized in both national and international law." Reciprocally speaking, this would apply to an American official seeking to assassinate a Chilean. Assassination was illegal both as a private and a public act when Henry Kissinger was in power and when the attacks on General Schneider of Chile and President Makarios of Cyprus took place.

As the Hinchey report to Congress in 2000 now demonstrates that US government agents were knowingly party to acts of torture, murder, and "disappearance" by Pinochet's death squads, Chilean citizens will be able to bring suit in America under the Alien Tort Claims Act, which grants US federal courts "subject-matter jurisdiction" over a claim when a non-US citizen sues for a civil wrong committed in violation of a US treaty or other international law. Chilean relatives of the "disappeared" and of General Schneider have recently expressed an interest in doing so, and I am advised by several international lawyers that Henry Kissinger would indeed be liable under such proceedings.

The Alien Tort Claims Act would also permit victims in other countries, such as Bangladesh or Cambodia, to seek damages from Kissinger, on the model of the recent lawsuit held in New York against Li Peng, among the Chinese Communist officials most accountable for the 1989 massacre in Tiananmen Square.

A significant body of legal theory can be brought to bear on the application of "customary law" to the bombardment of civilians in Indochina. The Genocide Convention was not ratified by the United States until 1988. In 1951, however, it was declared by the International Court of Justice to be customary international law. The work of the International Law Commission is in full agreement with this view. There would be argument over whether the numberless victims were a "protected group" under existing law, and also as to whether their treatment was sufficiently indiscriminate, but such argument would place heavy burdens on the defense as well as the prosecution.*

An important recent development is the enforcement by third countries—notably Spain—of the international laws that bind all states. Baltasar Garzón, the Spanish judge who initiated the successful prosecution of General Pinochet, has also secured the detention in Mexico of the Argentine torturer Ricardo Miguel Cavallo, who is now held in prison awaiting extradition. The parliament of Belgium has recently empowered Belgian courts to exercise jurisdiction over war crimes and breaches of the Geneva Convention committed anywhere in the world by a citizen of any country. This practice, which is on the increase, has at minimum the effect of limiting the ability of certain people to travel or to avoid extradition. The Netherlands, Switzerland, Denmark, and Germany have all recently employed the Geneva Conventions to prosecute war criminals for actions committed against non-nationals by non-nationals. The British House of Lords decision in the matter of Pinochet has also decisively negated the defense of "sovereign immunity" for acts committed by a

---

* See especially Nicole Barrett: "Holding Individual Leaders Responsible for Violations of Customary International Law," *Columbia Human Rights Law Review*, Spring 2001.

government or by those following a government's orders. This has led in turn to Pinochet's prosecution in his own country.

There remains the question of American law. Kissinger himself admits (see page 159) that he knowingly broke the law in continuing to supply American weapons to Indonesia, which in turn used them to violate the neutrality of a neighboring territory and to perpetrate gross crimes against humanity. Kissinger also faces legal trouble over his part in the ethnic cleansing of the British colonial island of Diego Garcia in the early 1970s, when indigenous inhabitants were displaced to make room for a United States military base. Lawyers for the Chagos Islanders have already won a judgment in the British courts on this matter, which now moves to a hearing in the United States. The torts cited are "forced relocation, torture, and genocide."

In this altered climate, the United States faces an interesting dilemma. At any moment, one of its most famous citizens may be found liable for terrorist actions under the Alien Tort Claims Act, or may be subject to an international request for extradition, or may be arrested if he travels to a foreign country, or may be cited for crimes against humanity by a court in an allied nation. The non-adherence by the United States to certain treaties and its reluctance to extradite make it improbable that American authorities would cooperate with such actions, though this would gravely undermine the righteousness with which Washington addresses other nations on the subject of human rights. There is also the option of bringing Kissinger to justice in an American court with an American prosecutor. Again the contingency seems a fantastically remote one, but, again, the failure to do so would expose the country to a much more obvious charge of double standards than would have been apparent even two years ago.

The burden therefore rests with the American legal community and with the American human-rights lobbies and non-governmental organizations. They can either persist in averting their gaze from the egregious impunity enjoyed by a notorious war criminal and lawbreaker, or they can become seized by the exalted standards to which they continually hold everyone else. The current state of suspended animation, however, cannot last. If the courts and lawyers of this country will not do their duty, we shall watch as the victims and survivors of this man pursue justice and vindication in their own dignified and painstaking way, and at their own expense, and we shall be put to shame.

Appendix I

A Fragrant Fragment

I am taking the liberty of reproducing a correspondence, initially between Henry Kissinger and
myself, which began in the *New York Times Book
Review* in the fall of the year 2000. In a review
(reprinted below) of *The Arrogance of Power*, the work
by Anthony Summers and Robbyn Swan to which
direct reference is made on page 12 of this book, I
had essentially summarized and condensed the case
against Nixon's and Kissinger's private and illicit
diplomacy during the 1968 election: a case made
much more fully in Chapter 1 here [see pages 1–17].
I also made reference to some other Nixon-era
crimes and misdemeanors.

This drew a rather lengthy and—to put it no
higher—distinctly bizarre reply from Kissinger.
Its full text is also appended, together with the
responses that it occasioned in its turn. (I have no
means of knowing why Kissinger recruited former
General Brent Scowcroft as his co-signer, unless it

was for the reassurance of human company as well as the solidarity of a well-rewarded partner in the firm of Kissinger Associates.)

The correspondence makes three convenient points. It undermines pseudo-lofty attempts by Kissinger and his defenders to pretend that this book, or better say the arguments contained in it, are beneath their notice. They have already attempted to engage, in other words, and have withdrawn in disorder. Second, it shows the extraordinary mendacity, and reliance upon mendacity and upon non-credible but hysterical denial, that characterizes the Kissinger style. Third, it supplies another small window into the nauseating record of "rogue state" internal affairs.

Review by Christopher Hitchens

The Arrogance of Power: The Secret World of Richard Nixon.
Anthony Summers with Robbyn Swan.

In one respect at least, the memoirs of Henry Kissinger agree with *Sideshow,* William Shawcross's report on the bombing of Cambodia. Both books confirm that Richard Nixon rather liked people to fear his own madness. In the fall of 1969, for example, he told Kissinger to warn the Soviet ambassador that the President was "out of control" on Indochina, and capable of anything. Kissinger claims that he regarded the assignment as "too dangerous" to carry out. But, as Anthony Summers now instructs us:

> Three months earlier, however, Kissinger had sent that very same message by proxy when he instructed Len Garment, about to leave on a trip to Moscow, to give the Soviets "the impression that Nixon is somewhat 'crazy'—immensely intelligent, well organized and experienced to be sure, but at moments of stress or personal challenge unpredictable and capable of the bloodiest brutality." Garment carried out the mission, telling a senior Brezhnev adviser that Nixon was "a dramatically disjointed personality... more than a little paranoid...when necessary, a cold-hearted butcher." The irony, the former aide reflected ruefully in 1997, was that everything he had told the Russians turned out to be "more or less true."

The great merit of *The Arrogance of Power* is that it takes much of what we already knew, or thought we knew (or darkly suspected), and refines and confirms and extends it. The inescapable conclusion, well bodyguarded by meticulous research and footnotes, is that in the Nixon era the United States was, in essence, a "rogue state." It had a ruthless, paranoid and unstable leader who did not hesitate to break the laws of his own country in order to violate the neutrality, menace the territorial integrity or destabilize the internal affairs of other nations. At the close of this man's reign, in an episode more typical of a banana republic or a "people's democracy," his own secretary of defense, James Schlesinger, had to instruct the Joint Chiefs of Staff to disregard any military order originating in the White House.

Schlesinger had excellent grounds for circumspection. Not only had he learned that Nixon had asked the Joint Chiefs "whether in a crunch there was support to keep him in power," but he had also been told the following by Joseph Laitin, public affairs spokesman of the Office of Management and Budget. On his way to the West Wing in the spring of 1974, Laitin recalls:

> I'd reached the basement, near the Situation Room. And just as I was about to ascend the stairway, a guy came running down the stairs two steps at a time. He had a frantic look on his face, wild-eyed, like a madman. And he bowled me over, so I kind of lost my balance. And before I could pick myself up, six athletic-looking young men leapt over me, pursuing him. I suddenly realized that they were Secret Service agents, that I'd been knocked over by the president of the United States.

APPENDIX I

Summers, a former BBC correspondent who has written biographies of Marilyn Monroe and J. Edgar Hoover, makes us almost spoiled for choice as we seek an explanation for this delirious interlude and others like it. Nixon might have been intoxicated; it took very little alcohol to make him belligerent, and he became even more thuggish and incoherent when he threw in a few sleeping pills as well. He might have been hypermedicated, and he may have helped himself to a very volatile anticonvulsant called Dilantin, given to him by a campaign donor rather than prescribed by a physician. He might have been in a depressive or psychotic state; for three decades and in great secrecy he consulted a psychotherapist named Dr. Arnold A. Hutschnecker. He may even have believed the Jews were after him; on numberless occasions he used his dirtiest mouth to curse at Jewish plots and individuals.

The most arresting chapter gives us conclusive reason to believe that Nixon and his associates—especially Attorney General John Mitchell and Vice President Spiro Agnew—consciously sabotaged the Vietnam peace negotiations in Paris in the fall of 1968. Elements of this story have surfaced before, in books by—among others—Clark Clifford and Richard Holbrooke, Seymour Hersh and William Bundy. But this is the most convincing account to

209

have appeared so far, relying as it does on wiretaps released to Summers by the Federal Bureau of Investigation. Many senior Democrats knew this ghastly secret but kept it to themselves, if only because L.B.J. had lawfully—if shamefacedly—bugged Nixon and his co-conspirators, as well as the South Vietnamese embassy. (The FBI intercept cables are reproduced here.)

Using a series of extremist and shady intermediaries, the Nixon campaign covertly assured the South Vietnamese generals that if they boycotted President Lyndon B. Johnson's dearly bought conference (which they ultimately did on the very eve of the election) they would get a more sympathetic administration. Irony is too feeble a word for what they actually got: a losing war, protracted for four years and concluded—with much additional humiliation—on the same terms that Johnson and Hubert Humphrey had been offering in 1968. Summers has spoken to all the surviving participants, including the dramatic go-between figure of Anna Chennault, who now regards even herself as one of those betrayed by this foul deal. Almost half the names on that wall in Washington are inscribed with a date after Nixon and Kissinger took office. We still cringe from counting the number of Vietnamese, Laotians and Cambodians. Nixon's illegal and surreptitious conduct not only prolonged an awful war but also corrupted and subverted a crucial presidential election: the combination must make it the most wicked action in American history.

Summers speculates that fear of disclosure might supply the motive for the Watergate burglary, an element in the tainting of yet a second election. Again, though, he spoils us for choice. If Nixon's mobsters were not looking for Democratic opposition research on the 1968 treason, they were looking for evidence that the Democrats either knew about bribes to the president from Howard Hughes or, much more probably, that they knew about secret subventions paid to Nixon and Agnew by the Greek military dictatorship. Nice choices, you will agree; it has taken some effort to narrow them down to those tasteful three (with a side bet on a prostitution racket that would have implicated both major parties).

For connoisseurs there is more detail—about the shenanigans of Nixon's crony, Bebe Rebozo, in the Bahamas; about underhand dealing with the Mafia in Cuba; and about the slow public martyrdom of Mrs. Nixon, who, Summers says, may have been a victim of physical as well as mental cruelty. Too often for my taste, Summers employs the weasel word "reportedly," which ought to be banned. But he usually goes no farther than his evidence. And two serious and consistent themes assert themselves. Richard Nixon was able, time and again, to employ overseas entanglements to make end runs around American democracy. Short of money? The shah, or the Greek junta, or some friendly but inconvenienced multinational, will provide the dough, redeemable in arms trades or rakeoffs or an imaginative new line on human rights. Stuck for an issue? Embrace the very despots—Brezhnev or Mao—whose demonization has fueled your career thus far. Polls narrowing? Sell your own country by conducting off-the-record two-track diplomacy with tinpot clients, as in 1968.

The second theme involves an attraction to violence that perhaps only Hutschnecker's posthumous notes will explain. Like many law-and-order types, Nixon had a relish for rough stuff and police provocation. He seems to have helped encourage the mayhem that both disfigured and transfigured his tour of Latin America as vice president in 1958. As president, he can be heard on tape agreeing to the employment of Teamster bullies to batter antiwar demonstrators ("Yeah.... They've got guys who'll go in and knock their heads off"). This is the same duplicitous, gloating, insecure man who embellished his own mediocre war record in order to run for Congress, who adored obscene talk but was a poor hand with the fair sex, and who affected cloth-coat austerity while dabbling all his life in slush funds. A small man who claimed to be for the little guy, but was at the service of the fat cats. A pseudo-intellectual who hated and resented the real thing. Summers has completed the work of many predecessors, and made the task of his successors very difficult. In the process, he has done an enormous service by describing, to the citizens of a nation founded on law and right, the precise obscenity of that moment when the jutting jaw of a would-be Caesar collapses into the slobbering underlip of a weak and self-pitying king.

In Defense of Nixon

To the Editor:

We would like to raise some questions of fact about Christopher Hitchens's tendentious account of a tendentious book, Anthony Summers's "Arrogance of Power" (Oct. 8).

1. Neither of us was associated with Richard Nixon during the 1968 election campaign, but the allegations that he blocked a Johnson administration Vietnam peace initiative remain, in our view, allegations unsubstantiated by persuasive evidence. In any case, the record shows that the South Vietnamese foot-dragging (alleged to be at the behest of Nixon underlings)—even if the account were true—could not have had the consequences that Summers claims. The expanded Paris peace talks began in early November, and any delay was therefore very brief; Nixon—as president-elect and at the peak of

his leverage—encouraged President Nguyen Van Thieu of South Vietnam to cooperate with the Johnson administration. Moreover, if the issue is political motivation, any discussion of this question has to begin with the indications from Soviet archives that Soviet leaders were led to believe that a main motive of rushing the bombing halt and peace talks was to get *Hubert Humphrey* elected.

2. It also needs to be borne in mind that the expanded Paris talks, once they began, were about procedure, not substance. Those talks immediately deadlocked, not on the substance of how to end the war but on whether the Vietcong guerrillas should have the same status at the table as the government of South Vietnam. No substantive proposal of any kind was put forward by the Johnson administration. It is therefore nonsense to assert that Nixon in 1972 achieved no better terms than what Lyndon Johnson was "offering" in 1968. (Hanoi rejected compromise terms until 1972.)

3. The reviewer plays the usual numbers game with American soldiers killed in action, claiming that nearly half occurred on Nixon's watch. One-third would be more nearly accurate. But that is not the essence of the misrepresentation. When Nixon came into office, America had already suffered 36,000 soldiers killed in action. Of the 20,000 killed in the Nixon period, 12,000 occurred in the first year before any new policy could take effect, 9,000

in the first six months—clear legacies of the previous administration. When Nixon came in, American soldiers killed in action had run at an average rate of 1,500 per month for a year. At the end of his first term, they had been reduced to 50 per month. When Nixon entered office, American troops in Vietnam stood at 525,000 and were still increasing according to plans made in the Johnson administration. In 1972, they had been reduced to 25,000.

4. The Nixon administration concluded the first strategic arms control agreement and the first agreement banning biological weapons; opened relations with China; ended the decades-long crisis over Berlin; launched the Arab-Israeli peace process; and initiated the Helsinki negotiations, generally accepted as weakening the Soviets' control of their satellite empire and fostering German unification. Are these the actions of a "rogue" leader, as Hitchens calls Nixon?

5. Nixon was a strategist. He did want the notion to get around, as a strategic ploy, that if provoked by a foreign aggressor, he might respond disproportionately. But it is important here to separate the Nixon who sometimes expressed extreme statements to his confidants for dramatic or rhetorical effect and the Nixon who never made a really serious international move without the most careful and cautious analysis. It is laughable to imagine Richard Nixon ordering a domestic coup. Defense Secretary James Schlesinger

did apparently in Nixon's last days direct the Joint Chiefs of Staff to ignore orders from their commander in chief—an unprecedented arrogation of authority. Whatever his motives, Schlesinger never came to either of us (or anyone else, so far as we know) with his concerns and what to do about them.

6. As for the story by Joe Laitin (a close associate of Schlesinger) that a frenetic Nixon came tearing down the stairs two at a time, pursued by six Secret Service agents, and literally knocked Laitin over—no way. Nixon could not have gone down a set of stairs two at a time if his life depended on it.

HENRY A. KISSINGER
New York
BRENT SCOWCROFT
Washington
[*November 5 2000*]

Nixon Descending

To the Editor:

In reading Henry A. Kissinger and Brent Scowcroft's spirited defense of Richard Nixon (Letters, Nov. 5), I was surprised that they felt it necessary in making their case to say I had fabricated the details of my strange encounter with the president. I was there; they weren't.

However, they miss the point. Whether the president bowled me over or not is unimportant. I cannot swear that he was descending the stairs two at a time, three at a time or one at a time. All I can say is that the desperate look on his face as he was pursued by the Secret Service agents alarmed me and prompted my call to Defense Secretary James Schlesinger. Because I had direct access to Schlesinger, having worked with him for years, I was able to report the raw details of the incident immediately after it happened. As Kissinger and Scowcroft well know, history cannot be tampered with, and suggesting I lied about my encounter with President Nixon can't change what actually took place.

JOE LAITIN
Bethesda, Md.
[*November 19 2000*]

Nixoniana

To the Editor:

In his and Brent Scowcroft's letter (Nov. 5), former Secretary of State Henry A. Kissinger denied having been associated with Defense Secretary James Schlesinger in directing the Joint Chiefs of Staff to ignore orders from President Richard Nixon. As one who during 1973–75 served on one of the Battle Staff units, on permanent standby to brief the president and top commanders in the event of a nuclear crisis, I know otherwise. As I have testified in secret debriefings and in both open and closed sessions of House and Senate committees as far back as 1975, Kissinger signed or countersigned at least three such orders in the final year of the Nixon presidency. I have so testified under penalty of perjury several times.

After the first such order in 1973 signed by Kissinger, the Joint Chiefs demanded that any subsequent ones be countersigned by at least one other Nixon cabinet officer. A second such order, again an instruction not to obey the president until further notice, was signed by Kissinger and, to the best of my recollection, Elliot Richardson. At least one other was jointly signed by Kissinger and Defense Secretary Schlesinger. Such orders were always sent "Top Secret, Eyes Only, Limited Distribution," bypassing other traffic. Sometimes they remained in effect for a week, most times only two to four days. The orders were issued at times of perceived Nixon mental instability, I repeatedly received them in my own hands, as did numerous others serving in sensitive nuclear control positions during that last horrific year of the Nixon presidency.

BARRY A. TOLL
Painesville, Ohio
[*December 12 2000*]

To the Editor:

The letter by Henry Kissinger and Brent Scowcroft, referring to our Nixon biography, "The Arrogance of Power," was an inept barrage. They assert that allegations of Nixonian sabotage of the 1968 Johnson peace effort are "unsubstantiated by persuasive evidence," then fail to counter any of our detailed analysis—which includes the recently released record of F.B.I. surveillance conducted on the eve of the election that brought Nixon to power.

Kissinger and Scowcroft cite Soviet archival sources, of all things, to insinuate that the Johnson peace initiative was just a political ploy "to get Hubert Humphrey elected." Any reading of the record of the pivotal White House meetings, available at the Johnson Library, dispels that notion. But even if that had been the case, it would not mitigate the offense indicated by the mass of information suggesting that Nixon did the unconscionable— as an unelected political candidate he meddled in the government's conduct of highly sensitive peace negotiations.

Readers of our book will find that we account, page by page, for our sources—which included more than a thousand interviews. Had Kissinger granted us an interview, we would have faithfully reported his views on relevant matters. We made nine written requests over a two-year period, but he ducked and weaved and never came through.

Anthony Summers
Robbyn Swan
Cappoquin, Ireland
[*December 12 2000*]

Unpublished

To the Editor:

I suppose it is a distinction of some sort to be attacked at such length by Henry Kissinger and (for some reason) his business partner General Brent Scowcroft. It is certainly fascinating to see the evident nervousness with which they approach the allegations I made.

The record of Henry Kissinger's underhand involvement with the Nixon presidential campaign of 1968 is so extensively documented by now, including by Nixon himself, that one rubs the bleary eyes to read a denial of it. "Neither of us," write the two men, "was associated" with that campaign. Misery is said to love company; I have never bothered to inquire whether General Scowcroft played any part in that unhappy episode but his own modesty—perhaps disappointment—only serves to put his co-author's credibility in starker contrast with the facts. Mr. Kissinger was hired as Nixon's principal adviser for national security as soon as the election was over, even though the two men had met only once. It was, moreover, Nixon's first appointment. Does Kissinger now deny that this was unconnected to the many surreptitious services performed by him, from Paris, for John Mitchell and for Nixon himself? If so, the flabbergasting denial of established facts would be interesting only insofar as it suggested something hitherto unguessed-at: the prickings of an uneasy conscience.

I make this perhaps unwarrantable suggestion because of a peculiar formulation later in the same paragraph, where Mr. Kissinger (I've done with Scowcroft for now), says that:

> the record shows that the South Vietnamese foot-dragging (alleged to be at the behest of Nixon underlings)—*even if the account were true*—could not have had the consequence that Summers claims. The expanded Paris peace talks began in early November, and any delay was therefore very brief; Nixon—as president-elect and at the peak of his leverage—encouraged President Nguyen Van Thieu of South Vietnam to cooperate with the Johnson administration. (Italics added.)

This is a finely crafted paragraph and no mistake. But it is also very dishonestly argued. The South Vietnamese foot-dragging is not "alleged" but has been asserted and extensively documented. If the other emphasis of "alleged" is the intended one, then it was not at the "behest of underlings"—the now-familiar "deniable" scheme whereby the chief is never told what his deputies do—but at the direct instigation of Nixon himself. This has been solidly phrased by many Democratic and Republican high-level participants in these momentous events, and is not challenged, let alone rebutted, by Kissinger. "Early November" may sound suitably autumnal as a description of the seasonal setting of these same events, but it stretches to cover the date of the election itself and is thus designed to obscure what it purports to illuminate. What Kissinger means is that in the short interval when the actual "foot-dragging" took place, and as a thinkable consequence of that precise interval, one regime replaced another in the White House. That is, after all, the whole hypothesis (and the whole accusation) in the first place. Once President, Nixon did indeed appear to hew to the Johnson line—which is another element in the case against him and his newly promoted "National Security Advisor," who had no principled differences with that line to begin with.

The preceding and succeeding passages also

betray unease. Kissinger does not say that there is no evidence for this grave allegation. He says that the evidence is not persuasive. Does he care to say what is unpersuasive about the evidence adduced by so many historians and participants, from the hawkish Bundy and Haldeman to the more skeptical Clark Clifford? Evidently he does not. Instead, there comes a breathtaking and highly suggestive change of subject:

> If the issue is political motivation, any discussion of this question has to begin with the indications from Soviet archives that Soviet leaders were led to believe that a main motive of rushing the bombing halt and peace talks was to get *Hubert Humphrey* elected. (Italics in original.)

This clumsily constructed sentence deserves a close parsing. Apparently, political motivation is an allowable subtext of the argument over the Paris negotiations after all, since if it can be alleged—actually only suggested—about the Democratic incumbents it can also surely be alleged about their Republican opponents. So one is grateful for Kissinger's perhaps inadvertent concession of common ground. However, if the Johnson-Humphrey regime sought to time the talks for their own electoral purposes (and this writer was not and is not in any position to approve of anything they undertook) then they did so in public view, and as the legally elected and constituted government of the United States. In that capacity, too, they would have been subject to the judgment of the voters as to their likely opportunism. Whereas Messrs. Nixon, Agnew, Mitchell and Kissinger (only one of them so far unindicted for one abuse of power or another) would have been conducting a "diplomacy" with unaccredited interlocutors, illegal under the Logan Act, concealed not only from both the public and denominated negotiators of the country but also from its electorate! This indeed is part of the essential *gravamen* of the charge. To put the two notions on the same footing, and to lard them with vague and unsupported innuendoes about "Soviet" knowledge, is to take the same attitude to the United States Constitution that Kissinger was later to adopt toward the Chilean one.

It is obviously true to say, in a military-technocratic sense, that there is some extensive cross-over between the war as waged by Johnson and Humphrey and the war as "inherited" by Nixon and Kissinger. To that extent, some of the assertions of point (3) need not be disputed. ("One-third would be more nearly accurate." Good grief—so Kissinger has been counting them after all, while daring to accuse me of playing "the usual numbers game.") However, if the "legacy" transmitted from one administration to the next was indeed passed through a filter of illegal secret dealing with an undisclosed third power—as has been authoritatively argued, and as the outgoing administration certainly believed—and if the effect of this was to enhance the level of violence rather than to diminish it, then the case for regarding Mr. Kissinger as a war criminal, careless only of *American* deaths, is complete on those terms alone.

Your readers might care to note that in seeking further to dilute the above implications, he says nothing to my original point about hugely increased Vietnamese, Cambodian and Laotian casualties during the years 1969–1975: a period when the war and its devastation was extended into large new tracts of formerly neutral and civilian territory. Such an omission cannot be accidental; it is the sort of "oversight" which results from a racist world-view and hopes—I am sure in vain—to concentrate the attention and sympathy of your audience only upon its "own" losses.

The remaining paragraphs of his letter are replete with boilerplate propaganda and pitiful falsehood, much of it ably disposed of by the later letters you have printed from Mr. Laitin and Mr. Toll. My forthcoming book *The Trial of Henry Kissinger* will, I hope, supply the refutation of the residual claims.

CHRISTOPHER HITCHENS
Washington, DC

[A PS for readers: I do not complain of not seeing my own letter in print; it was excessively lengthy and I had already had my say in the columns of the *Book Review*. I also delayed too long in sending it, in case Kissinger—or even the hapless Scowcroft—might choose to take on the annihilating replies they had received from Laitin and Toll. But answer came there none, so I allowed myself the satisfaction of finishing an argument Kissinger had started and then abandoned.]

Appendix II

The Demetracopoulos Letter

DOBROVIR & GEBHARDT

SUITE 1105

1025 VERMONT AVENUE, N.W.

WASHINGTON. D. C. 20005

12021 347-811b

TELEX: 6503136357

WILLIAM A DOBROVIR
JOSEPH D GEBHARDT
ROBERT L ISALIM
ROBIN A FRADKIN
NINA JOAN KIMBALL

COUNSEL BETH L DOH

OF COUNSEL
ELIZABETH L NEWMAN. P C

September 3, 1987

BY MESSENGER

Dr. Henry A. Kissinger
c/o James E. Wesner, Esq.
Ginsberg, Feldman, Weil & Bress
Suite 700
1250 Connecticut Avenue, N.W.
Washington, D.C. 20036

Dear Dr. Kissinger:

   You will recall correspondence I sent to
you, care of your attorney James Wesner, in

1980, concerning NSC documents referring to
Elias P. Demetracopoulos. You never replied
to those letters, in particular to the last,
October 24, 1980, letter. From what you had
told us through your attorney at that time,
we were led to believe that neither you nor
NSC possessed any of the described documents.
Events since then require us to renew this
matter with you.

1. Papers of Richard M. Nixon, released in
May 1987, included John Dean files relating to
Mr. Demetracopoulos, but no NSC files, as far
as we know.

2. As you know (since we sent you copies),
NSC released to us copies of computer indices
showing that while you were National Security
Advisor and Chairman of the "40 Committee,"
the NSC did have copies of documents relating
to Mr. Demetracopoulos. NSC informed us that
the documents, if not in the Nixon papers (as
they do not seem to be), were taken by you
and presumably repose in your personal files,
those files sent to the National Archives, or
those files you have deposited in the Library
of Congress but which are closed to the public
until 2001.

Dr. Henry A. Kissinger
September 3, 1987
Page 2

3. One of the NSC computer indices shows
a document, dated December 18, 1970, which
refers to "Mr. Demetracopoulos death in Athens
Prison." That was about the time that the first

attempts were made by the Greek dictatorship
to kidnap Mr. Demetracopoulos, then living in
this country, presumably to spirit him back to
Greece to his "death in [an] Athens prison."
This has recently been documented in sworn
statements of knowledgeable Greek officials.
The Senate Select Committee on Intelligence,
chaired by the late Sen. Frank Church, began
investigating the incident in connection with
its study of intelligence activities relating
to Greece: but, according to Committee sources,
as reported by Seymour Hersh in his book The
Price of Power, you urged the Committee to drop
the investigation, and it did so.

4. Documents released by the CIA since
1980 refer to briefings for then President
Ford in October 1974. The document refers to
a "trace paper" about Mr. Demetracopoulos,
a "derogatory blind memo" and "the long
Kissinger memo on Elias [Demetracopoulos],"
"left . . . with General Skowcroft." Copies of
pertinent documents are enclosed.

You should be aware that after a great
deal of discussion, correspondence and
congressional investigation, both the FBI
and then Director William Webster and the
CIA under the late Director William Casey,
acknowledged that their years of investigation
turned up not a shred of "derogatory"
information about Mr. Demetracopoulos. A copy
of a document is enclosed.

We cannot help but assume that you possess
at least a copy of "the long Kissinger memo"
on Mr. Demetracopoulos, and you may also

possess copies of the "trace paper" and the
"derogatory blind memo."

Dr. Henry A. Kissinger
September 3, 1987
Page 3

We ask that, in order to complete
the historical record you provide Mr.
Demetracopoulos promptly with copies of the
mentioned documents.

Sincerely Yours,

William A. Dobrovir

Enclosures
jk

Acknowledgments

When *Harper's* magazine was good enough to publish the two long essays that together became the core of this book, my friend and publisher Rick MacArthur sent an early copy round to ABC News in New York. Since we had criticized the deference of the American media quite as much as we had attacked the moral sloth of the overfed American "human rights" community, he thought it was only fair to give *Nightline*'s producer the right of reply. After an interval, we got our answer. "Is there," said the top man at that top-rated Kissinger-showcasing show, "anything new here?"

Rick and I hugged ourselves with promised laughter at that. In Washington and New York and Los Angeles and every other cultural capital, the shallow demand for novelty is also an ally of a favorite spintactic of the powerful, which is to confront a serious allegation not by refusing to deny it but instead by trying to reclassify it as "old news." And of course, the joke was therefore on the producer, who had come up with a stale and predictable and exhausted

ACKNOWLEDGMENTS

response. (We later asked him if there was anything fresh about his question.)

Had it been asked in good faith, of course, that same question would still require a straight answer. Here it is. The information in this book is not "new" to the people of East Timor and Cyprus and Bangladesh and Laos and Cambodia, whose societies were laid waste by a depraved statecraft. Nor is it "new" to the relatives of the tortured and disappeared and murdered in Chile. But it *would* be new to anyone who relied on ABC News for information. It is not new to the degraded statesmen who agree to appear on that network in return for being asked flattering questions. But some of it might come as news to the many decent Americans who saw their own laws and protections violated, and their own money spent in their name but without their leave, for atrocious purposes that could not be disclosed, by the Nixon-Kissinger gang. Oh yes, this is an old story all right. But I hope and intend to contribute to writing its ending.

As a matter of fact, there *are* a few disclosures in the book; some of the new material shocked even its author. But I'm not here to acknowledge my own work. Wherever possible, I give credit and attribution in the narrative itself. Some debts must still be mentioned.

Nobody in Washington who takes on the Kissinger

232

matter can ever be clear of debt to Seymour Hersh, who first contrasted the man's reputation with his actions, and by this method alone, as well as by heroic excavations of the record, began the slow process which will one day catch up with the worthless, evasive cleverness of official evil. This is a battle for transparency and for historical truth, among other things, and if Hersh has any rival in that area it is Scott Armstrong, founder of the National Security Archive, which has been deputizing as Washington's equivalent of a Truth and Justice Commission until the real thing comes along. ("Then let us pray that come it may...")

During their long absence from the moral radar-screen of the West, the people of East Timor could have had no better and braver friends than Amy Goodman and Allan Nairn. The family of Orlando Letelier, and the families of so many other Chilean victims, could always count on Peter Kornbluh, Saul Landau and John Dinges, who in Washington have helped keep alive a case of crucial importance that will one day be vindicated. Martin Edwin Anderson, Lucy Komisar, Mark Hertsgaard, Fred Branfman, Kevin Buckley, Lawrence Lifschultz will, I know, all recognize themselves in my borrowings from their more original and more courageous work.

Sometimes a chat with an editor can be encouraging; sometimes not. I was in the middle part of my first explanatory sentence with Lewis Lapham, editor of *Harper's* magazine, when he broke in to say: "Done. Write it. High time. We'll do it." I didn't trust myself then to thank him, as I do now. So instead I got on with it, which I could not have done without the unusual Ben Metcalf at the *Harper's* office. Together with Sarah Vos and Jennifer Szalai, punctilious fact-checkers, we went over it again and again, marvelously nauseated at the renewed realization that it was all true.

The current state of international human rights legislation is highly inchoate. But, in an uneven yet seemingly discernible fashion, it is evolving to the point where people like Kissinger are no longer above the law. Welcome and unexpected developments have had a vertiginous effect: I hope that my closing section on this area is out of date by the time it is published. For their help in guiding me through the existing statutes and precedents, I am enormously obliged to Nicole Barrett of Columbia University, to Jamin Raskin and Michael Tigar at the Washington College of Law at American University, and to Geoffrey Robertson QC.

Patrick Lannan and the Lannan Foundation were both enthusiastic and generous about this project, and kindly provided the seed money that will make its main conclusions available in television-documentary form.

ACKNOWLEDGMENTS

There are very few mirthful moments in these pages. Still, I remember so well the day in 1976 when Martin Amis, then my colleague at the *New Statesman*, told me that his literary pages would serialize Joseph Heller's *Good as Gold*. He showed me the proposed extract. Chapters 7 and 8 of that novel, in particular, are imperishable satire, and must be read and reread. (The relevant passage of sustained and obscene and well-reasoned abuse, which shames the publishing industry as well as the journalistic racket for its complicity with this deceitful and humorless toad, begins with the sentence: "Even that fat little fuck Henry Kissinger was writing a book!") I later became a friend of Joe Heller, whose death in 1999 was a calamity for so many of us, and my last acknowledgment is to the invigorating effect of his warm, broad-minded, hilarious, serious, and unquenchable indignation.

CHRISTOPHER HITCHENS
Washington, DC, 25 January 2001

Index

INDEX

INDEX

Panayotakos, Constantine, 183–84
Papadopoulos, Charalambos, 184–85
Papadopoulos, George, 168
Pappas, Thomas A., 131, 172–79
Pentagon Papers, 183
Pepsi Cola, 83
Phoenix Program, 59–60
Pike, Otis, xxxvii–xxxviii
Pinochet, Augusto, 102–8
  Contreras and CIA, 107–8, 113–15, 185–86
  Dorfman on, ix–xii, xiv
  international criminal law and, 200–203
  Kissinger's private meeting with, xxviii–xxix, 105–8
  release of secret files on, xliii–xlviii, 105–7
Pinto, Constancio, 142–43
Podhoretz, Norman, xlix
Portugal, and East Timor, 138–40, 144–46, 153–55, 165
Prats, Carlos, 104
Presidential Commission on Central America, xxxviii
Project FUBELT, 102

Qiao Guanhua, 136

Rahman, Mujibur, 66, 67, 73–76, 79–80
Rashid, Major, 76
Rebozo, Charles "Bebe," 50–51, 211
Reynolds, Russel B., 37
Richardson, Elliot, 218
RN: The Memoirs of Richard Nixon (Nixon), 9, 10, 11
Rockefeller, David, 83, 190
Rockefeller, Nelson, 10, 14–15, 22, 23
Rogers, William, xxvii–xxx, 50–51, 54, 178
Romania, 69
Rome Statute, 199
Rosenthal, Benjamin, 174–75, 177
Rostow, Walt, 7–8
Roufogalis, Michael, 168, 172
Rusk, Dean, 7–8
Ryan, Patrick, 102

Sampson, Nicos, 130–32, 136
Schanberg, Sydney, 56, 57–58
Schaufele, William, 160, 161
Schlesinger, James, xviii–xix, 208, 215–18
Schneider, René
  attempts to kidnap and kill, 84–101, 111–12, 185
  family files suit, xxxiv

About the Author

Christopher Hitchens (1949-2011) was a contributing editor to *Vanity Fair* and a columnist for *Slate*. He was the author of numerous books, including works on Thomas Jefferson, Thomas Paine, George Orwell, Mother Teresa, Henry Kissinger and Bill and Hillary Clinton, as well as his international bestseller and National Book Award nominee, *god Is Not Great*. His memoir, *Hitch-22*, was nominated for the Orwell Prize and was a finalist for the National Book Critics Circle Award. His last collection of essays, *Arguably* (Atlantic, 2011), was a *Sunday Times* bestseller. In 2012, Hitchens was awarded a memorial by the Orwell Prize.

THE
MISSIONARY
POSITION

Also by Christopher Hitchens

BOOKS

Hostage to History: Cyprus from the Ottomans to Kissinger
Blood, Class and Empire: The Enduring Anglo-American Relationship
Imperial Spoils: The Curious Case of the Elgin Marbles
Why Orwell Matters
No One Left to Lie To: The Triangulations of William Jefferson Clinton
Letters to a Young Contrarian
The Trial of Henry Kissinger
Thomas Jefferson: Author of America
Thomas Paine's "Rights of Man": A Biography
god Is Not Great: How Religion Poisons Everything
The Portable Atheist
Hitch-22: A Memoir
Arguably: Essays
Mortality

PAMPHLETS

Karl Marx and the Paris Commune
The Monarchy: A Critique of Britain's Favorite Fetish
The Missionary Position: Mother Teresa in Theory and Practice
A Long Short War: The Postponed Liberation of Iraq

ESSAYS

Prepared for the Worst: Essays and Minority Reports
For the Sake of Argument
Unacknowledged Legislation: Writers in the Public Sphere
Love, Poverty and War: Journeys and Essays

COLLABORATIONS

James Callaghan: The Road to Number Ten (with Peter Kellner)
Blaming the Victims (edited with Edward Said)
When the Borders Bleed: The Struggle of the Kurds (photographs by Ed Kash)
International Territory: The United Nations (photographs by Adam Bartos)
Vanity Fair's Hollywood (with Graydon Carter and David Friend)

THE
MISSIONARY
POSITION

MOTHER TERESA IN THEORY
AND PRACTICE

Foreword by Thomas Mallon

Christopher Hitchens

Atlantic Books
London

First published in 1995 by Verso, an imprint of New Left Books.

Published in hardback and e-book in Great Britain in 2012 by Atlantic Books, an imprint of Atlantic Books Ltd.

10 9 8 7 6 5 4 3 2 1

A CIP catalogue record for this book is available from the British Library.

E-book ISBN: 978-0-85789-840-1
Hardback ISBN: 978-0-85789-838-8

Printed in Great Britain by the MPG Books Group

Atlantic Books
An imprint of Atlantic Books Ltd
Ormond House
26–27 Boswell Street
London
WC1N 3JZ

www.atlantic-books.co.uk

For Edwin and Gertrude Blue:
saintly but secular.

Contents

Foreword

During the middle of the last decade, in his great period of political apostasy, Christopher Hitchens often entertained, along with his older left-leaning pals, a sprinkling of younger conservative journalists and operatives, all of them not only thrilled to be in his company—who ever wasn't?—but also grateful and deeply reassured to have such a blue-chip intellectual on their side of the Iraq War, that historical moment's great divide.

I would smile quietly while these young men cheered him on and *hear-hear*'d. Just wait, I'd think, knowing the moment would arrive when the ideological fiddler would have to be paid, when the host would change the topic and the earnest and happy young men would be reduced to looking at their shoes and muttering *Oh, well, yes, I suppose*. I like to think of this as the Mother Teresa Moment, named for Hitch's most incendiary cultural dissent but applicable to any subject that might startle the Christian soldiers of the Bush administration into remembering that, apart from Saddam Hussein, Hitch remained entirely his unreconstructed secular and socialist self.

Hitchens's disdain for the "thieving, fanatical Albanian dwarf"—i.e., Mother Teresa—became so famous that new readers of *The Missionary Position* may be surprised to discover that the phrase appears nowhere in this slender volume. If the book's main title produces a guffaw, its subhead ("Mother Teresa in Theory and Practice") more closely tracks its spirit. Far from being some cackle of defilement, or even just a bit of bad-boy blasphemy, *The Missionary Position* is, in fact, a modest, rational inquiry, a calm lifting of the veil that drapes its sacred subject. "Once the decision is taken to do without awe and reverence, if only for a moment," writes Hitchens, "the Mother Teresa phenomenon assumes the proportions of the ordinary and even the political." The author wishes to examine his subject's public pronouncements, her finances, projects and associates, and to judge "Mother Teresa's reputation by her actions and words rather than her actions and words by her reputation."

Does anyone have a problem with that?

What's under the veil turns out to be pretty unsightly: Mother Teresa's missions—backed by a yachtful of grifters from Haitian first lady Michèle Duvalier to 1980s S&L fleecer Charles Keating— are revealed to be less concerned with eliminating the poverty of the poor (and even their attendant physical pain) than with extending those things as their means toward salvation in the afterlife: "The point is not the honest relief of suffering but the promulgation of a cult based on death and suffering and subjection." Hitchens's most devastating source is "Mother" herself: She "has never pretended that her work is anything but a fundamentalist religious campaign," through which the poorest of the poor, the least of these, must grin and bear it until they're transmuted from being the last to the first.

Hitch being Hitch, he cannot, here and there, resist pouring it on for the reader's edified delight. Commenting upon the decision of advice columnist Ann Landers to share one of Mother's prescriptions for improving the world ("smile more"), he writes: "It is...doubtful whether a fortune-cookie maxim of such cretinous condescension would have been chosen even by Ann Landers unless it bore the imprimatur of Mother Teresa, one of the few untouchables in the mental universe of the mediocre and the credulous."

But *The Missionary Position* remains less a polemic than an investigation rooted in personal passion. In the manner of such intrepid, also-departed colleagues as Oriana Fallaci and Ryszard Kapuściński, Hitchens traveled the world toward eruptions of what fundamentally agitated him, and that was tyranny. "This is," he writes in the book's original foreword, "a small episode in an unending argument between those who *know* they are right and therefore claim the mandate of heaven, and those who suspect that the human race has nothing but the poor candle of reason by which to light its way." Preferring "anti-theist" to "atheist," Hitchens liked to draw comparisons between Christianity and North Korea, both mental kingdoms offering their inhabitants the chance to commit "thought crime" and to deliver "everlasting praise" of the leader.

This small book is part of a big career devoted to pulverizing cant, deflating oppression, and maximizing human liberty. Not a day went by that Hitch didn't enter the lists against some iniquity. Nearly all his causes were noble; a few were quixotic and probably not worth his time. I remember one piece he wrote a half-dozen years ago in defense of free speech for David Irving, the Holocaust-denying historian. Writing against the clock, with his usual urgency, he made a slip of the keyboard in an attempted reference to one of Irving's editors, putting down "Thomas Mallon" for "Thomas Dunne." Oh, joy, I thought, seeing my name mistakenly next to Irving's in the pages of *The Wall Street Journal*. I sent Hitch an e-mail that began, more or less: "I know that to the sons of British naval officers all of us Micks must seem the same, but...." He responded late that night with "Oh, fuck," or words to that effect—no apology, just an injunction to turn up, the next day, at a demonstration he was organizing to support the Danish cartoonists who'd recently had the temerity to draw the prophet Mohammed. I thought about going, knew that I should, and finally never made it. If you want one more epitaph to add to all the ones that already have been suggested for this dual man-of-letters/man-of-action, let it be: He Showed Up. Throughout his life and times, whenever and wherever something important was on the line, he presented himself.

The Missionary Position appeared in 1995, eight years before Mother Teresa's beatification, an occurrence that Hitchens had seen rushing our way. He notes in his text how Pope John Paul II was readying so many candidates so quickly for this enhanced status ("the ante-room to sainthood") that the process had begun to "[recall] the baptism by firehose with which Chinese generals Christianized their armies."

In the event, Hitchens played a necessary, if negative, role in Mother Teresa's elevation, testifying before an official church body as to her unworthiness. He explained the task, undertaken in 2001, in the magazine *Free Inquiry*: "The present pope...has abolished the traditional office of 'Devil's Advocate,' so I drew the job of representing the Evil One, as it were, pro bono. Fine by me—I don't believe in Satan either." The writer's wife, Carol, can recall sending Hitch off to Father David O'Connor of the Washington, D.C., archdiocese to perform this strange and futile exercise in debunking, and then welcoming him home to lunch in their apartment on Columbia Road, as if he'd just come back from a radio interview.

Another, even more significant, development—this one, too, coming years after *The Missionary Position*—was the publication of Mother Teresa's letters. The spiritual doubts they were discovered to contain created a sensation worthy of the cover of *Time*. Let me present just one extract: "Jesus has a very special love for you," Mother Teresa wrote to the Reverend Michael Van Der Peet in 1979, the year she received her Nobel Peace Prize. "As for me, the silence and the emptiness is so great that I look and do not see, listen and do not hear." No, let's quote one more passage, just in case this was some momentary slip: "I am told God loves me—and yet the reality of darkness & coldness & emptiness is so great that nothing touches my soul."

You mean you're not sure?

Had these letters been available to him in the 1990s, I can hear Hitchens asking Mother Teresa just that question, face-to-face, as she showed him around the Calcutta orphanage. And it seems to me that the existence of such doubts makes her enterprise all the more breathtakingly presumptuous: She

in fact was *not* one of "those who *know* they are right."
She felt no certainty that the poverty she was barely
palliating would lead its sufferers toward an eternal
reward. It is one thing to take Pascal's wager and bet
on the existence of God, no matter what one's doubts
may be. But to lead thousands of others to the gam-
ing table, insisting that they double down with their
one paltry handful of chips?

After his cancer diagnosis, I often prayed, on my
knees and through all my own doubts, for Hitch.
Not for his soul; just for his earthly continuation.
Nothing bothered me more during the long months
of his illness (and suffering) than having to watch
interviewers ask him if he might now not be ready
to change his mind on matters cosmic. He met such
inquiries with a sort of Christian forbearance, treated
them as one more teachable moment in which he
could explain his position. And throughout this grim
period, by his conduct and example, he provided me
with one specific religious certainty, the only one I've
had in a very long time: If God does exist, He would
have been deeply disappointed in any renunciation of
nonbelief by Christopher Hitchens, that spectacular
piece of His handicraft, the worthiest foe among all
His brilliant, wayward sons of the morning.

Thomas Mallon
February 2012

One may safely affirm that all popular theology has a kind of appetite for absurdity and contradiction.... While their gloomy apprehensions make them ascribe to Him measures of conduct which in human creatures would be blamed, they must still affect to praise and admire that conduct in the object of their devotional addresses. Thus it may safely be affirmed that popular religions are really, in the conception of their more vulgar votaries, a species of daemonism.

David Hume, *The Natural History of Religion*

Nothing to fear in God. Nothing to feel in death. Good can be attained. Evil can be endured.

Diogenes of Oenoanda

Where questions of religion are concerned, people are guilty of every possible sort of dishonesty and intellectual misdemeanor.

Sigmund Freud, *The Future of an Illusion*

Acknowledgments

Who would be so base as to pick on a wizened, shriveled old lady, well stricken in years, who has consecrated her entire life to the needy and the destitute? On the other hand, who would be so incurious as to leave unexamined the influence and motives of a woman who once boasted of operating more than five hundred convents in upward of 105 countries— "without counting India"? Lone self-sacrificing zealot, or chair of a missionary multinational? The scale alters with the perspective, and the perspective alters with the scale.

Once the decision is taken to do without awe and reverence, if only for a moment, the Mother Teresa phenomenon assumes the proportions of the ordinary and even the political. It is part of the combat of ideas and the clash of interpretations, and can make no serious claims to having invisible means of support. The first step, as so often, is the crucial one. It still seems astonishing to me that nobody had ever before decided to look at the saint of Calcutta as if, possibly, the supernatural had nothing to do with it.

I was very much discouraged—as I asked the most obvious questions and initiated what were, at the outset, the most perfunctory investigations—by almost everybody to whom I spoke. So I must mention several people who gave me heart, and who answered the implied question—Is nothing sacred?—with a stoical "No." Victor Navasky, editor of *The Nation*, and Graydon Carter, editor of *Vanity Fair*, both allowed me to write early polemics against Mother Teresa even though they had every reason to expect a hostile reader response (which, interestingly, failed to materialize). In making the Channel Four documentary *Hell's Angel*, which aired in Britain in the autumn of 1994 and which *did* lead to venomous and irrational attacks, I owe everything to Vania Del Borgo and Tariq Ali of Bandung Productions, whose idea it was, and to Waldemar Januszczak of Channel Four, who "took the heat," as the saying goes. A secular Muslim, a secular Jew and a secular Polish Catholic made excellent company in fending off the likes of Ms. Victoria Gillick, a pestilential morals campaigner who stated publicly that our program was a Jewish/Muslim conspiracy against the One True Faith. Colin Robinson and Mike Davis of Verso were unwavering in their belief that a few words are worth many pictures. Ben Metcalf was and is a splendid copy editor.

This is a small episode in an unending argument

ACKNOWLEDGMENTS

between those who *know* they are right and therefore claim the mandate of heaven, and those who suspect that the human race has nothing but the poor candle of reason by which to light its way. So I acknowledge as well the help and counsel and support of three heroes in this battle: Gore Vidal, Salman Rushdie and Israel Shahak. It was once well said, of the criticism of religion, that the critic should pluck the flowers from the chain, not in order that people should wear the chain without consolation but so that they might break the chain and cull the living flower. As fundamental monotheism and shallow cultism testify to one view of the human future, and as the millennium casts its shadow before us, it has been a privilege to soldier with such distinguished witnesses. If the baffled and fearful prehistory of our species ever comes to an end, and if we ever get off of our knees and cull those blooms, there will be no need for smoking altars and forbidding temples with which to honor the freethinking humanists, who scorned to use the fear of death to coerce and flatter the poor.

Ethiopians imagine their gods as black and snub-nosed; Thracians blue-eyed and red-haired. But if horses or lions had hands, or could draw and fashion works as men do, horses would draw the gods shaped like horses and lions like lions, making the gods resemble themselves.

Xenophanes

Introduction

On my table as I write is an old copy of *L'Assaut* ("The Attack"). It is, or more properly it was, a propaganda organ for the personal despotism of Jean-Claude Duvalier of Haiti. As the helplessly fat and jowly and stupid son of a very gaunt and ruthless and intelligent father (Jean-François "Papa Doc" Duvalier), the portly Dauphin was known to all, and to his evident embarrassment, as "Baby Doc." In an attempt to salvage some dignity and to establish an identity separate from that of the parental, *L'Assaut* carried the subtitle *"Organe de Jean-Claudisme."*

But this avoidance of the more accurate "Duvalierism" served only to underline the banana-republic, cult-of-dynasty impression that it sought to dispel. Below the headline appears a laughable bird, which resembles a very plump and nearly flightless pigeon but is clearly intended as a dove, judging by the stylized sprig of olive clamped in its beak. Beneath the dismal avian is a large slogan in Latin—*In Hoc Signo Vinces* ("In this sign shall ye conquer")—which appears to negate the pacific and herbivorous intentions of the logo. Early Christian symbols, such as the cross or the fish, sometimes bore this superscription. I have seen it annexed on pamphlets bearing other runes and fetishes, such as the swastika. For a certainty, nobody could conquer anything under a banner bearing the device reproduced here.

On the inside, next to a long and adoring account of the wedding anniversary of Haiti's bulbous First Citizen and his celebrated bride, Michèle Duvalier, is a large photograph. It shows Michèle, poised and cool and elegant in her capacity as leader of Haiti's white and Creole elite. Her bangled arms are being held in a loving clasp by another woman, who is offering up a gaze filled with respect and deference. Next to the picture is a quotation from this other woman, who clearly feels that her sycophantic gestures are not enough and that words must be offered as well: *"Madame la Présidente, c'est une personne qui sent, qui sait, qui veut prouver son amour non seulement par des mots*, mais aussi par des actions concrètes et tangibles."[1] The neighboring Society page takes up the cry, with the headline: *"Mme la Présidente, le pays resonne de votre œuvre."*[2]

The eye rests on the picture. The woman proposing these lavish compliments is the woman known

---

[1] "Madame President is someone who feels, who knows, who wishes to demonstrate her love not only with words *but also with concrete and tangible actions.*" [Emphasis added.]
[2] "Madame President, the country vibrates with your life work."

to millions as Mother Teresa of Calcutta. A number of questions obtrude themselves at once. First, is the picture by any chance a setup? Have the deft editors of *L'Assaut* made an exploited visitor out of an unsuspecting stranger, placed words in her mouth, put her in a vulnerable position? The answer appears to be in the negative, because the date of this issue is January 1981, and there exists film footage of Mother Teresa visiting Haiti that year. The footage, which was shown on the CBS documentary program *Sixty Minutes*, has Mother Teresa smiling into the camera and saying, of Michèle Duvalier, that while she had met kings and presidents aplenty in her time, she had "never seen the poor people being so familiar with their head of state as they were with her. It was a beautiful lesson for me." In return for these and other favors, Mother Teresa was awarded the Haitian *Légion d'honneur.* And her simple testimony, in warm encomium of the ruling couple, was shown on state-run television every night for at least a week. No protest against this footage is known to have been registered by Mother Teresa (who has ways of making her views widely available) between the time of the award and the time when the Haitian people became so "familiar" with Jean-Claude and Michèle that the couple had barely enough time to stuff their luggage with the National Treasury before fleeing forever to the French Riviera.

Other questions arise as well, all of them touching on matters of saintliness, modesty, humility and devotion to the poor. Apart from anything else, what was Mother Teresa doing in Port-au-Prince attending photo opportunities and award ceremonies with the local oligarchy? What, indeed, was she doing in Haiti at all? The world has a need to picture her in a pose of agonized yet willing subjection, washing the feet of Calcutta's poor. Politics is not her proper *métier*, and certainly not politics half a world away, in a sweltering Caribbean dictatorship. Haiti has been renowned for many years, and justly so, as the place where the wretched of the earth receive the cruelest and most capricious treatment. It is well and clearly understood, furthermore, that this is not the result of either natural disaster or unalterable misfortune. The island has been the property of an especially callous and greedy predatory class, which has employed pitiless force in order to keep the poor and the dispossessed in their place.

Let us look again at the photograph of the two smiling ladies. In terms of received ideas about Mother Teresa, it does not "fit." It does not, as people say nowadays, "compute." Image and perception are everything, and those who possess them have the ability to determine their own myth, to be taken at their own valuation. Actions and words are judged by reputations, and not the other way around. So hold the picture to the light for an instant, and try to take an impression of the "negative." Is it possible that the reverse black-and-white tells not a gray tale but a truer one?

Also before me as I write is a photograph of Mother Teresa standing, eyes modestly downcast, in friendly propinquity with a man known as "John-Roger." At first glance, it would seem to the casual viewer that they are standing in a Calcutta slum. A closer look makes it plain that the destitute figures in the background have been added in as a backdrop. The picture is a fake. So, for that matter, is John-Roger. As leader of the cult known sometimes as "Insight" but more accurately as MSIA (the "Movement of Spiritual Inner Awareness," pronounced "Messiah"), he is a fraud of Chaucerian proportions. Probably best known to the public for his lucrative connection to Arianna Stassinopoulos-Huffington—whose husband, Michael Huffington, spent $42 million of his own inherited money on an unsuccessful bid for a Senate seat in California—John-Roger has repeatedly claimed to be, and to have, a "spiritual consciousness" that is superior to that of Jesus Christ. Such a claim is hard to adjudicate. One might think, all the same, that it would be blasphemous to the simple outlook of Mother Teresa. Yet there she is, keeping him company and lending him the luster of her name and image. MSIA, it should be noted, has repeatedly been exposed in print as corrupt and fanatical, and the Cult Awareness Network lists the organization as "highly dangerous."

It turns out that the faked photograph records the momentous occasion of Mother Teresa's acceptance of a check for $10,000. It came in the form of an "Integrity Award" bestowed by John-Roger himself—a man who realized his own divinity in the aftermath of a visionary kidney operation. No doubt Mother Teresa's apologists will have their defense close at hand. Their heroine is too innocent to detect dishonesty in others. And $10,000 is $10,000 and, as Lenin was fond of saying (citing Juvenal), *pecunia non olet*: "money has no smell." So what is more natural than that she should quit Calcutta once more, journey to Tinseltown and share her aura with a guru claiming to outrank the Redeemer himself? We will discover Mother Teresa keeping company with several other frauds, crooks and exploiters as this little tale unfolds. At what point—her apologists might want to permit themselves this little tincture of skepticism—does such association cease to be coincidental?

One last set of photographs closes this portfolio. Behold Mother Teresa in prayerful attitude, flanked by Hillary Rodham Clinton and Marion Barry, as she opens an eight-bed adoption facility in the suburbs of Washington, D.C. It is a great day for Marion

Barry, who has led the capital city into beggary and corruption, and who covers his nakedness by calling for mandatory prayer in schools. It is a great day as well for Hillary Rodham Clinton, who almost single-handedly destroyed a coalition on national health care that had taken a quarter of a century to build and mature.

The seeds of this multiple photo opportunity, which occurred on 19 June 1995, were sown the preceding March, as the First Lady toured the Indian subcontinent. Molly Moore, the fine *Washington Post* reporter on the trip, made it clear in her dispatches that the visit was of a Potemkin nature:

> When the Clinton motorcade whisked through the Pakistani countryside yesterday, a long fence of brightly colored fabric shielded it from a sprawling, smoldering garbage dump where children combed through trash and several poor families had built huts from scraps of cardboard, rags and plastic.... In another instance, Pakistani officials, having heard rumors that the First Lady might take a hike into the scenic Margalla Hills overlooking the capital of Islamabad, rushed out and paved a 10-mile stretch of road to a village in the hills. She never took the hike (the Secret Service vetoed the proposal) but villagers got a paved road they'd been requesting for decades.

In such ways do Western leaders impress themselves momentarily upon the poor of the world, before flying home much purified and sobered by the experience. A stop at a Mother Teresa institution is absolutely *de rigueur* for all celebrities visiting the region, and Mrs. Clinton was not going to be the breaker of precedent. Having "raced past intersections where cars, buses, rickshaws and pedestrians were backed up as far as the eye could see," she arrived at Mother Teresa's New Delhi orphanage, where, again to quote from the reporter on the spot, "babies who normally wear nothing but thin cotton diapers that do little but promote rashes and exacerbate the reek of urine had been outfitted for the morning in American Pampers and newly-stitched floral pinafores."

One good turn deserves another, and so Mother Teresa's subsequent visit to Washington gave both Mrs. Clinton and Mayor Barry the occasion for some safe, free publicity. The new twelve-bed adoption center is in the rather leafy and decorous Chevy Chase suburb, and nobody was churlish enough to mention Mother Teresa's earlier trip to the city in October 1981, when she had turned the light of her countenance on the blighted ghetto of Anacostia. Situated in near segregation on the other side of the Potomac, Anacostia is the capital of black Washington, and there was suspicion at the time about the idea of a Missionaries of Charity operation there, because the inhabitants were known to resent the suggestion that they were helpless and abject Third Worlders. Indeed, just before her press conference, Mother Teresa found her office rudely invaded by a group of black men. Her assistant Kathy Sreedhar takes up the story:

> They were very upset.... They told Mother that Anacostia needed decent jobs, housing and services—not charity. Mother didn't argue with them; she just listened. Finally, one of them asked her what she was going to do here. Mother said: "First we must learn to love one another." They didn't know what to say to that.

Well, no. But possibly because they had heard it before. Anyway, when the press conference began, Mother Teresa was able to clear up any misunderstandings swiftly:

> "Mother Teresa, what do you hope to accomplish here?"
>   "The joy of loving and being loved."
>   "That takes a lot of money, doesn't it?"
>   "It takes a lot of sacrifice."
>   "Do you teach the poor to endure their lot?"
>   "I think it is very beautiful for the poor to accept

their lot, to share it with the passion of Christ. I think the world is being much helped by the suffering of the poor people."

Marion Barry graced the event with his presence, of course, as did Reverend George Stallings, the black pastor of St. Teresa's. Fourteen years later, Anacostia is an even worse slum and the Reverend Stallings has seceded from the Church in order to set up a blacks-only Catholicism devoted chiefly to himself. (He has also been in a spot of bother lately for allegedly outraging the innocence of a junior congregant.) Only Marion Barry, reborn in prison and re-elected as a demagogue, has really mastered the uses of redemption.

So behold again the photograph of Mother Teresa locked in a sisterly embrace with Michèle Duvalier, one of the modern world's most cynical, shallow and spoiled women: a whited sepulcher and a parasite on "the poor." The picture, and its context, announce Mother Teresa as what she is: a religious fundamentalist, a political operative, a primitive sermonizer and an accomplice of worldly, secular powers. Her mission has always been of this kind. The irony is that she has never been able to induce anybody to believe her. It is past time that she was duly honored, and taken at her word.

*　　*　　*

When I asked the electronic index at the Library of Congress to furnish me with a list of books on Mother Teresa, it printed out some twenty titles. There was *Mother Teresa: Helping the Poor*, by William Jay Jacobs; *Mother Teresa: The Glorious Years*, by Edward Le Jolly; *Mother Teresa: A Woman in Love*, which looked more promising but turned out to be by the same author in the same spirit; *Mother Teresa: Protector of the Sick*, by Linda Carlson Johnson; *Mother Teresa: Servant to the World's Suffering People*, by Susan Ullstein; *Mother Teresa: Friend of the Friendless*, by Carol Greene; and *Mother Teresa: Caring for All God's Children*, by Betsy Lee—to name but the most salient titles. Even the most neutral of these—*Mother Teresa: Her Life, Her Works*, by Dr. Lush Gjergji—proved to be a sort of devotional pamphlet in the guise of a biography, composed by one of Mother Teresa's Albanian co-religionists.

Indeed, the overall tone was so strongly devotional that it seemed almost normal for a moment. Yet if you review the above titles out loud—Mother Teresa, helper of the poor, protector of the sick, servant to the suffering, friend of the friendless—you are in fact mimicking an invocation of the Virgin and improvising your own "Ave Maria" or "Hail Mary." Note, too, the scale of the invocation—the *world's* suffering people, *all* God's children. What we have here is a saint in the making, whose sites and relics will one day be venerated and who is already the personal object of a following that is not much short of cultish.

The present Pope is unusually fond of the canonization process. In sixteen years he has created five times as many saints as all of his twentieth-century predecessors combined. He has also multiplied the number of beatifications, thus keeping the anteroom to sainthood well stocked. Between 1588 and 1988 the Vatican canonized 679 saints. In the reign of John Paul II alone (as of June 1995), there have been 271 canonizations and 631 beatifications. Several hundred cases are pending, including the petition to canonize Queen Isabella of Spain. So rapid and general is the approach that it recalls the baptism by firehose with which Chinese generals Christianized their armies; in one 1987 ceremony a grand total of 85 English, Scottish, Welsh and Irish martyrs were beatified in one day.

Sainthood is no small claim, because it brings with it the power to make intercession and it allows prayer to be directed at the said saint. Many popes have been slow to canonize, as the Church is generally slow to validate miracles and apparitions, because if divine intervention in human affairs is too promiscuously recognized, then an obvious danger arises. If one leper can be cured, the flock may inquire, then why not all lepers? Allow of a too-easy miracle and it becomes harder to answer questions about infant leukemia or mass poverty and injustice with unsatisfying formulae about the Lord's preference for moving in mysterious ways. This is an old problem, and it is unlikely to yield to mass-production methodology in the canonization division.

Although a "saint" traditionally is required to have performed at least one miracle, to have done "good works" and possessed "heroic virtues," and to have demonstrated the logistically difficult quality of ubiquity, many people who are not even Roman Catholics have already decided that Mother Teresa is a saint. Sources in the Vatican's "Congregation for Sainthood Causes" (which examines thorny cases like that of Queen Isabella) abandon their customary reticence and reserve in declaring Mother Teresa's beatification and eventual canonization to be certain. This consummation can hardly displease her, but it may not have been among her original objectives. Her life shows, rather, a determination to be the founder of a new order—her Missionaries of Charity organization currently numbers some 4,000 nuns and 40,000 lay workers—to be ranked with St. Francis and St. Benedict as the author of a "rule" and a "discipline."

Mother Teresa has a theory of poverty, which is also a theory of submission and gratitude. She has also a theory of power, which derives from St. Paul's neglected words about "the powers that be," which "are ordained of God." She is, finally, the emissary of a very determined and very politicized papacy. Her world travels are not the wanderings of a pilgrim but a campaign which accords with the requirements of power. Mother Teresa has a theory of morality too. It is not a difficult theory to comprehend, though it has its difficulties. And Mother Teresa understands very thoroughly the uses of the biblical passage concerning what is owed to Caesar.

As to what is owed to God, that is a matter for those who have faith, or for those who at any rate are relieved that others have it. The rich part of our world has a poor conscience, and it is no fault of an Albanian nun that so many otherwise contented people should decide to live vicariously through what they imagine to be her charity. What follows here is an argument not with a deceiver but with the deceived. If Mother Teresa is the adored object of many credulous and uncritical observers, then the blame is not hers, or hers alone. In the gradual manufacture of an illusion, the conjurer is only the instrument of the audience. He may even announce himself as a trickster and a clever prestidigitator and yet gull the crowd. *Populus vult decipi—ergo decipiatur.*

A Miracle

Convulsions in nature, disorders, prodigies, miracles, though the most opposite to the plan of a wise superintendent, impress mankind with the strongest sentiments of religion.

David Hume, *The Natural History of Religion*

Upon the whole, mystery, miracle and prophecy are appendages that belong to fabulous and not to true religion. They are the means by which so many Lo heres! and Lo theres! have been spread about the world, and religion been made into a trade. The success of one impostor gave encouragement to another, and the quieting salvo of doing some good by keeping up a pious fraud, protected them from remorse.

Tom Paine, *The Age of Reason*

Thus we call a belief an illusion when a wish-fulfillment is a prominent factor in its motivation, and in doing so we disregard its relations to reality just as the illusion itself sets no store by verification.

Sigmund Freud, *The Future of an Illusion*

Intercession, the hallmark of sainthood, requires the certification of a miracle. Mother Teresa is already worshipped as something more than human, but she has not transcended our common lot to the extent of being cited as a wonder-worker by Mother Church. The printout of the titles provided me by the Library of Congress showed that almost all were published in the 1980s and 1990s, and it wasn't until I had been through the list that I noticed what was not there: a 1971 book by Malcolm Muggeridge which argued, *inter alia*, that Mother Teresa's miracle had already taken place.

Muggeridge's book, *Something Beautiful for God*, was the outcome of a BBC documentary of the same name, screened in 1969. Muggeridge, who made something of a career out of ridiculing TV and showbiz values, claims that he began the project with no idea of the impression it would help to create. "Mother Teresa's way of looking at life is barren soil for copy-writers," he says, "and the poorest of the poor she cherishes offer little in the way of ratings." If that disingenuous disclaimer was true when filming began, it ceased to be true very shortly after transmission had occurred, for it is from this film and this book that we can date the arrival of Mother Teresa's "image" on the international retina.

Essential to Muggeridge's project, essential indeed to the whole Mother Teresa cult, is the impression that Calcutta is a hellhole:

> As it happened, I lived in Calcutta for eighteen months in the middle Thirties when I was working with the *Statesman* newspaper there, and found the place, even with all the comforts of a European's life—the refrigerator, the servants, the morning canter round the Maidan or out at the Jodhpur Club, and so on—barely tolerable.

Since Muggeridge's time, the city has not only had its own enormous difficulties to contend with but it has also been the scene of three major migrations of misery. Having been itself partitioned by a stupid British colonial decision before independence, Bengal took the brunt of the partitioning of all India into India and Pakistan in 1947. The Bangladesh war in 1971 and, later, the sectarian brushfires in Assam have swollen Calcutta's population to a number far greater than it can hope to accommodate. Photographs of people living on pavements have become internationally recognized emblems of destitution. Mother Teresa's emphasis on "the poorest of the poor and the lowest of the low" has served to reinforce the impression of Calcutta as a city of dreadful night, an impression which justly irritates many Bengalis.

The pleasant surprise that awaits the visitor to Calcutta is this: it is poor and crowded and dirty, in ways which are hard to exaggerate, *but it is anything but abject*. Its people are neither inert nor cringing. They work and they struggle, and as a general rule (especially as compared with ostensibly richer cities such as Bombay) they do not beg. This is the city of Tagore, of Ray and Bose and Mrinal Sen, and of a great flowering of culture and nationalism. There are films, theaters, university departments and magazines, all of a high quality. The photographs of Raghubir Singh are a testament to the vitality of the people, as well as to the beauty and variety of the architecture. Secular-leftist politics predominate, with a very strong internationalist temper: hardly unwelcome in a region so poisoned by brute religion.

When I paid my own visit to the city some years ago, I immediately felt rather cheated by the anti-Calcutta propaganda put out by the Muggeridges of the world. And when I made my way to the offices of the Missionaries of Charity on Bose Road, I received something of a shock. First was the inscription over the door, which read "He that loveth correction loveth knowledge." I don't know the provenance of the quotation, but it had something of the ring of the workhouse about it. Mother Teresa herself gave me a guided tour. I did not particularly care for the way that she took kisses bestowed on her sandaled feet as no more than her due, but I decided to suspend judgment on this—perhaps it was a local custom that I understood imperfectly. The orphanage, anyway, was moving and affecting. Very small (no shame in that) and very clean, it had an encouraging air and seemed to be run by charming and devoted people. One tiny cot stood empty, its occupant not having survived the night, and there was earnest discussion about a vacancy to be filled. I had begun to fumble for a contribution when Mother Teresa turned to me and said, with a gesture that seemed to take in the whole scene, "See, this is how we fight abortion and contraception."

If not for this, it would have been trifling to point out the drop-in-a-bucket contribution that such a small establishment makes to such a gigantic problem. But it is difficult to spend any time at all in Calcutta and conclude that what it most needs is a campaign against population control. Nor, of course, does

Mother Teresa make this judgment based on local conditions. She was opposed on principle to abortion and birth control long before she got there. For her, Calcutta is simply a front in a much larger war.

Muggeridge's fatalistic revulsion from the actual Calcutta made him all the more receptive to Mother Teresa's mystical prescription for the place, which is that it suffers from being too distant from Jesus. In consequence, his gullibility led him to write the following, which is worth quoting at length. (I should preface the quotation by saying that Muggeridge's BBC crew included a very distinguished cameraman named Ken Macmillan, who had earned a great reputation for his work on Lord Clark's art-history series *Civilisation*.)

This Home for the Dying is dimly lit by small windows high up in the walls, and Ken was adamant that filming was quite impossible there. We had only one small light with us, and to get the place adequately lighted in the time at our disposal was quite impossible. It was decided that, nonetheless, Ken should have a go, but by way of insurance he took, as well, some film in an outside courtyard where some of the inmates were sitting in the sun. In the processed film, the part taken inside was bathed in a particularly beautiful soft light, whereas the part taken outside was rather dim and confused.... I myself am absolutely convinced that the technically unaccountable light is, in fact, the Kindly Light [Cardinal] Newman refers to in his well-known exquisite hymn.

Nor was Muggeridge attempting to speak metaphorically. Of the love he observed in the home, he wrote that it was

> luminous, like the haloes artists have seen and made visible round the heads of the saints. I find it not at all surprising that the luminosity should register on a photographic film. The supernatural is only an infinite projection of the natural, as the furthest horizon is an image of eternity. Jesus put mud on a blind man's eyes and made him see.

Having gone on in this vein for some time, Muggeridge concluded:

> This is precisely what miracles are for—to reveal the inner reality of God's outward creation. *I am personally persuaded that Ken recorded the first authentic photographic miracle.* [Emphasis added.]

Muggeridge did not exaggerate when he wrote "I fear I talked and wrote about it to the point of tedium." So it is interesting to have the direct testimony of Ken Macmillan himself:

During *Something Beautiful for God*, there was an episode where we were taken to a building that Mother Teresa called the House of the Dying. Peter Chafer, the director, said, "Ah well, it's very dark in here. Do you think we can get something?" And we had just taken delivery at the BBC of some new film made by Kodak, which we hadn't had time to test before we left, so I said to Peter, "Well, we may as well have a go." So we shot it. And when we got back several weeks later, a month or two later, we are sitting in the rushes theater at Ealing Studios and eventually up came the shots of the House of the Dying. And it was surprising. You could see every detail. And I said, "That's amazing. That's extraordinary." And I was going to go on to say, you know, three cheers for Kodak. I didn't get a chance to say that though, because Malcolm, sitting in the front row, spun round and said: "It's divine light! It's Mother Teresa. You'll find that it's divine light, old boy." And three or four days later I found I was being phoned by journalists from London newspapers who were saying things like: "We hear you've just come back from India with Malcolm Muggeridge and you were the witness of a miracle."

And a star was born. Ken Macmillan's testimony came far, far too late to prevent the spread, largely by the televisual and mass-media methods that

Muggeridge affected to despise, of the reported "miracle." Rather than "the first authentic photographic miracle," this episode is actually something considerably more significant. It is the first unarguable refutation of a claimed miracle to come not merely from another supposed witness to said miracle but from its actual real-time author. As such, it deserves to be more widely known than it is. But modern technology and communications have ensured instead that rumor and myth can be transmitted with ever greater speed and efficiency to the eyes and ears of the credulous. How splendidly we progress. Ever since *Something Beautiful for God*, the critic of Mother Teresa, in small things as well as in great ones, has had to operate against an enormous weight of received opinion, a weight made no easier to shift by the fact that it is made up, quite literally, of illusion.

Muggeridge gave numerous other hostages to fortune during the course of his film and his book. Only his adoring gaze, for example, inhibited him from seeing the range of interpretation that might be placed on the following anecdote:

As Simone Weil says, Christianity is a religion for slaves; we have to make ourselves slaves and beggars to follow Christ. Despite the chronic financial stringency of the Missionaries of Charity, when I was instrumental in steering a few hundred pounds in Mother Teresa's direction, she astonished, and I must say enchanted, me by expending it on the chalice and ciborium for her new novitiate....Her action might, I suppose, be criticized on the same lines as the waste of spikenard ointment, but it gave me a great feeling of contentment at the time and subsequently.

Of course if the purpose of Mother Teresa's work is that of strict religious proselytization and the founding of an order toward that end, there can be no conceivable objection to her employing charitable donations in order to decorate an altarpiece with the things of this world. But those who make the donations are, it seems, not always aware that this is the essential point. Mother Teresa, to her credit, has never claimed otherwise. She did not even bother to use the biblical story of the spikenard ointment in reassuring Muggeridge, telling him instead that "you will be daily on the altar close to the Body of Christ." Muggeridge was not then a Catholic, so he had no grounds on which to object that this was a doubly tricky use of the notion of transubstantiation. He thought of the spikenard alibi all by himself. (This is the passage in which Jesus breaks a costly box of unguent exclusively on his own feet. To the naive objection that the luxury item might with greater effect have been sold for the relief of poverty, he rejoins, "The poor you have always with you." I remember as a child finding this famous crack rather unsatisfactory. Either one eschews luxury and serves the poor or one does not. If the poor are always with us, on the other hand, then there is no particular hurry and they can always be used to illustrate morality tales. In which case, it might be more honest for their prophetic benefactors to admit that the poor have *us* always with *them*.)

Modesty and humility are popularly supposed to be saintly attributes, yet Mother Teresa can scarcely grant an audience without claiming a special and personal relationship with Jesus Christ. In the following exchange between Muggeridge and his star, who is the one demonstrating the self-abnegating modesty?

MUGGERIDGE: When I think of Calcutta and of the appallingness of so much of it, it seems extraordinary that one person could just walk out and decide to tackle this thing.
MOTHER TERESA: I was sure then, and I'm still convinced, that it is He and not I.

Here is a perfect fit between interviewer and subject: Muggeridge finds the poor of Calcutta to be rife with "appallingness," and Mother Teresa says that there would be no point in trying if one was not mandated by heaven. A little further on in the interview, Muggeridge inquires as follows:

> So you wouldn't agree with people who say there are too many children in India?

> MOTHER TERESA: I do not agree because God always provides. He provides for the flowers and the birds, for everything in the world that he has created. And those little children are his life. There can never be enough.

Muggeridge approves of this reply, saying moistly that Mother Teresa might as well be asked if there are too many stars in the sky. The entire dialogue is conducted in a semi-surreal manner, as if nobody had ever made any reasoned point about family planning or population policy. To say that there *are* too many children is to miss the point, because they are born already. But to say that there *cannot be* too many people is (and not only in India) to commit at least the sin of hubris. Mrs. Indira Gandhi—a political patron of Mother Teresa's, incidentally—once embarked upon a criminal campaign of forced sterilization in India. Clearly there are many ways of getting the population question wrong. On the other hand, there is no rational way of saying that the question does not arise. And if it were true that God "always provides," then, obviously, there would be no need for the Missionaries of Charity in the first place.

Before leaving Muggeridge's milestone behind us, it is necessary to record one more of the interchanges between him and his guru:

MUGGERIDGE: You don't think that there's a danger that people might mistake the means for the end, and feel that serving their fellow men was an end in itself? Do you think there's danger of that?

MOTHER TERESA: There is always the danger that we may become only social workers or just do the work for the sake of the work....It is a danger; if we forget to whom we are doing it. Our works are only an expression of our love for Christ. Our hearts need to be full of love for him, and since we have to express that love in action, naturally then the poorest of the poor are the means of expressing our love for God.

In the film of *Something Beautiful for God*, there is a sequence in which Mother Teresa takes an abandoned and undernourished child in her arms. The child is sickly looking and wizened and without much of the charm that babies possess at that age, but the old lady looks down at her with dauntless encouragement and enthusiasm and says, "See. There *is* life in her." It is an undeniably affirmative moment. We would not be worse off if there were many more like it. But, just as Mother Teresa rather spoiled her own best moment for me by implying that her life's work was a mere exercise in propaganda for the Vatican's population policy, she cheapens her own example by telling us, as above, that humanism and altruism are "dangers" to be sedulously avoided. Mother Teresa has never pretended that her work is anything but a fundamentalist religious campaign. And in the excerpt above we have it on her own authority that "the poorest of the poor" are the instruments of this; an occasion for piety.

Good Works
and
Heroic Virtues

Fan Ch'ih asked about wisdom. The master said: "To work for the things the common people have a right to, and to keep one's distance from the gods and spirits while showing them reverence can be called wisdom."

Confucius, *Analects Book VI, 22*

No Philosopher was on hand to tell him that there is no strong sentiment without some terror, as there is no real religion without a little fetishism.

Joseph Conrad, *Victory*

Star light, star bright... we look up and we hope the stars look down, we pray that there may be stars for us to follow, stars moving across the heavens and leading up to our destiny, but it's only our vanity. We look at the galaxy and fall in love, but the universe cares less about us than we do about it, and the stars stay in their courses however much we may wish upon them to do otherwise. It's true that if you watch the sky-wheel turn for a while you'll see a meteor fall, flame and die. That's not a star worth following; it's just an unlucky rock. Our fates are here on earth. There are no guiding stars.

Salman Rushdie, *The Moor's Last Sigh*

I

Those prepared to listen to criticism of Mother Teresa's questionable motives and patently confused sociological policy are still inclined to believe that her work is essentially humane. Surely, they reason, there is something morally impressive in a life consecrated to charity. If it were not for the testimony of those who have seen the shortcomings and contradictions of her work firsthand, it might be sufficient argument, on the grounds that Mother Teresa *must* have done some genuine good for the world's suffering people.

However, even here the record is somewhat murky and uneven, and it is qualified by the same limitations as apply to the rest of Mother Teresa's work: that such work is undertaken not for its own sake but to propagandize one highly subjective view of human nature and need, so that she may one day be counted as the beatific founder of a new order and discipline within the Church itself. Even in the quotidian details of ostensibly "charitable" labor, this unresolved contradiction repeatedly discloses itself.

Take, as one unremarked example, the visit of Dr. Robin Fox to the Mother Teresa operation in Calcutta in 1994. As editor of *The Lancet*, perhaps the world's leading medical journal, Dr. Fox was professionally interested in, and qualified to pronounce upon, the standards of care. The opening paragraphs of his report in the journal's 17 September 1994 issue also make it clear that he paid his visit with every expectation of being favorably impressed. Indeed, his tone of slightly raised-eyebrow politeness never deserts him:

> There are doctors who call in from time to time but usually the sisters and volunteers (some of whom have medical knowledge) make decisions as best they can. I saw a young man who had been admitted in poor shape with high fever, and the drugs prescribed had been tetracycline and paracetamol. Later a visiting doctor diagnosed probable malaria and substituted chloroquine. Could not someone have looked at a blood film? Investigations, I was told, are seldom permissible. How about simple algorithms that might help the sisters and volunteers distinguish the curable from the incurable? Again no. *Such systematic approaches are alien to the ethos of the home. Mother*

Teresa prefers providence to planning; her rules are designed to prevent any drift towards materialism: the sisters must remain on equal terms with the poor.... Finally, how competent are the sisters at managing pain? On a short visit, I could not judge the power of their spiritual approach, but I was disturbed to learn that the formulary includes no strong analgesics. Along with the neglect of diagnosis, the lack of good analgesia marks Mother Teresa's approach as clearly separate from the hospice movement. I know which I prefer. [Emphasis added.]

It should be underlined that the state of affairs described by Dr. Fox was not that obtaining in some amateur, impoverished clinic in a disaster zone. Mother Teresa has been working in Calcutta for four and a half decades, and for nearly three of them she has been favored with immense quantities of money and material. Her "Home for the Dying," which was the part of her dominion visited by Dr. Fox, is in no straitened condition. It is as he described it because that is how Mother Teresa wishes it to be. The neglect of what is commonly understood as proper medicine or care is not a superficial contradiction. It is the essence of the endeavor, the same essence that is evident in a cheerful sign which has been filmed on the wall of Mother Teresa's morgue. It reads "I am going to heaven today."

According to many other former volunteers, Dr. Fox may have paid his visit on an unusually good day, or may have been unusually well looked after. Mary Loudon, a volunteer in Calcutta who has since written extensively about the lives of nuns and religious women, has this testimony to offer about the Home for the Dying:

My initial impression was of all the photographs and footage I've ever seen of Belsen and places like that, because all the patients had shaved heads. No chairs anywhere, there were just these stretcher beds. They're like First World War stretcher beds. There's no garden, no yard even. No nothing. And I thought what is this? This is two rooms with fifty to sixty men in one, fifty to sixty women in another. They're dying. They're not being given a great deal of medical care. They're not being given painkillers really beyond aspirin and maybe if you're lucky some Brufen or something, for the sort of pain that goes with terminal cancer and the things they were dying of…

They didn't have enough drips. The needles they used and re-used over and over and over and you would see some of the nuns rinsing needles under the cold water tap. And I asked one of them why she was doing it and she said: "Well to clean it." And I said, "Yes, but why are you not sterilizing it; why are

you not boiling water and sterilizing your needles?"
She said: "There's no point. There's no time."

The first day I was there when I'd finished working in the women's ward I went and waited on the
edge of the men's ward for my boyfriend, who was
looking after a boy of fifteen who was dying, and an
American doctor told me that she had been trying
to treat this boy. And that he had a really relatively
simple kidney complaint that had simply got worse
and worse and worse because he hadn't had antibiotics. And he actually needed an operation. I don't
recall what the problem was, but she did tell me. And
she was so angry, but also very resigned which so
many people become in that situation. And she said,
"Well, they won't take him to hospital." And I said:
"Why? All you have to do is get a cab. Take him to
the nearest hospital, demand that he has treatment.
Get him an operation." She said: "They don't do it.
They won't do it. If they do it for one, they do it for
everybody." And I thought—but this kid is fifteen.

Bear in mind that Mother Teresa's global income
is more than enough to outfit several first-class clinics in Bengal. The decision not to do so, and indeed
to run instead a haphazard and cranky institution
which would expose itself to litigation and protest
were it run by any branch of the medical profession,
is a deliberate one. The point is not the honest relief

of suffering but the promulgation of a cult based on death and suffering and subjection. Mother Teresa (who herself, it should be noted, has checked into some of the finest and costliest clinics and hospitals in the West during her bouts with heart trouble and old age) once gave this game away in a filmed interview. She described a person who was in the last agonies of cancer and suffering unbearable pain. With a smile, Mother Teresa told the camera what she told this terminal patient: "You are suffering like Christ on the cross. So Jesus must be kissing you." Unconscious of the account to which this irony might be charged, she then told of the sufferer's reply: "Then please tell him to stop kissing me." There are many people in the direst need and pain who have had cause to wish, in their own extremity, that Mother Teresa was less free with her own metaphysical caresses and a little more attentive to actual suffering.

After I had helped to make *Hell's Angel*, a documentary about Mother Teresa's shortcomings which was screened on Channel Four in England in the autumn of 1994, I received a number of communications from former volunteers and even from former members of the Missionaries of Charity. Some wished to remain anonymous and some seemed actuated by motives of revenge or other personal disorders. My practice in citing the ones I consider to be genuine is as follows: the person must have been willing to be quoted by name and to give bona fide answers to some background questions. Let me instance Ms. Elgy Gillespie, author, journalist and sometime editor of *The San Francisco Review of Books*. Experienced in the care of AIDS patients, she spent some time at Mother Teresa's San Francisco branch:

> Sent to cook in her hostel, tactfully named "The Gift of Love" (it is for homeless men with HIV), I found a dozen or so very sick men; but those who weren't very sick were exceptionally depressed, because they were not allowed to watch TV or smoke or drink or have friends over. Even when they are dying, close friends are not allowed. They are never allowed to drink, even (or especially) at the funerals of their friends and roommates and some have been thrown out for coming home in drag! When I mentioned the Olympics to them, they looked even more depressed. "We are not watching the Olympics," said a sister from Bombay, "because we are making our Lenten sacrifice." When they're very sick and very religious (which is often the case...) this doesn't matter, but with brighter men or older men it seems intolerable.
>
> A Guatemalan writer that I befriended there was desperate to get out, so a friend of mine who also

cooks there (an African American who is a practicing Catholic) adopted him for as long as she could. He became much sicker and when she begged him to go back because she couldn't mind him, he begged her to keep him because he knew they didn't medicate enough, or properly, and was afraid he would have to die without morphine...I am now cooking occasionally for the homeless men at the Franciscans where one of the patients, Bruce, is an ex-Mother Teresa and neither he nor the priest have a good word to say for the Sisters at "The Gift of Love."

Many volunteers at hostels and clinics from Calcutta to San Francisco have comparable tales to relate. Especially impressive is the testimony of Susan Shields, who for nine and a half years worked as a member of Mother Teresa's order, living the daily discipline of a Missionary of Charity in the Bronx, in Rome and in San Francisco. I have her permission to quote from her unpublished manuscript, *In Mother's House*, which is an honest, well-written account, offered by a woman who left the Missionaries of Charity for the same reason that she joined it—a love of her fellow humans.[3] If her memoir reads like the testimony of a former cult member, this is

---

[3] It seems to me a disgrace that such an original piece of courageous work should have failed to find a publisher when the Pope can receive an advance of around $5 million for a book he did not write.

because in many ways it is. She relates that, within the order, total obedience to the dictates of a single woman is enforced at every level. Questioning of authority is not an option.

> I was able to keep my complaining conscience quiet because we had been taught that the Holy Spirit was guiding Mother. To doubt her was a sign that we were lacking in trust and, even worse, guilty of the sin of pride. I shelved my objections and hoped that one day I would understand the many things that seemed to be contradictions.
>
> ...
>
> One summer the sisters in the Rome novitiate were given a great quantity of tomatoes. They couldn't give the tomatoes away because all their neighbors had grown their own. The superior decided that the sisters would can the tomatoes and eat them in the winter. When Mother came to visit and saw the canned tomatoes, she was very displeased. Missionaries of Charity do not store things but must rely only on God's providence.
>
> ...
>
> In San Francisco the sisters were given use of a three-storey convent with many large rooms, long hallways, two staircases and an immense basement.... The sisters lost no time in disposing of the unwanted furnishing. They removed the benches

from the chapel and pulled up all the carpeting in the rooms and hallways. They pushed thick mattresses out the windows and removed all the sofas, chairs and curtains from the premises. People from the neighborhood stood on the sidewalk and watched in amazement.

The beautifully constructed house was made to conform to a way of life intended to help the sisters become holy. Large sitting rooms were turned into dormitories where beds were crowded together.... The heat remained off all winter in this exceedingly damp house. Several sisters got TB during the time I lived there.

. . .

In the Bronx, plans were being made to establish a new home for the poor. Many of the homeless were sick and needed more permanent accommodation than that offered by our night shelter. We had bought a large abandoned building from the city for one dollar. A co-worker offered to be the contractor and arranged for an architect to draw up plans for the renovations. Government regulations required that an elevator be installed for the use of the disabled. Mother would not allow an elevator. The city offered to pay for the elevator. Its offer was refused. After all the negotiations and plans, the project for the poor was abandoned because an elevator for the handicapped was unacceptable.

This last anecdote may be familiar to some readers, because the New York press (which is fanatically loyal to Mother Teresa, as are most branches of the journalistic profession) wrote up the incident as a case of "politically correct" bureaucracy insisting on the rights of the disabled and negating the efforts of the missionaries. The truth is the exact reverse.

It might be argued that extreme simplicity, even primitivism, is to be preferred to a luxurious or corrupting style of the sort that has overtaken religious orders in the past. Ms. Shields told herself things like this for years. However, she realized that, rather than a life of asceticism, theirs was a regime of austerity, rigidity, harshness and confusion. As might be expected, when the requirements of dogma clash with the needs of the poor, it is the latter which give way.

She was disturbed that the poor were the ones who suffered from the sisters' self-righteous adherence to "poverty." She knew of immense quantities of money, donated in all sincerity by people "from all walks of life," which lingered unproductively in bank accounts, the size of which even many of the sisters knew nothing about. The sisters were rarely allowed to spend money on the poor they were trying to help. Instead they were forced to plead poverty, thus manipulating generous, credulous people and enterprises into giving more goods, services and cash. Ms. Shields became uncomfortable with the deceit, pretense and hypocrisy—the ancient problem of the Pharisees and the too-ostentatious public worshippers:

> The flood of donations was considered to be a sign of God's approval of Mother Teresa's congregation. We were told that we received more gifts than other religious congregations because God was pleased with Mother, and because the Missionaries of Charity were the sisters who were faithful to the true spirit of religious life. Our bank account was already the size of a great fortune and increased with every postal service delivery. Around $50 million had collected in one checking account in the Bronx.... Those of us who worked in the office regularly understood that we were not to speak about our work. The donations rolled in and were deposited in the bank, but they had no effect on our ascetic lives or on the lives of the poor we were trying to help.

Without an audit, it is impossible to say with certainty what becomes of Mother Teresa's hoards of money, but it *is* possible to say what the true purpose and nature of the order is, and to what end the donations are accepted in the first place. Susan Shields again:

For Mother, it was the spiritual well-being of the poor that mattered most. Material aid was a means of reaching their souls, of showing the poor that God loved them. In the homes for the dying, Mother taught the sisters how to secretly baptize those who were dying. Sisters were to ask each person in danger of death if he wanted a "ticket to heaven." An affirmative reply was to mean consent to baptism. The sister was then to pretend she was just cooling the person's forehead with a wet cloth, while in fact she was baptizing him, saying quietly the necessary words. Secrecy was important so that it would not come to be known that Mother Teresa's sisters were baptizing Hindus and Moslems.

Thus the smaller hypocrisy conceals a much greater one. "Our Constitution forbade us to beg for more than we needed, but the money in the bank was treated as if it did not exist." And thus the affectation of modesty and humility masks both greed and ambition, not to say arrogance.

I also have permission to quote from a letter I received from Emily Lewis, a seventy-five-year-old nurse who has worked in many of the most desperate quarters of the earth. At the time she wrote to me, she had just returned from a very arduous stint in Rwanda (a country about which Mother Teresa has been silent, perhaps because the Roman Catholic leadership in that country was complicit in the attempted genocide of the Tutsi people in the summer of 1994). Ms. Lewis's testimony follows:

My own experience of Mother Teresa occurred when she was being honored at the 1989 luncheon meeting of the International Health Organization in Washington, D.C. During her acceptance speech, she spoke at length of her opposition to contraception and her activities to save the unwanted products of heterosexual activity. (She also touched on AIDS, saying she did not want to label it a scourge of God but that it did seem like a just retribution for improper sexual conduct.) Although she said that God could find it in his heart to forgive all sinners, she herself would never allow a woman or a couple who had had an abortion to adopt one of "her" babies. In her speech Mother Teresa frequently referred to what God wants us to think or do. As my table-mate (an MD from Aid to International Development) remarked to me: "Do you think it takes a certain amount of arrogance to assume that you have a direct line to God's mind?"

Is it going too far to liken Mother Teresa to some of our infamous televangelists, turning their audiences on to what is in God's heart and mind while encouraging and accepting all donations?

The rich world likes and wishes to believe that someone, somewhere, is doing something for the Third World. For this reason, it does not inquire too closely into the motives or practices of anyone who fulfills, however vicariously, this mandate. The great white hope meets the great black hole; the mission to the heathen blends with the comforting myth of Florence Nightingale. As ever, the true address of the missionary is to the self-satisfaction of the sponsor and the donor, and not to the needs of the downtrodden. Helpless infants, abandoned derelicts, lepers and the terminally ill are the raw material for demonstrations of compassion. They are in no position to complain, and their passivity and abjection is considered a sterling trait. It is time to recognize that the world's leading exponent of this false consolation is herself a demagogue, an obscurantist and a servant of earthly powers.

II

The Catholic Church is a limitless source of fascination, to believers as well as to doubters and unbelievers, because of its attitude toward sex and procreation. Its official dogmas, derived in the main from St. Paul but elaborated down the centuries, forbid clergy from being married and prohibit women from being clergy. Homosexual acts are condemned, as in a way are homosexual persons. Heterosexual acts taking place outside the bond of lawful matrimony are condemned, whether premarital or extramarital. The sexual act within marriage is frowned upon unless it has reproduction as its object. Solitary sex is taboo. The preaching of such a range of prohibitions, and its enforcement by male and female celibates, has been the fertile soil for innumerable reflections, autobiographies and polemics from the *Confessions* of St. Augustine to Mary McCarthy's *Memoirs of a Catholic Girlhood*.

Reverence for life, especially in its vulnerable condition *in utero*, is a *sine qua non* of Catholic teaching, and one which possesses a great moral strength even in its extreme forms. A woman experiencing danger in childbirth, for example, is supposed to sacrifice her own life for that of the child. (Judaism, which has codes no less ethical, tends to mandate the opposite decision, for the greater good of the family.) When mass rapes occurred in the course of aggressive war in Bangladesh and later in Bosnia, Mother Teresa in the first case and the Pope in the second made strenuous appeals to the victims not to abort the seed of the invader and the violator. Give the child up for adoption, or raise it in a spirit unlike the one in which it was conceived—this was the injunction. While it can be seen as grotesque to lecture women who are in such desperate dilemmas, there is none the less something impressive and noble in the high priority the Church gives to potential life. Humans, it says, blaspheme when they throw away a fetus, because they cannot assume the right to dispose of another's life and they cannot presume to know the future. Children born with appalling deformities in sordid and overcrowded homes have been known time and again, after all, to defy all material odds and become exemplary, or merely human.

But the nobility of this essential teaching is compromised by the fact that it depends on an unnecessary theological assumption about "ensoulment"—the point at which Thomas Aquinas maintained that a life became human and immortal. Two objections can be made here, the first being that human life can and should be respected whether or not it is constituted by a creator with an immortal soul; to make the one position dependent upon the other is to make the respect in some way contingent. Second, if a fertilized egg is fully human, then all terminations of pregnancy at any stage and for any reason are to be regarded as murder. This offends against the natural or instinctive feeling in favor of the pregnant woman and the occupant of her womb, because it blurs the distinction between an embryonic group of cells and a human with a central nervous system. The distinction between abortions in the first and third trimesters, a distinction which speaks both to our ability to avoid casuistry and to our inborn wish to have a say in our own fates, is therefore null and void in Catholic teaching. Some of the coarsening in arguments on the other side of the case—arguments which bluntly and unscientifically define the fetus as a mere appendix to the woman's body—no doubt result from confrontation with this absolutist edict.

Then there is the fact that Catholic prohibition on abortion comes indissolubly linked to a prohibition on birth control and contraception. Again, more is involved than the technical and dogmatic finding that certain forms of contraception, such as some versions of the intrauterine device which expels fertilized ova, actually are abortifacient in the fundamentalist definition of the term: the ban extends to all means and methods of avoiding conception, and indeed to the very intention of doing so. It is as "natural" in humans to seek control over their biological fecundity as it is for them to wish to have children in the first place. The Roman Catholic Church stands alone in condemning the desire to remove oneself from the caprices of nature and evolution, and the Roman Catholic Church has great political power over millions of poor and fertile people.

The Church's teaching seems to deny any connection at all between the rapid exponential growth in human population and the spread and persistence of disease, famine, squalor, ignorance and environmental calamity. One need not be a follower of the grim Reverend Malthus to deduce that there is indeed such a connection and that, moreover, it works in the other direction as well. In every developing country that has been studied, a clear correlation can be found between the limitation of family size and the life chances of the family members. Where such measures cannot be freely taken, by means of education and example, they have been enforced in desperation by authoritarian regimes. We have before us the forbidding example of the People's Republic of China, which limits families to one child apiece and is thus, in the name of Communism, preparing a future in which the words "brother" and "sister" will have no literal meaning. And we have the instance of Mother Teresa's friend and admirer Indira Gandhi, who launched a demagogic and brutal attempt to bring about male sterilization by a combination of bullying and bribery. (Salman Rushdie's short story "The Free Radio" in *East, West* brilliantly shows the pathos and emptiness of this effort.) Certainly these are not kind solutions, but they evidence the severity of a problem which the Church has chosen entirely to ignore.

Over the past decades, and particularly since the Second Vatican Council, the Roman Catholic Church has been faced with nearly every sort of cultural, doctrinal and political dissent. In Latin America, where it faces an unprecedented challenge from evangelical Protestantism and from the populist challenge of so-called "liberation theology," the need to renew the priesthood has led to questioning of the celibacy requirement. In the United States and Western Europe, the congregation appears to conduct its affairs without reference to canonical teaching on birth control. Homosexual groups have petitioned for the right to be considered true Catholics, since if God did not create their condition there seems to be an interesting question as to who did. Even prominent Catholic writers of the conservative wing, such as William Buckley and Clare Booth Luce, have made the obvious point that an unyielding opposition to contraception, and the ranking of it as a sin more or less equivalent to abortion, is, among other things, a cheapening of the moral position on abortion itself.

In all of these debates, the most consistently reactionary figure has been Mother Teresa. The fundamentalist faction within the Vatican has found her useful in two ways—first as an advertisement for the good works of the Church to non-Catholics; and second as a potent instrument of moral suasion within the ranks of the existing faithful. She has missed no opportunity to restate elementary dogmas (much as she once told an interviewer that, if faced with a choice between Galileo and the authority of the Inquisition, she would have sided with the Church authorities). She has inveighed against abortion, against contraception and against the idea that there should be any limit whatsoever to the growth of world population.[4]

---

[4] In the course of preparing for the 1994 United Nations World Population Conference in Cairo, the Vatican went so far as to make a temporary alliance with those forces of Shi'a Islam, chiefly represented by the mullahs of Iran, which denounced population control as an imperialist conspiracy. The apple of dogma had, at least in this case, fallen some distance from the tree of proselytization and the crusades.

*   *   *

When Mother Teresa was awarded the Nobel Peace Prize in 1979, few people had the poor taste to ask what she had ever done, or even *claimed* to do, for the cause of peace. Her address to the ceremony of investiture did little to resolve any doubt on this score and much to increase it. She began the speech with a literal-minded account of the myth of Christ's conception, perhaps in honor of that day's festal character: the Feast of the Immaculate Conception. Then she began her diatribe:

> I was amazed when I learned that in the West so many young people are on drugs. I tried to understand the reason for this. Why? The answer is, "because in the family there is nobody who cares about them." Fathers and mothers are so busy they have no time. Young parents work, and the child lives in the street and goes his own way. We speak of peace. These are the things that threaten peace. I think that today peace is threatened by abortion, too, which is a true war, the direct killing of a child by its own mother. In the Bible we read that God clearly said: "Even though a mother did forget her infant, I will not forget him."
>
> Today, abortion is the worst evil, and the greatest enemy of peace. We who are here today were wanted by our parents. We would not be here if our parents had not wanted us.

We want children, and we love them. But what about the other millions? Many are concerned about the children, like those in Africa, who die in great numbers either from hunger or for other reasons. But millions of children die intentionally, by the will of their mothers. Because if a mother can kill her own child, what will prevent us from killing ourselves, or one another? Nothing.

There is not much necessity for identifying the fallacies and distortions which are piled upon one another here. Few women who have had abortions, even those who still feel remorse or regret, will recognize themselves as having committed actual infanticide. If there are "millions" of children being slain in this way, so that they compare to the millions of children dying of malnutrition and pestilence, then there is clearly no hope for Mother Teresa's adoption solution. (She claims to have rescued only three or four dozen orphans from the entire Bangladesh calamity, for example.) Moreover, these impressive figures should be enough at least to impel reconsideration in those who proclaim that all pregnancies are "wanted" by definition and that there can be no excess population.

At a vast open-air mass in Knock, Ireland, in 1992, Mother Teresa made it plain yet again that there is no connection at all in her mind between the conditions of poverty and misery that she "combats" and the inability of the very poor to reach the plateau on which limitation of family size becomes a rational choice. Addressing a crowd of the devout, she said, "Let us promise Our Lady who loves Ireland so much that we will never allow in this country a single abortion. And no contraceptives."

In this instance, she fell into the last great fallacy and offense to which Church teaching on this subject is prone. Ireland is now, to a great extent, a secular society. It is also a society which has to seek an accommodation with its huge Protestant-majority province. The Church claims the right to make law, in states where it is strong enough, for believers and unbelievers alike. Mother Teresa's "pacific" humanitarianism and charity therefore translate directly into an injunction to the faithful to breed without hindrance, an admonishment to the rest to live under laws not made by them, and an attack on the idea of a non-sectarian state. What this does for the cause of peace does not, in Ireland, take long to estimate. What it does for suffering humanity is to criminalize, or at least to ration and restrict, one of the few means ever devised for its self-emancipation. It is often said, inside the Church and out of it, that there is something grotesque about lectures on the sexual life when delivered by those who have shunned it. Given the way that the Church forbids women to preach, this point is usually made about men. But given how much this Church allows the fanatical Mother Teresa to preach, it might be added that the call to go forth and multiply, and to take no thought for the morrow, sounds grotesque when uttered by an elderly virgin whose chief claim to reverence is that she ministers to the inevitable losers in this very lottery.

III

In her reputation-making interview with Malcolm Muggeridge during *Something Beautiful for God*, Mother Teresa made the following large claim:

> We have to do God's will in everything. We also take a special vow which other congregations don't take; that of giving wholehearted free service to the poor. This vow means that we cannot work for the rich; neither can we accept any money for the work we do. Ours has to be a free service, and to the poor.

For the many ethical humanists, as well as for the many vaguely religious people who support or endorse what they imagine to be Mother Teresa's mission, the above statement is quite an important one. It seems to spare the Missionaries of Charity from the worldliness and financial cunning which have so disfigured Christianity in the past. And it insists that no service is furnished to the rich—a claim which might lead the unwary to conclude that no contributions are solicited from them.

In point of fact, the Missionaries of Charity have for decades been the recipients of the extraordinary largesse of governments, large foundations, corporations and private citizens. The affectation of poverty, which is so attractive to some observers, has obscured this relative plenty. And so has another affectation—one very well known to missionary fund-raisers down through the years. In this story, which has become solemnized by repetition at a thousand tent meetings, the necessary donation arrives just at the moment when the need for it is greatest. Was a consignment of blankets the pressing need, with a hard winter coming on? Sure enough, an anonymous benefactor chose that very night to leave a truckload of blankets on the doorstep of the mission. Dr. Lush Gjergji gives an especially touching example of the genre in his book, an example no less touching for its being written as if the notion had never been tried out in print before:

One day Sister Frances, from the city of Agra, phoned Mother Teresa asking for urgent help.

"Mother, I need 50,000 rupees. Over here there is a crying and urgent need to start a house for the children."

Mother Teresa replied: "That is too much, my daughter, I will call you back; for the moment we have nothing…" A short time later the phone rang again. It was a press agency. "Mother Teresa? This is the editor of the agency. The Philippine government has just awarded you the Magsaysay Prize. Heartfelt compliments! It involves a considerable sum."

Mother Teresa: "Thanks for letting me know."

The editor: "What do you plan on doing with the 50,000 rupees from the prize?"

Mother Teresa: "What did you say? 50,000 rupees? I think the Lord wants us to build a home for children at Agra."

As her television reputation spread, Mother Teresa found herself accepting more and more awards and benefactions. The Indian government invested her with the Prize of the Miraculous Lotus. In 1971 the Vatican gave her the John XXIII Prize for Peace (Dr. Gjergji hastens to inform us that on this occasion "the prize winner herself had come to the Vatican on the city bus, and was wearing her Indian sari, worth about one dollar." If true, this was ostentatious of her.) In Boston in the same year she accepted the "Good Samaritan" award, again with many words of self-deprecation. Then straight to Washington, to receive the John F. Kennedy award on 16 October. The next year, with the auction in full swing, the government of India improved on its relatively lowly Miraculous Lotus prize and gave her a larger one, in a ceremony at which Indira Gandhi publicly wept. In 1973 it was Prince Philip's turn to make an emotional demonstration, which he did while presenting the Templeton Prize "for the promotion of faith in the world." In the presence of his wife, who holds the title of "Defender of the Faith" against all the works of Rome and who heads a family which is barred from making a marriage to a Roman Catholic, the royal consort handed over £34,000. The United Nations Food and Agriculture Organization went one better two years later by striking a special medal with the goddess Ceres brandishing a stalk of wheat at Mother Teresa and, on the obverse, the inscription "Food For All: Holy Year 1975." Revenue from the sale of the medals went to the Missionaries of Charity. It was only a step up from this to the Albert Schweitzer Prize, and then to yet another recognition from the Indian government—this time an honorary degree presented by Indira Gandhi herself. (The future patroness of compulsory sterilization had become, in the meantime, head of the government.) In March 1979, the International Balzan Prize, worth a quarter of a million lire, was presented by the president of Italy. The Pope, by then John Paul II, took the opportunity of her visit to receive her in private audience. All things thereby pressed toward the ultimate event of the prize-giving machine, which was to make Mother Teresa the Nobel Laureate for Peace and to invest her with the prize and the check in December 1979.

Nobody has troubled to total the amount of prize money received from governments and quasi-government organizations by the Missionaries of Charity, and nobody has ever asked what became of the funds. It is safe to say, however, that if all the money had been used on one project it would have been possible, say, to give Calcutta the finest teaching hospital in the entire Third World. That such is neither Mother Teresa's intention nor her desire may be inferred from the Muggeridge incident. It may also be inferred from her preference for spreading the money thin and for devoting it to religious and missionary work rather than the sustained relief of deprivation. In any event, if she is claiming that the order does not solicit money from the rich and powerful, or accept it from them, this is easily shown to be false.

The apologists generally claim that Mother Teresa is too innocent to count money or to take the measure of those who offer it, or to reckon that they obtain some benefit from their supposed generosity in the form of virtue-by-association. Forgetting for a moment her boast that she does not accept eye-of-the-needle subventions in the first place, we might agree that this argument had merit in the case of the late Robert Maxwell. Mr. Maxwell inveigled a not-unwilling Mother Teresa into a fund-raising scheme run by his newspaper group, and then, it seems (having got her to join him in some remarkable publicity photographs), he made off with the money. But Maxwell did succeed in fooling some very experienced and unsentimental people in his day, and although it might be asked how Mother Teresa had time to spare for such a wicked and greedy man, it can still be argued with some degree of plausibility that she was a blameless party to his cynical manipulations.

However, it is difficult, if not impossible, to assert this in the case of Mr. Charles Keating. Keating is now serving a ten-year sentence for his part in the Savings and Loan scandal—undoubtedly one of the greatest frauds in American history. In the early 1980s, during the booming, deregulated years of Reagan's first term, Keating, among other operators, mounted a sustained and criminal assault on the deposits of America's small investors. His methods were those of the false prospectus and the political bribe. (Washington vernacular still contains the expression "the Keating Five," in honor of the five United States senators who did him favors while receiving vast campaign donations in the form of other people's money.) Keating had political ambitions as well as financial ones, and as a conservative Catholic fundamentalist had served Richard Nixon

as a member of a much-mocked commission to
investigate the ill effects of pornography.

At the height of his success as a thief, Keating
made donations (not out of his own pocket, of course)
to Mother Teresa in the sum of one and a quarter
million dollars. He also granted her the use of his
private jet. In return, Mother Teresa allowed Keating to make use of her prestige on several important occasions and gave him a personalized crucifix
which he took everywhere with him.

In 1992, after a series of political and financial
crises and the most expensive bailout operation in
the history of the American taxpayer, Keating was
finally brought to trial. He appeared before the
Superior Court in Los Angeles (his "Lincoln Savings and Loan" had been a largely Californian operation) where he was heard by the later-notorious Judge
Lance Ito. The trial could have only one outcome: the
maximum sentence allowable under California law.

During the course of the trial, Mother Teresa
wrote to the court seeking clemency for Mr. Keating.
She gave no explanation of her original involvement
with the defendant and offered no direct testimony
mitigating his looting of the thrift industry. The letter, in its original form, appears opposite.

One is struck immediately by two things. First,
though the claim about "free service to the poorest

"As long as you did it to one of these My least brethren. You did it to Me"

FILED

Honorable Lance Ito
Superior Court
210 West Temple Street
Dept. 123,   13th floor
Los Angeles, Calif. 90012

JAN 27 1992

HANK S COURT. COUNTY CLERK
BY _____
DEPUTY

18/1/92

Dear Honorable Lance Ito,

We do not mix up in Business or Politicts or
courts. Our work, as Missionaries of Charity is to give
wholehearted and free service to the poorest of the poor.

I do not know anything about Mr. Charles Keating's
work or his business or the matters you are dealing with.

I only know that he has alway been kind and
generous to God's poor, and always ready to help whenever
there was a need.   It is for this reason that I do not want
to forget him now while he and his family are suffering.
Jesus has told us "Whatever you do to the least of my
brethern...YOU DID IT TO ME. Mr. Keating has done much to
help the poor, which is why I am writing to you on his
behalf.

Whenever someone asks me to speak to a judge, I
always tell them the same thing. I ask them to pray, to look
into thier heart, and to do what Jesus would do in that
circumstance. And this is what I am asking of you, your
Honor.

My gratitude to you is my prayer for you, and your
work, your family and the people with whom you are working.

God bless you
M. Teresa mc

71

of the poor" is made in almost the same words as it was made to Muggeridge, the related claim that the rich receive no quid pro quo seems to have disappeared. Then there is the astonishing artlessness of the letter, both as composed and as presented. One might think it a missive from an innocent old woman who knows nothing of cupidity and scandal, and who naively wishes to intercede for reasons of rather woolly compassion. The transcript of Mother Teresa's highly ideological Nobel Prize speech, for example, does *not* read like this. It is professionally written and presented. And many of her other public interventions demonstrate a much sharper sense of the real world, even when Mother Teresa is choosing to speak on matters, such as sexuality and reproduction, where she must necessarily admit to being disqualified by inexperience.

The suspicion that there might be something *faux naïf* about the appeal occurred also to Mr. Paul Turley who, in his capacity as Deputy District Attorney for Los Angeles, was Mr. Keating's co-prosecutor. On his own initiative, and as a private citizen, he wrote and dispatched a careful reply. I reproduce it below for the first time:

Dear Mother Teresa:
    I am a Deputy District Attorney in Los Angeles County and one of the persons who worked

on the prosecution of your benefactor, Charles H. Keating, Jr. I read your letter to Judge Ito, written on behalf of Mr. Keating, which includes your admission that you know nothing about Mr. Keating's business or the criminal charges presented to Judge Ito. I am writing to you to provide a brief explanation of the crimes of which Mr. Keating has been convicted, to give you an understanding of the source of the money that Mr. Keating gave to you, and to suggest that you perform the moral and ethical act of returning the money to its rightful owners.

Mr. Keating was convicted of defrauding 17 individuals of more than $900,000. These 17 persons were representative of 17,000 individuals from whom Mr. Keating stole $252,000,000. Mr. Keating's specific acts of fraud were that he was the source of a series of fraudulent representations made to persons who bought bonds from his company and he also was the repository of crucial information which he chose to withhold from bond purchasers, thereby luring his victims into believing they were making a safe, low-risk investment. In truth and in fact, their money was being used to fund Mr. Keating's exorbitant and extravagant lifestyle.

The victims of Mr. Keating's fraud come from a wide spectrum of society. Some were wealthy and well-educated. Most were people of modest means and unfamiliar with high finance. One was, indeed, a poor carpenter who did not speak English and had his life savings stolen by Mr. Keating's fraud.

The biblical slogan of your organization is "As long as you did it to one of these My least brethren. You did it to Me." The "least" of the brethren are among those whom Mr. Keating fleeced without flinching. As you well know, divine forgiveness is available to all, but forgiveness must be preceded by admission of sin. Not only has Mr. Keating failed to admit his sins and his crimes, he persists in self-righteously blaming others for his own misdeeds. Your experience is, admirably, with the poor. My experience has been with the "con" man and the perpetrator of the fraud. It is not uncommon for "con" men to be generous with family, friends and charities. Perhaps they believe that their generosity will purchase love, respect or forgiveness. However, the time when the purchase of "indulgences" was an acceptable method of seeking forgiveness died with the Reformation. No church, no charity, no organization should allow itself to be used as salve for the conscience of the criminal. We all are grateful that forgiveness is available but we all, also, must perform our duty.

That includes the Judge and the Jury. I remind myself of the biblical admonition of the Prophet Micah: "O man, what is good and what does the Lord require of you. To do justice, love mercy and walk humbly."

We are urged to love mercy but we must *do* justice.

You urge Judge Ito to look into his heart—as he sentences Charles Keating—and do what Jesus would do. I submit the same challenge to you. Ask yourself what Jesus would do if he were given the fruits of a crime; what Jesus would do if he were in possession of money that had been stolen; what Jesus would do if he were being exploited by a thief to ease his conscience?

I submit that Jesus would promptly and unhesitatingly return the stolen property to its rightful owners. You should do the same. You have been given money by Mr. Keating that he has been convicted of stealing by fraud. Do not permit him the "indulgence" he desires. Do not keep the money. Return it to those who worked for it and earned it!

If you contact me I will put you in direct contact with the rightful owners of the property now in your possession.

Sincerely,
Paul W. Turley

Three years later, Mr. Turley has received no reply to his letter. Nor can anybody account for the missing money: saints, it seems, are immune to audit.

This is by no means the only example of Mother Teresa's surreptitious attitude to money, nor of her hypocritical protestations about the beauty of poverty, whether self-imposed or otherwise. But it is the clearest and best-documented instance, and it is proof against the customary apologetics about innocence and unworldliness. In her dealings with pelf, as in her transactions with power, Mother Teresa reigns in a kingdom that is very much of this world.

Ubiquity

Naturally, there are puzzles. I would like to know whether or not the universe is finite or infinite. I would like even better to be assured that the two words are meaningless. But excepting the sort of puzzle which makes our passage here interesting and gives incentive to our questioning games, I see no mystery at the heart of things and take comfort from Wittgenstein's profoundly unpopular dictum, "Philosophy simply puts everything before us, and neither explains nor deduces anything. Since everything lies open to view there is nothing to explain. For what is hidden, for example, is of no interest to us."

Gore Vidal, *Two Sisters*

The Bible commands us to love our enemies. I love the Pope very much.

Father Jean-Bertrand Aristide,
president of Haiti

I

At a certain point in the period of its medieval ascendancy, the Church of Rome was forced to confront a problem of theory and of practice. If a human soul could only be redeemed by acceptance of the New Testament canon—the birth, life, death and resurrection of Jesus Christ—then what was to become of those who had never heard the news? These were not heretics or infidels to be slain or burned but people who suffered from "invincible ignorance." They fell into two categories: those who lived in parts of the world unvisited and untouched by the faith, and those who had died before the Christian era began. (There was also a third category, namely the disciples of Jesus himself, who had never read the Bible story, either. But they were, and remain, exempt.) Not much could be done for those who had expired before the birth of Christ, though Dante did his best for them and there are passages in the Creeds which speak of Jesus descending into hell in order to carry out some retrospective redemption. But for those who lived in non-Christian lands, it was decreed that the work of conversion was an imperative.

It is, in a sense, a pity that this work will always be remembered for its association either with conquest, with religious fratricide or with imperialism. Very frequently, the main consequence was sanguinary conflict between different branches of Christianity itself. (Long after the Catholic Crusaders got to Jerusalem, for example, they sacked Orthodox and Byzantine Constantinople.) In later epochs, both Catholic and Protestant missionaries penetrated the interiors of China and Japan and the remotest parts of Africa and South America, but their presence was indissoluble from that of the trading post and the garrison. In the course of a profitable partnership with slavery, colonialism and forced labor, the Christian "civilizing mission" often came up against strongly entrenched local religions. Where it did not adapt to these, or eliminate their believers, it made little headway. In India, which was disputed as a prize between four principal European powers before passing under British suzerainty, the effect of Christianity has been relatively slight. The Indian authorities, who are suspicious to this day of the link between proselytization and foreign interference, have generally dis-

couraged missionary activity. They have left Mother
Teresa's Missionaries of Charity largely alone, however, in deference to the worldwide reputation of
their founder. The Mother Teresa establishment in
Calcutta, therefore, possesses elements of pathos and
nostalgia: it is the chief and lonely relic of what was
once a vast enterprise of conquest and crusading.
When the girl Agnes Bojaxhiu was born on 27
August 1910 in Skopje, to an Albanian Catholic
family, the idea of the "mission" as a vocation was
still very much alive. And in that region, yesterday
as today, allegiance to the Church was more than
a merely confessional matter. It was, and is, imbri-
cated with a series of loyalties to nation, region and
even party. We know little enough of Agnes's early
life, and the devotional tracts written about her are
not very illuminating, but it seems that her father
Nikola, a prosperous shopkeeper, died in a nationalist squabble when the girl was only eight. The family
was strongly religious and adhered to the Parish of
the Sacred Heart, which in Skopje was synonymous
with Albanian identity. Through the influence of
a Jesuit priest she became interested in missionary
work and at the age of twelve, on her own account,
she first received the idea that her life should be dedicated to spreading the word among the poor. But
she told Malcolm Muggeridge that "at the beginning, between twelve and eighteen, I didn't want to

become a nun. We were a very happy family. But when I was eighteen, I decided to leave my home and become a nun." Having entered a convent—the Congregation of the Sisters of the Blessed Virgin Mary of Loreto—she left Skopje for Zagreb, and from there traveled to Dublin, where the Loreto Sisters have their headquarters to this day. Shortly after Christmas Day 1928, her ship made landfall in Colombo, en route to the Loreto mission in Bengal.

The account of Agnes's early life given by Dr. Gjergji is intriguing for its fragmentary character. We learn, for example, that the future Mother Teresa's brother, Lazzaro, "went to Italy in 1939, remained there during and after the war, and finally died there." We learn also that "when, in the fall of 1910, the Serbians reached Skopje, the missionaries had to limit their pastoral action to the city itself. Things got worse at the outbreak of war in 1914." From this terse account we can only guess at the impact on the fervent Bojaxhiu family of the second Balkan war and the two world wars. However, a certain amount of background can be inferred.

Albanians divide between members of the Tosk and Gheg peoples, separated south and north, respectively, by the Shkumbini river. Most are Muslim, with an Orthodox Christian minority among the Tosks and a Roman Catholic one among the Ghegs. The Ghegs, who include the Bojaxhiu family, populate the much-disputed region of Kosovo. Now an "autonomous region" of Serbia, Kosovo has an Albanian majority, but it is also home to the Orthodox Serbs' holiest battlefield—the site of a fourteenth-century rout by the Turks.

In 1927 King Zog of Albania signed a treaty with Benito Mussolini which made Albania into an effective protectorate of Italian fascism. The treaty provided for the training of the Albanian military by Italian officers and the relocation of the Bank of Albania to Rome. Even before the subsequent Concordat signed between Mussolini and the Vatican, which gave papal imprimatur to the fascist project, the treaty established favorable conditions for the adoption of Roman Catholicism throughout Albania. The Church was permitted to open numerous schools, while the schools run by Greek Orthodox authorities were closed. (Greece took Albania to the World Court on this matter and in 1933 won a landmark case defining the rights of minorities to their own language and religion.) Nor did the advent of the Second World War diminish the enthusiasm of "Greater Albania" for the Axis. Even as Hitler was taking over Athens, a delegation of Albanian notables waited upon Mussolini in order to present him with the crown of Skanderbeg, the Albanian national hero.

A striking fact about this period is the fealty of all Albanian extremists to the idea of "Mother Albania."

When Mussolini finally collapsed, the Albanian Communists, under the leadership of Enver Hoxha, echoed, at a meeting of Albanian political groups that included the fascists, the demand that Kosovo be incorporated into Albania after the war. Tito's partisans were strong enough and (then) weighty enough in Moscow to negate this demand. But many of Hoxha's postwar cabinet members were unpurged members of the Albanian Youth of the Lictor, a prewar fascist movement which cherished the idea of military expansion. (Hoxha's successor as dictator, Ramiz Alia, was one of those who made this bizarre yet seemingly consistent traverse of the political spectrum.)

Before the war, the ideas of fascism, Catholicism, Albanianism and Albano-Italian unity were closely identified. Afterward, religious identity was officially suppressed by Hoxha's proclamation of the "world's first atheist state." None the less, the evidence implies that irredentist ideology persisted under Stalinist disguise and had at least as much to do with Albania's foreign-policy alignments as did any supposed doctrinal schism over the canonical texts of Marx and Lenin. An Albanian Catholic nationalist, in other words, might, on "patriotic" questions, still feel loyal to an ostensibly materialist Communist regime.

How else are we to explain the following entry from the *Yearbook on International Communist Affairs 1990*, published by the Hoover Institution at Stanford University and reviewing developments in all countries of the Communist world?

After numerous previous attempts to secure a visa had been denied, in August the government allowed Mother Teresa to visit Tirana....Although the visit was called "private," Mother Teresa was received by Mrs. Hoxha, Foreign Minister Reis Malile, Minister of Health Ahmet Kamberi, the Chairman of the People's Assembly Petro Dode, and other state and party officials. Dutifully, the Albanian-born nun and Nobel peace prize laureate placed a wreath at the monument of "Mother Albania" and "paid homage and laid a bouquet of flowers on the grave of Comrade Enver Hoxha." The world-renowned Catholic nun did not utter a word of criticism against the regime for its brutal suppression of religion.

The "Mother Albania" monument, it might be worth emphasizing, is not an abstract symbol of sentimental nationhood. It is the emblem of the cause of Greater Albania. A nearby museum displays the boundaries of this ambition in the form of a map. "Mother Albania" turns out to comprise—in addition to the martyred province of Kosovo—a large piece of Serbia and Montenegro, a substantial chunk of formerly Yugoslav Macedonia and most of that part of modern Greece now known as Epirus.

I possess a film of "Mother Teresa" making her homage to "Mother Albania"—as well as to its patron, the pitiless thug Enver Hoxha—and it invites the same question as does the infamous embrace in Haiti: What is a woman of unworldly innocence and charity doing *dans cette galère*? Apologists have said, of the Albanian case, that it was only natural for Mother Teresa to make a few obeisances in order to visit the graves of her ancestors and, of the second, that a few compromises were necessary so that her order would be allowed to work freely in Haiti. Interestingly enough, these are not excuses that have been tendered by Mother Teresa herself, who keeps her own counsel on both matters (and on many others besides).

It is at least worth considering whether Mother Teresa made both of these trips (and many others) in furtherance of the more flinty political stands taken by hard-liners in her own Church. The personal conduct and the questionable policy are at least congruent in each instance. In the case of Haiti, the Vatican had long taken a position in favor of the "Duvalierist" oligarchy. When the Reverend Father Jean-Bertrand Aristide began his campaign of charismatic populism against the regime, he encountered instant hostility from the Church hierarchy, which eventually suspended him from his order. By the time that Aristide had been triumphantly elected, ignominiously deposed by a military junta and finally restored to power by international intervention, the Vatican was the only government in the world which still retained formal diplomatic relations with the usurping dictatorship. Mother Teresa's activism, then, was representative of the most dogmatic line taken by her Church.

Similarly in the Balkans, the collapse and disintegration of Yugoslavia led to a recrudescence of essentially prewar rivalries. Croatia, with the support of the Vatican and Germany, declared itself an independent state and restored many of the signs and emblems of the wartime republic led by Ante Pavelic. Protected by the Vatican and the Third Reich, this government had massacred its Jews and embarked on a program of forced conversion of Orthodox Serbs; those who resisted the crusade had been put to death. This memory alone, and the evident lack of regret for it, contributed to the evolution of a nationalist-religious paranoia among the Serbs, who subsequently launched a war of territorial and sectarian aggrandizement, destroying the cities of Vukovar and Sarajevo in the process. The Croatian ruling party, led by Franjo Tudjman, responded by carving out its own slice of Bosnia and demolishing the city of Mostar.

Even more ominously there existed, and still exists, the possibility that a generalized war could destroy the boundaries of the former Yugoslavia and once again pit Catholic against Orthodox as well as both, in various local combinations, against Islam. In Tetovo, the Albanian center of western Macedonia, and in Kosovo too, local zealots speak of Greater Albania as the response to Greater Serbia, and they flourish their pictures of Mother Teresa.

II

Intervention, whether moral or political, is always and everywhere a matter of the most exquisite timing. The choice of time and the selection of place can be most eloquent. So indeed may be the moments when nothing is said or done. Mother Teresa is fond of claiming to be not so much *above* politics as actually *beyond* them, operating in a manner that is transcendental. All claims by public persons to be apolitical deserve critical scrutiny, and all claims made by those who affect a merely "spiritual" influence deserve a doubly critical scrutiny. The naive and simple are seldom as naive and simple as they seem, and this suspicion is reinforced by those who proclaim their own naïveté and simplicity. There is no conceit equal to false modesty, and there is no politics like antipolitics, just as there is no worldliness to compare with ostentatious antimaterialism.

Mother Teresa's timing shows every sign of

instinctive genius. She possesses an intuition about the need for her message and about the way in which this message should be delivered. To take a relatively small example: In 1984 the Indian town of Bhopal was the scene of an appalling industrial calamity. The Union Carbide plant, which had been located in the town to take advantage of low labor costs and government tax incentives, exploded and spilled toxic chemicals over a large swath of the citizenry. Two and a half thousand persons perished almost at once, and many thousands more were choked by lung-searing emissions and had their health permanently impaired. The subsequent investigation revealed a pattern of negligence and showed that previous safety warnings at the plant had been shelved or ignored. Here was no "Act of God," as the insurance companies like to phrase it in the fine print of their contracts, but a shocking case of callousness on the part of a giant multinational corporation. Mother Teresa was on the next plane to Bhopal. At the airport, greeted by throngs of angry relatives of the victims, she was pressed to give her advice and counsel, and she did so unhesitatingly. I have a videotape of the moment. "Forgive," she said. "Forgive, forgive."

On the face of it, a strange injunction. How did she know there was anything to forgive? Had anybody asked for forgiveness? What are the duties of the poor to the rich in such a situation? And who is authorized to recommend, or to dispense, forgiveness?[5] In the absence of any answer to these questions, Mother Teresa's flying visit to Bhopal read like a hasty exercise in damage control, the expedient containment of righteous secular indignation.

Here is another film clip, this time of Mother Teresa at the airport in Madrid. She has flown in to lend her support to the clerical forces who are contesting the post-Franco legislation enabling divorce, abortion and birth control. The crowd at the terminal is composed of the highly traditional Spanish Right, with here and there a blue shirt, and a right arm flung skyward. This is one of the first political votes to decide whether or not Spain will evolve into a secular society. Mother Teresa has taken her stand in this debate, and she has taken it unequivocally on the conservative side—all the while claiming to remain above politics. Any exertion of this privilege is really an abuse, just as it was in Knock.

In London in 1988, Mother Teresa paid a visit ostensibly to discuss the growing problem of the

---

[5] If I may add a personal anecdote here: Mother Teresa was in the autumn of 1994 asked by the Calcutta newspapers to comment on *Hell's Angel*, the critical documentary which I and others had made on her work. She had not seen the documentary but her response was to say that she "forgave" us for making it. This was odd, since we had not sought forgiveness from her or from anyone else. Odder still if you have any inclination to ask by what right she assumes the power to forgive. There are even some conscientious Christians who would say that forgiveness, like the astringent of revenge, is reserved to a higher power.

city's homeless, who had forced the phrase "Cardboard City" into the language by dwelling in cardboard structures in parks and on the Embankment. Having spoken briefly on this topic, Mother Teresa was ushered into 10 Downing Street to meet in private with Prime Minister Margaret Thatcher. Mrs. Thatcher was famously unsentimental about the denizens of "Cardboard City" and indeed about most other forms of human failure and defeat, and it was not in any case the plight of the homeless that Mother Teresa wished to discuss. The two women went into conclave on the matter of abortion, which was then the subject of a private member's bill in the House of Commons, sponsored by the Liberal MP David Alton. Mr. Alton, who had sought to limit the availability of abortion, was in no doubt of the value of Mother Teresa's intervention. He told reporters that her meeting with Margaret Thatcher was an immense boost to his campaign, and he took credit for arranging the womanly summit. Whatever else may be said of this meeting, which occurred on the eve of a decisive parliamentary vote and was attended by a circus of cameras and scribes, the term "nonpolitical" does not apply to it very easily.

And now a photograph, or pair of photographs. Mother Teresa is seated in earnest conversation with Ronald Reagan and his chief of staff, Donald Regan. Both men wear expressions of the most determined sincerity. The photo opportunity occurs inside the White House in May 1985. Mother Teresa has been chosen to receive the Presidential Medal of Freedom. Her companions for the day are Frank Sinatra, James Stewart and Jeane Kirkpatrick, among other recipients. At the moment when the shutter falls on this shot, Ronald Reagan has every reason to be careful of Catholic susceptibility. His policy in Central America, which has resulted in his Cabinet officers defending the murders of four American nuns and the Archbishop of San Salvador, is deeply unpopular with the voters. One of his more daring lies—the claim that he had received a personal message from the Pope supporting his policy in the isthmus—has had to be retracted after causing considerable embarrassment. In the basement of the very building where Mother Teresa sits, a Marine Colonel named Oliver North (who forsook the Catholic Church for evangelical Pentecostalism after being vouchsafed a personal vision) is toiling away on an enterprise which will nearly succeed in destroying the Presidency that spawned it.

Stepping onto the portico of the White House, flanked by Ronald and Nancy, Mother Teresa knows just what to say:

I am most unworthy of this generous gift of our President, Mr. Reagan, and his wife and you people of the United States. But I accept it for the greater glory of God and in the name of the millions of poor people that this gift, in spirit and in love, will penetrate the hearts of the people.

This kind of modesty—speaking for God and for the poor—is now so standard on her part that nobody even notices it. Then:

> I've never realized that you loved the people so tenderly. I had the experience, I was last time here, a sister from Ethiopia found me and said "Our people are dying. Our children are dying. Mother, do something." And the only person that came in my mind while she was talking, it was the President. And immediately I wrote to him, and I said, "I don't know, but this is what happened to me." And next day it was that immediately he arranged to bring food to our people.... Together, we are doing something beautiful for God.

Here was greater praise than Reagan could possibly have asked or hoped for. Not only was he told that he "loved the people so tenderly" but he was congratulated for his policy in Ethiopia. That policy, as it happened, was to support the claim of the Ethiopian ruling junta—the Dergue—to the supposed "territorial integrity" of the Ethiopian empire, which included (then) the insurgent people of Eritrea. General Mengistu Haile Mariam had deliberately used the weapon of starvation not just against Eritrea but also against domestic and regional dissent in other regions of the country. This had not prevented Mother Teresa from dancing attendance upon him and thereby shocking the human-rights community, which had sought to isolate his regime. That very isolation, however, had provided opportunities for "missionary work" to those few prepared to compromise. To invest such temporal and temporizing politics with the faint odor of sanctity, let alone with Mother Teresa's now-familiar suggestion of the operations of divine providence ("And next day it was…") is political in the extreme, but the White House press corps, deliberately ignorant of such considerations, duly gave the visit and the presentation its standard uncritical treatment.

During this same period, Mother Teresa visited Nicaragua and contrived to admonish the Sandinista revolutionary party. The Cardinal Archbishop of Managua, Miguel Obando y Bravo, was at that time the official patron and confessor of the *contras*, and was paid an admitted and regular stipend by the Central Intelligence Agency. Also at that time, the *contras* conceived it as their task to make a special target of clinics, schools, dairies and other "soft target" elements of the Nicaraguan system. And the *contras* believed—almost predictably—that they had on their side a miraculous Virgin who had appeared in the remote northern regions of the country. What they assuredly did have on their side was the most powerful state on earth, which openly announced that it would bring Nicaragua to heel by increasing the poverty and destitution of its wavering citizens. A consistent case might be made for following such a policy and for employing the Church in support of it, but however reasonable that case might be it could by no stretch of the imagination be described as a non-political one, or one animated by a love of the poor.

More lives were taken on purpose in the war on Nicaraguan "subversion" than have been saved by all the missionaries in Calcutta even by accident. Yet this brute utilitarian calculus is never employed against Mother Teresa, even by the sort of sophists who would deploy its moral and physical equivalent in her favor. So: silence on the death squads and on the Duvaliers and noisy complaint against the Sandinistas, and the whole act baptized as an apolitical intervention by someone whose kingdom is not of this world.

Visiting Guatemala during the same period, at a time when the killing fields were becoming too hideous even for the local oligarchy and its foreign patrons, and at a time when the planned extirpation of the Guatemalan Indians had finally become a global headline, Mother Teresa purred: "Everything was peaceful in the parts of the country we visited. I do not get involved in that sort of politics." At least, for once, she did not say that everything was "beautiful."

Afterword

We believe that taking that kind of position, Charlie, is not a Democrat or Republican issue. We think it's an issue of what's moral; it's about what's compassionate; it's the kind of values that Mother Teresa represents.

> Ralph Reed, chairman of Pat Robertson's "Christian Coalition," on *Charlie Rose*, 21 February 1995

DEAR ANN LANDERS:

Often the simple things in life can make the most difference. For example, when someone asked Mother Teresa how people without money or power can make the world a better place, she replied, "They should smile more." —Prince George, B.C.

DEAR PRINCE:

What a splendid response. Thank you.

22 May 1995

Every day, the troubled and the despairing and the bewildered write their humble, nervous letters to the Ann Landers agony column. And every day, they are urged to seek counseling, to talk things over with their ministers, to pull their socks up, to play by the rules and look on the bright side. Most mornings, the jaunty column ends its brisk summary of the conventional wisdom with a "Gem of the Day," some fragment of cracker-barrel sapience or wry, *Reader's Digest*-style positive thinking. Recently, the above item was selected as the daily gem. Many Americans, schooled in the national dream of promise and abundance and opportunity, are condemned to experience life as a disappointment and to wonder if the fault is in themselves or in their stars that they are perpetual underlings. If this were not so, Ann Landers would be out of a job in the same way that so many of her readers are. But it is difficult to imagine many losers facing the day with a squarer jaw or a firmer, springier step as a consequence of imbibing this particular piece of counsel over their nutrition-free breakfast cereal. It is also doubtful whether a fortune-cookie maxim of such cretinous condescension would have been chosen even by Ann Landers unless it bore the imprimatur of Mother Teresa, one of the few untouchables in the mental universe of the mediocre and the credulous.

Intellectual snobbery? Only if the task of intellectuals is to urge Mr. and Mrs. Average to settle for little, or for less. Time and again, since I began the project of judging Mother Teresa's reputation by her actions and words rather than her actions and words by her reputation, I have been rebuked and admonished for ridiculing the household gods of the simple folk; for sneering at a woman who, to employ an old citation, "gives those in the gutter a glimpse of the stars." But is it not here that authentic intellectual snobbery exposes itself? We ourselves are far too sophisticated to believe in God and creationism and all that, say the more advanced defenders of the Teresa cult. But we *do* believe in religion—at least for other people. It is a means of marketing hope, and of instilling ethical precepts on the cheap. It is also a form of discipline. The followers of the late American guru Leo Strauss—a man who had a profound influence on the Republican Right wing—make this cynical point explicit in their otherwise arcane texts. There should be philosophy and knowledge for the elect, religion and sentimentality for the masses. By a bizarre coincidence of political opportunism, these Straussian forces are today ranged in alliance with the Christian fundamentalist cohort, founded by Pat Robertson but represented in public by the more cosmetic Ralph Reed. As can be seen from the excerpt above, Mr. Reed knows how to use a script when he is in a tight corner. Challenged on his prospectus for a

"Christian America" that cares for people before they are born and after they are dead but is only interested in clerical coercion for the years in between, Mr. Reed immediately reaches for the Gorgon's head of Mother Teresa and turns his questioners into stone. This would be even funnier if the Christian Coalition did not have its roots in the most vulgar strain of anti-Catholicism, but as Mother Teresa has shown in her moments with John-Roger and Michèle Duvalier, and as her Church has shown in its alliance with mullahs and ayatollahs, there exists a sort of reverse ecumenicism which unites all versions of the "faithful" against any version of the dreaded "secular humanist" Enlightenment.

Agnes Bojaxhiu knows perfectly well that she is conscripted by people like Ralph Reed, that she is a fund-raising icon for clerical nationalists in the Balkans, that she has furnished PR-type cover for all manner of cultists and shady businessmen (who are often the same thing), that her face is on vast highway billboards urging the state to take on the responsibility of safeguarding the womb. By no word or gesture has she ever repudiated any of these connections or alliances. Nor has she ever deigned to respond to questions about her friendship with despots. She merely desires to be taken at her own valuation and to be addressed universally as "Mother Teresa." Her success is not, therefore, a triumph of humility and simplicity. It is another chapter in a millennial story which stretches back to the superstitious childhood of our species, and which depends on the exploitation of the simple and the humble by the cunning and the single-minded.

As Edward Gibbon observed about the modes of worship prevalent in the Roman world, they were "considered by the people as equally true, by the philosopher as equally false and by the magistrate as equally useful." Mother Teresa descends from each element in this grisly triptych. She has herself purposely blurred the supposed distinction between the sacred and the profane, to say nothing of the line that separates the sublime from the ridiculous. It is past time that she was subjected to the rational critique that she has evaded so arrogantly and for so long.

About the Author

Christopher Hitchens (1949-2011) was a contributing editor to *Vanity Fair* and a columnist for *Slate*. He was the author of numerous books, including works on Thomas Jefferson, Thomas Paine, George Orwell, Mother Teresa, Henry Kissinger and Bill and Hillary Clinton, as well as his international bestseller and National Book Award nominee, *god Is Not Great*. His memoir, *Hitch-22*, was nominated for the Orwell Prize and was a finalist for the National Book Critics Circle Award. His last collection of essays, *Arguably* (Atlantic, 2011), was a *Sunday Times* bestseller. In 2012, Hitchens was awarded a memorial by the Orwell Prize.